THE
OXFORD
World STUDY
ATLAS

© Oxford University Press 1994
© Maps copyright Oxford University Press

Oxford University Press, Great Clarendon Street, Oxford, OX2 6DP

Oxford New York
Athens Auckland Bangkok Bogotá Buenos Aires
Calcutta Cape Town Chennai Dar es Salaam
Delhi Florence Hong Kong Istanbul Karachi
Kuala Lumpur Madrid Melbourne Mexico City
Mumbai Nairobi Paris São Paulo Singapore
Taipei Tokyo Toronto Warsaw

and associated companies in
Berlin Ibadan

Oxford is a trade mark of Oxford University Press

ISBN 0 19 831858 8   pbk

First published 1994
Reprinted 1995, July 1996 with corrections, May 1997,
January 1999

Printed in Hong Kong

Oxford University Press

2 Contents

Asia

Europe

Contents 3

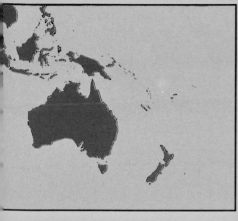

Country	Land Area thousand sq km	Capital city	Total Population millions	Density of Population per sq km	Birth Rate per thousand	Death Rate per thousand	People living in cities percent	GNP per capita US $
Afghanistan	652	Kābul	16.9	26	51	23	18	450
Albania	27	Tiranë	3.3	113	23	6	36	800
Algeria	2382	Algers (Algiers)	26.0	11	35	8	50	2060
Andorra	0.5	Andorra-la-Vella	0.05	104	13	4	...	...
Angola	1247	Luanda	8.9	8	47	19	26	620
Anguilla	0.16	The Valley	0.007	77	25	10	...	...
Antigua & Barbuda	0.4	St. John's	0.1	190	15	5	58	4600
Argentina	2767	Buenos Aires	33.1	12	21	9	86	2370
Armenia	30	Yerevan	3.5	...	24	7	68	...
Australia	7687	Canberra	17.8	2	15	8	85	17080
Austria	84	Wien (Vienna)	7.9	89	12	12	55	19240
Azerbaijan	87	Baku	7.1	...	26	6	53	...
Bahamas, The	14	Nassau	0.3	18	20	5	75	11510
Bahrain	0.6	Al'Manāmah (Manama)	0.5	829	27	3	81	6610
Bangladesh	144	Dhaka	111.4	803	41	15	14	200
Barbados	0.4	Bridgetown	0.3	606	16	9	32	6540
Belarus	207	Minsk	10.3	...	14	11	67	...
Belgium	31	Bruxelles (Brussels)	10.0	326	12	12	95	15440
Belize	23	Belmopan	0.2	8	37	6	50	1970
Benin	113	Porto Novo	5.0	42	49	19	39	360
Bermuda	0.05	Hamilton	0.058	1160	16	7	100	25000
Bhutan	47	Thimphu	0.7	32	38	16	13	190
Bolivia	1099	La Paz	7.8	7	42	13	51	620
Bosnia-Herzegovina	51	Sarajevo	4.2	...	14	6	36	...
Botswana	582	Gaborone	1.4	2	46	11	24	2040
Brazil	8512	Brasília	150.8	18	27	8	74	2680
Brunei Darussalam	6	Bandar Seri Begawan	0.3	42	29	3	59	14120
Bulgaria	111	Sofiya	8.9	81	13	12	68	2210
Burkina	274	Ougadougou	9.6	33	47	18	18	330
Burundi	28	Bujumbura	5.8	196	47	17	5	210
Cambodia	181	Phnom Penh	9.1	46	39	16	13	75
Cameroon	475	Yaoundé	12.7	24	47	14	42	940
Canada	9976	Ottawa	27.4	3	14	8	78	20450
Cape Verde Islands	4	Praia	0.4	94	38	10	33	890
Cayman Islands	0.3	George Town	0.25	...	15	4	100	...
Central African Republic	623	Bangui	3.2	5	45	17	43	390
Chad	1284	Ndjamena	5.2	4	44	19	30	190
Chile	757	Santiago	13.6	17	23	6	85	1940
China	9597	Beijing (Peking)	1165.8	118	21	7	26	370
Colombia	1139	Bogotá	34.3	28	27	6	68	1240
Comoros	2	Moroni	0.5	239	47	13	26	480
Congo	342	Brazzaville	2.4	6	46	14	41	1010
Cook Islands	0.3	Rarotonga	0.018	90	24	5	35	...
Costa Rica	51	San José	3.2	59	27	4	45	1910
Côte d'Ivoire	322	Yamoussoukro	13.0	39	50	14	43	730
Croatia	56	Zagreb	4.6	...	12	11	51	...
Cuba	111	La Habana (Havana)	10.8	93	18	7	73	1500
Cyprus	9	Nicosia	0.7	76	19	7	62	8040
Czech Republic	79	Praha (Prague)	15.7	...	14	12	347	3140
Denmark	43	København (Copenhagen)	5.2	119	11	11	85	22090
Djibouti	22	Djibouti	0.4	18	47	18	79	1000
Dominica	0.7	Roseau	0.1	109	26	5	...	1940
Dominican Republic	49	Santo Domingo	7.5	147	30	7	58	820
Ecuador	284	Quito	10.2	38	32	7	55	960
Egypt	1001	El Qâ'hira (Cairo)	55.7	54	33	10	45	600
El Salvador	21	San Salvador	5.6	250	36	8	48	1100
Equatorial Guinea	28	Malabo	0.4	16	43	17	28	330
Eritrea	117	Asmera	3	...	...	...	...	...
Estonia	45	Tallinn	1.6	...	16	12	71	...
Ethiopia	1105	Ādis Ābeba (Addis Ababa)	54.3	15	...	...	...	120
Fiji	18	Suva	0.8	41	27	6	39	1770
Finland	338	Helsinki	5.0	15	12	10	62	26070
France	547	Paris	56.9	103	14	10	73	19480
French Polynesia	4	Papeete	0.2	56	28	5	62	6000
Gabon	268	Libreville	1.1	4	41	16	43	3220
Gambia, The	11	Banjul	0.9	76	47	21	22	260
Georgia	70	Tbilisi	5.5	...	17	9	56	...
Germany	357	Berlin	80.6	218	11	12	90	20750
Ghana	239	Accra	16.0	63	44	13	32	390
Greece	132	Athínai (Athens)	10.3	76	12	10	58	6000
Grenada	0.4	St George's	0.1	247	37	7	...	2120
Guam	0.5	Agaña	0.1	218	27	4	...	...
Guatemala	109	Guatemala	9.7	84	40	8	39	900
Guinea	246	Conakry	7.8	28	51	21	22	480
Guinea Bissau	36	Bissau	1.0	27	43	22	27	180
Guyana	215	Georgetown	0.8	5	24	5	35	370
Haiti	28	Port-au-Prince	6.4	234	36	13	28	370
Honduras	112	Tegucigalpa	5.5	46	39	8	44	590
Hong Kong	1	Victoria	5.7	5589	13	6	93	11540
Hungary	93	Budapest	10.3	113	12	13	63	2780
Iceland	103	Reykjavik	0.3	2	19	7	90	21150
India	3288	New Delhi	882.6	260	32	11	26	350
Indonesia	1905	Jakarta	184.5	9	28	9	31	560
Iran	1648	Tehrān	59.7	34	34	7	54	2450
Iraq	438	Baghdād	18.2	44	42	7	73	2000
Irish Republic	70	Dublin	3.5	53	18	9	56	9550
Israel	21	Jerusalem	5.2	221	22	7	91	10970
Italy	301	Roma (Rome)	58.0	190	10	10	72	16850
Jamaica	11	Kingston	2.5	229	23	6	51	1510
Japan	378	Tōkyō	124.4	327	11	7	77	25430
Jordan	98	Amman	3.6	44	39	6	70	1240
Kazakhstan	2717	Alma-Ata	16.9	...	22	8	58	...
Kenya	580	Nairobi	26.2	43	47	11	22	370
Kirgyzstan	199	Bishkek	4.5	...	29	7	38	...
Kiribati	0.7	Tarawa	0.06	92	...	...	36	760
Korea, North	121	Pyongyang	22.2	190	24	5	64	700
Korea, South	99	Soul (Seoul)	44.3	443	16	6	74	5400
Kuwait	18	Al Kuwayt	1.4	117	27	2	96	16380
Laos	237	Viangchan (Vientiane)	4.4	17	45	16	16	200
Latvia	65	Riga	2.7	...	15	12	71	...
Lebanon	10	Beyrouth (Beirut)	3.4	285	31	8	84	2000
Lesotho	30	Maseru	1.9	58	41	12	19	470
Liberia	98	Monrovia	2.8	23	47	15	44	500
Libya	1760	Tarābulus (Tripoli)	4.5	3	44	9	76	6000
Liechtenstein	0.2	Vaduz	0.03	175	14	6	28	16600

Country	Land Area thousand sq km	Capital city	Total Population millions	Density of Population per sq·km	Birth Rate per thousand	Death Rate per thousand	People living in cities percent	GNP per capita US $
Lithuania	65	Vilnius	3.7	...	15	10	69	...
Luxembourg	3	Luxembourg	0.4	142	12	10	78	28770
Macao	0.02	Macau City	0.5	20826	17	3	99	2000
Macedonia	26	Skopje	1.9	...	17	7	54	1.9
Madagascar	587	Antananarivo	11.9	20	45	13	23	230
Malawi	118	Lilongwe	8.7	71	56	20	15	200
Malaysia	330	Kuala Lumpur	18.7	53	30	5	35	2340
Maldives	0.3	Malé	0.2	717	46	9	28	440
Mali	1240	Bamako	8.5	8	51	20	22	270
Malta	0.3	Valletta	0.4	1117	16	8	85	6630
Marshall Islands	0.2	Majuro	0.1	...	31	5	...	...
Mauritania	1031	Nouakchott	2.1	2	46	18	41	500
Mauritius	2	Port Louis	1.1	539	18	6	41	2250
Mexico	1973	México	87.7	45	28	6	71	2490
Micronesia, Federated States of	0.7	Kolonia	0.1	...	...	...	...	...
Moldova	34	Kishinev	4.4	...	18	10	48	...
Monaco	(195 hectares)	Monaco	0.03	14737	20	17	100	...
Mongolia	1585	Ulaanbaatar (Ulan Bator)	2.3	1	35	8	42	400
Montserrat	0.1	Plymouth	0.008	120	17	10	12	11000
Morocco	447	Rabat-Salé	26.2	56	34	9	46	950
Mozambique	802	Maputo	16.6	20	45	18	23	80
Myanmar (Burma)	677	Rangoon (Yangon)	42.5	62	30	9	24	...
Namibia	824	Windhoek	1.5	2	43	11	27	1300
Nauru	0.02	Yaren	0.009	450	23	5	...	...
Nepal	141	Kathmandu	19.98	136	38	14	8	170
Netherlands	37	Amsterdam	15.2	361	13	9	89	17330
New Caledonia	19	Nouméa	0.2	9	25	6	58	4000
New Zealand	269	Wellington	3.4	13	16	8	84	12680
Nicaragua	130	Managua	4.1	30	40	7	57	830
Niger	1267	Niamey	8.3	6	52	20	15	310
Nigeria	924	Lagos & Abuja	90.1	122	48	15	16	370
Niue	0.3	Alofi	0.003	12	21	5	23	...
Northern Marianas	0.5	Susupe	0.02	...	...	...	...	4240
Norway	324	Oslo	4.3	13	13	11	71	23120
Oman	212	Masqat (Muscat)	1.6	7	44	7	11	5070
Pakistan	804	Islamabad	121.7	154	44	12	28	380
Palau (Belau)	0.5	Koror	0.02	...	...	...	...	1100
Panama	77	Panamá	2.4	31	26	5	53	1830
Papua New Guinea	463	Port Moresby	3.9	9	34	11	13	860
Paraguay	407	Asunción	4.5	11	34	7	43	1110
Peru	1285	Lima	22.5	17	30	8	70	1160
Philippines	300	Manila	63.7	208	32	7	43	730
Pitcairn Island	(4.6 sq km)	Adamstown	(59 people)	12	...	...	...	...
Poland	313	Warszawa (Warsaw)	38.4	123	16	10	61	1700
Portugal	92	Lisboa (Lisbon)	10.5	112	13	10	30	4890
Puerto Rico	9	San Juan	3.7	417	18	8	72	6470
Qatar	11	Ad Dawhah (Doha)	0.5	33	25	2	90	15860
Romania	238	Bucureşti (Bucharest)	23.2	98	15	11	54	1640
Russian Federation (Russia)	17078	Moskva (Moscow)	149.3	...	14	11	74	...
Rwanda	26	Kigali	7.7	275	51	16	7	310
St Kitts-Nevis	0.3	Basseterre	0.04	168	23	11	45	3330
St Lucia	0.6	Castries	0.2	244	28	6	46	1900
St Vincent & The Grenadines	0.4	Kingstown	0.1	299	25	6	21	1610
Samoa, American	0.2	Fagotogo	0.05	60	...	...	...	...
San Marino	0.06	San Marino	0.02	377	11	7	...	...
São Tomé & Príncipe	1	São Tomé	0.1	126	36	9	38	380
Saudi Arabia	2150	Ar Riyad (Riyadh)	16.1	7	42	7	77	6230
Senegal	197	Dakar	7.9	38	45	17	37	710
Seychelles	0.4	Victoria	0.1	152	25	8	52	4670
Sierra Leone	72	Freetown	4.4	58	48	23	30	240
Singapore	1	Singapore City	2.8	4650	17	5	100	12310
Slovakia	49	Bratislava	1.5	...	...	...	...	...
Slovenia	20	Ljubljana	1.9	...	...	...	49	...
Solomon Islands	28	Honiara	0.4	10	41	5	9	580
Somalia	638	Muqdisho (Mogadishu)	8.3	12	49	19	24	150
South Africa, Republic of	1221	Pretoria	41.7	29	31	9	56	2520
Spain	505	Madrid	38.6	78	13	9	91	10920
Sri Lanka	66	Colombo	17.6	262	22	6	22	470
Sudan	2506	Khartoum	26.5	10	44	15	20	340
Surinam	163	Paramaribo	0.4	2	27	6	48	3050
Swaziland	17	Mbabane	0.8	45	46	15	23	820
Sweden	450	Stockholm	8.7	19	13	12	83	23860
Switzerland	41	Berne	6.9	158	12	10	60	32790
Syria	185	Dimashq (Damascus)	13.7	68	44	6	50	990
Taiwan	36	T'ai-pei	20.8	556	17	5	62	6600
Tajikistan	143	Dushanbe	5.5	...	38	6	31	...
Tanzania	945	Dodoma	27.4	39	50	13	21	120
Thailand	513	Bangkok	56.3	108	21	7	18	1420
Togo	57	Lomé	3.8	61	45	13	24	410
Tonga	0.7	Nuku'alofa	0.1	127	29	4	21	660
Trinidad & Tobago	5	Port-of-Spain	1.3	250	25	6	64	3470
Tunisia	164	Tunis	8.4	50	29	7	53	1420
Turkey	781	Ankara	59.2	71	28	8	59	1630
Turkmenistan	488	Ashkhabad	3.9	72	34	7	45	...
Turks & Caicos	0.4	Grand Turk	0.012	23	26	4	51	...
Tuvalu	0.03	Fongafale (Funafuti)	0.008	23	29	4	...	...
Uganda	236	Kampala	17.5	78	52	15	10	220
Ukraine	604	Kiyev (Kiev)	52.1	...	134	12	68	...
United Arab Emirates	78	Abu Zabi (Abu Dhabi)	2.5	19	22	4	78	19860
United Kingdom (UK)	245	London	57.8	233	14	12	90	16070
United States of America (USA)	9363	Washington D.C.	255.6	27	15	9	75	21700
Uruguay	177	Montevideo	3.1	18	17	10	89	2560
Uzbekistan	447	Tashkent	21.3	...	33	6	40	...
Vanuatu	12	Vila	0.2	12	37	7	18	1060
Venezuela	912	Caracas	18.9	22	30	5	84	2560
Vietnam	329	Hanoi	69.2	204	31	9	20	...
Virgin Islands, British	0.1	Road Town	0.015	...	...	...	...	10000
Wallis & Futuna	0.2	Mata-Utu	0.015	...	...	...	...	...
Western Sahara	267	Laayoune (El Aaiun)	0.2	...	...	...	57	800
Western Samoa	2.8	Apia	0.2	...	...	7	21	730
Yemen Republic	528	San'a	10.4	41	51	16	25	397
Yugoslavia	102	Beograd (Belgrade)	10.3	...	...	...	47	...
Zaire	2345	Kinshasa	37.9	15	46	14	40	230
Zambia	753	Lusaka	8.4	11	51	13	49	420
Zimbabwe	391	Harare	10.3	25	41	10	26	640

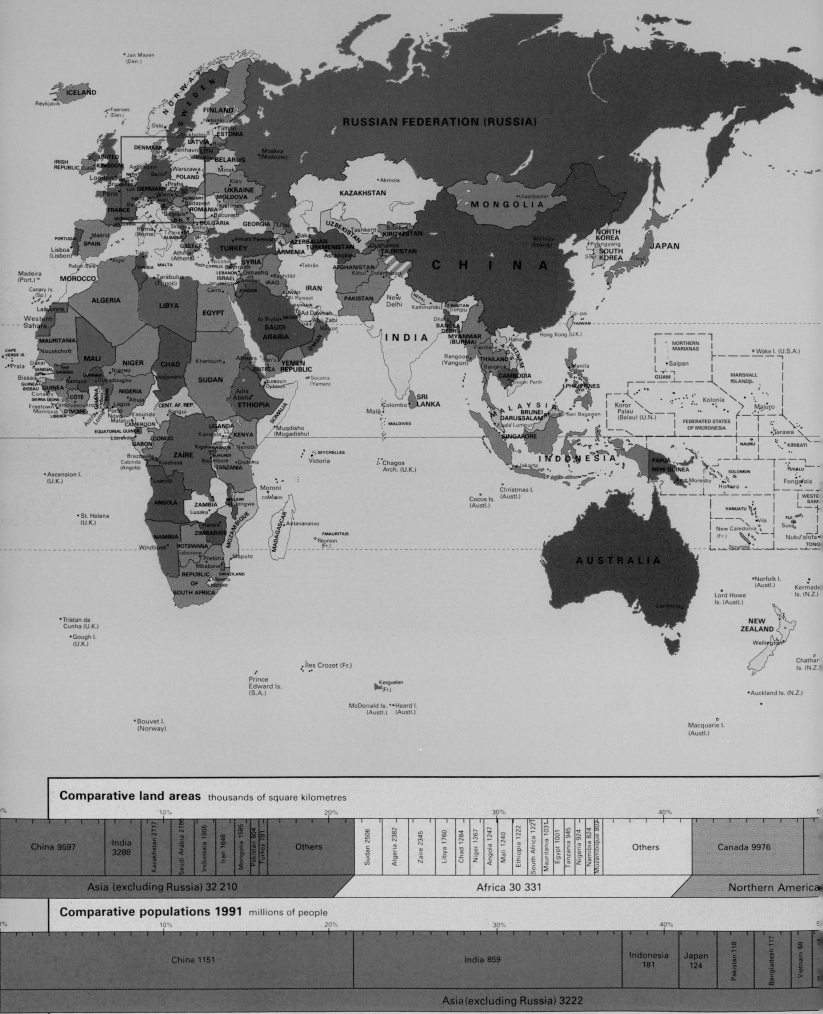

Comparative land areas thousands of square kilometres

0%	10%	20%	30%	40%	50%

| China 9597 | India 3288 | Kazakhstan 2717 | Saudi Arabia 2150 | Indonesia 1905 | Iran 1648 | Mongolia 1585 | Pakistan 804 | Turkey 781 | Others | Sudan 2506 | Algeria 2382 | Zaire 2345 | Libya 1760 | Chad 1284 | Niger 1267 | Angola 1247 | Mali 1240 | Ethiopia 1222 | South Africa 1221 | Mauritania 1031 | Tanzania 945 | Egypt 1001 | Nigeria 924 | Namibia 824 | Mozambique 802 | Others | Canada 9976 |

| Asia (excluding Russia) 32 210 | | | | | | | | | | Africa 30 331 | | | | | | | | | | | | | | | | | Northern America |

Comparative populations 1991 millions of people

0%	10%	20%	30%	40%	50%

| China 1151 | India 859 | Indonesia 181 | Japan 124 | Pakistan 118 | Bangladesh 117 | Vietnam 68 |

| Asia (excluding Russia) 3222 | | | | | | |

Plate tectonics

The present positions of the major tectonic plates are shown with the white areas representing the smaller plates

Plate boundaries

- subduction zones
- ridge zones
- transform zones
- direction of sea-floor spreading
- major fracture zones

Gall Projection

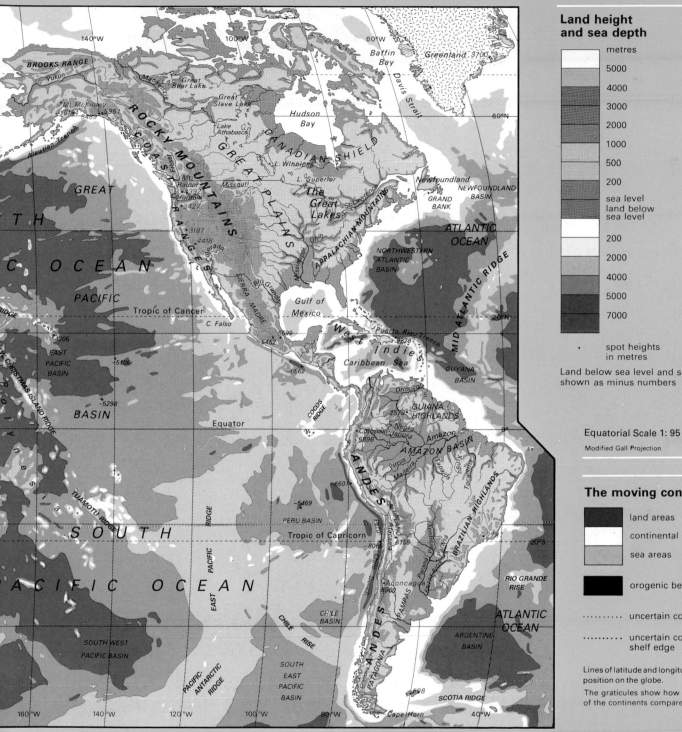

Land height and sea depth

metres

	5000
	4000
	3000
	2000
	1000
	500
	200
	sea level
	land below sea level
	200
	2000
	4000
	5000
	7000

- spot heights in metres

Land below sea level and sea depths shown as minus numbers

Equatorial Scale 1: 95 000 000

Modified Gall Projection

The moving continents

	land areas
	continental shelf
	sea areas
	orogenic belts

·········· uncertain coastline

········· uncertain continental shelf edge

Lines of latitude and longitude indicate position on the globe.

The graticules show how earlier positions of the continents compare with the present

Map labels: BROOKS RANGE, Yukon, Mackenzie, Great Bear Lake, Great Slave Lake, Hudson Bay, Baffin Bay, Greenland, Davis Strait, Mt McKinley 6194, 5489, 5951, ROCKY MOUNTAINS, COAST RANGES, Lake Athabasca, CANADIAN SHIELD, GREAT PLAINS, L. Winnipeg, L. Superior, The Great Lakes, Fraser, Columbia, Mt Rainier 4392, 3427, Missouri, St Lawrence, APPALACHIAN MOUNTAINS, Newfoundland, GRAND BANK, NEWFOUNDLAND BASIN, ATLANTIC OCEAN, GREAT, NORTH OCEAN, PACIFIC, 3187, 4418, Colorado, SIERRA MADRE, Rio Grande, Tropic of Cancer, C. Falso, 5452, -5699, Gulf of Mexico, NORTHWESTERN ATLANTIC BASIN, MID ATLANTIC RIDGE, West Indies, Caribbean Sea, Puerto Rico Trench -8320, GUYANA BASIN, Orinoco, GUIANA HIGHLANDS, 2570, EAST PACIFIC BASIN, -5206, -5105, COCOS RIDGE, Negro, Cotopaxi 5896, Japura, Amazon, AMAZON BASIN, Purus, Madeira, Tapajós, Xingu, Tocantins, Equator, -5298, BASIN, -6662, -6601, -5469, PERU BASIN, ANDES, Peru, Atacama, Ucayali, BRAZILIAN HIGHLANDS, Tropic of Capricorn, Paraguay, Paraná, -8065, 6155, RIO GRANDE RISE, ATLANTIC OCEAN, Aconcagua 6960, PAMPAS, Uruguay, ARGENTINE BASIN, SOUTH PACIFIC OCEAN, TUAMOTU RIDGE, EAST PACIFIC RISE, CHILE BASIN, CHILE RISE, SOUTH WEST PACIFIC BASIN, PACIFIC-ANTARCTIC RIDGE, SOUTH EAST PACIFIC BASIN, PATAGONIA, -698, Cape Horn, SCOTIA RIDGE, Polynesia, CHRISTMAS ISLAND RIDGE

140°W, 100°W, 60°W, 60°N, 20°N, 0°, 20°S, 40°W, 160°W, 120°W, 100°W, 80°W

resent day

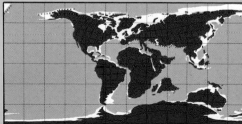

100 million years ago

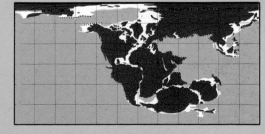

200 million years ago

Oxford University Press

Rainfall
and other forms of precipitation

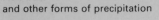

	mm
	over 400
	250–400
	150–250
	50–150
	25–50
	under 25

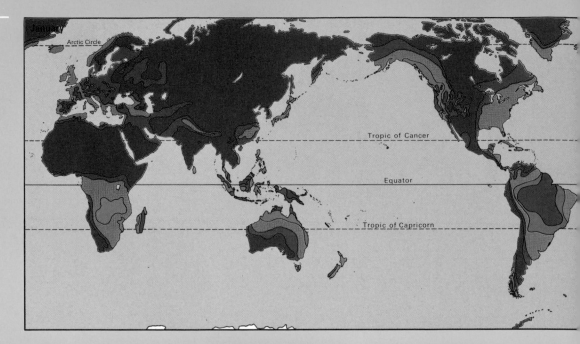

Temperature, ocean currents

actual temperature °C

	32
	24
	16
	8
	0
	−8
	−16
	−24

Ocean currents

cold ————▶

warm ━━━▶

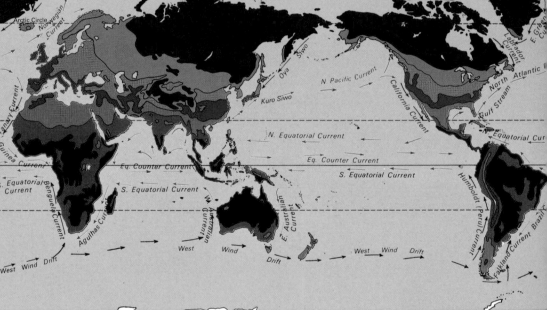

Pressure and winds

Pressure reduced to sea level

1035 millibars
1030
1025
1020
1015
1010
1005
1000
 995

H high pressure cell

L low pressure cell

Prevailing winds
Arrows fly with the wind:
the heavier the arrow, the
more regular ('constant')
the direction of the wind

Equatorial scale 1: 240 000 000

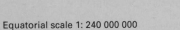
Modified Gall Projection

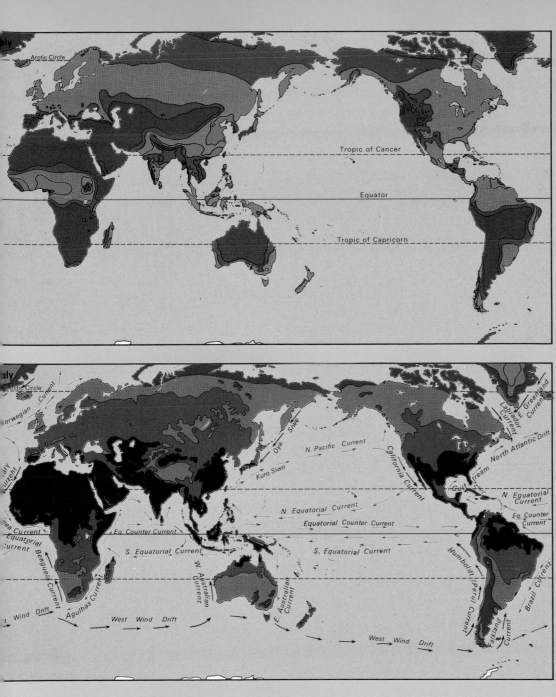

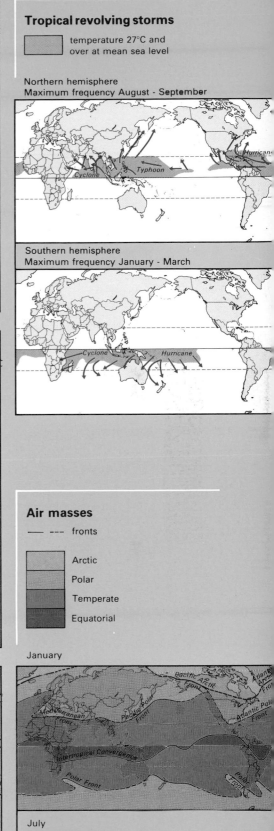

Tropical revolving storms

temperature 27°C and over at mean sea level

Northern hemisphere
Maximum frequency August - September

Cyclone · *Typhoon* · *Hurricane*

Southern hemisphere
Maximum frequency January - March

Cyclone · *Hurricane*

Air masses

--- fronts

Arctic

Polar

Temperate

Equatorial

January

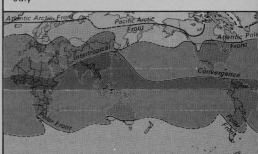

July

Distribution of the earth's water

	Volume (km³)	Average residence time
Oceans and seas	1 370 000 000	4 000+ years
Glaciers and ice caps	30 000 000	1000's of years
Groundwater	4 000 000 60 000 000	from days to tens of thousands of years
Atmospheric water	113 000	8 to 10 days
Freshwater lakes	125 000	days to years
Saline lakes and inland seas	104 000	—
River channels	1 700	2 weeks
Swamps and marshes	3 600	years
Biological water (in plants and animals)	65 000	a few days
Moisture in soil	65 000	2 weeks to 1 year

Water

Surplus

Enough water to support vegetation and crops without irrigation

large surplus

surplus

Deficiency

Not enough water to support vegetation and crops without irrigation. After long periods of deficiency these areas may lose their natural vegetation.

deficiency

chronic deficiency

Equatorial Scale 1: 385 000 000

Climatic regions (basis of classification)

Region		Mean monthly temperature (°C)		Mean monthly precipitation (mm)
		minimum	maximum	
Polar	Arctic	<2	<6	
	Sub-polar	<2	6 – 10	
Middle latitude	Oceanic	2 – 13 seasonal range <12	10 – 20	
	Continental	<2 seasonal range 12 - 36	>10	
	Extreme continental	<2 seasonal range > 36	>10	
Sub-tropical	Humid	2 – 13	>20	>50 for 8 – 12 months
	Distinct wet and dry seasons*	2 – 13	>20	>50 for 1 – 7 months
Tropical	Humid		>13	>50 for 8 – 12 months
	Distinct wet and dry seasons*		>13	>50 for 1 – 7 months
Arid	Desert and semi-desert*			<50 in any month
High altitude	Temperature decreases with altitude			shares characteristics of neighbouring regions

*Regions vulnerable to prolonged drought cycles

Equatorial Scale 1: 135 000 000

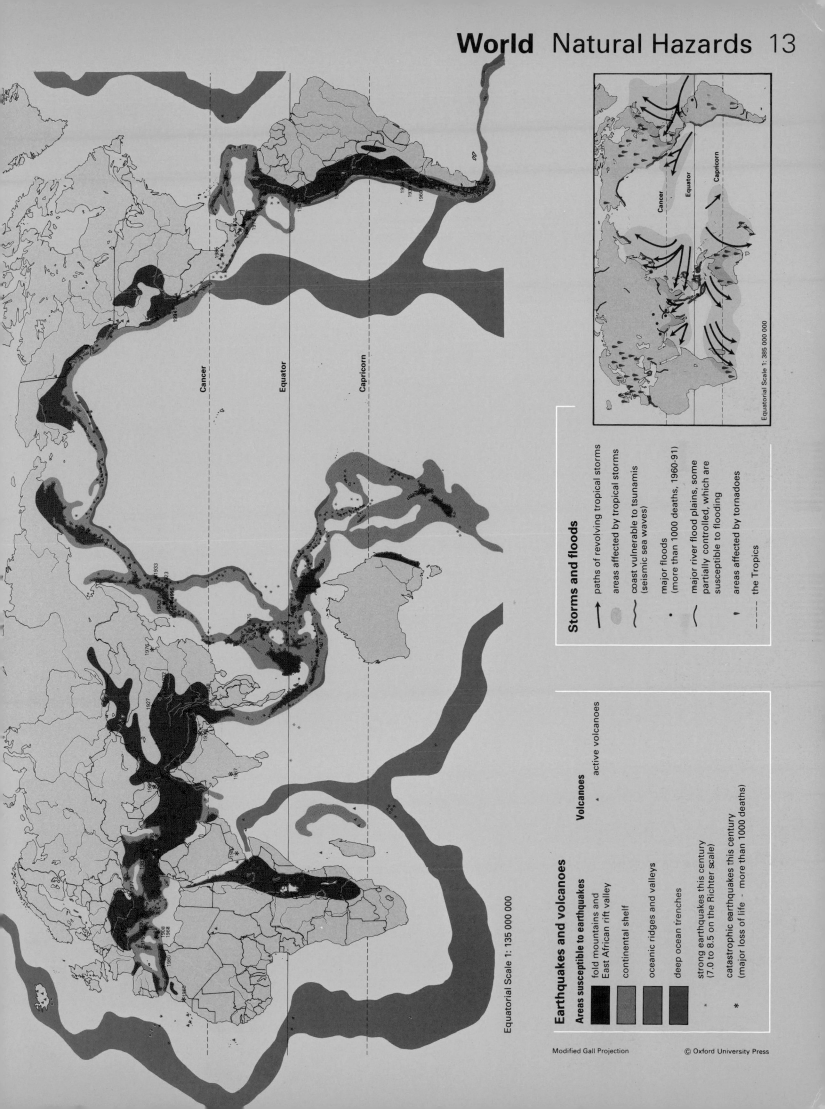

Equatorial Scale 1: 385 000 000

Storms and floods

→ paths of revolving tropical storms

areas affected by tropical storms

) coast vulnerable to tsunamis (seismic sea waves)

• major floods (more than 1000 deaths, 1960-91)

) major river flood plains, some partially controlled, which are susceptible to flooding

• areas affected by tornadoes

--- the Tropics

Earthquakes and volcanoes

Equatorial Scale 1: 135 000 000

Areas susceptible to earthquakes

fold mountains and East African rift valley

continental shelf

oceanic ridges and valleys

deep ocean trenches

Volcanoes

▲ active volcanoes

* strong earthquakes this century (7.0 to 8.5 on the Richter scale)

* catastrophic earthquakes this century (major loss of life - more than 1000 deaths)

Cancer

Equator

Capricorn

Modified Gall Projection

© Oxford University Press

Manchester
London
Essen
Berlin
Petersburg
Milan
Madrid
Barcelona
Rome
Istanbul
Athens
Tehrān
Baghdād
Cairo
Lagos
Kinshasa
Karachi
Lahore
Delhi
Ahmadabad
Bombay
Hyderabad
Bangalore
Madras
Calcutta
Dhaka
Bangkok
Ho Chi Minh
Jakarta
Surabaya
Shenyang
Beijing
Tianjin
Sŏul
Pusan
Nagoya
Tōkyō-Yokohama
Osaka-Kōbe-Kyōto
Wuhan
Shanghai
Guangzhou
T'aip-ei
Hong Kong
Manila
Sydney

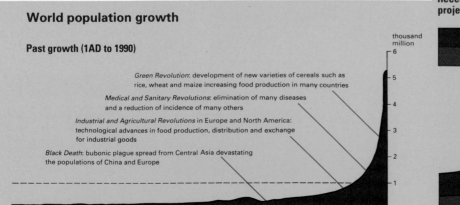

World population growth

Past growth (1AD to 1990)

Green Revolution: development of new varieties of cereals such as
rice, wheat and maize increasing food production in many countries

Medical and Sanitary Revolutions: elimination of many diseases
and a reduction of incidence of many others

Industrial and Agricultural Revolutions in Europe and North America:
technological advances in food production, distribution and exchange
for industrial goods

Black Death: bubonic plague spread from Central Asia devastating
the populations of China and Europe

thousand
million
6
5
4
3
2
1

1AD 100 200 300 400 500 600 700 800 900 1000 1100 1200 1300 1400 1500 1600 1700 1800 1900 1990

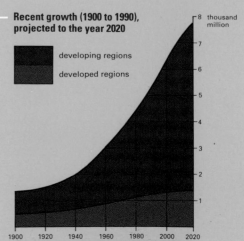

**Recent growth (1900 to 1990),
projected to the year 2020**

developing regions

developed regions

8 thousand
million
7
6
5
4
3
2
1

1900 1920 1940 1960 1980 2000 2020

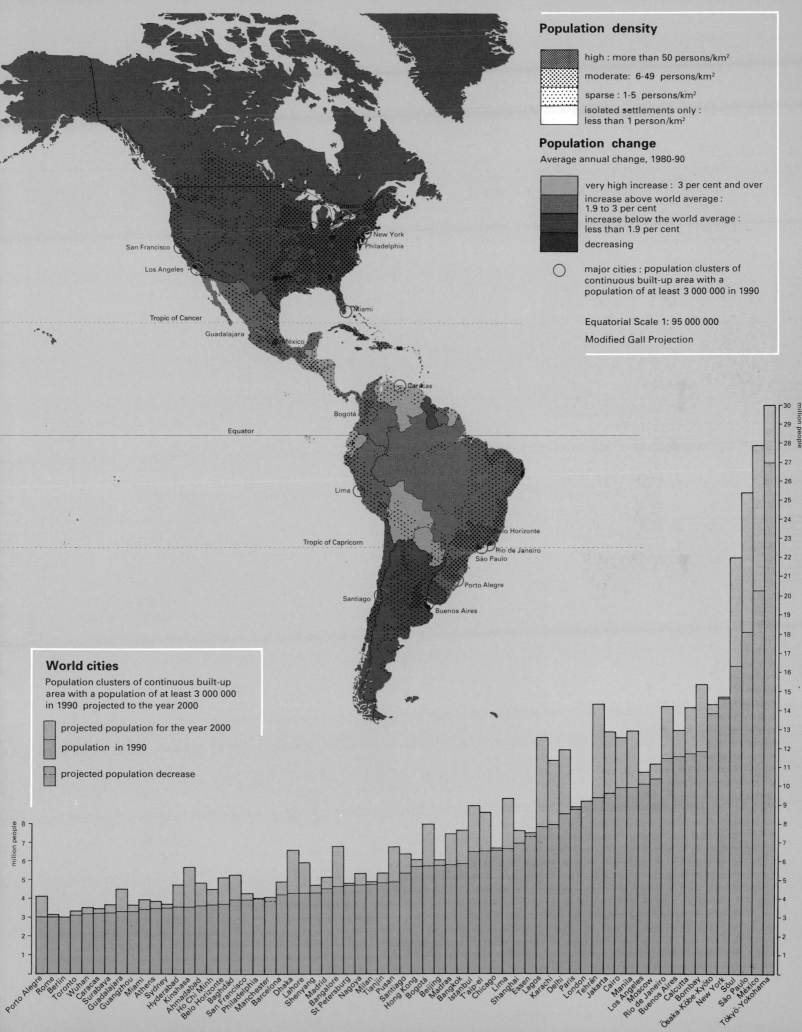

Population density

	high : more than 50 persons/km²
	moderate: 6-49 persons/km²
	sparse : 1-5 persons/km²
	isolated settlements only : less than 1 person/km²

Population change

Average annual change, 1980-90

	very high increase : 3 per cent and over
	increase above world average : 1.9 to 3 per cent
	increase below the world average : less than 1.9 per cent
	decreasing

○ major cities : population clusters of continuous built-up area with a population of at least 3 000 000 in 1990

Equatorial Scale 1: 95 000 000

Modified Gall Projection

World cities

Population clusters of continuous built-up area with a population of at least 3 000 000 in 1990 projected to the year 2000

	projected population for the year 2000
	population in 1990
	projected population decrease

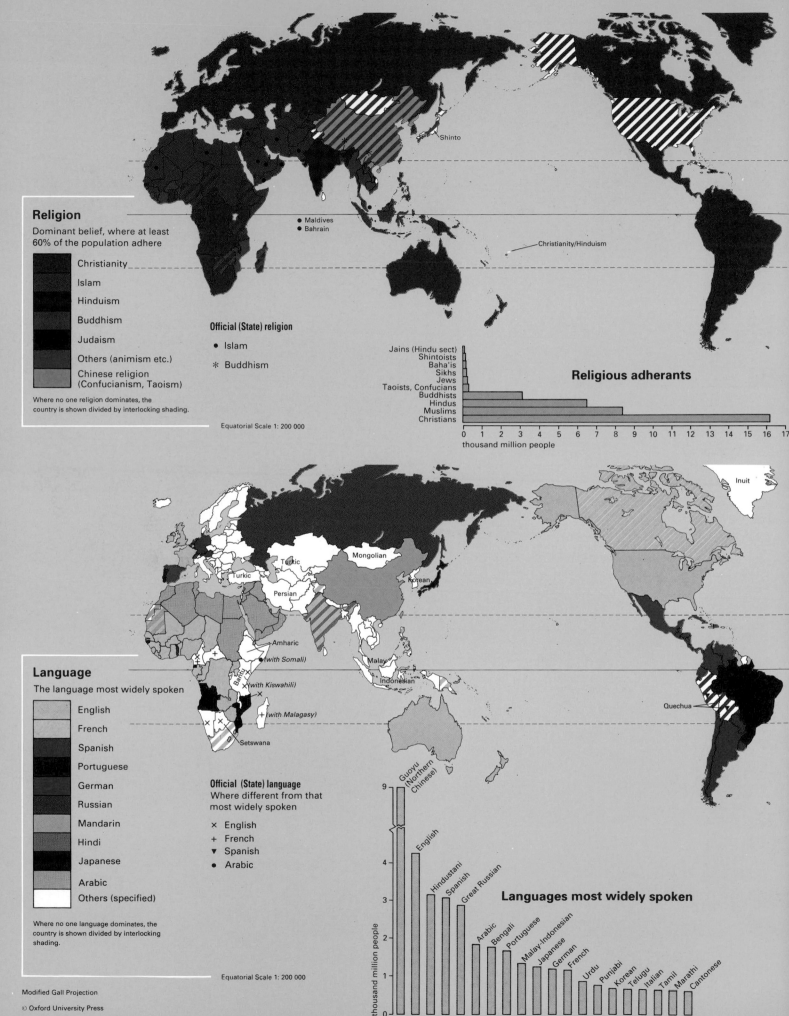

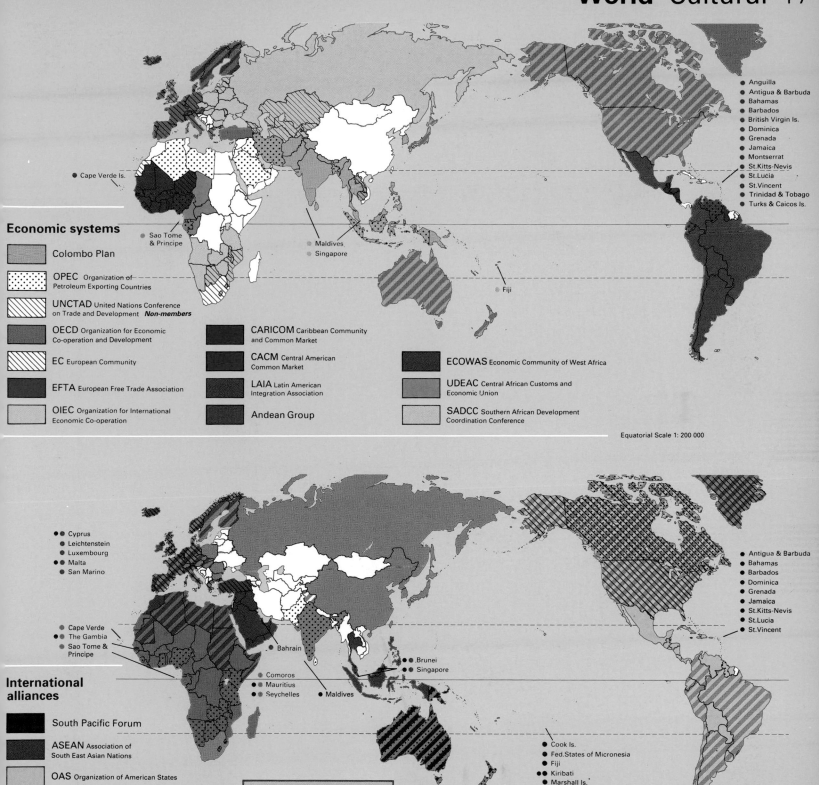

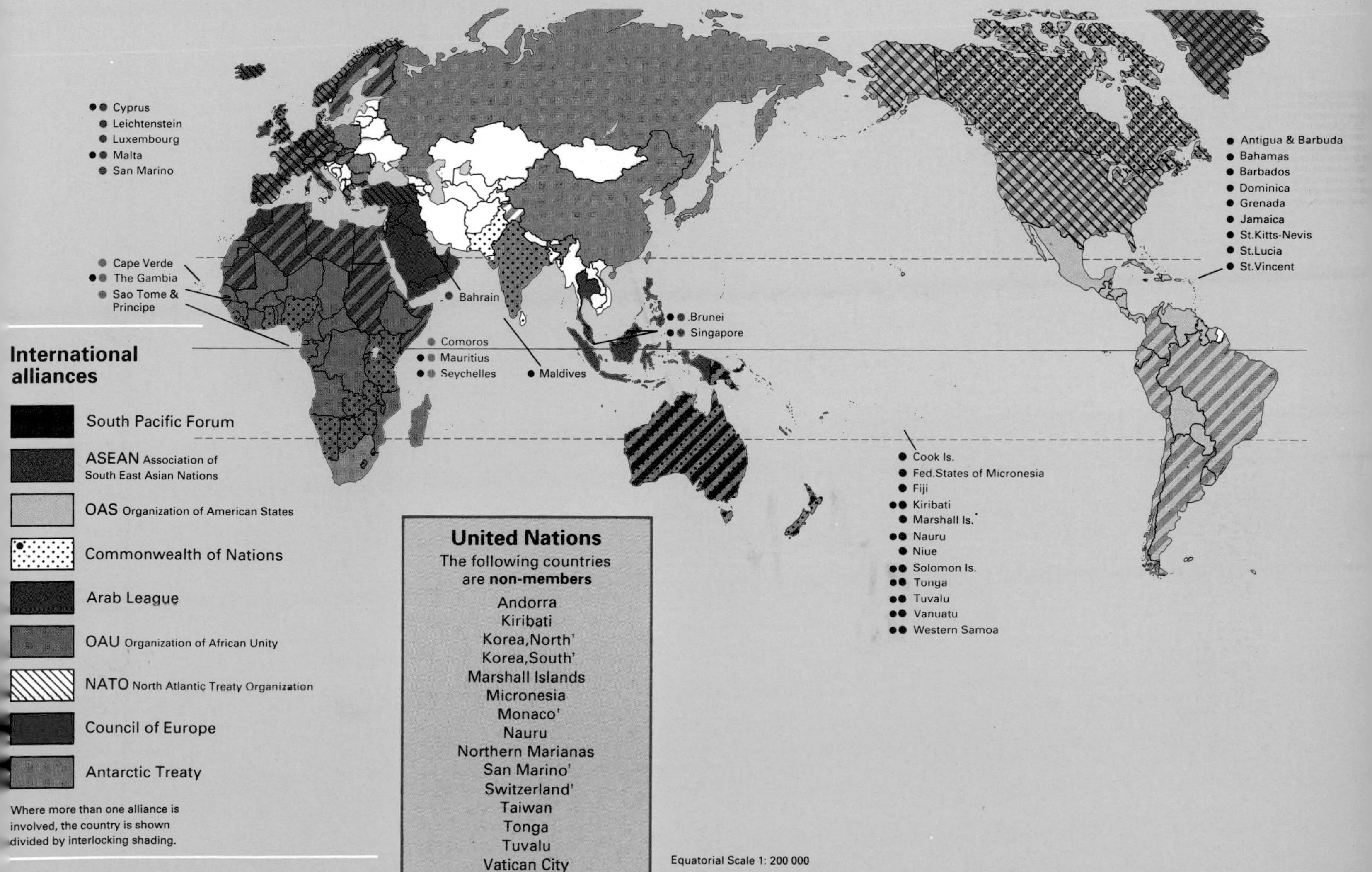

Economic systems

- Colombo Plan
- OPEC Organization of Petroleum Exporting Countries
- UNCTAD United Nations Conference on Trade and Development **Non-members**
- OECD Organization for Economic Co-operation and Development
- EC European Community
- EFTA European Free Trade Association
- OIEC Organization for International Economic Co-operation
- CARICOM Caribbean Community and Common Market
- CACM Central American Common Market
- LAIA Latin American Integration Association
- Andean Group
- ECOWAS Economic Community of West Africa
- UDEAC Central African Customs and Economic Union
- SADCC Southern African Development Coordination Conference

Equatorial Scale 1: 200 000

Labels on maps:
- Cape Verde Is.
- Sao Tome & Principe
- Maldives
- Singapore
- Fiji

- Anguilla
- Antigua & Barbuda
- Bahamas
- Barbados
- British Virgin Is.
- Dominica
- Grenada
- Jamaica
- Montserrat
- St.Kitts-Nevis
- St.Lucia
- St.Vincent
- Trinidad & Tobago
- Turks & Caicos Is.

International alliances

- South Pacific Forum
- ASEAN Association of South East Asian Nations
- OAS Organization of American States
- Commonwealth of Nations
- Arab League
- OAU Organization of African Unity
- NATO North Atlantic Treaty Organization
- Council of Europe
- Antarctic Treaty

Where more than one alliance is involved, the country is shown divided by interlocking shading.

Labels on maps:
- Cyprus
- Leichtenstein
- Luxembourg
- Malta
- San Marino
- Cape Verde
- The Gambia
- Sao Tome & Principe
- Bahrain
- Comoros
- Mauritius
- Seychelles
- Maldives
- Brunei
- Singapore

- Antigua & Barbuda
- Bahamas
- Barbados
- Dominica
- Grenada
- Jamaica
- St.Kitts-Nevis
- St.Lucia
- St.Vincent

- Cook Is.
- Fed.States of Micronesia
- Fiji
- Kiribati
- Marshall Is.
- Nauru
- Niue
- Solomon Is.
- Tonga
- Tuvalu
- Vanuatu
- Western Samoa

United Nations
The following countries are **non-members**

Andorra
Kiribati
Korea,North'
Korea,South'
Marshall Islands
Micronesia
Monaco'
Nauru
Northern Marianas
San Marino'
Switzerland'
Taiwan
Tonga
Tuvalu
Vatican City
Western Sahara

Information correct as of April 1993.

'observer status

Equatorial Scale 1: 200 000

odified Gall Projection

Oxford University Press

¹Now the independent republics of Armenia, Azerbaijan, Belarus, Estonia, Georgia, Kazakhstan, Kirgyzstan, Latvia, Lithuania, Moldova, Russia, Tajikistan, Turkmenistan, Ukraine and Uzbekistan.

²Now the Czech Republic and Slovakia.

³Now Bosnia-Herzegovina, Croatia, Macedonia, Slovenia and Yugoslavia.

Share of world trade, 1981-91

growth
- 49 percent and over
- 5-49 percent

little or no change
- 0-5 percent growth or decline

decline
- 5-49 percent
- 49 percent and over

World trade, 1991

On this map the size of each country represents the share that country has of total world trade, rather than the area of land that the country occupies.

Only those countries with more than 0.01% of world trade are shown

a country shown by a square of this size would have 1% of world trade

a country shown by a square of this size would have 0.01% of world trade

Share of world trade for selected countries, 1981-91

percentage growth — 150, 100, 49, 5 0 5, 49, 100 — percentage decline

Vietnam, Hong Kong, China, Portugal, Spain, Botswana, Mali, Japan, UK, USA, Australia, Greece, New Zealand, Indonesia, Argentina, South Africa, Nigeria, Saudi Arabia, Romania, Iraq

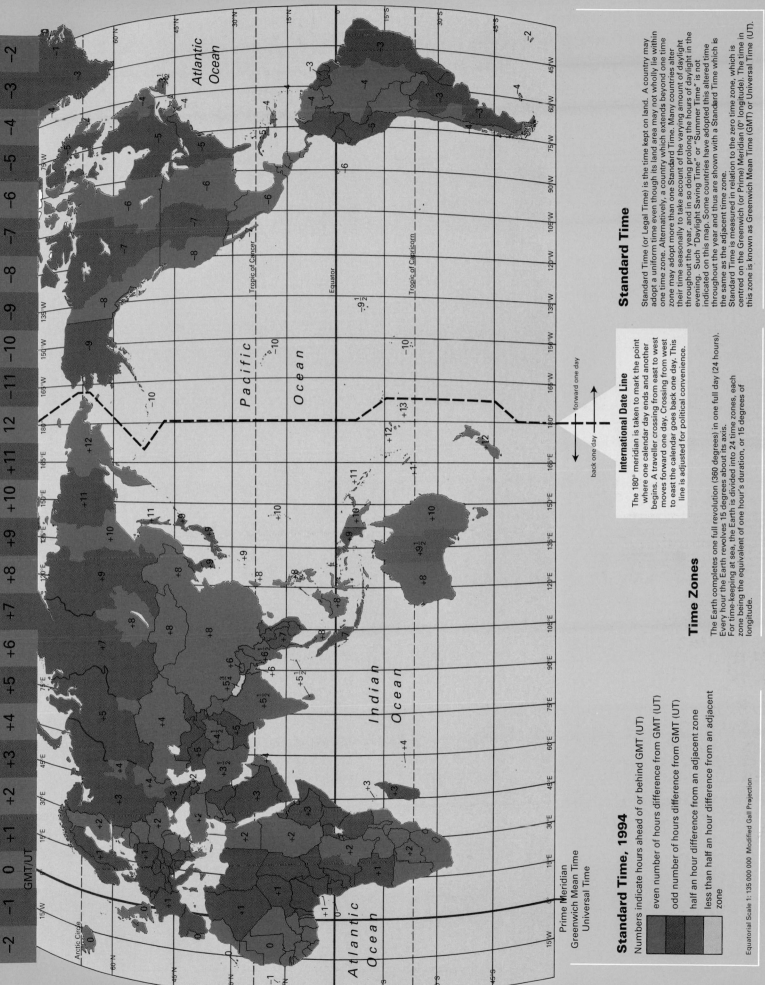

-2 **-1** **0** **+1** **+2** **+3** **+4** **+5** **+6** **+7** **+8** **+9** **+10** **+11** **+12** **-11** **-10** **-9** **-8** **-7** **-6** **-5** **-4** **-3** **-2**

GMT/UT

Standard Time

Standard Time (or Legal Time) is the time kept on land. A country may adopt a uniform time even though its land area may not wholly lie within one time zone. Alternatively, a country which extends beyond one time zone may adopt more than one Standard Time. Many countries alter their time seasonally to take account of the varying amount of daylight throughout the year, and in so doing prolong the hours of daylight in the evening. Such "Daylight Saving Time" or "Summer Time" is not indicated on this map. Some countries have adopted this altered time throughout the year and thus are shown with a Standard Time which is not the same as the adjacent time zone.
Standard Time is measured in relation to the zero time zone, which is centred on the Greenwich (or Prime) Meridian (0° longitude). The time in this zone is known as Greenwich Mean Time (GMT) or Universal Time (UT).

International Date Line

The 180° meridian is taken to mark the point where one calendar day ends and another begins. A traveller crossing from east to west moves forward one day. Crossing from west to east the calendar goes back one day. This line is adjusted for political convenience.

forward one day

back one day

Time Zones

The Earth completes one full revolution (360 degrees) in one full day (24 hours). Every hour the Earth revolves 15 degrees about its axis. For time-keeping at sea, the Earth is divided into 24 time zones, each zone being the equivalent of one hour's duration, or 15 degrees of longitude.

Standard Time, 1994

Numbers indicate hours ahead of or behind GMT (UT)

even number of hours difference from GMT (UT)

odd number of hours difference from GMT (UT)

half an hour difference from an adjacent zone

less than half an hour difference from an adjacent zone

Equatorial Scale 1: 135 000 000 Modified Gall Projection

Prime Meridian
Greenwich Mean Time
Universal Time

© Oxford University Press

Boundaries

international

state

Communications

major road

railway

canal

✈ major airport

Cities and towns

■ over 1 million
   inhabitants

● more than 100 000
   inhabitants

• smaller towns

Physical features

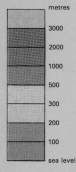 ice cap

Land height

metres
3000
2000
1000
500
300
200
100
sea level

Sea depth

sea level
200
3000
4000
5000

▲ spot height
   in metres

sea depths shown
as minus numbers

Sea ice

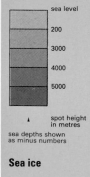

unnavigable

pack ice –
autumn minimum

pack ice –
spring maximum

Scale 1:25 000 000

0   250   500 km

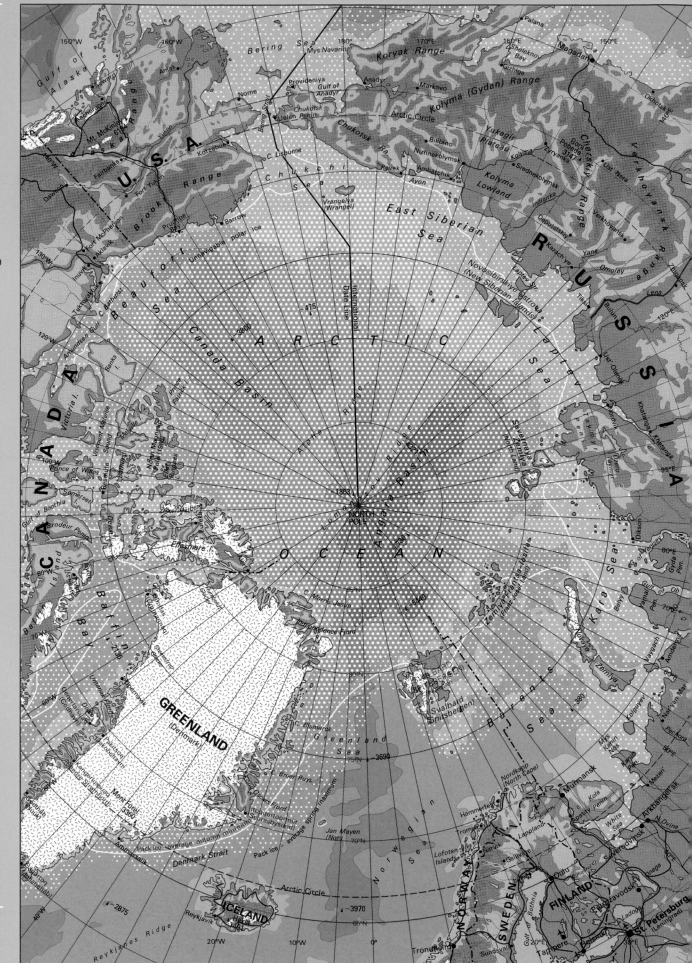

Zenithal Equidistant Projection

© Oxford University Press

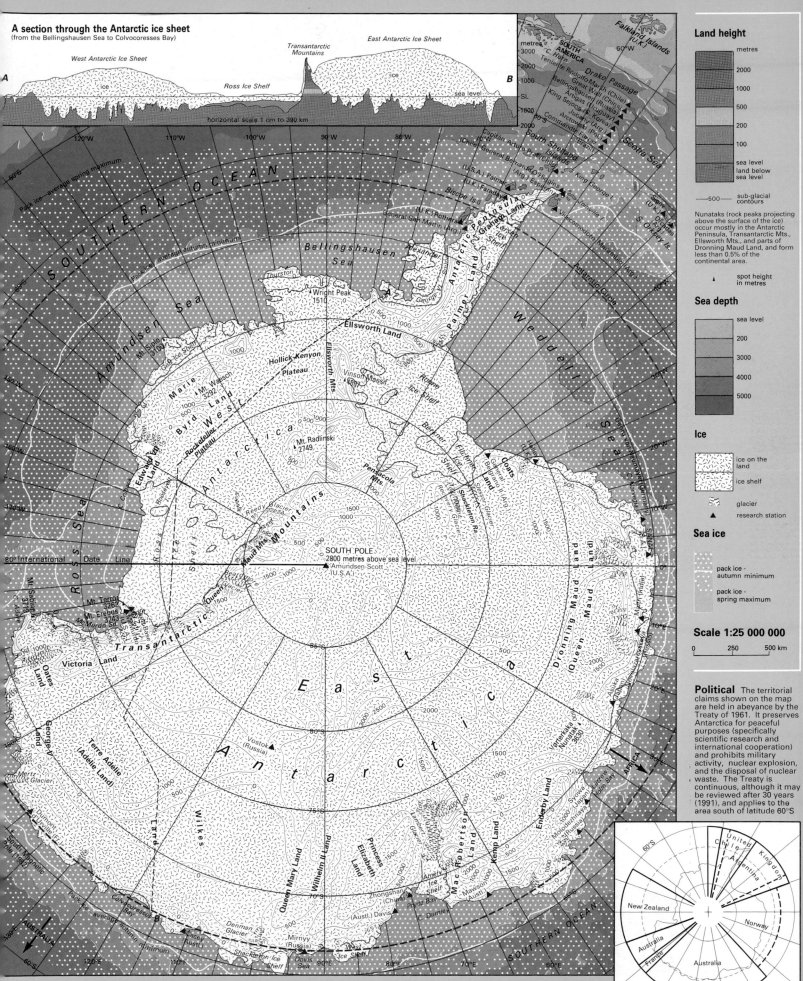

A section through the Antarctic ice sheet (from the Bellingshausen Sea to Colvocoresses Bay)

Zenithal Equidistant Projection
© Oxford University Press

Boundaries

international

political group
(not recognized
territorial boundaries)

Communications

major road*

✈ major airport*

Physical features

ice cap

Land height

metres
5000
3000
2000
1000
500
300
200
100
sea level

* Hawaiian Islands inset
only

Cities and towns

built-up areas

over 1 million
inhabitants

more than 100 000
inhabitants

smaller towns

national capitals
are underlined

Sea ice

pack ice
autumn minimum

pack ice
spring maximum

Sea depth

metres below sea level
200
3000
4000
5000
6000

▲ spot height
in metres

sea depths shown as
minus numbers

Ocean currents

→ warm

⇢ cold

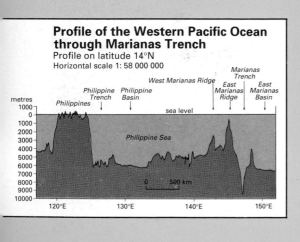

Profile of the Western Pacific Ocean through Marianas Trench

Profile on latitude 14°N
Horizontal scale 1: 58 000 000

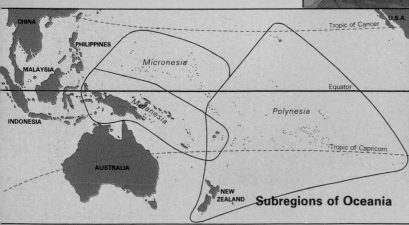

Subregions of Oceania

Modified Zenithal Equidistant Project

Hawaiian Islands (U.S.A.)

Kilauea • Kapaa
Kaalualakahi Channel • Kapaa
Niihau Channel Kauai
Kaula
Waialua Wahiawa
Oahu Kaneohe
Pearl Harbor Honolulu Hoolehua
Molokai C. Halawa
Lanai City Lahaina Maui
Lanai Wailuku 3055
Kahoolawe Alenuihaha Channel
Upolu Pt.
Kawaihae Honokaa
Mauna Kea Honokaa
Hawaii 4205 Hilo
Kailua Kailua
Napoopoo Mauna Loa C.
Papa Kumukahi
Pahala 4169
Kalae (South Cape)

Scale 1 : 7 500 000 | 0 ——— 100 km

ALASKA (U.S.A.)
Mt. McKinley 6194
Mt. Logan 5951
Anchorage
Kodiak I.
Gulf of Alaska
Queen Charlotte Is.

CANADA
Rocky Mountains
Great Slave Lake
Saskatchewan
Canadian Shield
Churchill
Hudson Bay
Winnipeg
Vancouver I.
Vancouver
Seattle
Minneapolis St. Paul
Great Lakes
Toronto
Chicago

UNITED STATES
Salt Lake City
Mt. Elbert 4399
San Francisco
Los Angeles
Houston
New Orleans
Rio Grande
Miami
THE BAHAMAS
La Habana
CUBA
Gulf of Mexico

MÉXICO
Guadalajara
México 5452
Acapulco
Middle America
GUATEMALA
Guatemala
Belize
Cayman Trench
JAMAICA Kingston
HAITI
DOMINICAN REPUBLIC
PUERTO RICO (U.S.A.)
9220 Puerto Rico Trench
Leeward Is.
DOMINICA
ST. LUCIA
BARBADOS
GRENADA
TRINIDAD & TOBAGO

NORTH ATLANTIC OCEAN
Tropic of Cancer
North Equatorial Current

PACIFIC OCEAN
-6474
-6108
Honolulu
Hawaiian Is. (U.S.A.)
Necker
Nihoa
Niihau
Hawaii
Johnston Atoll (U.S.A.)
East Pacific Basin
-5106
Clarion Fracture Zone
Clipperton I. (France)
JANUARY
JULY
-5298
Clipperton Fracture Zone JULY
Equatorial Counter Current
Christmas Island
JANUARY
JULY
Palmyra Atoll (U.S.A.)
Tabuaeran I. (Kiribati)
Kiritimati I. (Kiribati)
Jarvis Is. (U.S.A.)
KIRIBATI
Malden I.
Caroline I.
-6594
Marquesas Islands (France)
French Polynesia (France)
Tuamotu Archipelago (France)
Society Is. (France)
Tahiti
Tuamotu Ridge
Tubuai Is. (France)
Gambier Is. (France)
Austral Ridge
-6144
Palmerston Atoll (N.Z.)
Cook Is. (N.Z.)
Niue (N.Z.)
American Samoa (U.S.A.)

SOUTH PACIFIC OCEAN
-1088
South West Pacific Basin
JULY
JANUARY
Henderson I. (U.S.A.)
Ducie I.
Oeno I. Pitcairn Islands (U.K.)
Easter I. (Chile)
Salay Gomez (Chile)
Easter Island Fracture Zone
Peru Basin
-5469

HONDURAS
Tegucigalpa
6662
EL SALVADOR
NICARAGUA
Managua
San José
COSTA RICA
Guatemala Basin
America Trench
Guatemala Basin
Pacific Rise
Cocos Ridge
Barranquilla
Maracaibo
Caracas
VENEZUELA
Medellín
COLOMBIA
Bogotá
Cali -5750
Quito -6310
ECUADOR
Islas Galápagos (Ecuador)
Carnegie Ridge
I. del Coco (Costa Rica)
PANAMA
Panama
Venezuelan Sea
Caribbean Sea
Windward Is.
Guyana Basin
Orinoco
Llanos
GUYANA
SURINAM
FRENCH GUIANA
Georgetown
Paramaribo
Cayenne

BRAZIL
Manaus
Amazonas
Galápagos Rise
-6601
-6768
Nazca Ridge
Lima
Peru
PERU
Titicaca
La Paz -6388
BOLIVIA
Santa Cruz
Mato Grosso
Chaco
Brasília
-8066
-6755
PARAGUAY
Gran Chaco
Asunción
Rio de Janeiro
São Paulo
Tropic of Capricorn
ARGENTINA
URUGUAY
Córdoba -6960
Valparaíso
Santiago
Concepción
Rosario
Buenos Aires
Montevideo
Porto Alegre
Paraná
Brazil Current
Rio Grande Rise
Chile Basin
Isla de Chiloé
Isla Wellington
Chile Rise
South East Pacific Basin
Valdivia
Santa Cruz
Falkland Current
West Wind Drift
Isla Grande de Tierra del Fuego
C. de Hornos
Falkland Is. (U.K.)
Argentine Basin
Patagonia
Pacific Antarctic Ridge
Eltanin Fracture Zone
West Wind Drift
Antarctic Circle
Pack ice
spring maximum
autumn minimum

Bering Strait
Nunivak I.
St. Lawrence I.
Arctic Circle
Mendocino Seascarp
Murray Seascarp
Gorda Rise
Guadalupe (Mexico)
Roca Alijos
Is. Revillagigedo (Mexico)
California Current
Colorado
Mississippi
Missouri
Yucatan Basin

Scale 1 : 63 000 000 | 0 —— 500 — 1000 — 1500 km

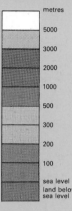

Boundaries

international

disputed

Cities and towns

■ over 1 million inhabitants

● more than 100 000 inhabitants

• smaller towns

national capitals are <u>underlined</u>

Land height

metres
5000
3000
2000
1000
500
300
200
100
sea level
land below sea level

Sea depth

metres below sea level
200
3000
4000
5000
6000

▲ spot height in metres

sea depths shown as minus numbers

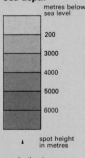

Sea Ice

pack ice autumn minimum

pack ice spring maximum

Ocean currents

→ warm

--→ cold

Scale 1 : 63 000 000

0   500   1000   1500 km

Modified Zenithal Equidistant Projection

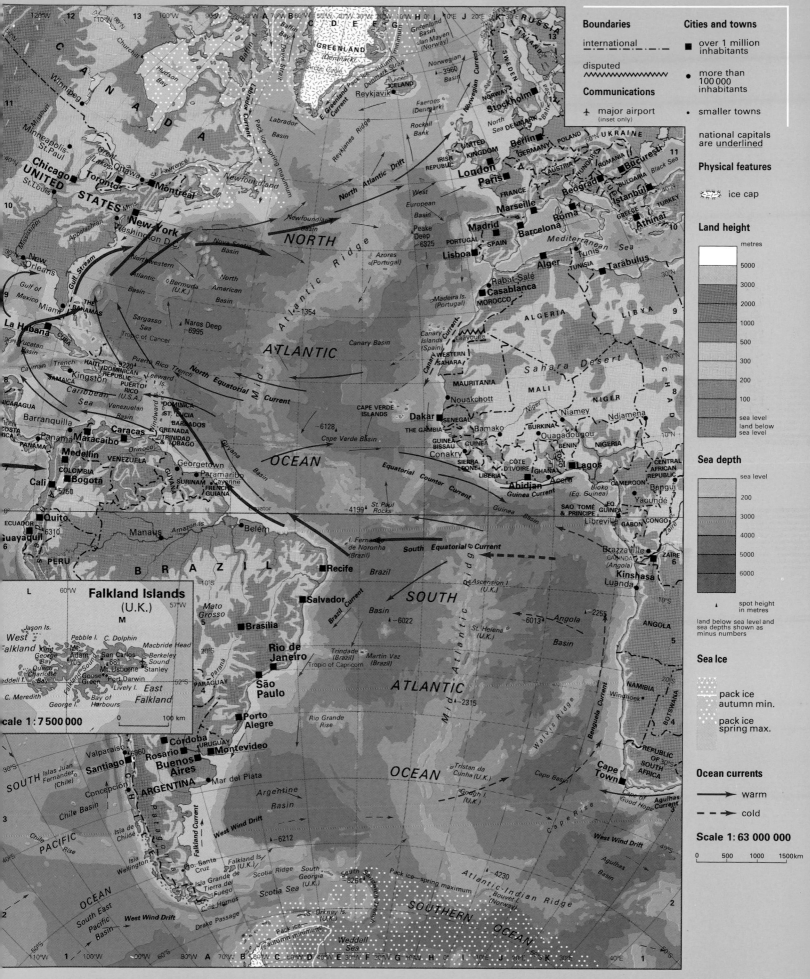

Boundaries

international ----

disputed ~~~~~~

Communications

✈ major airport (inset only)

Cities and towns

■ over 1 million inhabitants

● more than 100 000 inhabitants

• smaller towns

national capitals are <u>underlined</u>

Physical features

ice cap

Land height

	metres
	5000
	3000
	2000
	1000
	500
	300
	200
	100
	sea level
	land below sea level

Sea depth

	sea level
	200
	3000
	4000
	5000
	6000

▲ spot height in metres

land below sea level and sea depths shown as minus numbers

Sea Ice

pack ice autumn min.

pack ice spring max.

Ocean currents

→ warm

--→ cold

Scale 1: 63 000 000

0   500   1000   1500km

Falkland Islands (U.K.)

Scale 1: 7 500 000

0   100 km

Modified Zenithal Equidistant Projection

© Oxford University Press

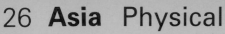

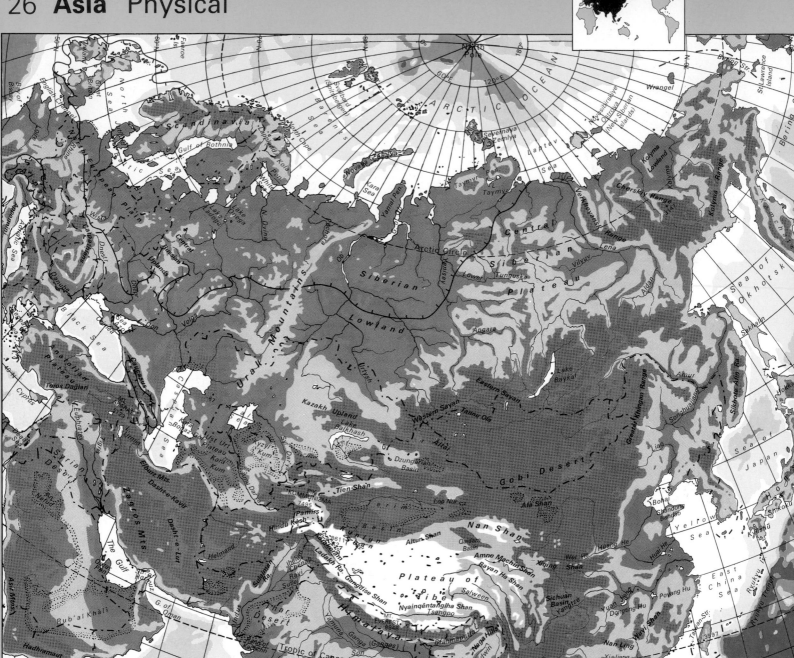

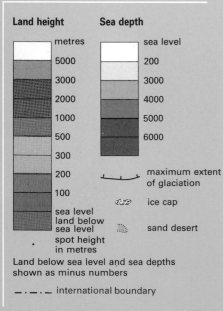

Land height

metres
5000
3000
2000
1000
500
300
200
100
sea level
land below
sea level
spot height
in metres

Sea depth

sea level
200
3000
4000
5000
6000

maximum extent
of glaciation

ice cap

sand desert

Land below sea level and sea depths
shown as minus numbers

— · — · — international boundary

Scale 1 : 44 000 000

0   500   1000 km

Zenithal Equal Area Proj

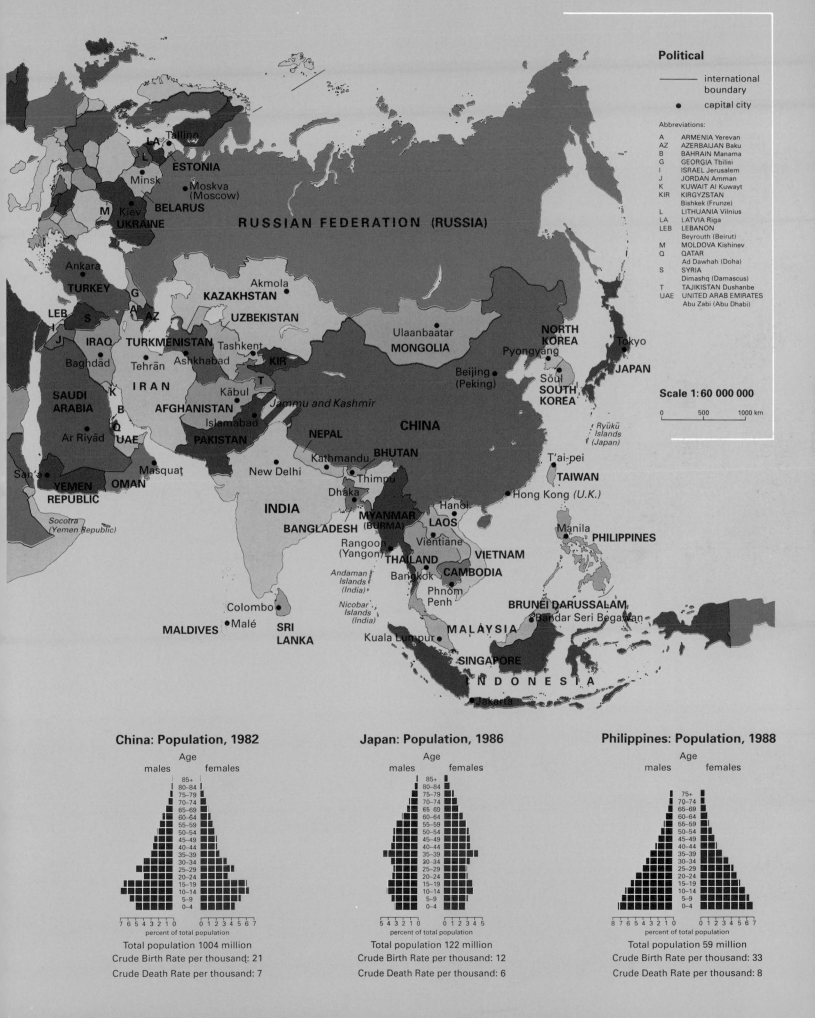

Political

— international boundary
• capital city

Abbreviations:

A	ARMENIA Yerevan
AZ	AZERBAIJAN Baku
B	BAHRAIN Manama
G	GEORGIA Tbilisi
I	ISRAEL Jerusalem
J	JORDAN Amman
K	KUWAIT Al Kuwayt
KIR	KIRGYZSTAN Bishkek (Frunze)
L	LITHUANIA Vilnius
LA	LATVIA Riga
LEB	LEBANON Beyrouth (Beirut)
M	MOLDOVA Kishinev
Q	QATAR Ad Dawhah (Doha)
S	SYRIA Dimashq (Damascus)
T	TAJIKISTAN Dushanbe
UAE	UNITED ARAB EMIRATES Abu Zabi (Abu Dhabi)

Scale 1: 60 000 000

0   500   1000 km

China: Population, 1982

Age
males   females

85+
80–84
75–79
70–74
65–69
60–64
55–59
50–54
45–49
40–44
35–39
30–34
25–29
20–24
15–19
10–14
5–9
0–4

7 6 5 4 3 2 1 0   0 1 2 3 4 5 6 7
percent of total population

Total population 1004 million
Crude Birth Rate per thousand: 21
Crude Death Rate per thousand: 7

Japan: Population, 1986

Age
males   females

85+
80–84
75–79
70–74
65 69
60–64
55–59
50–54
45–49
40–44
35–39
30–34
25–29
20–24
15–19
10–14
5–9
0–4

5 4 3 2 1 0   0 1 2 3 4 5
percent of total population

Total population 122 million
Crude Birth Rate per thousand: 12
Crude Death Rate per thousand: 6

Philippines: Population, 1988

Age
males   females

75+
70–74
65–69
60–64
55–59
50–54
45–49
40–44
35–39
30–34
25–29
20–24
15–19
10–14
5–9
0–4

8 7 6 5 4 3 2 1 0   0 1 2 3 4 5 6 7
percent of total population

Total population 59 million
Crude Birth Rate per thousand: 33
Crude Death Rate per thousand: 8

Asia Natural Vegetation

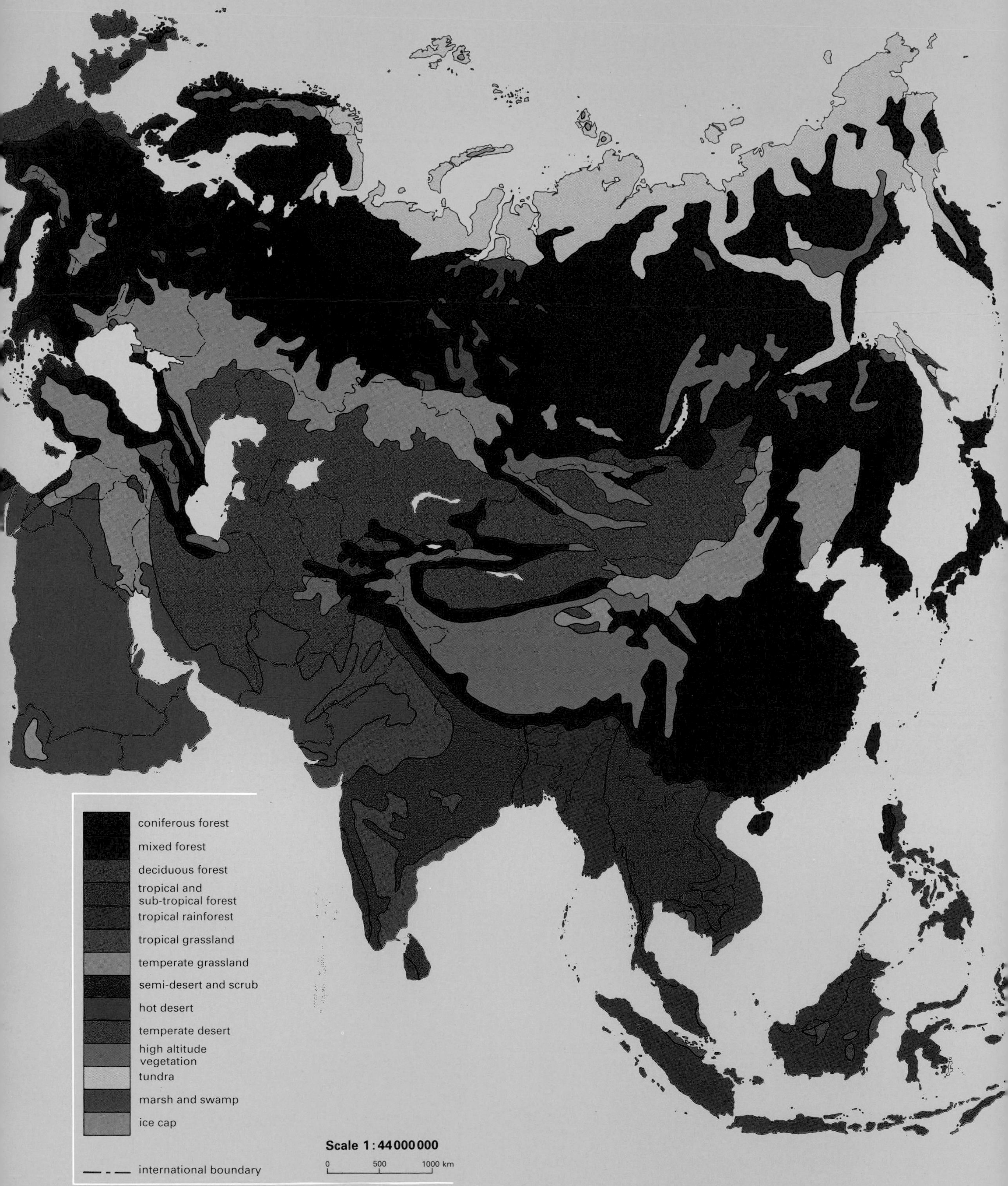

coniferous forest
mixed forest
deciduous forest
tropical and sub-tropical forest
tropical rainforest
tropical grassland
temperate grassland
semi-desert and scrub
hot desert
temperate desert
high altitude vegetation
tundra
marsh and swamp
ice cap
international boundary
Scale 1:44 000 000
0
500
1000 km

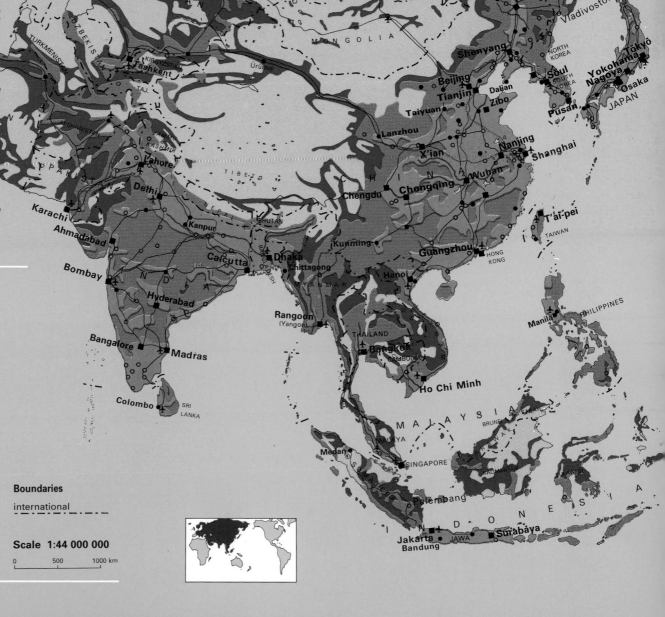

Population density
people per square kilometre

over 100

10–100

1–9

under 1

Cities

■ over 2 million inhabitants

● 1–2 million inhabitants

○ 0.5–1 million inhabitants

Communications

principal roads

principal railways

✈ principal airports

navigable rivers

Boundaries

international

Scale 1:44 000 000

0   500   1000 km

Zenithal Equal Area Projection

© Oxford University Press

arable, predominantly cereals

arable, predominantly paddy

general arable

arable with cash crops

irrigated crops

grazing and dry farming

deciduous forest, farming and grazing

mixed forest, farming and grazing

tropical rain forest, lumbering, crops

coniferous forest, lumbering

desert, nomadic herding

marsh or swamp

tundra and high altitude desert

ice cap

Scale 1:44 000 000

0   500   1000 km

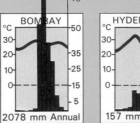

BOMBAY

2078 mm Annual

HYDERABAD

157 mm Annual

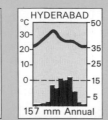

SINGAPORE

2282 mm Annual

Rainfall figures on graphs in tens of millimetres except for annual totals

Zenithal Equal Area Project

© Oxford University Pre

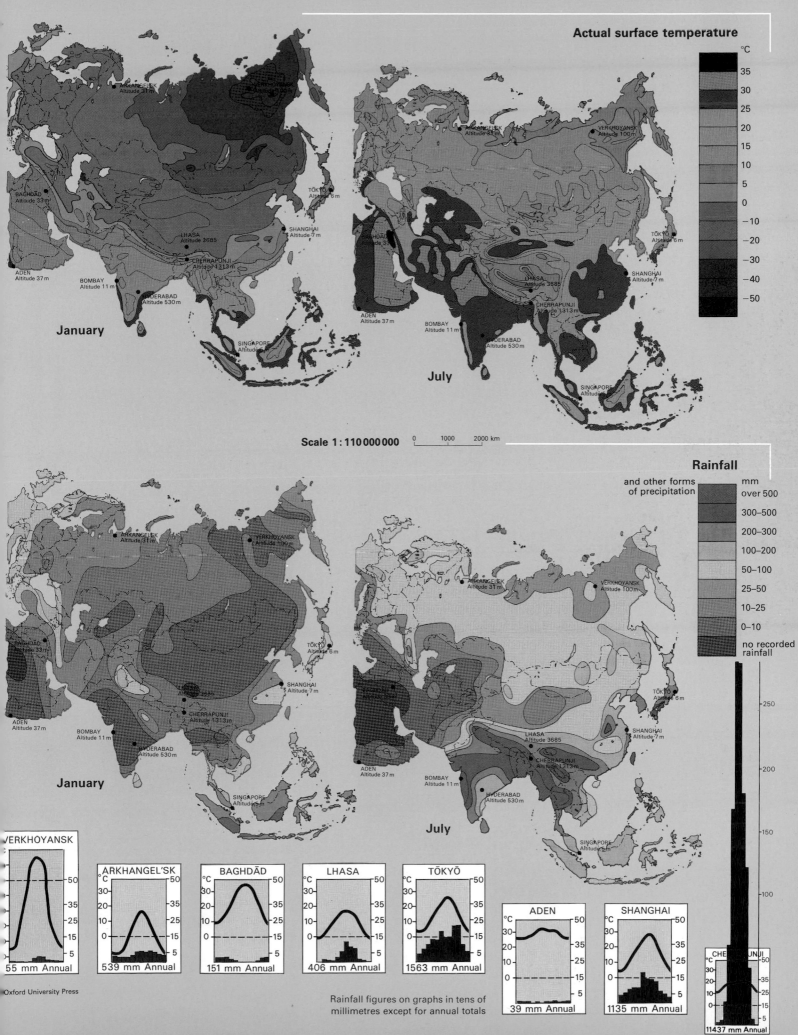

Actual surface temperature

°C
35
30
25
20
15
10
5
0
−10
−20
−30
−40
−50

January

July

Scale 1 : 110 000 000

0   1000   2000 km

Rainfall

and other forms
of precipitation

mm
over 500
300–500
200–300
100–200
50–100
25–50
10–25
0–10

no recorded
rainfall

January

July

VERKHOYANSK
55 mm Annual

ARKHANGEL'SK
539 mm Annual

BAGHDĀD
151 mm Annual

LHASA
406 mm Annual

TŌKYŌ
1563 mm Annual

ADEN
39 mm Annual

SHANGHAI
1135 mm Annual

CHERRAPUNJI
11437 mm Annual

Rainfall figures on graphs in tens of
millimetres except for annual totals

Oxford University Press

Physical features

- seasonal river/lake
- marsh
- salt pan
- ice cap

Boundaries
- international
- disputed
- internal

Communications
- major road
- railway
- canal
- major airport

Cities and towns
- ■ over 1 million inhabitants
- ● more than 100 000 inhabitants
- · smaller towns

Land height

metres
5000
3000
2000
1000
500
300
200
100
sea level
land below sea level
spot height in metres

Scale 1:19 000 000

Conical Orthomorphic Projection
© Oxford University Press

Annual rainfall

	mm
	over 4000
	3000–4000
	2000–3000
	1000–2000
	under 1000

Scale 1: 60 000 000

0   1000 km

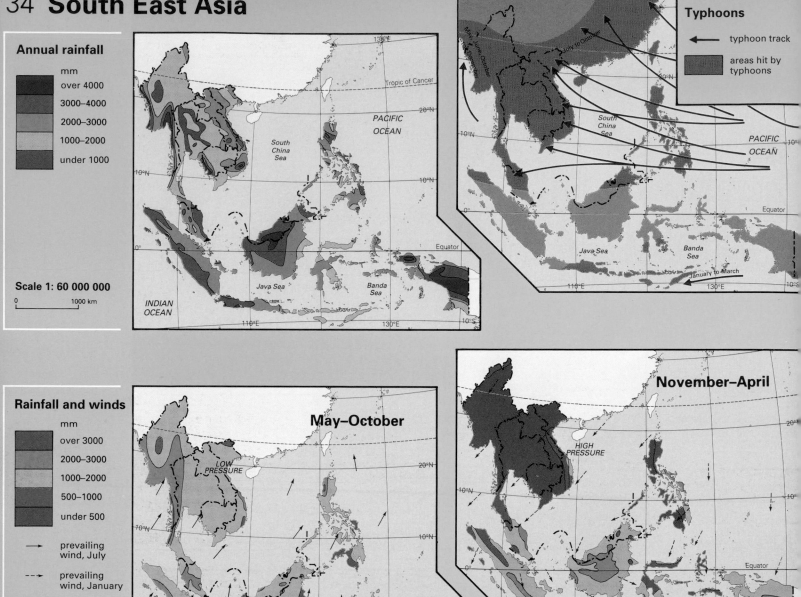

Typhoons

→ typhoon track

    areas hit by typhoons

Rainfall and winds

	mm
	over 3000
	2000–3000
	1000–2000
	500–1000
	under 500

→   prevailing wind, July

--→   prevailing wind, January

Scale 1: 60 000 000

0   1000 km

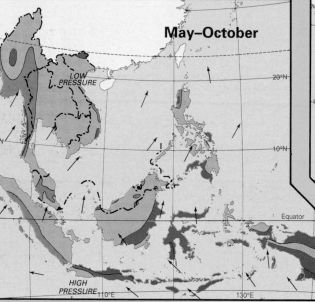

May–October

November–April

Temperature

	°C
	29
	27
	25
	23
	21
	19
	17

Scale 1: 60 000 000

0   1000 km

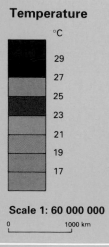

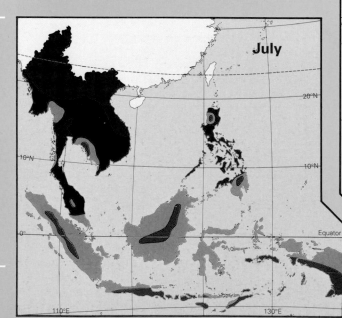

July

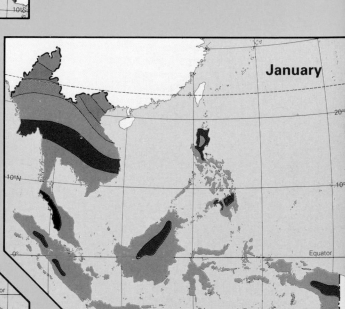

January

Oblique Mercator Projection

© Oxford University Press

Land use

- cultivated land
- cultivated land, rice dominant
- scrub, non-agricultural land
- forest and jungle
- swamp forest and swamp

- shifting cultivation
- plantations

Scale 1: 30 000 000

0   300   600 km

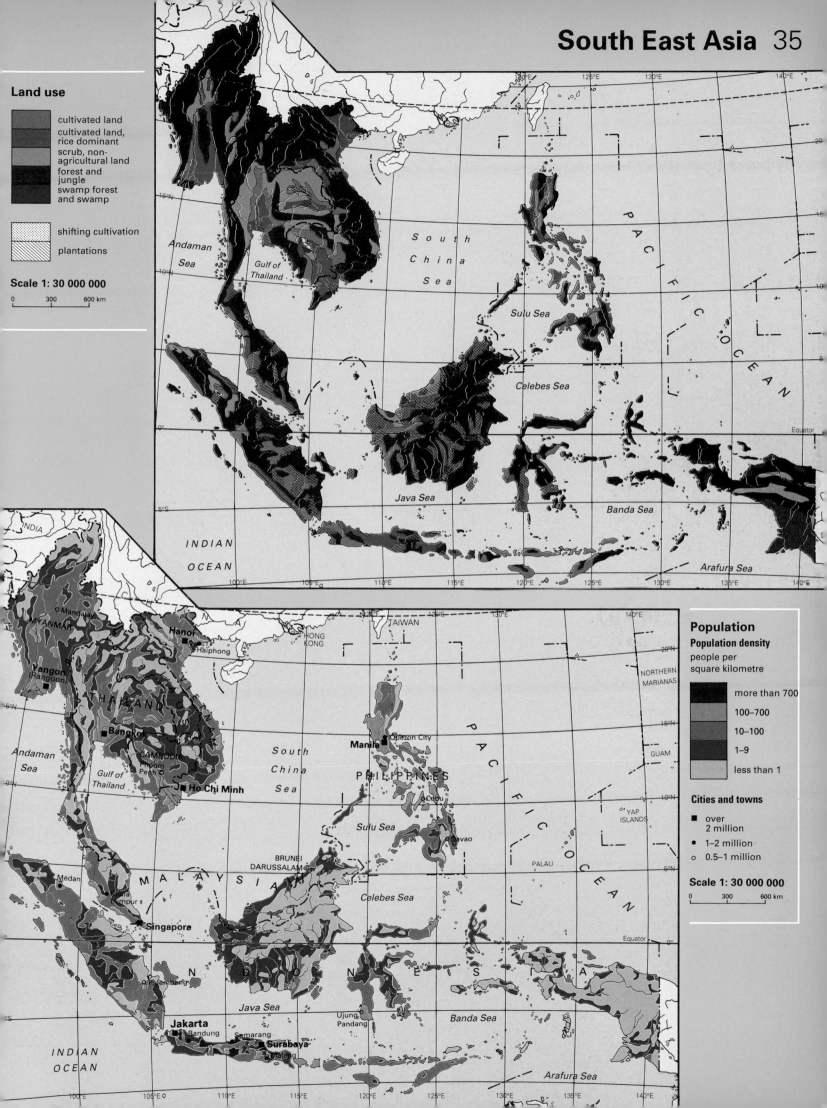

Andaman Sea

Gulf of Thailand

South China Sea

Sulu Sea

Celebes Sea

Java Sea

Banda Sea

Equator

Arafura Sea

INDIAN OCEAN

Population

Population density

people per square kilometre

- more than 700
- 100–700
- 10–100
- 1–9
- less than 1

Cities and towns

- ■ over 2 million
- ● 1–2 million
- ○ 0.5–1 million

Scale 1: 30 000 000

0   300   600 km

INDIA

MYANMAR

Mandalay

Hanoi

Haiphong

Yangon (Rangoon)

HONG KONG

TAIWAN

NORTHERN MARIANAS

THAILAND

Bangkok

CAMBODIA

Phnom Penh

Ho Chi Minh

Andaman Sea

Gulf of Thailand

South China Sea

Manila

Quezon City

PHILIPPINES

GUAM

Cebu

YAP ISLANDS

Davao

Sulu Sea

BRUNEI DARUSSALAM

PALAU

Celebes Sea

M A L A Y S I A

Medan

Kuala Lumpur

Singapore

I N D O N E S I A

Palembang

Java Sea

Ujung Pandang

Banda Sea

Jakarta

Bandung

Semarang

Surabaya

Malang

Equator

PACIFIC OCEAN

INDIAN OCEAN

Arafura Sea

Scale 1: 12 500 000

0   200   400 km

Transverse Mercator Projection

© Oxford University Press

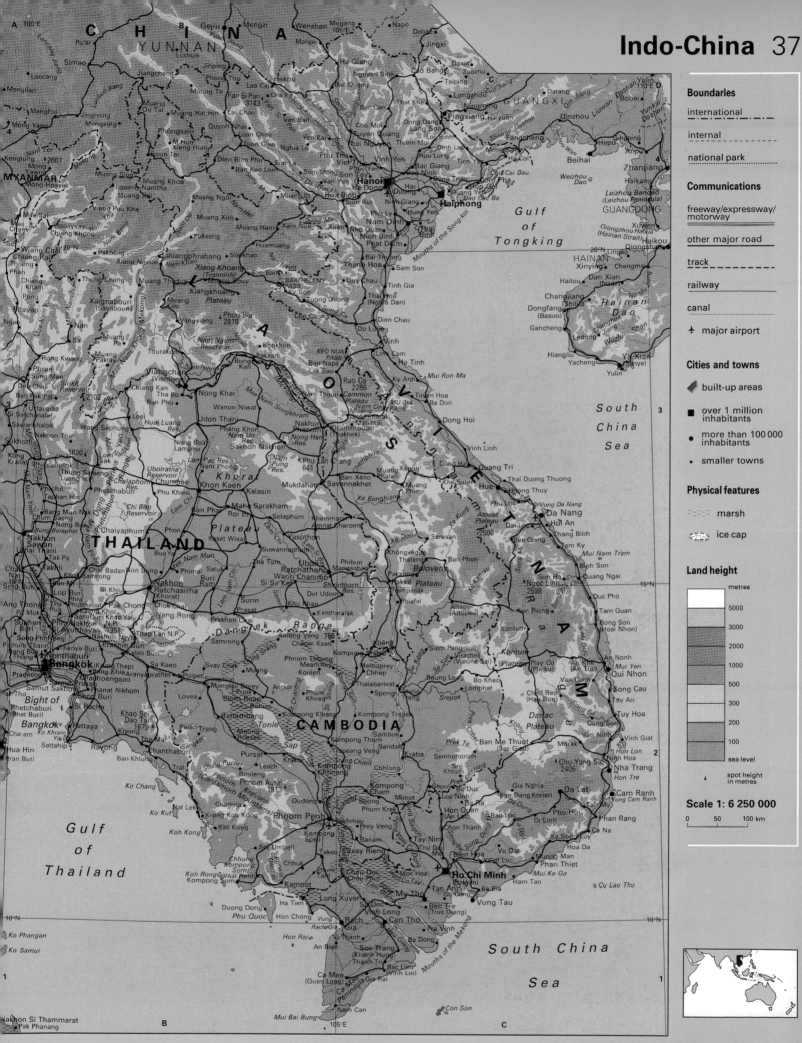

Boundaries

international

disputed

internal

national park

Communications

freeway/expressway/
motorway

other major road

track

railway

canal

✈ major airport

Cities and towns

◥ built-up areas

■ over 1 million
inhabitants

● more than 100 000
inhabitants

• smaller towns

Physical features

seasonal
river/lake

marsh

ice cap

Land height

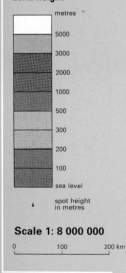

metres

5000

3000

2000

1000

500

300

200

100

sea level

▲ spot height
in metres

Scale 1 : 8 000 000

0   100   200 km

Conic Projection
© Oxford University Press

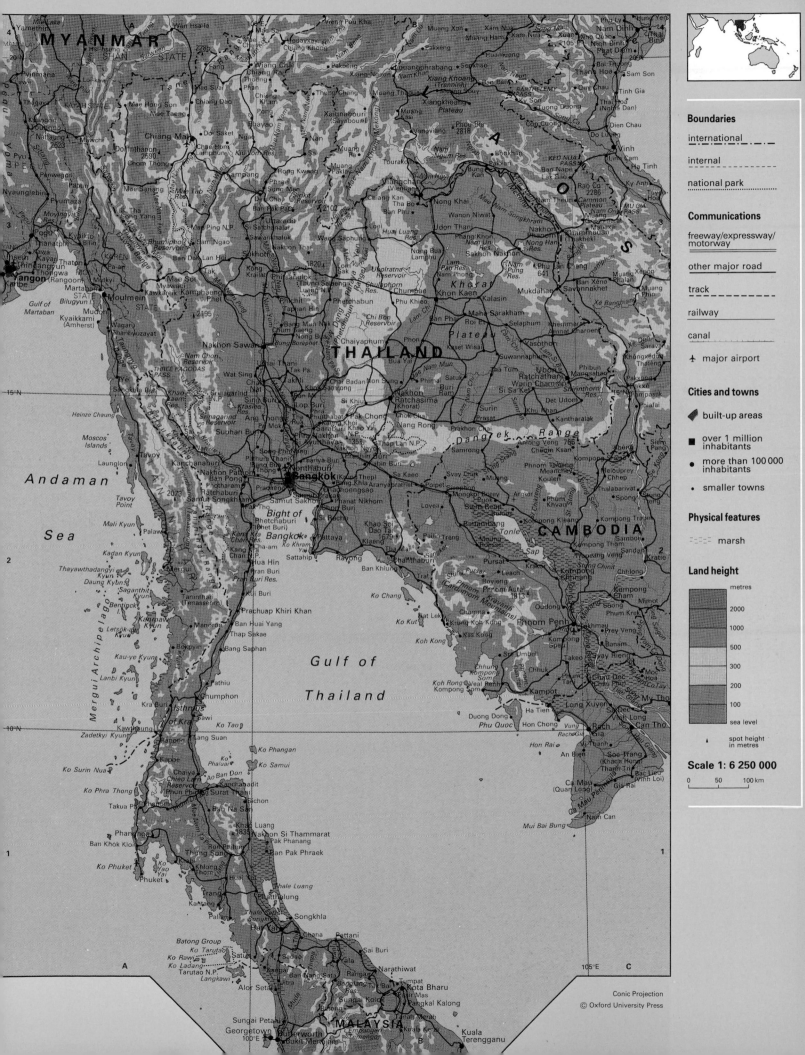

Boundaries

international

internal

national park

Communications

freeway/expressway/
motorway

other major road

track

railway

canal

✈ major airport

Cities and towns

◤ built-up areas

■ over 1 million
inhabitants

● more than 100 000
inhabitants

• smaller towns

Physical features

▭▭▭ marsh

Land height

metres

2000

1000

500

300

200

100

sea level

▲ spot height
in metres

Scale 1: 6 250 000

0   50   100 km

Conic Projection

© Oxford University Press

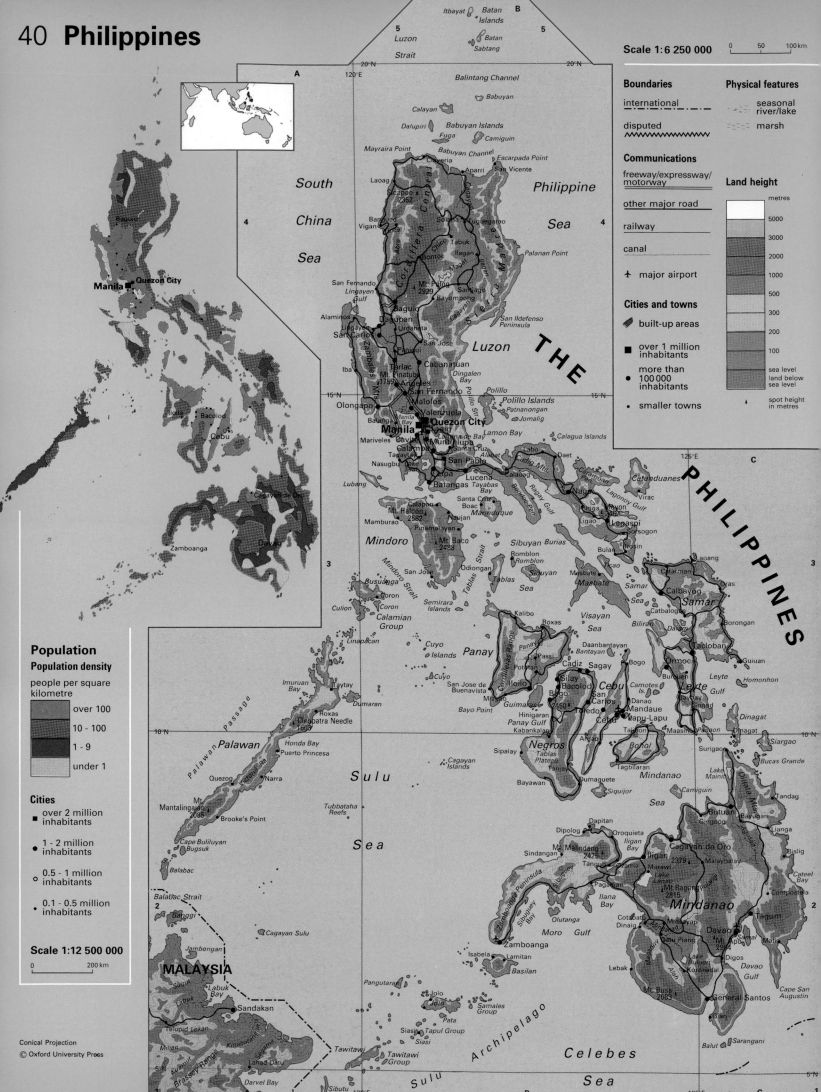

Scale 1:6 250 000

0   50   100km

Boundaries

international

disputed

Communications

freeway/expressway/motorway

other major road

railway

canal

✈ major airport

Cities and towns

built-up areas

■ over 1 million inhabitants

● more than 100 000 inhabitants

• smaller towns

Physical features

seasonal river/lake

marsh

Land height

metres

5000
3000
2000
1000
500
300
200
100
sea level
land below sea level

▲ spot height in metres

Population

Population density

people per square kilometre

over 100

10 - 100

1 - 9

under 1

Cities

■ over 2 million inhabitants

● 1 - 2 million inhabitants

○ 0.5 - 1 million inhabitants

• 0.1 - 0.5 million inhabitants

Scale 1:12 500 000

0   200 km

Conical Projection

© Oxford University Press

THE PHILIPPINES

South China Sea

Philippine Sea

Luzon

Mindoro

Panay

Negros

Palawan

Sulu Sea

Celebes Sea

Mindanao

MALAYSIA

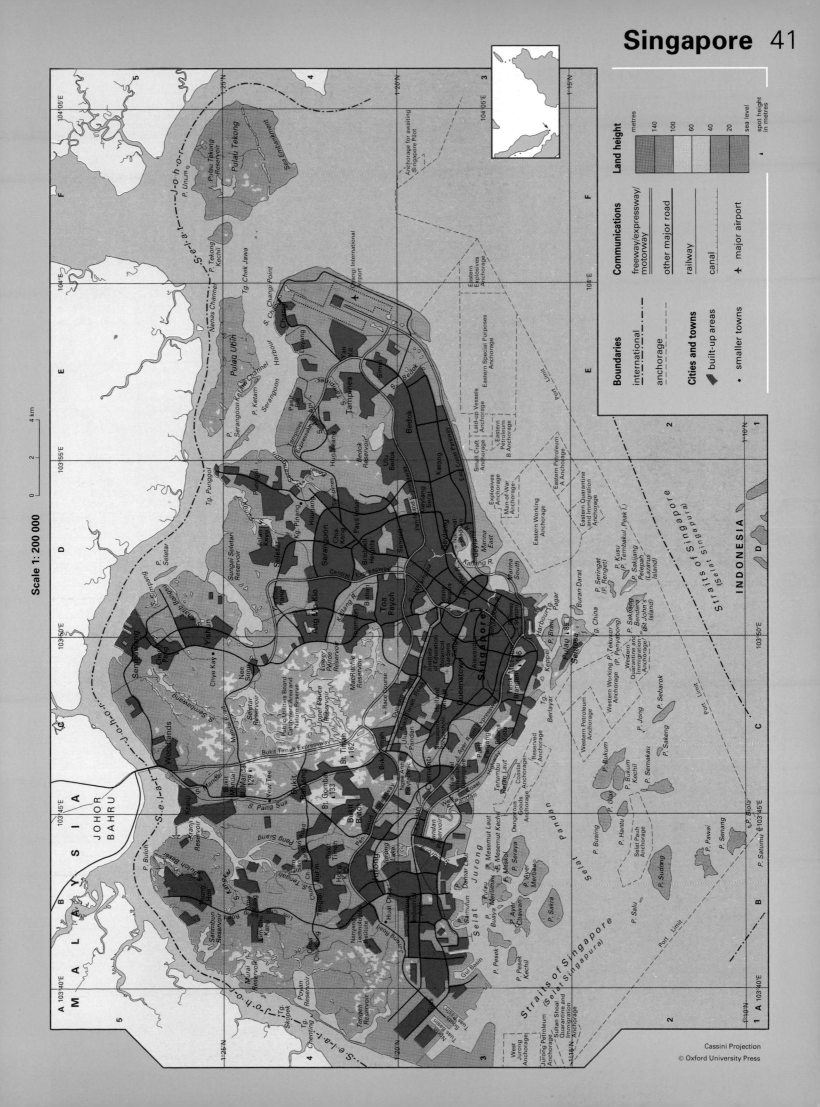

Scale 1: 200 000

0   2   4 km

Land height

metres
140
100
60
40
20
sea level
spot height in metres

Communications

freeway/expressway/motorway
other major road
railway
canal
✈ major airport

Boundaries

international
anchorage

Cities and towns

built-up areas
• smaller towns

Cassini Projection
© Oxford University Press

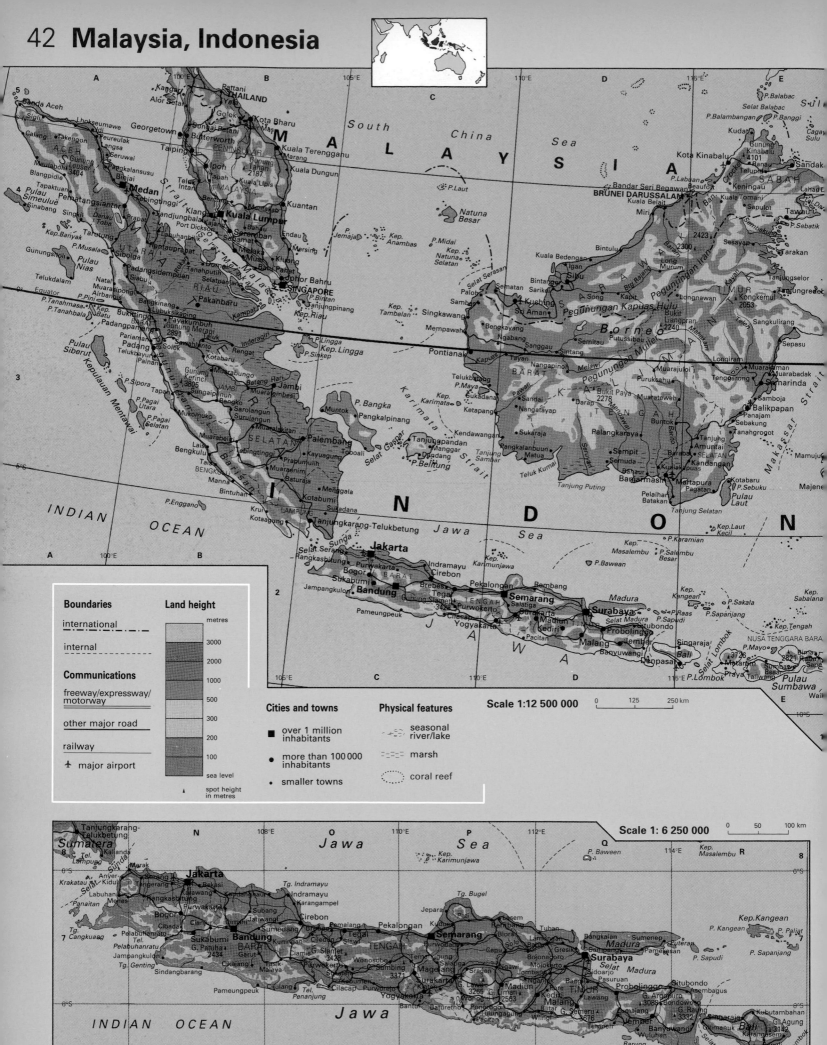

Boundaries

international

internal

Communications

freeway/expressway/
motorway

other major road

railway

+ major airport

Land height

metres

3000
2000
1000
500
300
200
100

sea level

spot height
in metres

Cities and towns

■ over 1 million
inhabitants

● more than 100 000
inhabitants

• smaller towns

Physical features

seasonal
river/lake

marsh

coral reef

Scale 1:12 500 000

0   125   250 km

Scale 1: 6 250 000

0   50   100 km

Jawa and Bali

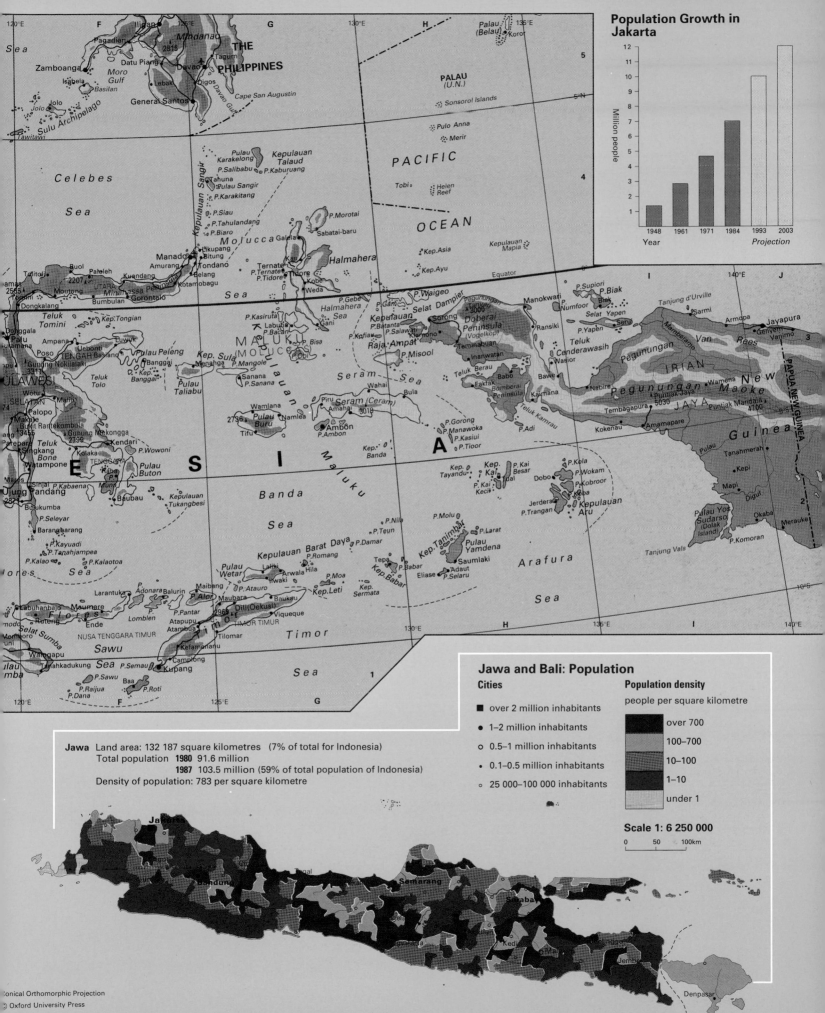

Population Growth in Jakarta

Million people / Year

1948, 1961, 1971, 1984, 1993, 2003 (Projection)

Jawa and Bali: Population

Cities

- ■ over 2 million inhabitants
- ● 1–2 million inhabitants
- ○ 0.5–1 million inhabitants
- · 0.1–0.5 million inhabitants
- ○ 25 000–100 000 inhabitants

Population density

people per square kilometre

- over 700
- 100–700
- 10–100
- 1–10
- under 1

Scale 1: 6 250 000

0   50   100km

Jawa Land area: 132 187 square kilometres (7% of total for Indonesia)
Total population **1980** 91.6 million
  1987 103.5 million (59% of total population of Indonesia)
Density of population: 783 per square kilometre

Conical Orthomorphic Projection
© Oxford University Press

Boundaries

international

internal

national park

Communications

major road

✈ major airport

Cities and towns

● more than 100 000 inhabitants

• smaller towns

Physical features

seasonal river/lake

marsh

Scale 1: 8 000 000
Conical Equidistant Projection

0   100 km

Land height

metres
5000
3000
2000
1000
500
300
200
100
sea level

▲ spot height in metres

Irian Jaya Economic

areas considered for transmigration settlement (see map on page 65)

– – – oil concession boundaries

+ alluvial extraction of minerals

● mineral mines

* major mining prospect

logging concession area

Timor Gap Treaty, 1988

1971 1972 Australian-Indonesian seabed boundary agreements

.... the "Timor Gap"

Zone of cooperation, sub-areas:

area subject to Indonesian laws covering petroleum exploration and exploitation

central area, subject to Australian/Indonesian development regime, regulated by a ministerial council and a joint authority

area subject to Australian laws covering petroleum exploration and exploitation

Scale 1: 14 000 000

0   200   400 km

Scale 1: 11 500 000

Net internal migration, 1980
percent by province

Political Boundaries
international
province
district

Headquarters
● provincial
• district
Daru provincial/district

Population, 1995
estimate by province
Thousand people
more than 400
325–400
250–325
175–250
100–175
25–100

District	Headquarters		
1 GEMBOGL	Gembogl	15 PORGERA	Porgera
2 KUNDIAWA	Kundiawa	16 KANDEP	Kandep
3 SINA SINA	Kamtai	17 WAPENAMANDA	Wapenamanda
4 CHUAVE	Chuave	18 TAMBUL	Tambul
5 GUMINE	Gumine	19 HAGEN CENTRAL	Mt.Hagen
6 KEROWAGI	Kerowagi	20 MENDI	Mendi
7 WAHGI	Minj	21 IALIBU	Ialibu
8 JIMI	Tabibuga	22 PANGIA	Pangia
9 HAGEN NORTH	Muglamp	23 KARIMUI	Karimui
10 LUFA	Lufa	24 OKAPA	Okapa
11 HENGANOFI	Henganofi	25 GOROKA	Goroka
12 KOMPIAM	Kompiam	26 KAINANTU	Kainantu
13 WABAG	Wabag	27 MARAWAKA	Marawaka
14 LAGAIP	Laiagam	28 KIRA	Kira

Boundaries

international

disputed
~~~~~~~~~~~~~~

internal

Communications

freeway/expressway/
motorway

other major road

railway

canal

✈ major airport

Cities and towns

■ over 1 million
  inhabitants

● more than
  100 000
  inhabitants

• smaller towns

Physical features

~~~ seasonal
    river/lake

---- marsh

salt pan

ice cap

sand dunes

Land height

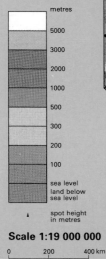

metres

5000

3000

2000

1000

500

300

200

100

sea level
land below
sea level

▲ spot height
  in metres

Scale 1:19 000 000

0   200   400 km

Conical Orthomorphic Projection

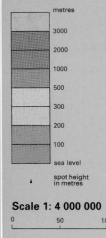

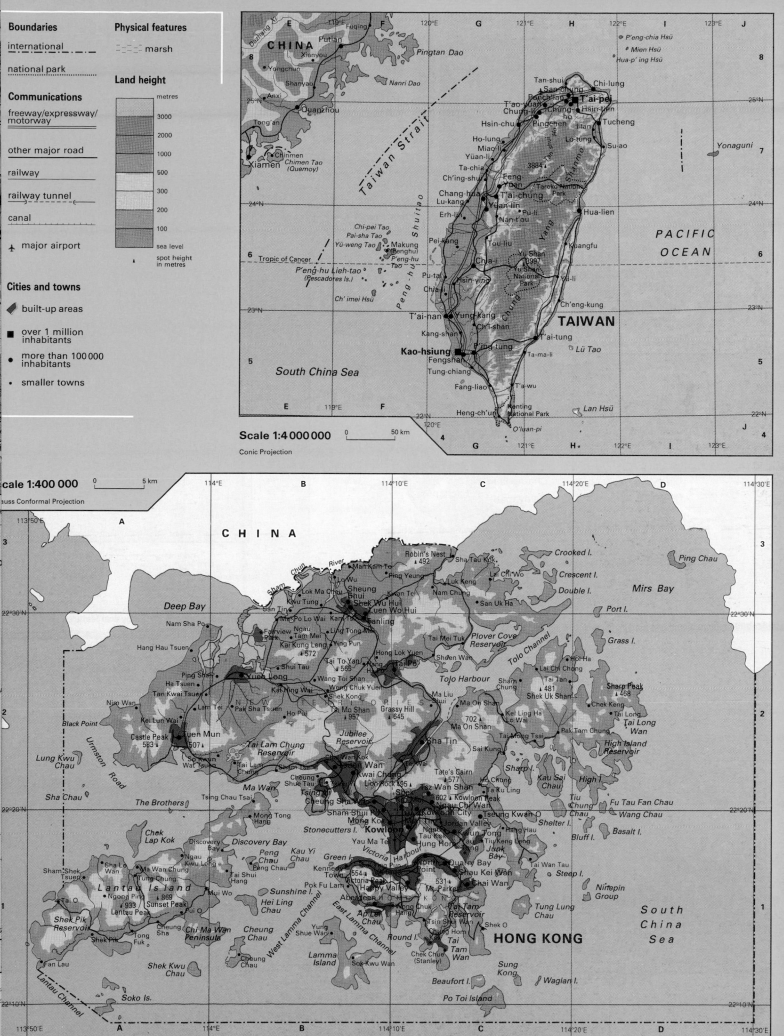

Boundaries

international

national park

Communications

freeway/expressway/
motorway

other major road

railway

railway tunnel

canal

✈ major airport

Cities and towns

◤ built-up areas

■ over 1 million
inhabitants

● more than 100 000
inhabitants

● smaller towns

Physical features

marsh

Land height

metres
3000
2000
1000
500
300
200
100
sea level
▲ spot height
in metres

Scale 1:4 000 000

Conic Projection

Scale 1:400 000

Gauss Conformal Projection

Israel & Lebanon

Scale 1:4 000 000

0   50   100 km

Conical Orthomorphic Projection

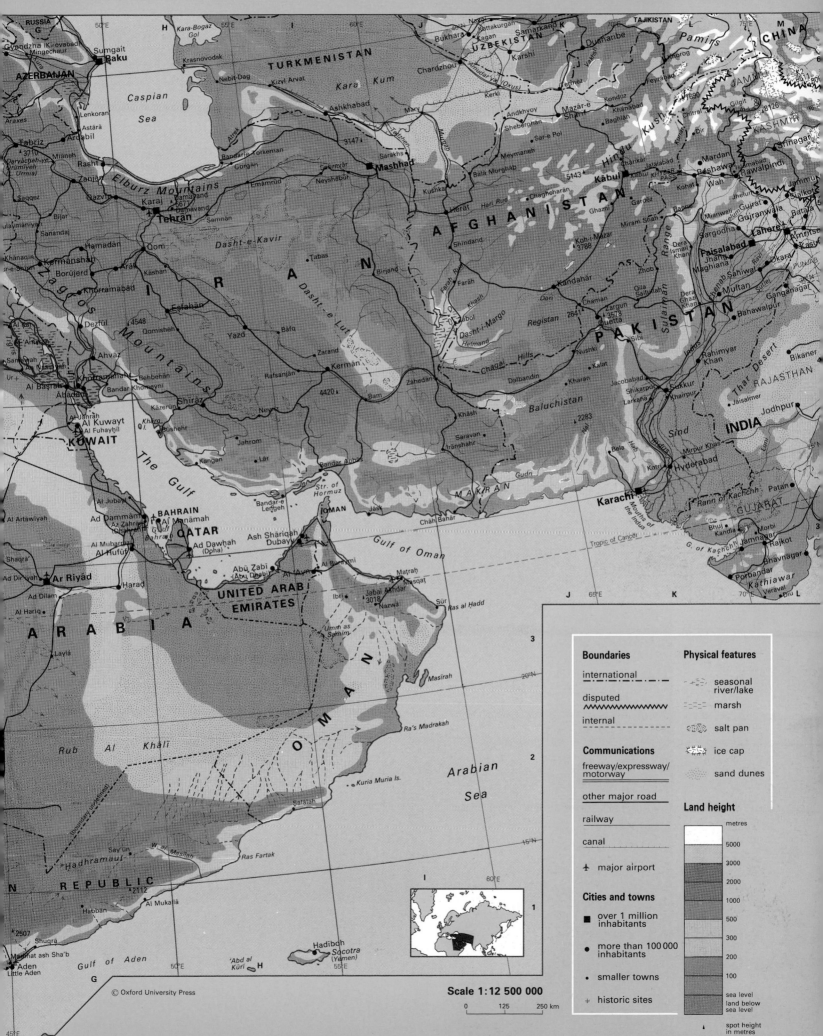

Boundaries

international

disputed ∿∿∿∿∿

internal ─ ─ ─ ─

Communications

freeway/expressway/
motorway

other major road

railway

canal

✈ major airport

Cities and towns

■ over 1 million
inhabitants

● more than 100 000
inhabitants

• smaller towns

+ historic sites

Physical features

seasonal
river/lake

marsh

salt pan

ice cap

sand dunes

Land height

metres
5000
3000
2000
1000
500
300
200
100
sea level
land below sea level

▲ spot height
in metres

Scale 1:12 500 000

0   125   250 km

© Oxford University Press

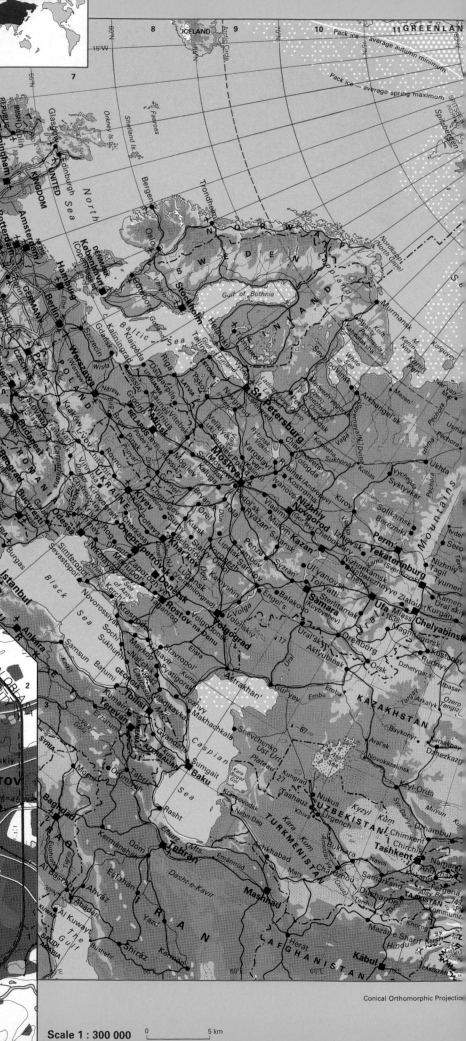

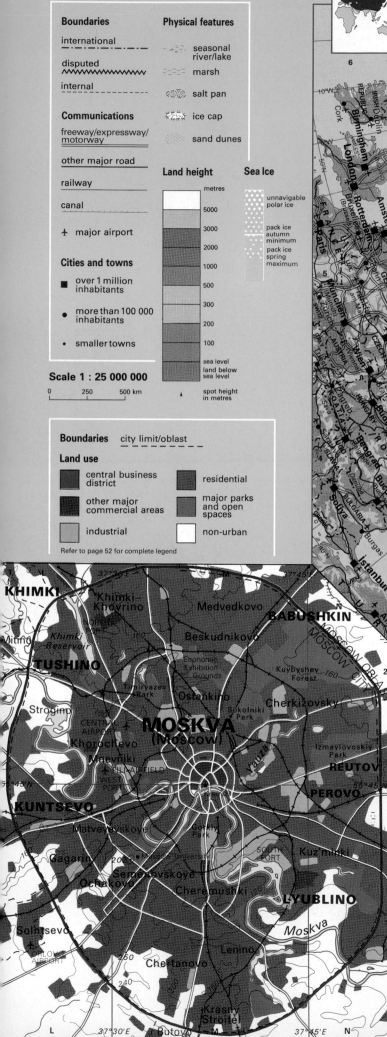

Boundaries

international

disputed

internal

Communications

freeway/expressway/
motorway

other major road

railway

canal

✈ major airport

Cities and towns

■ over 1 million
inhabitants

● more than 100 000
inhabitants

• smaller towns

Scale 1 : 25 000 000

0   250   500 km

Physical features

seasonal
river/lake

marsh

salt pan

ice cap

sand dunes

Land height

metres

5000

3000

2000

1000

500

300

200

100

sea level

land below
sea level

▲ spot height
in metres

Sea Ice

unnavigable
polar ice

pack ice
autumn
minimum

pack ice
spring
maximum

Boundaries   city limit/oblast

Land use

■ central business
district

■ other major
commercial areas

■ industrial

■ residential

■ major parks
and open
spaces

□ non-urban

Refer to page 52 for complete legend

Scale 1 : 300 000

0   5 km

Conical Orthomorphic Projection

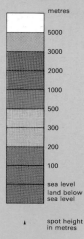

Boundaries

international — ·· — ·· —

disputed ∿∿∿∿∿∿

Communications

freeway/expressway/
motorway

other major road

railway

canal

✈ major airport

Cities and towns

■ over 1 million
inhabitants

● more than 100 000
inhabitants

• smaller towns

Physical features

seasonal
river/lake

marsh

salt pan

ice cap

sand dunes

salt lake

Sea Ice

pack ice
spring max.

Land height

metres

5000
3000
2000
1000
500
300
200
100
sea level
land below
sea level

▲ spot height
in metres

Scale 1: 12 500 000

0   100   200   300 km

Conical Orthomorphic Projection

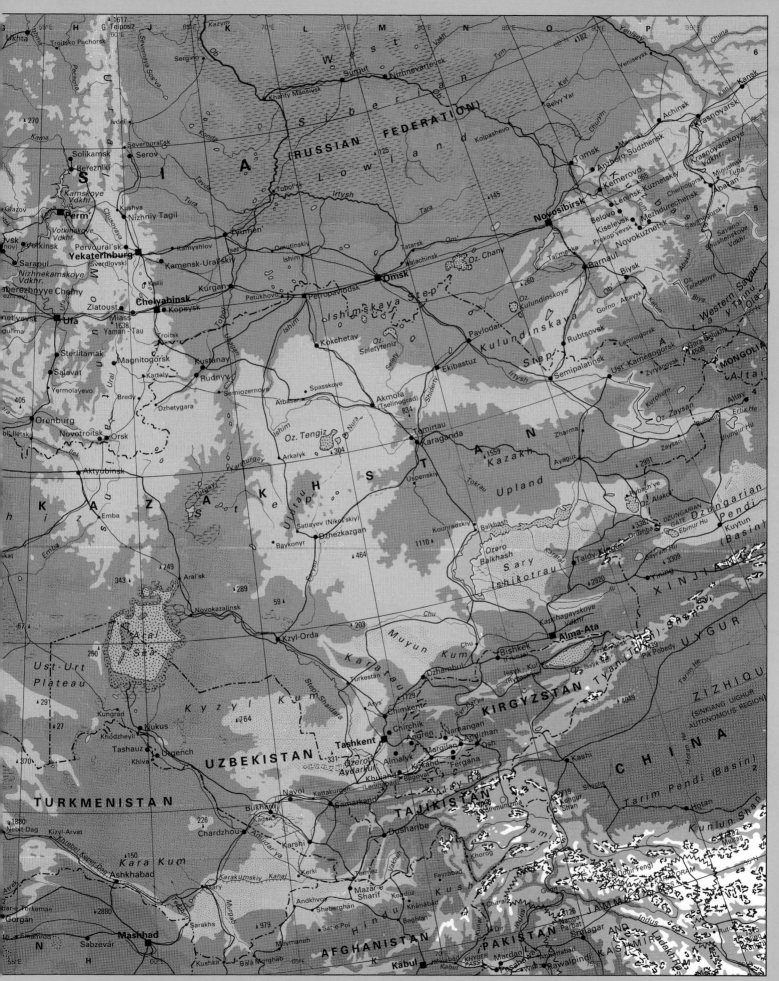

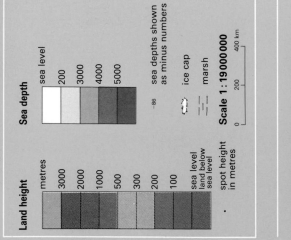

Land height

metres	
3000	
2000	
1000	
500	
300	
200	
100	
sea level land below sea level	
•	spot height in metres

Sea depth

	sea level
	200
	3000
	4000
	5000

sea depths shown as minus numbers

-86

ice cap
marsh

Scale 1:19 000 000

0   200   400 km

European Economic Organizations

European Community (EC)
Headquarters: Brussels

European Free Trade Association (EFTA)
Headquarters: Geneva

—— international boundary
• national capital

Scale 1:44 000 000

0   400 km

Oxford University Press
Central Orthographic Projection

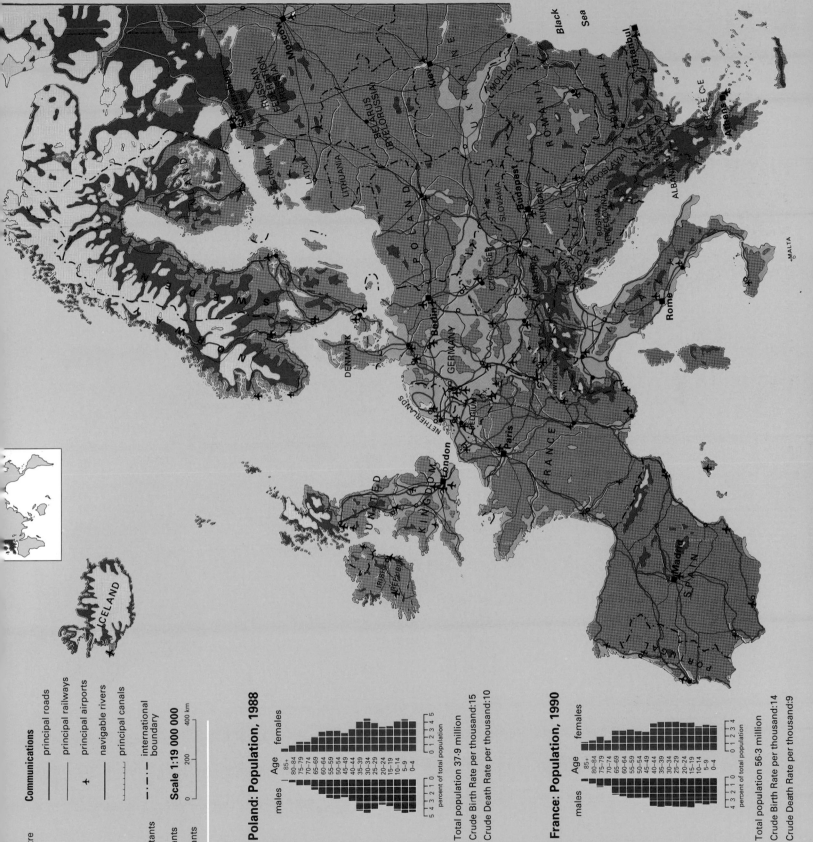

Population density

people per square kilometre

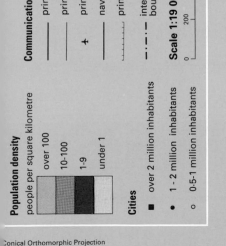

over 100
10-100
1-9
under 1

Cities

■ over 2 million inhabitants

● 1 - 2 million inhabitants

○ 0.5-1 million inhabitants

Communications

— principal roads

— principal railways

✈ principal airports

— navigable rivers

— principal canals

– · – international boundary

Scale 1:19 000 000

0   200   400 km

Italy: Population, 1988

males   Age   females

85+
80-84
75-79
70-74
65-69
60-64
55-59
50-54
45-49
40-44
35-39
30-34
25-29
20-24
15-19
10-14
5-9
0-4

5 4 3 2 1 0   0 1 2 3 4 5

percent of total population

Total population 57.4 million

Crude Birth Rate per thousand:10

Crude Death Rate per thousand:9

Poland: Population, 1988

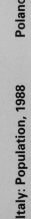

males   Age   females

85+
80-84
75-79
70-74
65-69
60-64
55-59
50-54
45-49
40-44
35-39
30-34
25-29
20-24
15-19
10-14
5-9
0-4

5 4 3 2 1 0   0 1 2 3 4 5

percent of total population

Total population 37.9 million

Crude Birth Rate per thousand:15

Crude Death Rate per thousand:10

UK: Population, 1988

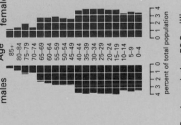

males   Age   females

85+
80-84
75-79
70-74
65-69
60-64
55-59
50-54
45-49
40-44
35-39
30-34
25-29
20-24
15-19
10-14
5-9
0-4

5 4 3 2 1 0   0 1 2 3 4 5

percent of total population

Total population 57 million

Crude Birth Rate per thousand:14

Crude Death Rate per thousand:12

France: Population, 1990

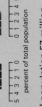

males   Age   females

85+
80-84
75-79
70-74
65-69
60-64
55-59
50-54
45-49
40-44
35-39
30-34
25-29
20-24
15-19
10-14
5-9
0-4

4 3 2 1 0   0 1 2 3 4

percent of total population

Total population 56.3 million

Crude Birth Rate per thousand:14

Crude Death Rate per thousand:9

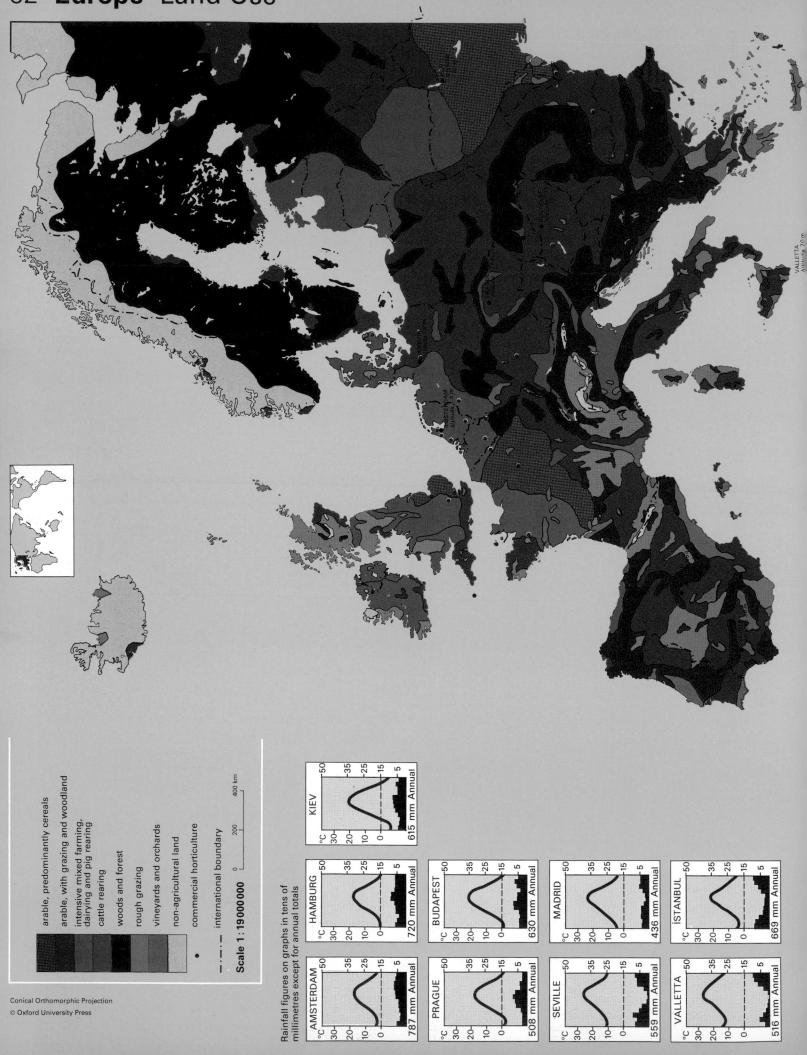

arable, predominantly cereals

arable, with grazing and woodland

intensive mixed farming,
dairying and pig rearing

cattle rearing

woods and forest

rough grazing

vineyards and orchards

non-agricultural land

commercial horticulture

– · – · – · international boundary

Scale 1:19 000 000

0   200   400 km

Conical Orthomorphic Projection

© Oxford University Press

Rainfall figures on graphs in tens of
millimetres except for annual totals

KIEV   °C   50   °C 30   35   20   25   10   15   0   5   615 mm Annual

HAMBURG   °C   50   °C 30   35   20   25   10   15   0   5   720 mm Annual

BUDAPEST   °C   50   °C 30   35   20   25   10   15   0   5   630 mm Annual

MADRID   °C   50   °C 30   35   20   25   10   15   0   5   436 mm Annual

İSTANBUL   °C   50   °C 30   35   20   25   10   15   0   5   669 mm Annual

AMSTERDAM   °C   50   °C 30   35   20   25   10   15   0   5   787 mm Annual

PRAGUE   °C   50   °C 30   35   20   25   10   15   0   5   508 mm Annual

SEVILLE   °C   50   °C 30   35   20   25   10   15   0   5   559 mm Annual

VALLETTA   °C   50   °C 30   35   20   25   10   15   0   5   516 mm Annual

VALLETTA
Altitude 70 m

AMSTERDAM
Altitude 15 m

January

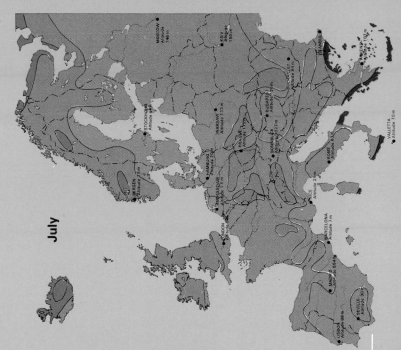

July

Actual surface temperature

°C

25
20
15
10
5
0
-5
-10
-15

Scale 1:40 000 000

0   200   400 km

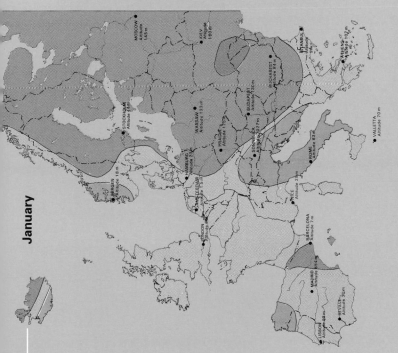

January

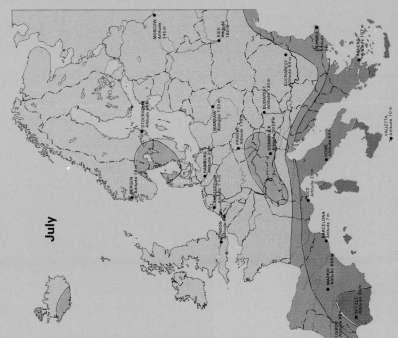

July

Rainfall
and other forms
of precipitation

mm
over 100
50-100
25-50
10-25
0-10

Scale 1:40 000 000

0   200   400 km

Conical Orthomorphic Projection
© Oxford University Press

Rainfall figures on graphs in tens of
millimetres except for annual totals

STOCKHOLM
°C
50
35
25
15
5
30
20
10
0
555 mm Annual

MOSCOW
°C
50
35
25
15
5
30
20
10
0
575 mm Annual

NICE
°C
50
35
25
15
5
30
20
10
0
862 mm Annual

ROME
°C
50
35
25
15
5
30
20
10
0
749 mm Annual

BARCELONA
°C
50
35
25
15
5
30
20
10
0
598 mm Annual

ATHENS
°C
50
35
25
15
5
30
20
10
0
402 mm Annual

BERGEN
°C
50
35
25
15
5
30
20
10
0
1958 mm Annual

WARSAW
°C
50
35
25
15
5
30
20
10
0
471 mm Annual

LONDON
°C
50
35
25
15
5
30
20
10
0
594 mm Annual

SONNBLICK
°C
50
35
25
15
5
30
20
10
0
1495 mm Annual

LISBON
°C
50
35
25
15
5
30
20
10
0
708 mm Annual

BUCHAREST
°C
50
35
25
15
5
30
20
10
0
578 mm Annual

Boundaries

international

disputed .

internal

Communications

freeway/expressway/
motorway

other major road

railway

canal

✈ major airport

Cities and towns

■ over 1 million
inhabitants

● more than 100 000
inhabitants

• smaller towns

Physical features

seasonal
river/lake

marsh

salt pan

ice cap

sand dunes

Sea Ice

pack ice
spring max.

Land height

	metres
	3000
	2000
	1000
	500
	300
	200
	100
	sea level
	land below sea level

▲ spot height
in metres

Scale 1 : 12 500 000

0   125   250 km

Conical Orthomorphic Projection

66 London

Boundaries
county

Communications
freeway/
expressway/
motorway

other major road

major railway

canal

✈ major
airport

✈ other
airport

Physical features
river

contours

·155 spot height
in metres

Land use

central
business
district

other major
commercial
areas

industrial

residential

major parks
and open
spaces

non-urban

This image of London, United
Kingdom was produced by a Landsat
satellite orbiting the earth at an
altitude of approximately 900 km.

Scale 1:600 000

Scale 1:300 000

0   5 km

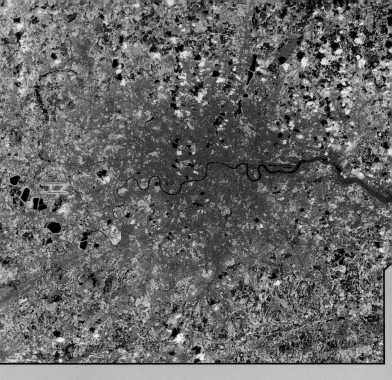

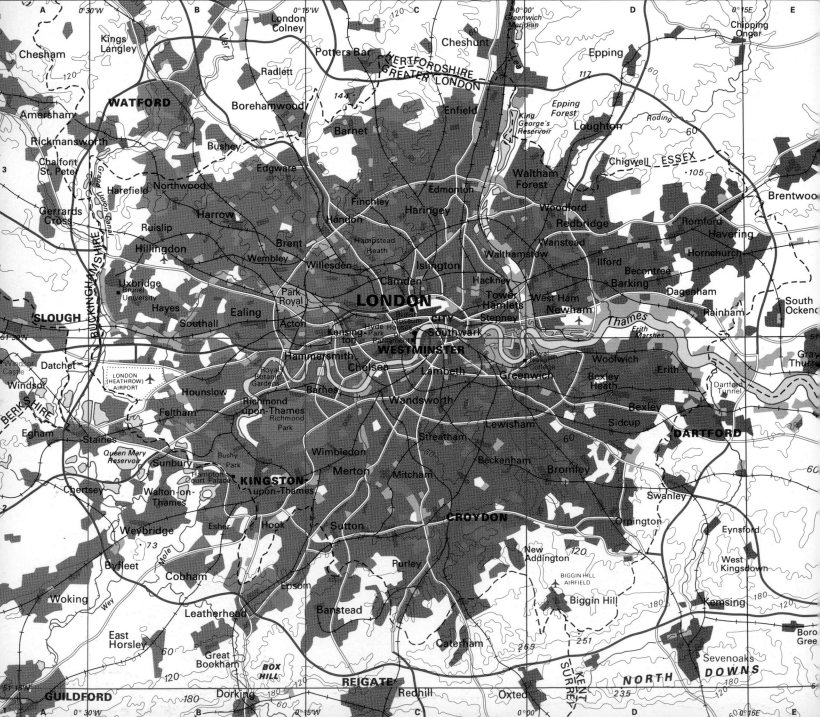

Chesham
Kings
Langley
London
Colney
Potters Bar
Cheshunt
Greenwich
Meridian
Chipping
Ongar
HERTFORDSHIRE
GREATER LONDON
Epping
Radlett
WATFORD
Amersham
Borehamwood
Enfield
Epping
Forest
King
George's
Reservoir
Roding
Loughton
Rickmansworth
Barnet
Chalfont
St. Peter
Bushey
Edgware
Chigwell   ESSEX
·105
Waltham
Forest
Harefield
Northwood
Gerrards
Cross
Finchley
Haringey
Edmonton
Woodford
Redbridge
Brentwood
Harrow
Hendon
Ruislip
Romford
Hillingdon
Brent
Hampstead
Heath
Wanstead
Havering
Wembley
Islington
Walthamstow
Ilford
Hornchurch
Becontree
BUCKINGHAMSHIRE
Uxbridge
Brunel
University
Willesden
Camden
Hackney
Barking
Dagenham
LONDON
SLOUGH
Hayes
Park
Royal
Tower
Hamlets
West Ham
Newham
Ealing
Acton
CITY
Stepney
Rainham
South
Ockendon
Southall
Kensing-
ton
Hyde
Park
British
Museum
Houses of
Parliament
Southwark
Thames
Erith
Marshes
Windsor
Castle
Datchet
Hammersmith
WESTMINSTER
Royal
Naval
College
Woolwich
Erith
Windsor
Chelsea
Lambeth
Greenwich
Bexley
Heath
Dartford
Tunnel
Gravesend
Thurrock
BERKSHIRE
LONDON
(HEATHROW)
AIRPORT
Royal
Botanic
Gardens
Barnes
Wandsworth
Bexley
Egham
Hounslow
Lewisham
Sidcup
DARTFORD
Staines
Feltham
Richmond
upon-Thames
Richmond
Park
Streatham
60
Queen Mary
Reservoir
Bushy
Park
Wimbledon
Beckenham
Bromley
Sunbury
Hampton
Court Palace
KINGSTON-
upon-Thames
Merton
Mitcham
Swanley
Chertsey
Walton-on-
Thames
Orpington
Weybridge
Esher
Hook
Sutton
CROYDON
Eynsford
West
Kingsdown
Byfleet
Cobham
Purley
New
Addington
120
Woking
Epsom
Banstead
BIGGIN HILL
AIRFIELD
Biggin Hill
Kemsing
Leatherhead
180
East
Horsley
Caterham
269
251
Sevenoaks
NORTH   DOWNS
Great
Bookham
BOX
HILL
REIGATE
235
Boro
Gree
GUILDFORD
Dorking
Redhill
Oxted
KENT SURREY

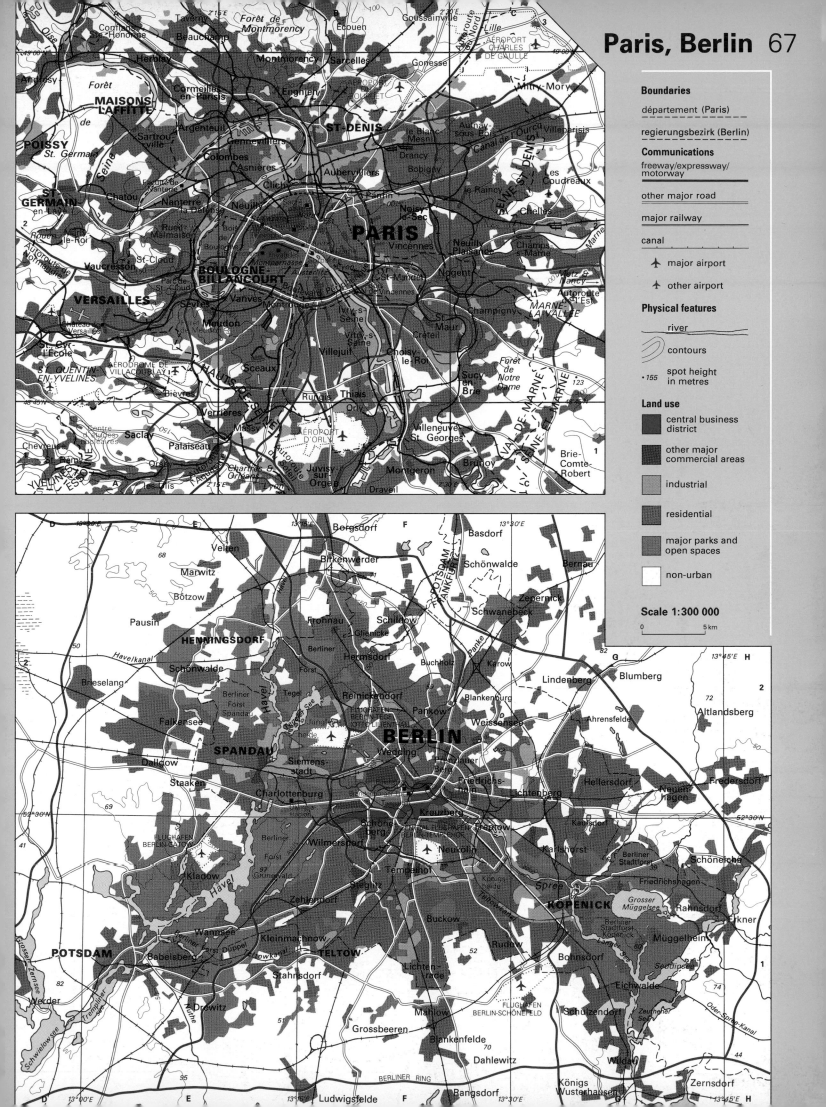

68 British Isles

Boundaries

international	———
internal	---------

Communications

freeway/expressway/motorway

other major road

railway

canal

✈ major airport

Cities and towns

■ over 1 million inhabitants

● more than 100 000 inhabitants

· smaller towns

Physical features

- - - marsh

ice cap

Land height

metres
2000
1000
500
300
200
100
sea level
land below sea level

▲ spot height in metres

Scale 1:8 500 000

100   200 km

Modified Conical
Orthomorphic Projection
© Oxford University Press

ICELAND

ARCTIC OCEAN

Barents Sea

Nordkapp (North Cape)

Murmansk

R U S S I A (RUSSIAN FEDERATION)

L a p p l a n d

N O R W A Y

S W E D E N

F I N L A N D

Gulf of Bothnia

Gulf of Finland

St. Petersburg (Leningrad)

Helsinki (Helsingfors)

Stockholm

ESTONIA

RUSSIA

Baltic Sea

LATVIA

Gulf of Riga

DENMARK

København (Copenhagen)

LITHUANIA

North Sea

Skagerrak

Kattegat

Oslo

Göteborg

GERMANY

Hamburg

POLAND

Gdańsk

KALININGRAD (RUSSIA)

BELARUS (BYELORUSSIA)

Minsk

Vilnius

Benelux: Political

Boundaries

international

région

province

Cities

■ national capital

• provincial capital

Scale 1:4 000 000

0   50   100 km

Boundaries

international

internal

Communications

freeway/expressway/
motorway

other major road

railway

canal

✈ major airport

Physical features

≈≈≈ marsh

Cities and towns

🔺 built-up areas

■ over 1 million
inhabitants

● more than
100 000
inhabitants

• smaller towns

Land height

metres

500

300

200

100

sea level

land below
sea level

▲ spot height
in metres

Scale 1:2 000 000

0   25   50 km

Conical Orthomorphic Projection

© Oxford University Press

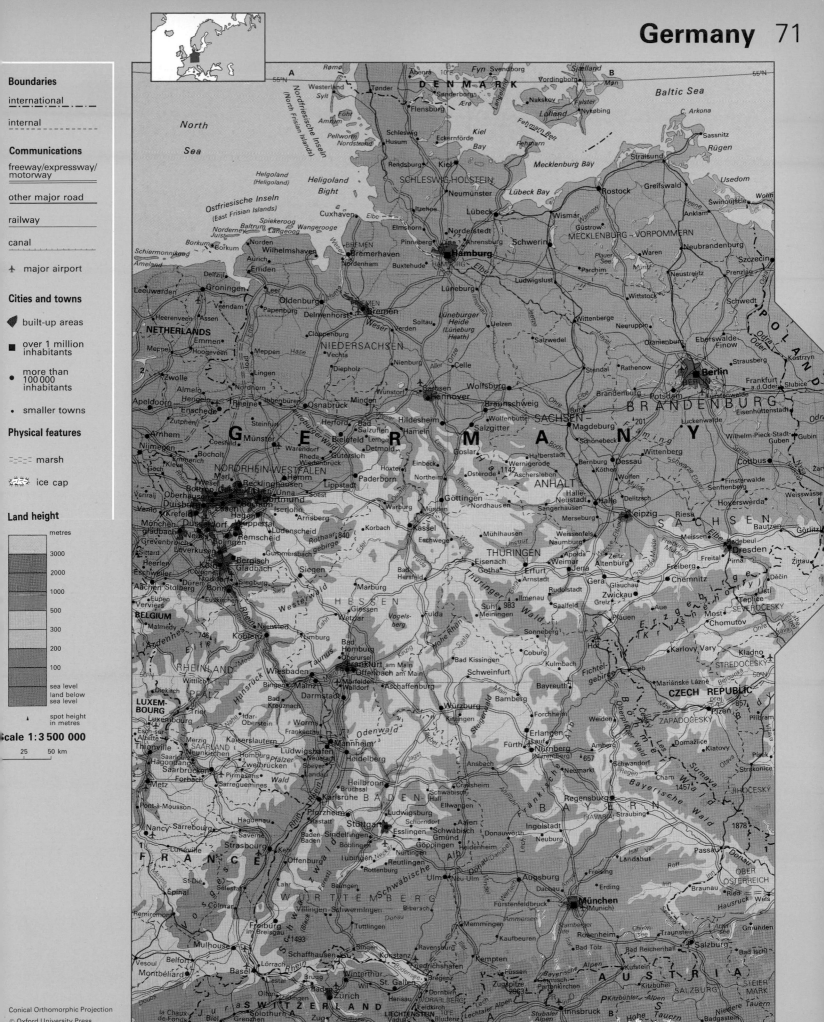

Boundaries

international

internal

Communications

freeway/expressway/
motorway

other major road

railway

canal

✈ major airport

Cities and towns

◤ built-up areas

■ over 1 million
inhabitants

● more than
100 000
inhabitants

• smaller towns

Physical features

marsh

ice cap

Land height

metres

3000
2000
1000
500
300
200
100

sea level
land below
sea level

▲ spot height
in metres

Scale 1:3 500 000

25   50 km

Conical Orthomorphic Projection

© Oxford University Press

Bay of Biscay

FRANCE

Pyrénées / **Pirineos**

ANDORRA Andorra la Vella

SPAIN

PORTUGAL

Lisboa (Lisbon)

Madrid

Barcelona

Zaragoza

Sevilla (Seville)

Valencia

GIBRALTAR (U.K.)

ATLANTIC OCEAN

Mediterranean Sea

Balearic Islands (Spain)

Mallorca

Menorca

Ibiza

Formentera

MOROCCO

ALGERIA

Alger (Algiers)

Oran

Scale 1 : 6 250 000

0   50   100 km

Boundaries

international

Communications

freeway/expressway/
motorway

other major road

railway

canal

major airport

Cities and towns

built-up areas

over 1 million inhabitants

more than 100 000 inhabitants

smaller towns

Land height

metres
3000
2000
1000
500
300
200
100
sea level

spot height in metres

Physical features

seasonal river/lake

marsh

Balearic Islands (Spain)

Mallorca (Majorca)

Menorca (Minorca)

Ibiza

Formentera

Mediterranean Sea

Scale 1 : 3 000 000

0   25   50 km

Conical Orthomorphic Projection

© Oxford University Press

Boundaries

international

Communications

freeway/expressway/motorway

other major road

railway

canal

✈ major airport

Cities and towns

🍃 built-up areas

■ over 1 million inhabitants

● more than 100 000 inhabitants

• smaller towns

Physical features

marsh

ice cap

Land height

metres

3000
2000
1000
500
300
200
100
sea level
land below sea level

▲ spot height in metres

Scale 1: 5 000 000

0   50   100 km

Conical Orthomorphic Projection   © Oxford University Press

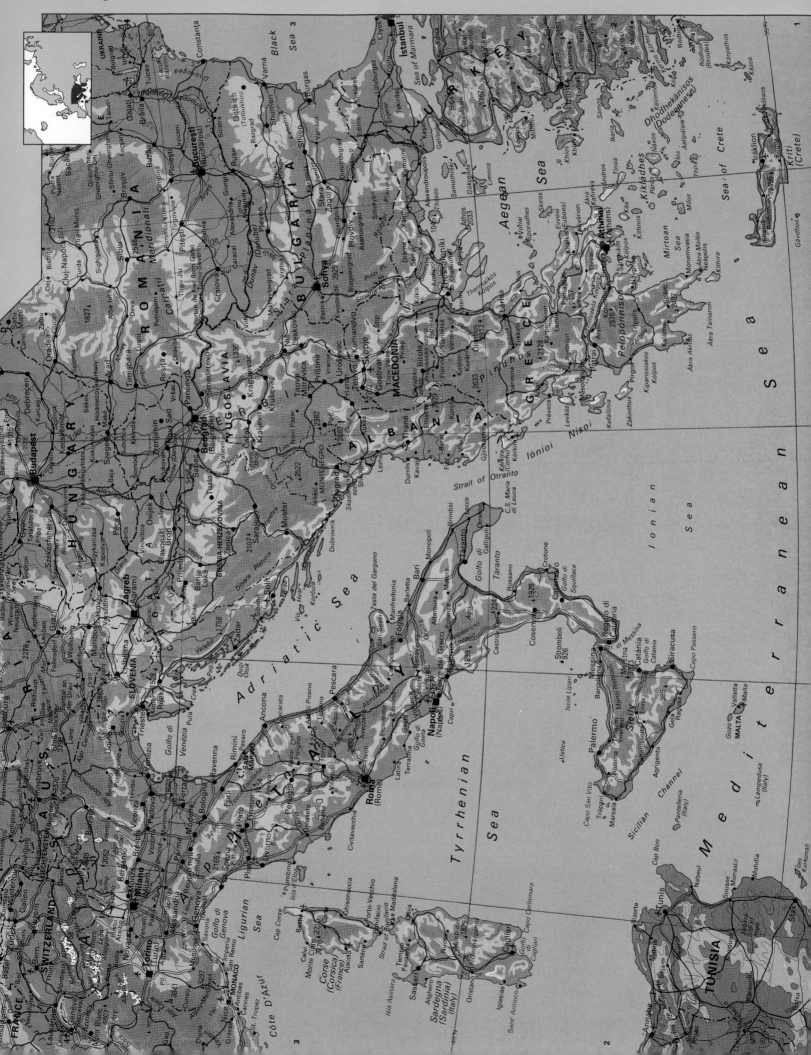

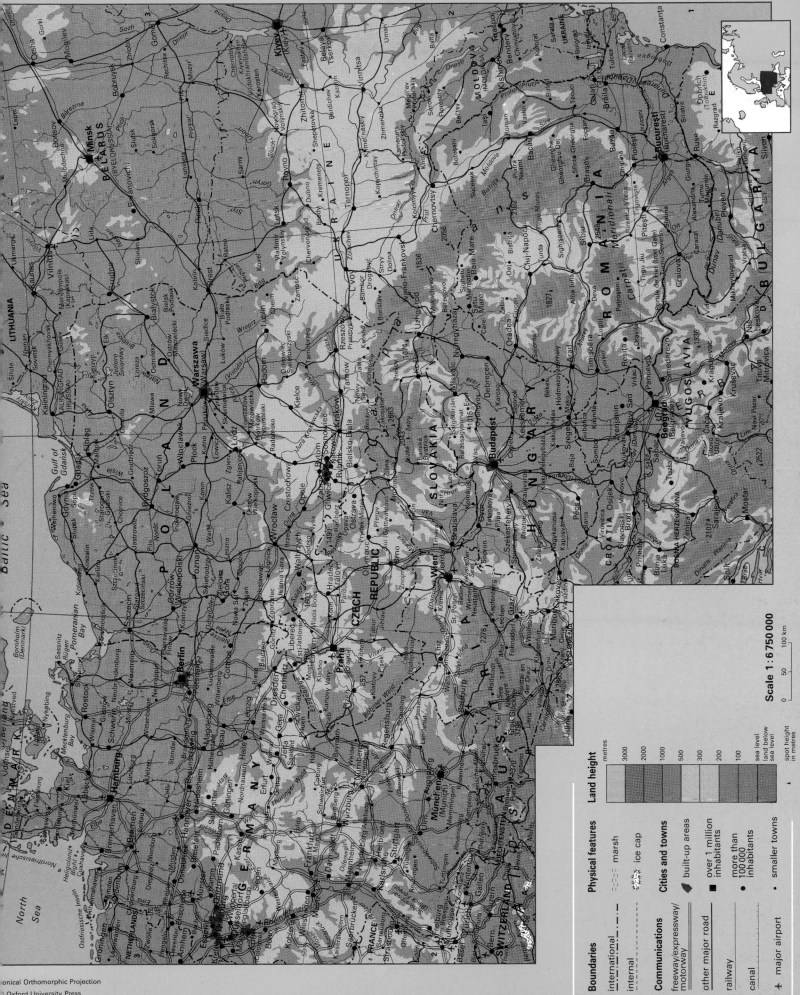

Scale 1 : 6 750 000

0   50   100 km

Boundaries

international

internal

Communications

freeway/expressway/
motorway

other major road

railway

canal

Physical features

marsh

ice cap

Cities and towns

built-up areas

over 1 million
inhabitants

more than
100 000
inhabitants

smaller towns

major airport

Land height

metres

3000

2000

1000

500

300

200

100

sea level

land below
sea level

spot height
in metres

Conical Orthomorphic Projection

© Oxford University Press

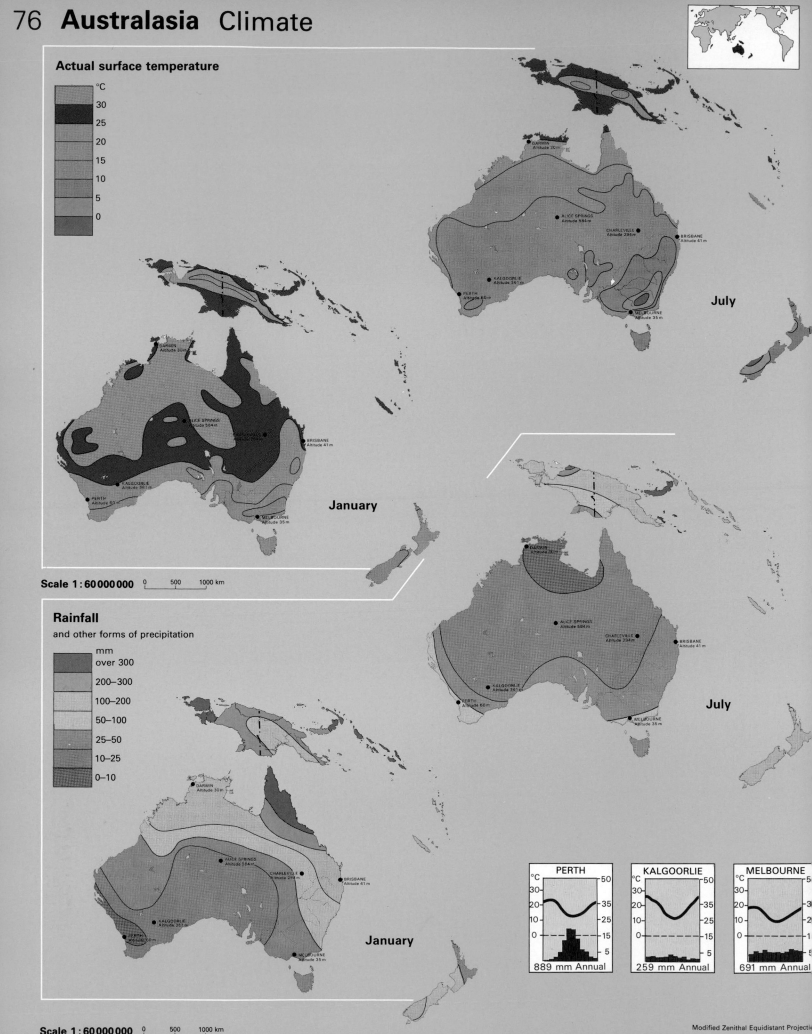

Actual surface temperature

°C
30
25
20
15
10
5
0

July

January

Scale 1:60 000 000 | 0 | 500 | 1000 km

Rainfall
and other forms of precipitation

mm
over 300
200–300
100–200
50–100
25–50
10–25
0–10

July

January

Scale 1:60 000 000 | 0 | 500 | 1000 km

DARWIN Altitude 30 m
ALICE SPRINGS Altitude 584 m
CHARLEVILLE Altitude 294 m
BRISBANE Altitude 41 m
KALGOORLIE Altitude 361 m
PERTH Altitude 60 m
MELBOURNE Altitude 35 m

PERTH
°C
30
20
10
0
50
35
25
15
5
889 mm Annual

KALGOORLIE
°C
30
20
10
0
50
35
25
15
5
259 mm Annual

MELBOURNE
°C
30
20
10
0
691 mm Annual

Modified Zenithal Equidistant Projection

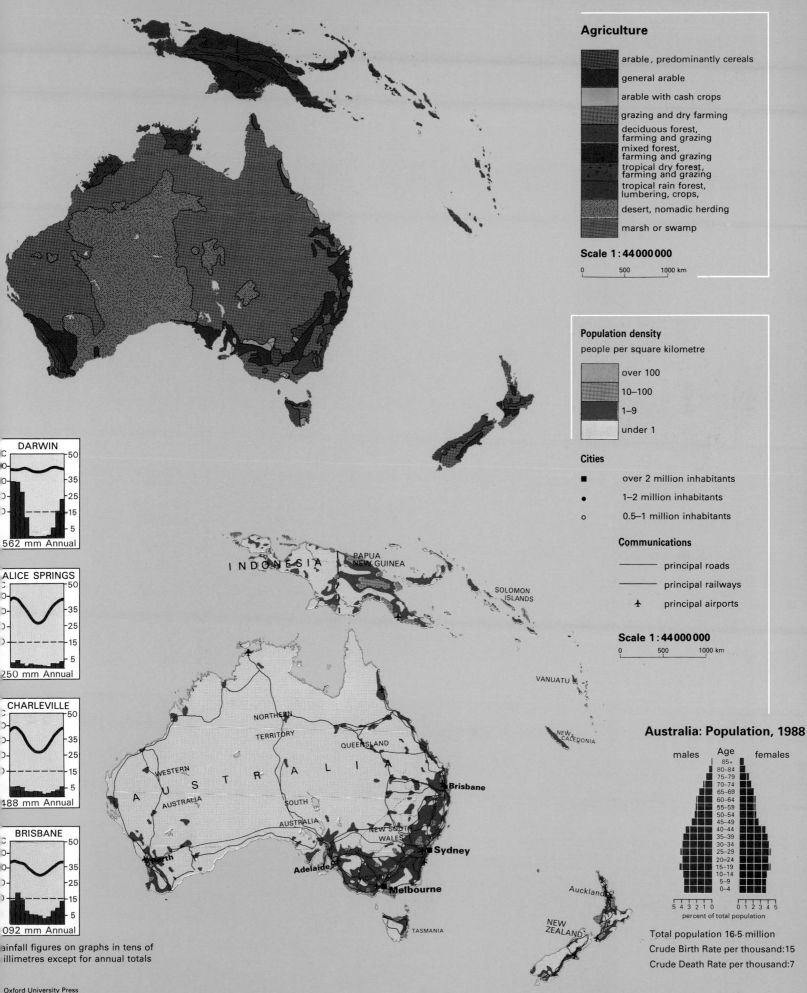

Agriculture

arable, predominantly cereals

general arable

arable with cash crops

grazing and dry farming

deciduous forest, farming and grazing

mixed forest, farming and grazing

tropical dry forest, farming and grazing

tropical rain forest, lumbering, crops,

desert, nomadic herding

marsh or swamp

Scale 1 : 44 000 000

0   500   1000 km

Population density

people per square kilometre

over 100

10–100

1–9

under 1

Cities

■   over 2 million inhabitants

●   1–2 million inhabitants

○   0.5–1 million inhabitants

Communications

───   principal roads

───   principal railways

✈   principal airports

Scale 1 : 44 000 000

0   500   1000 km

DARWIN

562 mm Annual

ALICE SPRINGS

250 mm Annual

CHARLEVILLE

188 mm Annual

BRISBANE

092 mm Annual

ainfall figures on graphs in tens of
illimetres except for annual totals

INDONESIA

PAPUA NEW GUINEA

SOLOMON ISLANDS

VANUATU

NEW CALEDONIA

NORTHERN TERRITORY

QUEENSLAND

WESTERN AUSTRALIA

AUSTRALIA

SOUTH AUSTRALIA

NEW SOUTH WALES

Perth

Adelaide

Brisbane

Sydney

Melbourne

Auckland

TASMANIA

NEW ZEALAND

Australia: Population, 1988

males   Age   females

85+
80–84
75–79
70–74
65–69
60–64
55–59
50–54
45–49
40–44
35–39
30–34
25–29
20–24
15–19
10–14
5–9
0–4

5 4 3 2 1 0   0 1 2 3 4 5
percent of total population

Total population 16·5 million

Crude Birth Rate per thousand:15

Crude Death Rate per thousand:7

Oxford University Press

Boundaries
international
internal

Communications
major road
railway

Cities and towns
■ over 1 million inhabitants
● more than 100 000 inhabitants
• smaller towns

Physical features
seasonal river/lake
marsh
sand dunes

Land height
metres
3000
2000
1000
500
300
200
100
sea level
land below sea level

+ major airport

Scale 1:22 000 000

Zenithal Equidistant Project

© Oxford University Pr

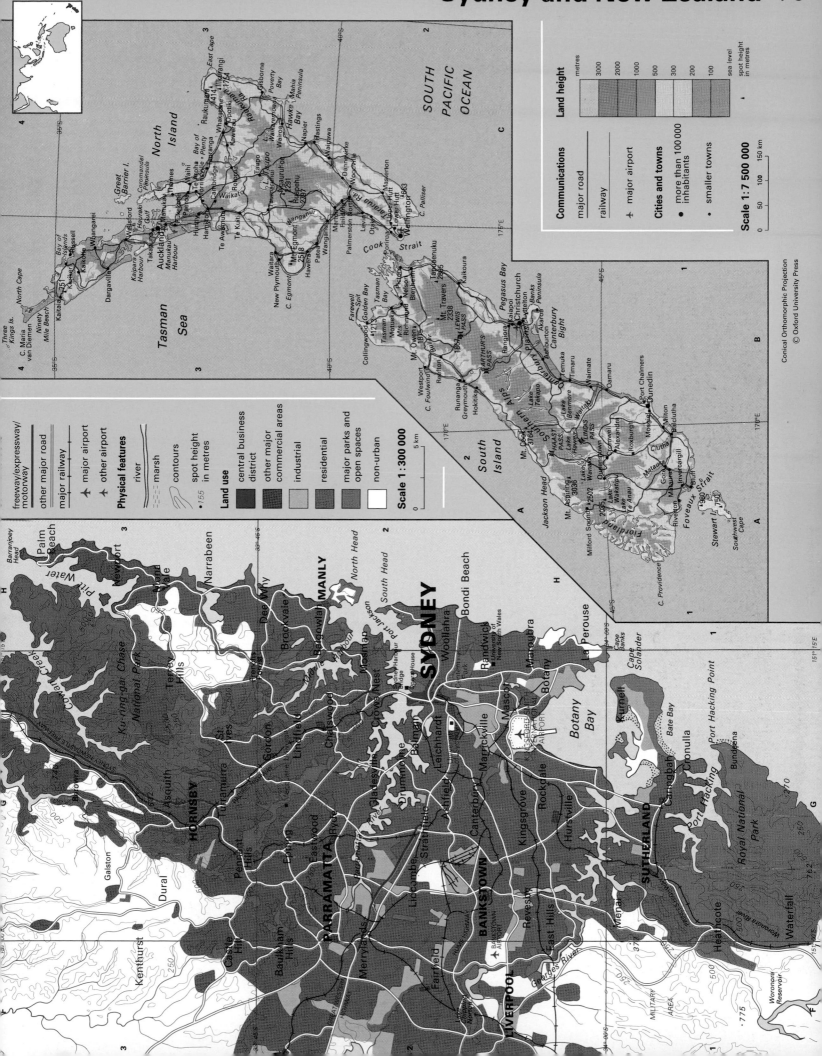

Land height

	metres
	3000
	2000
	1000
	500
	300
	200
	100
	sea level
▲	spot height in metres

Communications

major road
railway
✈ major airport

Cities and towns

● more than 100 000 inhabitants
• smaller towns

Scale 1:7 500 000

0   50   100   150 km

Conical Orthomorphic Projection
© Oxford University Press

---

freeway/expressway/motorway
other major road
major railway
✈ major airport
✈ other airport

Physical features

river
marsh
contours
▲155 spot height in metres

Land use

central business district
other major commercial areas
industrial
residential
major parks and open spaces
non-urban

Scale 1:300 000

0   5 km

North Island

Three Kings Is.
North Cape
C. Maria van Diemen
Ninety Mile Beach
Kaitaia
Kaikohe
Bay of Islands
Russell
Kerikeri
Whangarei
Dargaville
Kaipara Harbour
Wellsford
Great Barrier I.
Coromandel Peninsula
Hauraki Gulf
Auckland
Manukau
Manukau Harbour
Takapuna
Thames
Whakatane
Bay of Plenty
Tauranga
Waihi
Te Aroha
Paeroa
Huntly
Hamilton
Cambridge
Te Kuiti
Te Awamutu
Waikato
Rotorua
Lake Taupo
Taupo
Ngauruhoe 2291
Ruapehu 2797
Mt Egmont 2518
New Plymouth
C. Egmont
Waitara
Hawera
Patea
Wanganui
Raukumara
East Cape
Mt Hikurangi e.1754
Whakatane
Opotiki
Waioeka
Gisborne
Poverty Bay
Wairoa
Mahia Peninsula
Hawke Bay
Napier
Hastings
Waipawa
Dannevirke
Woodville
Masterton
Palmerston North
Feilding
Marton
Waiouru
Ruahine Ra.
Tararua Ra.
Levin
Otaki
Upper Hutt
Lower Hutt 663
Wellington
C. Palliser
Cook Strait

Tasman Sea

South Pacific Ocean

South Island

Farewell Spit
Golden Bay
Collingwood
Tasman Bay
Nelson
Motueka
Picton
Blenheim
Tasman Mts
Mt Owen 1875
Mt Richmond
Richmond
C. Foulwind
Westport
Buller
Reefton
Mt Travers 2338
Murchison
Lewis Pass
Tapuaenuku 2885
Kaikoura
Greymouth
Hokitika
Arthurs Pass 1817
Rangiora
Kaiapoi
Pegasus Bay
Christchurch
Lyttelton
Banks Peninsula
Akaroa
Southern Alps
Mt Cook 3764
Haast Pass
Mt Aspiring 3036
Jackson Head
Milford Sound
Lindis Pass
Lake Wanaka
Lake Hawea
Wanaka
Cromwell
Alexandra
Roxburgh
Canterbury Plains
Ashburton
Geraldine
Temuka
Timaru
Waimate
Oamaru
Port Chalmers
Dunedin
Mosgiel
Milton
Balclutha
Clutha
Lake Te Anau
Lake Manapouri
Fiordland
C. Providence
Queenstown
Lake Wakatipu
Lake Benmore
Lake Tekapo
Mt Travers
Kaikoura
Lake Wakatipu 2502
Gore
Mataura
Invercargill
Riverton
Bluff
Foveaux Strait
Stewart I. 980
Southwest Cape

Canterbury Bight

Sydney

Barranjoey Head
Palm Beach
Pitt Water
Cowan Creek
Newport
Mona Vale
Narrabeen
Ku-ring-gai Chase National Park
Dee Why
Terrey Hills
Brookvale
French's Forest
Balgowlah
MANLY
North Head
South Head
Middle Harbour
St Ives
Gordon
Chatswood
Crows Nest
Mosman
Port Jackson
Sydney Harbour Bridge
Opera House
SYDNEY
Woollahra
Bondi Beach
Galston
Dural
Kenthurst
HORNSBY
Asquith
Hornsby
Turramurra
Lindfield
Gladesville
Drummoyne
Balmain
Leichhardt
University of New South Wales
Randwick
La Perouse
Maroubra
Botany
Coogee
Castle Hill
Baulkham Hills
PARRAMATTA
Ryde
Parramatta River
Eastwood
Epping
Pennant Hills
Ermington
Concord
Strathfield
Ashfield
Marrickville
Canterbury
Rockdale
Botany Bay
Kurnell
Kingsford Smith Airport (Mascot)
Mascot
Bate Bay
Cronulla
Port Hacking
Port Hacking Point
Bundeena
Royal National Park
Liverpool
Fairfield
Merrylands
Lidcombe
BANKSTOWN
Bankstown Airport
Revesby
East Hills
Georges River
Hurstville
Kingsgrove
Menai
SUTHERLAND
Sutherland
Heathcote
Waterfall
Woronora Reservoir
Woronora River
MILITARY AREA
Great Western Highway

151°15'E

Scale 1: 35 000 000

0   500   1000 km

Modified Gall Projection
© Oxford University Press

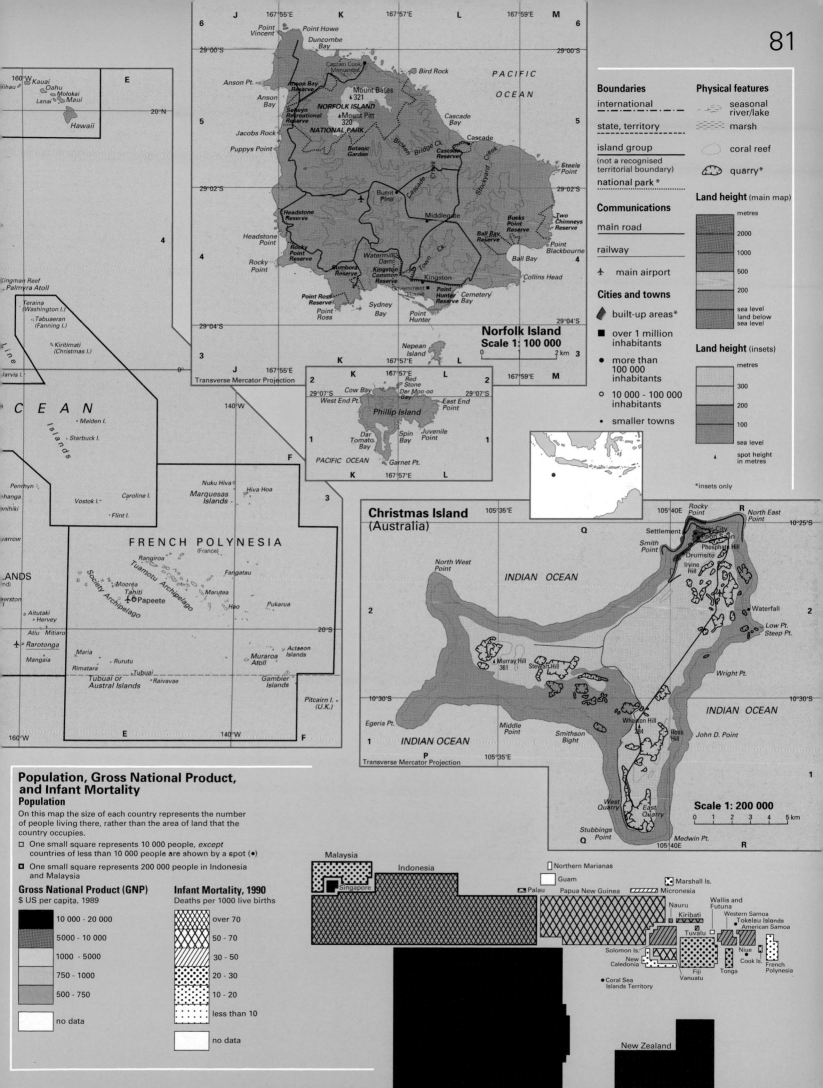

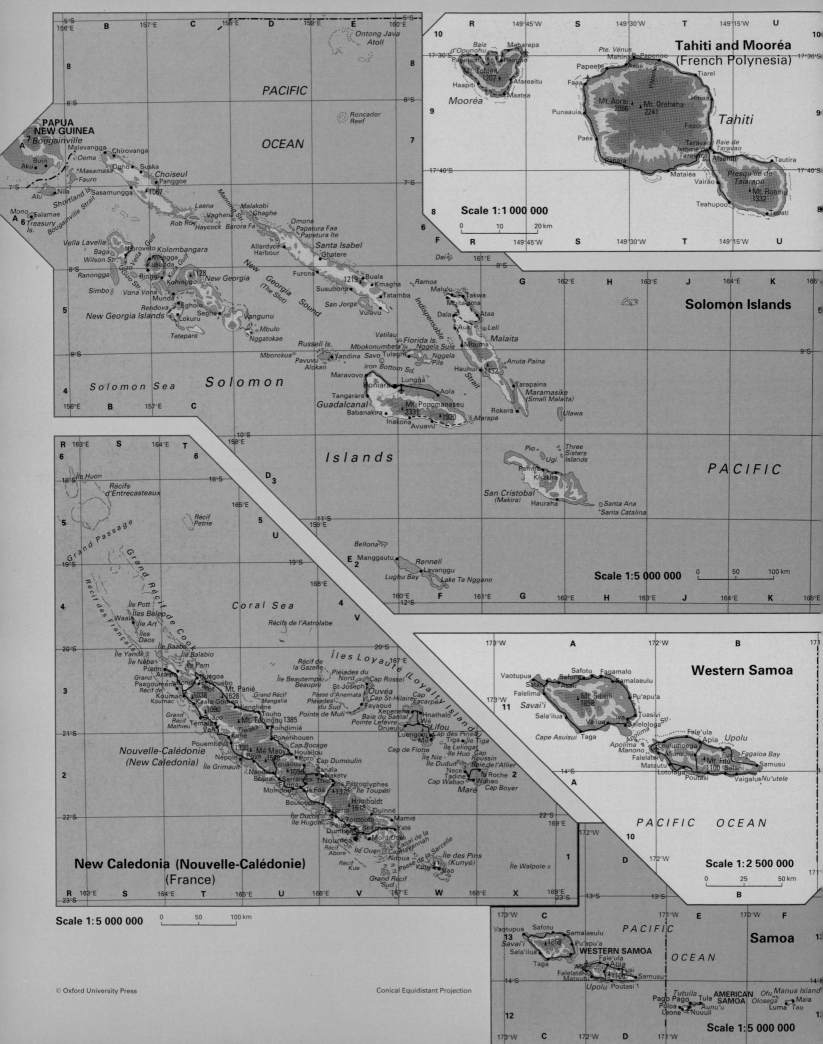

Tahiti and Mooréa (French Polynesia)

Scale 1:1 000 000

Solomon Islands

Western Samoa

New Caledonia (Nouvelle-Calédonie) (France)

Scale 1:5 000 000

Scale 1:5 000 000

Scale 1:2 500 000

Samoa

Scale 1:5 000 000

© Oxford University Press

Conical Equidistant Projection

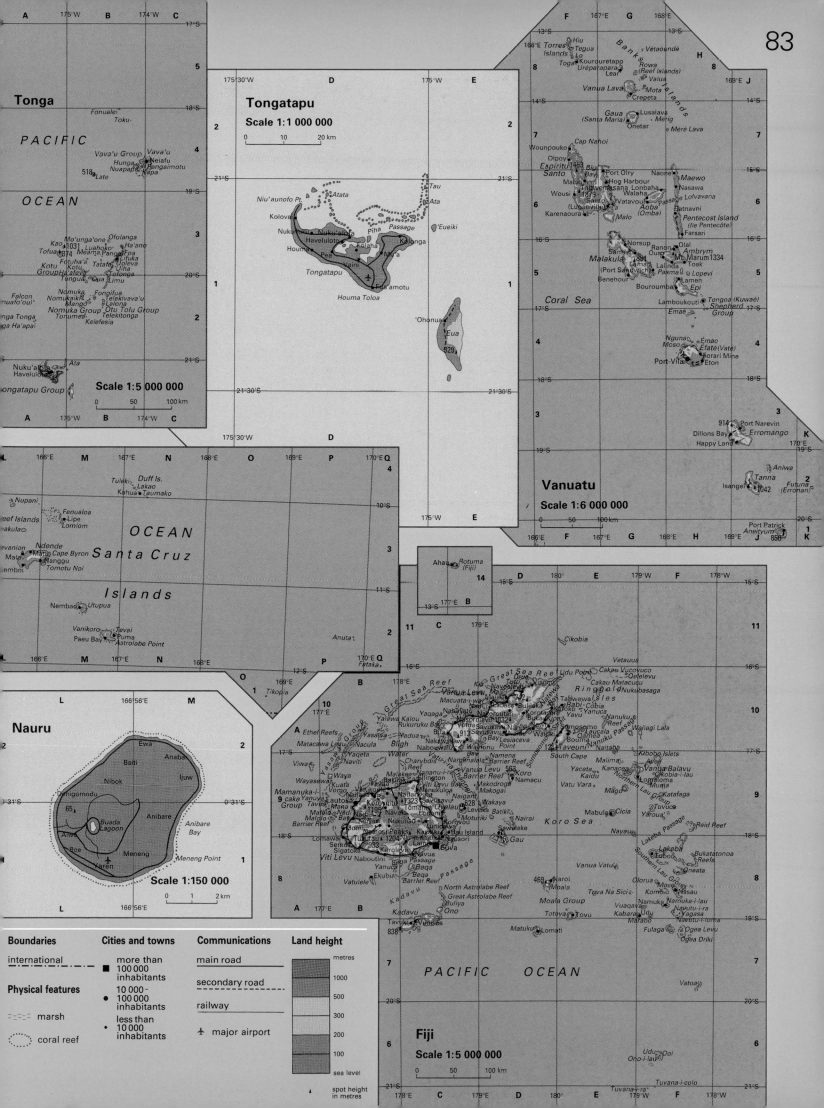

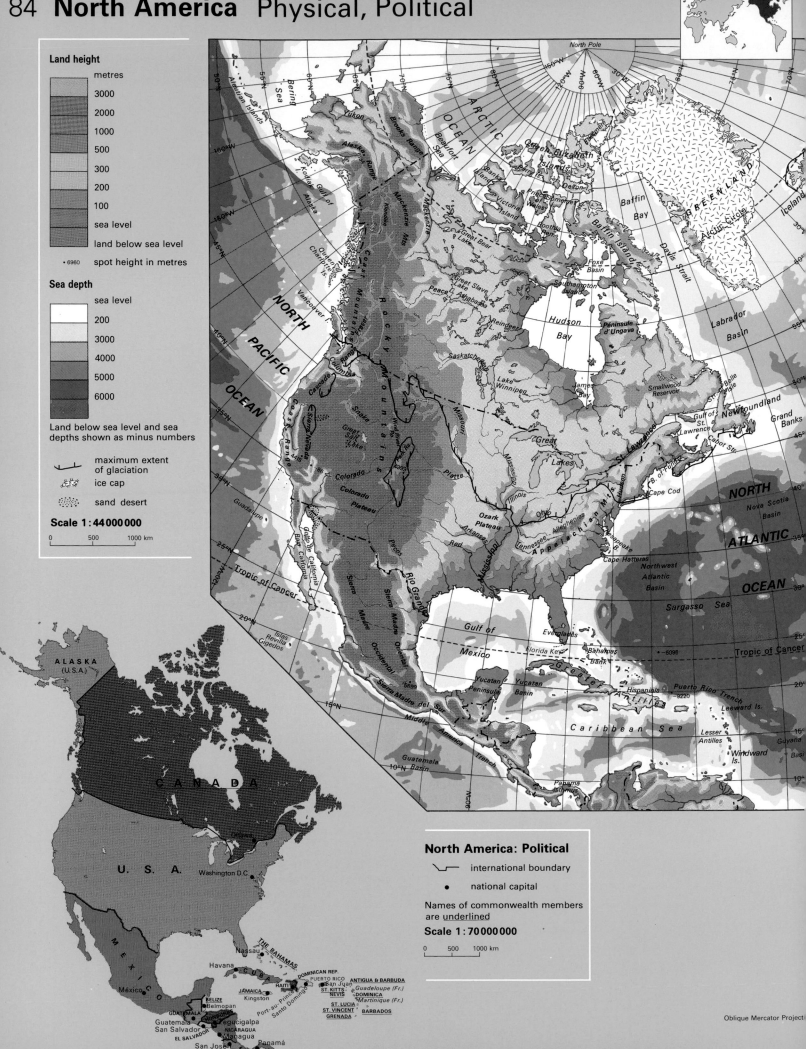

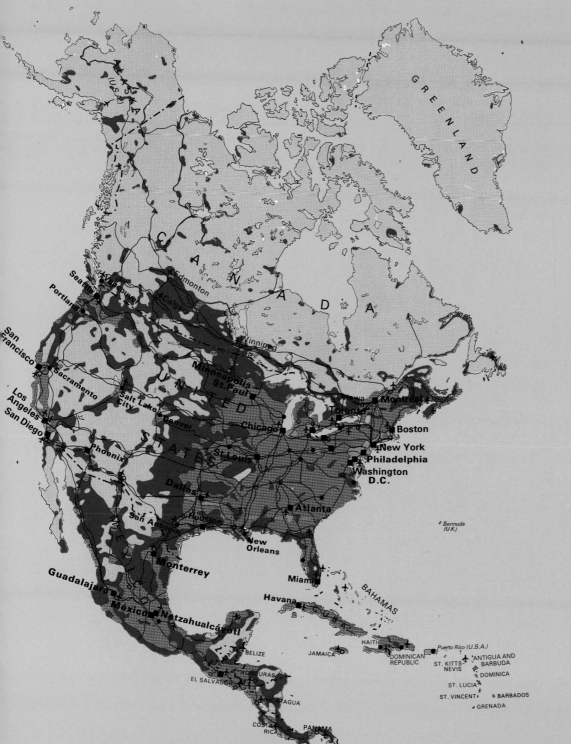

Population density
people per square kilometre

- over 100
- 10–100
- 1–9
- under 1

Cities

- ■ over 2 million inhabitants
- ● 1–2 million inhabitants
- ○ 0.5–1 million inhabitants

Communications

- —— principal roads
- —— principal railways
- ✈ principal airports
- —— navigable rivers

Boundaries

international —·—·—

Scale 1 : 44 000 000

0   500   1000 km

Canada:Population,1990

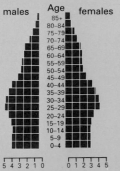

males   Age   females

85+
80–84
75–79
70–74
65–69
60–64
55–59
50–54
45–49
40–44
35–39
30–34
25–29
20–24
15–19
10–14
5–9
0–4

5 4 3 2 1 0   0 1 2 3 4 5
percent of total population

Total population:26.6 million

Crude Birth Rate per thousand:15

Crude Death Rate per thousand:7

Mexico:Population,1985

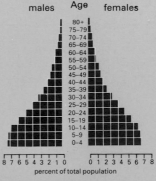

males   Age   females

80+
75–79
70–74
65–69
60–64
55–59
50–54
45–49
40–44
35–39
30–34
25–29
20–24
15–19
10–14
5–9
0–4

8 7 6 5 4 3 2 1 0   0 1 2 3 4 5 6 7 8
percent of total population

Total population:78.5 million

Crude Birth Rate per thousand:29

Crude Death Rate per thousand:6

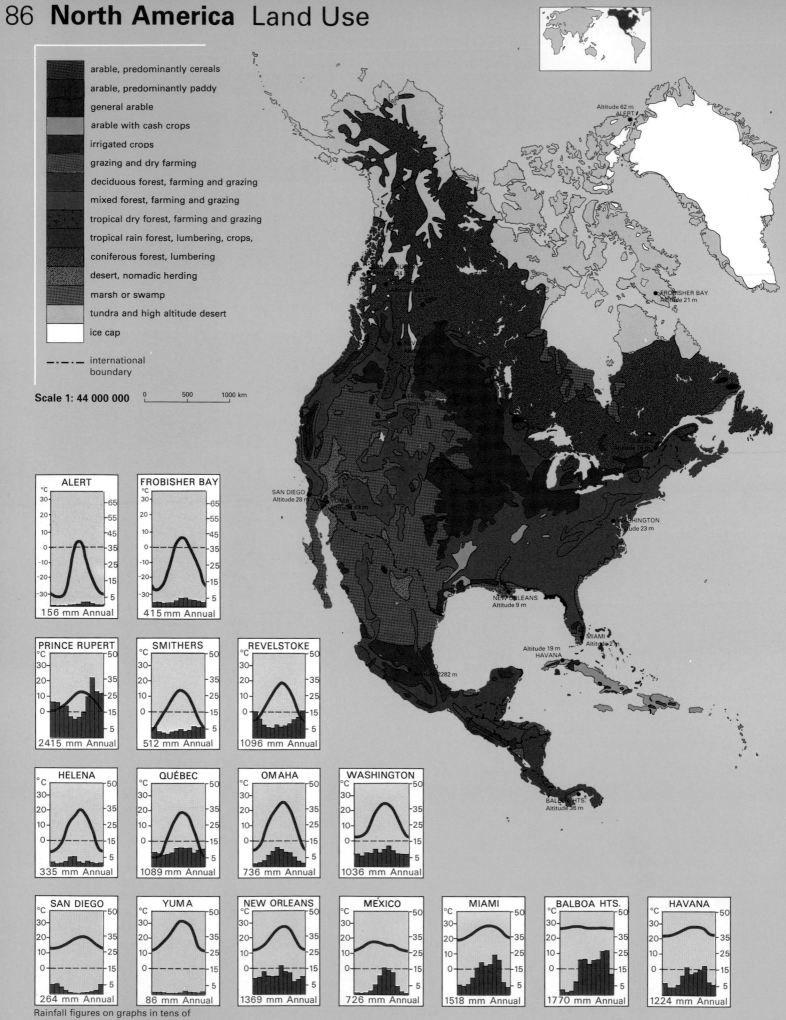

arable, predominantly cereals

arable, predominantly paddy

general arable

arable with cash crops

irrigated crops

grazing and dry farming

deciduous forest, farming and grazing

mixed forest, farming and grazing

tropical dry forest, farming and grazing

tropical rain forest, lumbering, crops,

coniferous forest, lumbering

desert, nomadic herding

marsh or swamp

tundra and high altitude desert

ice cap

–·–·– international
boundary

Scale 1: 44 000 000

0   500   1000 km

ALERT
°C
156 mm Annual

FROBISHER BAY
°C
415 mm Annual

PRINCE RUPERT
°C
2415 mm Annual

SMITHERS
°C
512 mm Annual

REVELSTOKE
°C
1096 mm Annual

HELENA
°C
335 mm Annual

QUÉBEC
°C
1089 mm Annual

OMAHA
°C
736 mm Annual

WASHINGTON
°C
1036 mm Annual

SAN DIEGO
°C
264 mm Annual

YUMA
°C
86 mm Annual

NEW ORLEANS
°C
1369 mm Annual

MÉXICO
°C
726 mm Annual

MIAMI
°C
1518 mm Annual

BALBOA HTS.
°C
1770 mm Annual

HAVANA
°C
1224 mm Annual

Rainfall figures on graphs in tens of
millimetres except for annual totals

Oblique Mercator Projection

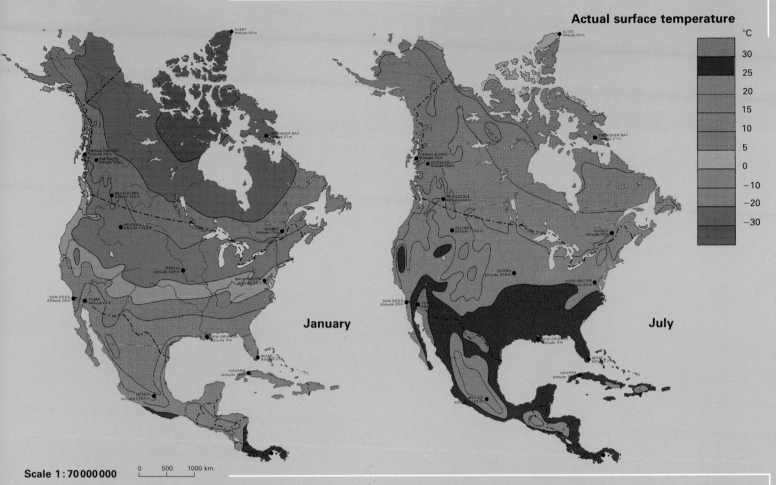

Actual surface temperature

°C
30
25
20
15
10
5
0
-10
-20
-30

January

July

Scale 1 : 70 000 000

0   500   1000 km

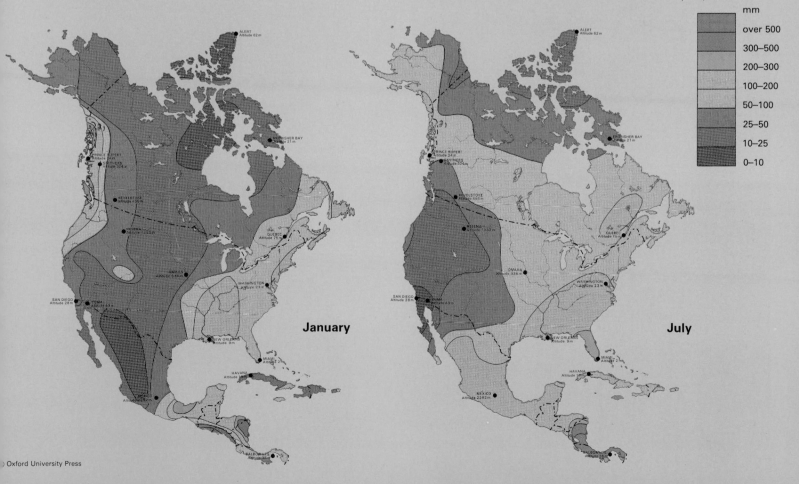

Rainfall
and other forms of precipitation

mm
over 500
300–500
200–300
100–200
50–100
25–50
10–25
0–10

January

July

Scale 1:19 000 000

0   200   400 km

Zenithal Equidistant Projection

120°W 100°W 80°W 60°W 50°W 40°W 8 30°W 20°W 7 20°W 6 5

Arctic Circle

GREENLAND
(Denmark)

Kong Christian X. Land
Kong Oscars Fj.
Scoresbysund

Pack ice — average autumn minimum

ICELAND
Reykjavik
Hafnarfjördur

Queen Elizabeth Islands
Axel Heiberg Island
Ellef Ringnes Amund Ringnes
Bathurst

Parry Islands
Cornwallis I. Resolute
Viscount Melville Sound
McClintock Channel
Prince of Wales Island
Peel Sound
Somerset Island
Boothia Penin.
Brodeur Penin.
Borden Penin. 7621
Arctic Bay

Ellesmere Island
Nares Strait
Hayes
Thule (Qaanaaq)
Halvø
Dundas (Uummannaq)
Melville Bugt

Steenstrup Glacier

Jakobshavn
Mont Fjord 3360

Denmark Strait

EE
60°N
DD
25°W

Devon Island
Jones Sound
Lancaster Sound
Bylot Island
Pond Inlet

Baffin Bay

Upernavik
Umanak Fjord
Nuussuaq
Oqaatsut
Disko Bugt
Godhavn (Qeqertarsuaq)

30°W
4
CC
35°W

Cambridge Bay
Victoria Str. King William Island
Gjoa Haven
Queen Maud Gulf
Spence Bay
Gulf of Boothia
Boothia Penin.

Clyde
Home Bay
Barnes Ice Cap 250

Baffin Island

Auyuittuq National Park
Cumberland Penin.
Pangnirtung
Cape Dyer

Davis Strait

Holsteinsborg
Sukkertoppen
Godthåb (Nuuk)

55°N
BB
40°W

Melville Peninsula
Prince Charles I.
Foxe Basin
Nettilling Lake

Cumberland Sound

Frederikshåb
Grønnedal
Julianehåb
Nanortalik
Narsarssuaq
Kap Farvel (Cape Farewell)

NORTH ATLANTIC OCEAN

WEST RIES
Pelly L.
Garry Lake
Back
Thelon
Dubawnt Lake
Wager Bay
Baker Lake
Baker L.

Southampton Island
Coral Harbour
Salisbury I.
Nottingham I. Hudson Strait
Amadjuak Foxe Penin.
Cape Dorset
Iqaluit (Frobisher Bay)
Hall Penin.
Frobisher Bay
Meta Incognita Penin.
Lake Harbour

C. Chidley
Torngat Mts.
Nutak

Labrador Sea

45°N
AA
3

Yathkyed Lake
Rankin Inlet
Eskimo Point
Nueltin Lake

Ross Welcome Sd.
Fisher Str. Evans Str.
Coats I.
Mansel I.

Péninsule d'Ungava

Ivujivik
Déception
Akpatok I.
C. Hopes Advance

Ungava Bay (Baie d'Ungava)
Rivière George
Rivière aux Feuilles

Davis Inlet
Makkovik

Pack ice — average spring maximum

NEWFO
45°W
50°N
Z
2

Hudson Bay

Povphgnituk
Inukjuak
Lac Payne
Lac Minto

Nain
Hamilton Inlet
Cartwright

Reindeer Lake
Wollaston L.
Wollaston Lake
Seal R.
North River
C. Churchill
Churchill
Churchill R.
C. Tatnam

Ottawa Is.
Les Îles Belcher
C. Henrietta Maria

Kuujjuarapik
Grande Rivière de la Baleine
Résr. La Grande 2
Grande Rivière La Grande 3

Lac à l'Eau Claire
Lac Bienville
Rivière (Fort George)

Schefferville
Kawawachikamach
Réservoir Caniapiscau
Labrador City
Wabush

Churchill Falls
Atikonak Lake
Smallwood Reservoir
Melville
Happy Valley Goose Bay

St. Anthony
White Bay Notre Dame Bay
Springdale

55°N
Y
1

N
Lynn Lake
Granville Lake
Southern Indian Lake
Thompson
Sipiwesk
Gillam
York Factory
Nelson R.
Fort Severn
Severn R.

D A
Akimiski I.
James Bay
Eastmain
Fort Rupert

Lac Mistassini
Chibougamau

Réservoir Manicouagan
Monts Otish 1128
Réservoir Gouin

Harrington Harbour
Mingan Natashquan
Wolf Bay
Sept-Îles

St. John's
Cape Race
Trepassey
Placentia
Ferryland

ONTARIO
Norway House
Gods L.
Big Trout Lake
Winisk L.
Lansdowne House
Sandy Lake
Pickle Lake
Fort Hope
Ogoki
Attawapiskat River
Attawapiskat
Albany River
Moosonee

Matagami
Val-d'Or
Rouyn-Noranda
Chibougamau

QUÉBEC

Jacques-Cartier Pa.
Baie Comeau
Rivière-du-Loup
Chandler
Gaspé
Gulf of St. Lawrence
Matane
Mont-Joli
Chicoutimi
Lac St-Jean
Roberval
Jonquière

NEW BRUNSWICK
Bathurst
PRINCE EDWARD
Charlottetown
Summerside
Îles de la Madeleine

NOVA SCOTIA
Sydney
Cape Breton I.
Glace Bay
Port Hawkesbury
Canso
Sable I.

35°W
W

MANITOBA
Winnipeg
Lake Winnipeg
Selkirk
Portage la Prairie
Dauphin
Riverton
Lake Manitoba
Lac Seul
Lake St. Joseph

Pikangikum Lake
Pickle Lake
Osnaburgh
Sioux Lookout
Nakina
Geraldton
Longlac
Hearst
Kapuskasing
Cochrane
Timmins
Kirkland Lake
New Liskeard

La Tuque
Shawinigan
Trois-Rivières
Québec
Lévis
Drummondville
Sherbrooke
Sorel

MAINE
Fredericton
Saint John
Woodstock
Edmundston

Moncton
Amherst
Truro
Halifax
Dartmouth
Lunenburg
Yarmouth
Shelburne

Bay of Fundy

NORTH ATLANTIC OCEAN

40°N
X

NORTH DAKOTA
Grand Forks
Jamestown
Bismarck
Fargo
Moorhead
Fergus Falls
MINNESOTA
Duluth
Superior
Brainerd
St. Cloud
Willmar

WISCONSIN
Green Bay
Eau Claire
La Crosse
Madison
Milwaukee

Lake Superior
Thunder Bay
Nipigon
Terrace Bay
White River
Wawa
Michipicoten
Sault Ste. Marie
Blind River
Manitoulin I.
Sudbury
North Bay
Parry Sound
Georgian Bay
Owen Sound
Midland
Barrie

Ottawa
Pembroke
Renfrew
Cornwall
Brockville
Kingston
Peterborough
Lake Ontario
Toronto
Oshawa
Hamilton
Guelph
Kitchener
London
Sarnia
Windsor

NEW YORK
Watertown
Utica
Syracuse
Rochester
Buffalo
Albany
Binghamton
Elmira

VERMONT
Burlington
NEW HAMPSHIRE
Concord
Portland
Portsmouth
MASSACHUSETTS
Boston
Worcester
Providence
New Haven
Hartford
Bridgeport
New York
Newark
Atlantic City

SOUTH DAKOTA
Watertown
Brookings
Mitchell
Sioux Falls
Yankton
Sioux City

IOWA
Cedar Rapids
Council Bluffs
Des Moines
Davenport

ILLINOIS
Rockford
Chicago
Gary

MICHIGAN
Grand Rapids
Lansing
Flint
Detroit
Kalamazoo
Jackson
Lake Michigan
Lake Huron
Lake Erie
Toledo
Cleveland
Youngstown

OHIO
Akron
Canton
Pittsburgh
PENNSYLVANIA
Harrisburg
York
Allentown
Philadelphia
Baltimore
NEW JERSEY

35°N

NEBRASKA
Norfolk
Columbus
North Platte

KANSAS
MISSOURI

100°W 95°W 85°W 80°W 75°W 70°W 65°W 60°W

© Oxford University Press

Boundaries

international

internal

national park

Communications

freeway/expressway/
motorway

other major road

railway

canal

✈ major airport

Cities and towns

◣ built-up areas

■ over 1 million
inhabitants

● more than 100 000
inhabitants

• smaller towns

Physical features

seasonal
river/lake

marsh

Land height

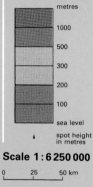

metres
1000
500
300
200
100
sea level

▲ spot height
in metres

Scale 1 : 6 250 000

0   25   50 km

RICHMOND · Staten Island · Long Island · Atlantic Ocean · Lower Bay · NEW YORK

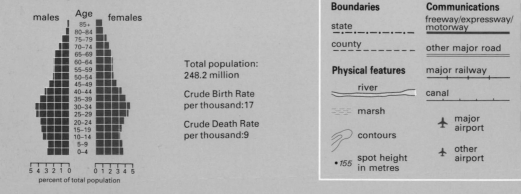

USA:Population,1989

males | Age | females
85+
80–84
75–79
70–74
65–69
60–64
55–59
50–54
45–49
40–44
35–39
30–34
25–29
20–24
15–19
10–14
5–9
0–4

5 4 3 2 1 0 | 0 1 2 3 4 5
percent of total population

Total population:
248.2 million

Crude Birth Rate
per thousand:17

Crude Death Rate
per thousand:9

Boundaries
state
county

Physical features
river
marsh
contours
•155 spot height in metres

Communications
freeway/expressway/motorway
other major road
major railway
canal
✈ major airport
✈ other airport

Land use
central business district
other major commercial areas
industrial
residential
major parks and open spaces
non-urban

Scale 1 : 300 000

0   5 km

Oxford University Press

Boundaries

international

internal

national park

Communications

freeway/expressway/
motorway

other major road

track

railway

canal

✈ major airport

Cities and towns

⬗ built-up areas

■ over 1 million
inhabitants

● more than 100 000
inhabitants

• smaller towns

Physical features

seasonal
river/lake

marsh

sand dunes

Land height

metres

3000
2000
1000
500
300
200
100
sea level
land below
sea level

▲ spot height
in metres

Scale 1:16 000 000

0   200   400km

main map only

Scale 1:1 250 000

0   25 km

Trinidad

Barbados

Scale 1:1 000 000

0   25 km

Panama Canal
Scale 1:1 500 000

0   25 km

Caribbean Sea

Portobelo
Punta Manzanillo
979
Colón
Puerto Pilón
Gatún Locks
Gatún
Madden Lake
1006
Palmas Bellas
Escobal
Gamboa
Gatún Lake
Gaillard Cut
Pedro Miguel Locks
Miraflores Locks
Panamá
Balboa
PACIFIC OCEAN
La Chorrera

Gaillard Cut
maximum elevation 95 m

CARIBBEAN SEA   minimum depth 12 m   PACIFIC OCEAN

sea level   sea level

0   15   30   45   60   75km

Gatún Locks (3 pairs)	Pedro Miguel Locks (1 pair)	Miraflores Locks (2 pairs)
length 305 m	length 305 m	length 305 m
width 33.5 m	width 33.5 m	width 33.5 m
total lift 25.9 m	total lift 9.1 m	total lift 16.8 m

The canal, opened in 1914, is 82 km long, including approaches (actual canal 64 km). Minimum depth 12 m, minimum width 152 m (Gaillard Cut). Time of passage 8 hours. In 1990 11 941 vessels used the canal carrying 157 072 978 tonnes of cargo. In 1979 Panama assumed control of the former Canal Zone, with the USA retaining majority representation on the Panama Commission until 1989. US military forces will remain in Panama until the year 2000 and the USA will be entitled to defend the Canal's neutrality thereafter.

NORTH ATLANTIC OCEAN

INDIANA
OHIO
Dayton
Cincinnati
Louisville
KENTUCKY
Lexington
Huntington
WEST VIRGINIA
Charleston
Parkersburg
Baltimore
Washington D.C.
MARYLAND
DELAWARE
Annapolis
Richmond
VIRGINIA
Lynchburg
Roanoke
Danville
Newport News
Portsmouth
Norfolk
Chesapeake
Hampton
Cape Hatteras
Winston-Salem
Greensboro
Raleigh
NORTH CAROLINA
Charlotte
Fayetteville
Wilmington
Rock Hill
Columbia
SOUTH CAROLINA
Charleston
Nashville
Knoxville
Chattanooga
TENNESSEE
Asheville
Greenville
Athens
Atlanta
GEORGIA
Augusta
Macon
Columbus
Montgomery
ALABAMA
Birmingham
Anniston
Huntsville
Savannah
Jacksonville
Tallahassee
Fort Walton Beach
Gainesville
St. Augustine
Ocala
Daytona Beach
Orlando
Melbourne
C. Canaveral
Tampa
St. Petersburg
Sarasota
Fort Myers
L. Okeechobee
West Palm Beach
Miami
FLORIDA
Key West
Straits of Florida
Mexico
Cape Catoche
Pen. de Morelos
I. de Cozumel

THE BAHAMAS
Grand Bahama
Great Abaco
New Providence
Nassau
Eleuthera
Andros
Cat I.
San Salvador
Great Exuma
Long Island
Crooked I.
Acklins I.
Mayaguana
Caicos Passage
Great Inagua
Turks & Caicos Is. (UK)
Tropic of Cancer

La Habana (Havana)
Pinar del Río
La Fe
Matanzas
Güines
Santa Clara
Cienfuegos
Sagua la Grande
Morón
Ciego de Ávila
CUBA
Trinidad
Camagüey
Holguín
Bayamo
Guantánamo
Manzanillo
Nuevitas
2005
Santiago de Cuba
Isla de la Juventud
Grand Cayman (UK)

West Indies
Windward Passage
Cap-Haïtien
Port-de-Paix
San Francisco
Santiago
Vega
DOMINICAN REPUBLIC
San Pedro
Aguadilla
San Juan
PUERTO RICO (USA)
St. Thomas
Virgin Is. (USA/UK)
Anguilla (UK)
ANTIGUA & BARBUDA
Codrington
Barbuda
ST. KITTS-NEVIS
Antigua
St. John's
Grande Terre
Guadeloupe (Fr.)
Pointe-à-Pitre
Basse Terre
Montserrat (UK)
3175
HAITI
Jérémie
Port-au-Prince
Santo Domingo
La Romana
Mayagüez
Ponce
Caguas
San Germán
St. Croix (USA)
Les Cayes
Jacmel
2680
Barahona
Hispaniola
Greater Antilles
Montego Bay
JAMAICA
Spanish Town
Kingston
DOMINICA
Roseau
1397
Martinique (Fr.)
Fort-de-France
Castries
ST. LUCIA
336
ST. VINCENT & THE GRENADINES
Kingstown
St. Vincent
BARBADOS
Bridgetown
840
GRENADA
St. George's

Caribbean Sea
Lesser Antilles
Leeward Is.
Windward Is.

HONDURAS
de la Bahía
La Ceiba
Laguna Caratasca
Cabo Gracias á Dios
Pto. Cabezas
Prinzapolca
NICARAGUA
Matagalpa
Managua
Masaya
Granada
Bluefields
Lago de Nicaragua
Punta del Mono
Laguna de Perlas
COSTA RICA
Alajuela
3432
San José
Cartago
Limón
Puntarenas
Palmar Sur
Pto. Armuelles
David
PANAMA
Santiago
Penonomé
Colón
Panamá
Canal
Balboa
Golfo de Panamá
Pen. de Azuero
Isla de Coiba
Cabo Blanco

Punta Gallinas
Riohacha
Santa Marta
Barranquilla
Sabanalarga
Cartagena
Arjona
Calamar
Sincelejo
Lorica
Magangué
El Banco
Montería
Ocaña
Bucaramanga
Yarumal
Sogamoso
COLOMBIA
Magdalena
Pico Cristóbal 5800

Golfo de Venezuela
Punto Fijo
Coro
Churuguara
Maracaibo
Cabimas
Lagunillas
San Felipe
Valencia
Barquisimeto
Trujillo
Valera
Acarigua
San Carlos
Guanare
VENEZUELA
ARUBA
Curaçao (Neths.)
Bonaire (Neths.)
Willemstad
Pto. Cumarebo
Pto. Cabello
Maracay
Caracas
La Guaira
Los Teques
Barcelona
Cumaná
Carúpano
Caripito
Maturín
Tucupita
Isla Margarita
La Asunción
Porlamar
Güiria
Trinidad
TRINIDAD & TOBAGO
Port of Spain
San Fernando
Tobago
Los Morros
San Juan de los Morros
Calabozo
Valle de la Pascua
El Tigre
Zaraza
Río Orinoco
Ciudad Bolívar
Ciudad Guayana
Barrancas
Embalse de Guri
Upata
El Callao
Cuyuni
GUYANA
Georgetown
New Amsterdam
Port Kaituma

Scale 1:3 000 000

0   25   50 km

Zenithal Equidistant Projection
Oxford University Press

Jamaica

Montego Bay
Falmouth
St. Ann's Bay
Galina Point
Port Maria
Lucea
Brown's Town
Ocho Rios
Grange Hill
Cambridge
Highgate
Annotto Bay
Buff Bay
South Negril Point
Christiana
Frankfield
Ewarton
Linstead
Port Antonio
Savanna la Mar
Santa Cruz
Mandeville
Chapelton
Bog Walk
The Blue Mts.
Black River
Porus
May Pen
Spanish Town
2256
Kingston
Port Royal
Bath
Great Pedro Bluff
Old Harbour Town
Old Harbour Bay
Morant Point
Port Morant
Morant Bay
Portland Point

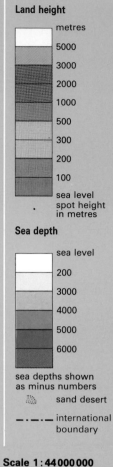

Land height

metres
	5000
	3000
	2000
	1000
	500
	300
	200
	100
	sea level

. spot height
in metres

Sea depth

	sea level
	200
	3000
	4000
	5000
	6000

sea depths shown
as minus numbers

sand desert

-·-·- international
boundary

Scale 1 : 44 000 000

0   500   1000 km

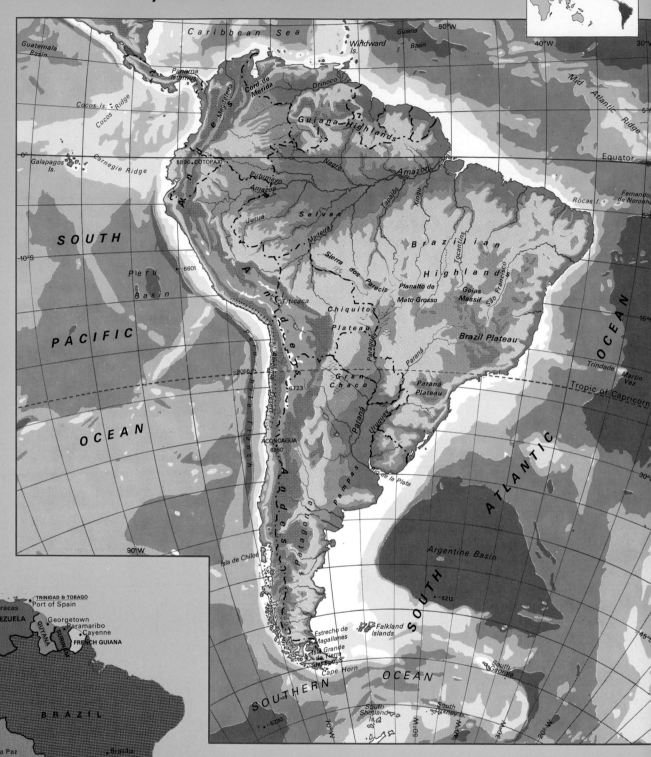

Oblique Mercator Project

South America: Political

——— international boundary

• national capital

Names of commonwealth members
are underlined

Scale 1 : 70 000 000

0   500   1000 km

Oblique Mercator Projection

Oxford University Press

Population density

people per square kilometre

- over 100
- 10–100
- 1–9
- under 1

Cities

- ■ over 2 million inhabitants
- ● 1–2 million inhabitants
- ○ 0.5–1 million inhabitants

Communications

—— principal roads

—— principal railways

✈ principal airports

—— navigable rivers

Boundaries

international

Scale 1 : 44 000 000

0   500   1000 km

Venezuela: Population, 1986

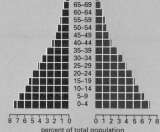

males   Age   females

Total population 17.8 million
Crude Birth Rate per thousand: 32
Crude Death Rate per thousand: 5

percent of total population

Argentina: Population, 1985

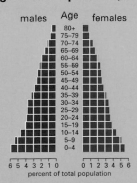

males   Age   females

percent of total population

Total population 30.6 million
Crude Birth Rate per thousand: 24
Crude Death Rate per thousand: 9

Brazil:Population,1988

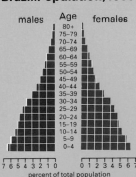

males   Age   females

percent of total population

Total population 144.4 million
Crude Birth Rate per thousand:27
Crude Death Rate per thousand:8

Peru: Population, 1985

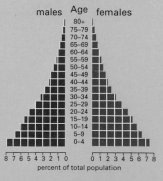

males   Age   females

percent of total population

Total population 19.7 million
Crude Birth Rate per thousand: 33
Crude Death Rate per thousand:10

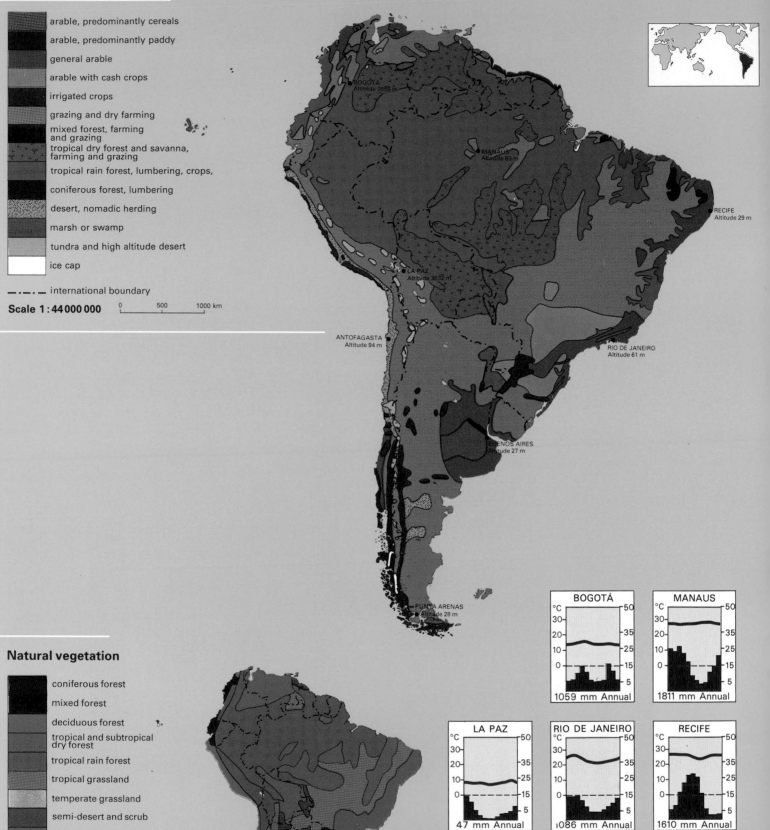

Land Use legend

	arable, predominantly cereals
	arable, predominantly paddy
	general arable
	arable with cash crops
	irrigated crops
	grazing and dry farming
	mixed forest, farming and grazing
	tropical dry forest and savanna, farming and grazing
	tropical rain forest, lumbering, crops,
	coniferous forest, lumbering
	desert, nomadic herding
	marsh or swamp
	tundra and high altitude desert
	ice cap
–·–·–	international boundary

Scale 1 : 44 000 000

0   500   1000 km

BOGOTÁ
Altitude 2659 m
MANAUS
Altitude 83 m
LA PAZ
Altitude 3632 m
ANTOFAGASTA
Altitude 94 m
RIO DE JANEIRO
Altitude 61 m
RECIFE
Altitude 29 m
BUENOS AIRES
Altitude 27 m
PUNTA ARENAS
Altitude 28 m

Natural vegetation

	coniferous forest
	mixed forest
	deciduous forest
	tropical and subtropical dry forest
	tropical rain forest
	tropical grassland
	temperate grassland
	semi-desert and scrub
	hot desert
	temperate desert
	high altitude vegetation
	marsh and swamp
–·–·–	international boundary

Scale 1 : 88 000 000

0   1000 km

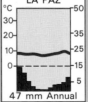

BOGOTÁ
°C
30
20
10
0
50
35
25
15
5
1059 mm Annual

MANAUS
°C
30
20
10
0
50
35
25
15
5
1811 mm Annual

LA PAZ
°C
30
20
10
0
50
35
25
15
5
47 mm Annual

RIO DE JANEIRO
°C
30
20
10
0
50
35
25
15
5
1086 mm Annual

RECIFE
°C
30
20
10
0
50
35
25
15
5
1610 mm Annual

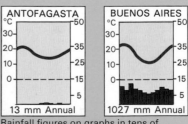

ANTOFAGASTA
°C
30
20
10
0
50
35
25
15
5
13 mm Annual

BUENOS AIRES
°C
30
20
10
0
50
35
25
15
5
1027 mm Annual

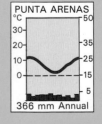

PUNTA ARENAS
°C
30
20
10
0
50
35
25
15
5
366 mm Annual

Rainfall figures on graphs in tens of millimetres except for annual totals

Oblique Mercator Projecti

© Oxford University Pre

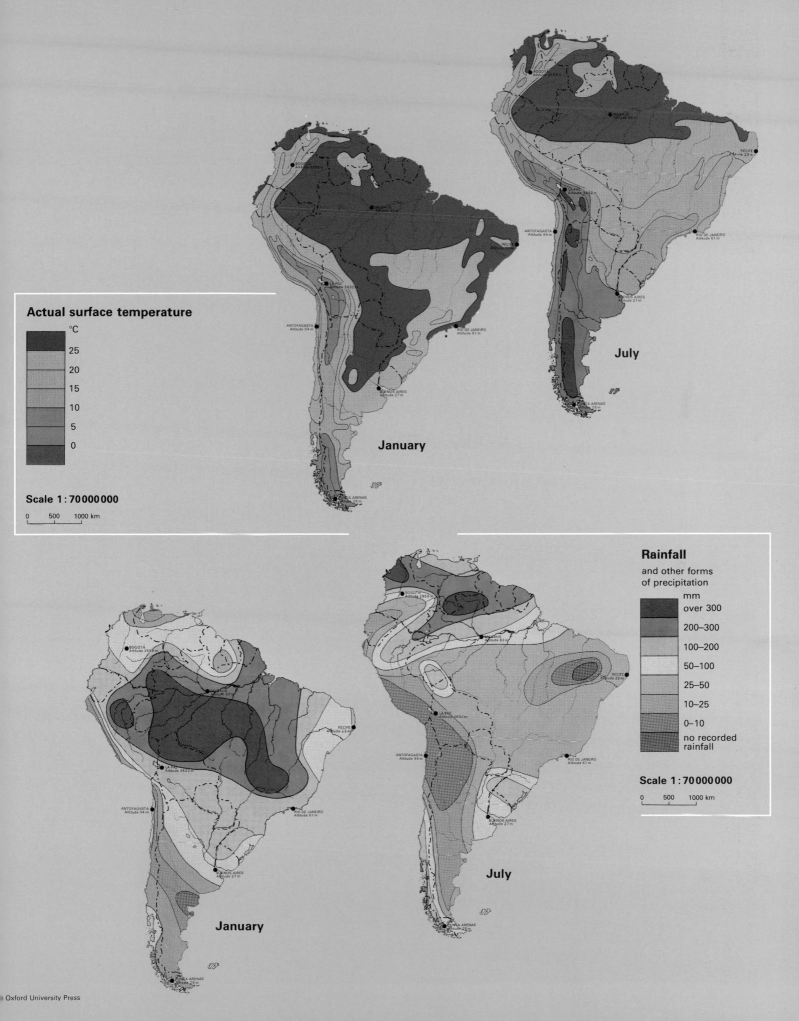

Actual surface temperature

°C
25
20
15
10
5
0

Scale 1 : 70 000 000

0   500   1000 km

July

January

Rainfall

and other forms
of precipitation

mm
over 300
200–300
100–200
50–100
25–50
10–25
0–10
no recorded
rainfall

Scale 1 : 70 000 000

0   500   1000 km

July

January

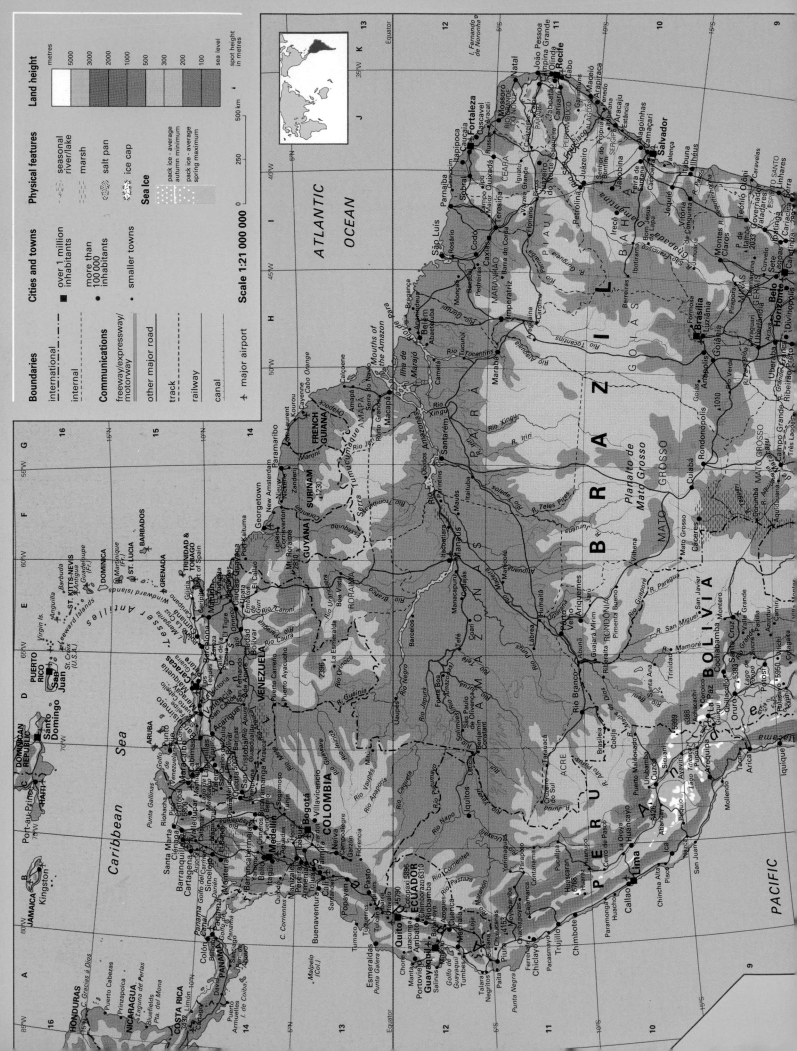

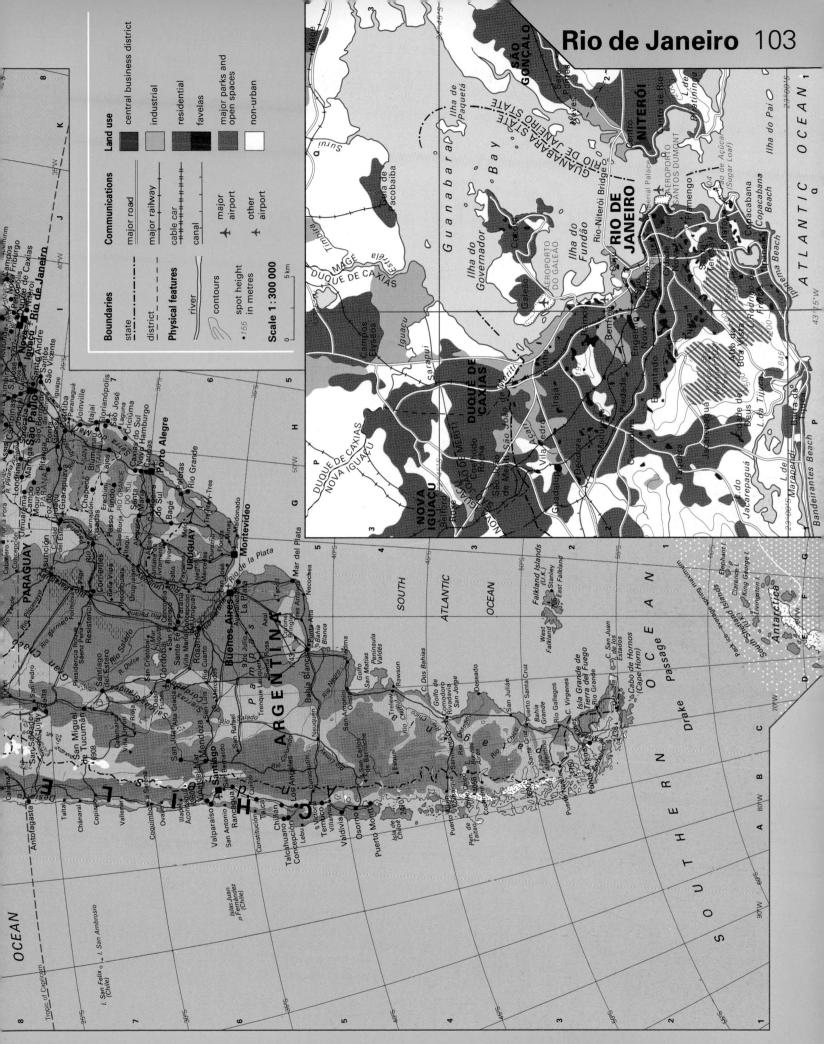

Land use

- central business district
- industrial
- residential
- favelas
- major parks and open spaces
- non-urban

Boundaries

- state
- district

Physical features

- river
- contours
- •155 spot height in metres

Communications

- major road
- major railway
- cable car
- canal
- ✈ major airport
- ✦ other airport

Scale 1:300 000

0   5 km

Transverse Mercator Projection

Oxford University Press

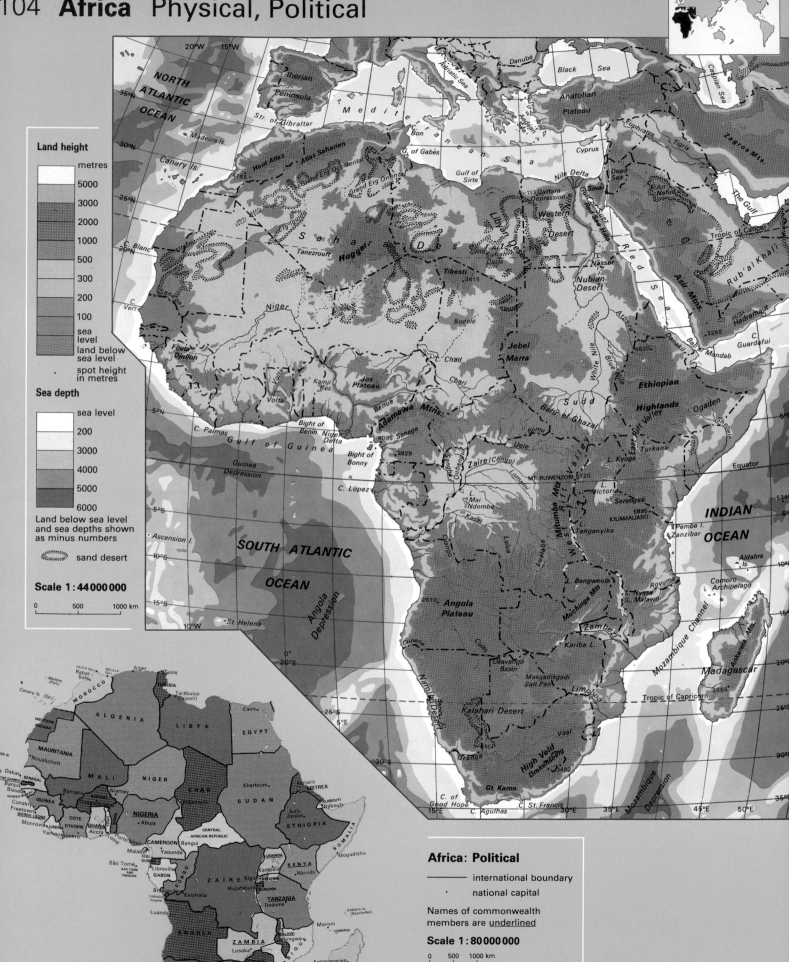

Land height

metres
5000
3000
2000
1000
500
300
200
100
sea level
land below sea level

· spot height in metres

Sea depth

sea level
200
3000
4000
5000
6000

Land below sea level and sea depths shown as minus numbers

sand desert

Scale 1:44 000 000

0   500   1000 km

Africa: Political

——— international boundary

· national capital

Names of commonwealth members are <u>underlined</u>

Scale 1:80 000 000

0   500   1000 km

Zenithal Equal Area Projection

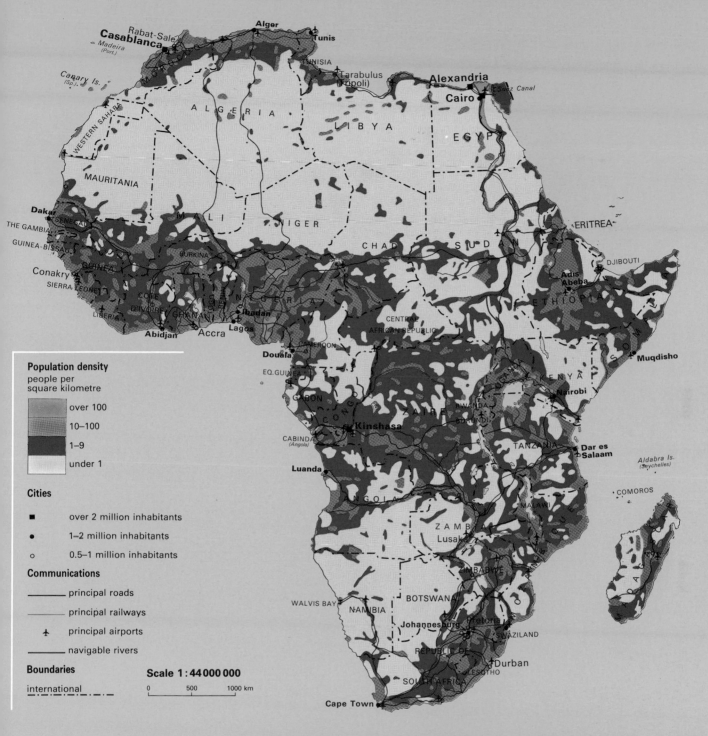

Population density

people per
square kilometre

over 100

10–100

1–9

under 1

Cities

■   over 2 million inhabitants

●   1–2 million inhabitants

○   0.5–1 million inhabitants

Communications

────── principal roads

────── principal railways

✈   principal airports

────── navigable rivers

Boundaries

Scale 1 : 44 000 000

international

0   500   1000 km

Algeria:Population,1984

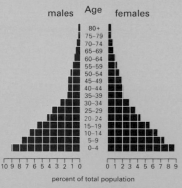

males   Age   females

80+
75–79
70–74
65–69
60–64
55–59
50–54
45–49
40–44
35–39
30–34
25–29
20–24
15–19
10–14
5–9
0–4

10 9 8 7 6 5 4 3 2 1 0   0 1 2 3 4 5 6 7 8 9

percent of total population

Total Population:20.8 million

Crude Birth Rate per thousand:37

Crude Death Rate per thousand:10

Ethiopia:Population,1989

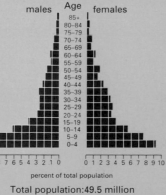

males   Age   females

85+
80–84
75–79
70–74
65–69
60–64
55–59
50–54
45–49
40–44
35–39
30–34
25–29
20–24
15–19
10–14
5–9
0–4

10 9 8 7 6 5 4 3 2 1 0   0 1 2 3 4 5 6 7 8 9 10

percent of total population

Total population:49.5 million

Crude Birth Rate per thousand:49

Crude Death Rate per thousand:20

Zaïre:Population,1985

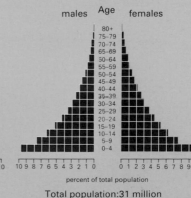

males   Age   females

80+
75–79
70–74
65–69
60–64
55–59
50–54
45–49
40–44
35–39
30–34
25–29
20–24
15–19
10–14
5–9
0–4

10 9 8 7 6 5 4 3 2 1 0   0 1 2 3 4 5 6 7 8 9 10

percent of total population

Total population:31 million

Crude Birth Rate per thousand:46

Crude Death Rate per thousand:14

South Africa:Population,1985

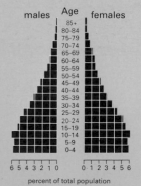

males   Age   females

85+
80–84
75–79
70–74
65–69
60–64
55–59
50–54
45–49
40–44
35–39
30–34
25–29
20–24
15–19
10–14
5–9
0–4

6 5 4 3 2 1 0   0 1 2 3 4 5 6

percent of total population

Total population:23.4 million

Crude Birth Rate per thousand:35

Crude Death Rate per thousand:8

Oxford University Press

Legend:
- arable, predominantly cereals
- arable, predominantly paddy
- general arable
- arable with cash crops
- irrigated crops
- grazing and dry farming
- deciduous forest, farming and grazing
- mixed forest, farming and grazing
- tropical dry forest and savanna, farming and grazing
- tropical rain forest, lumbering, crops,
- desert, nomadic herding
- marsh or swamp

Scale 1:44 000 000

0   500   1000 km

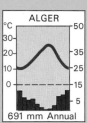

Tsetse fly
- infected areas

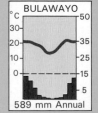

ALGER
°C
30
20
10
0
691 mm Annual

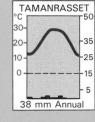

TAMANRASSET
38 mm Annual

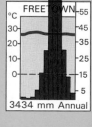

FREETOWN
3434 mm Annual

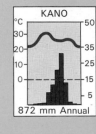

KANO
872 mm Annual

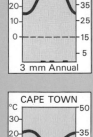

KINSHASA
1371 mm Annual

WADI HALFA
3 mm Annual

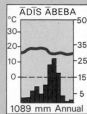

ĀDĪS ĀBEBA
1089 mm Annual

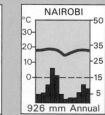

NAIROBI
926 mm Annual

BULAWAYO
589 mm Annual

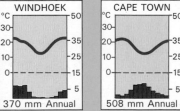

WINDHOEK
370 mm Annual

CAPE TOWN
508 mm Annual

Rainfall figures on graphs in tens of millimetres except for annual totals

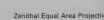

Zenithal Equal Area Projection

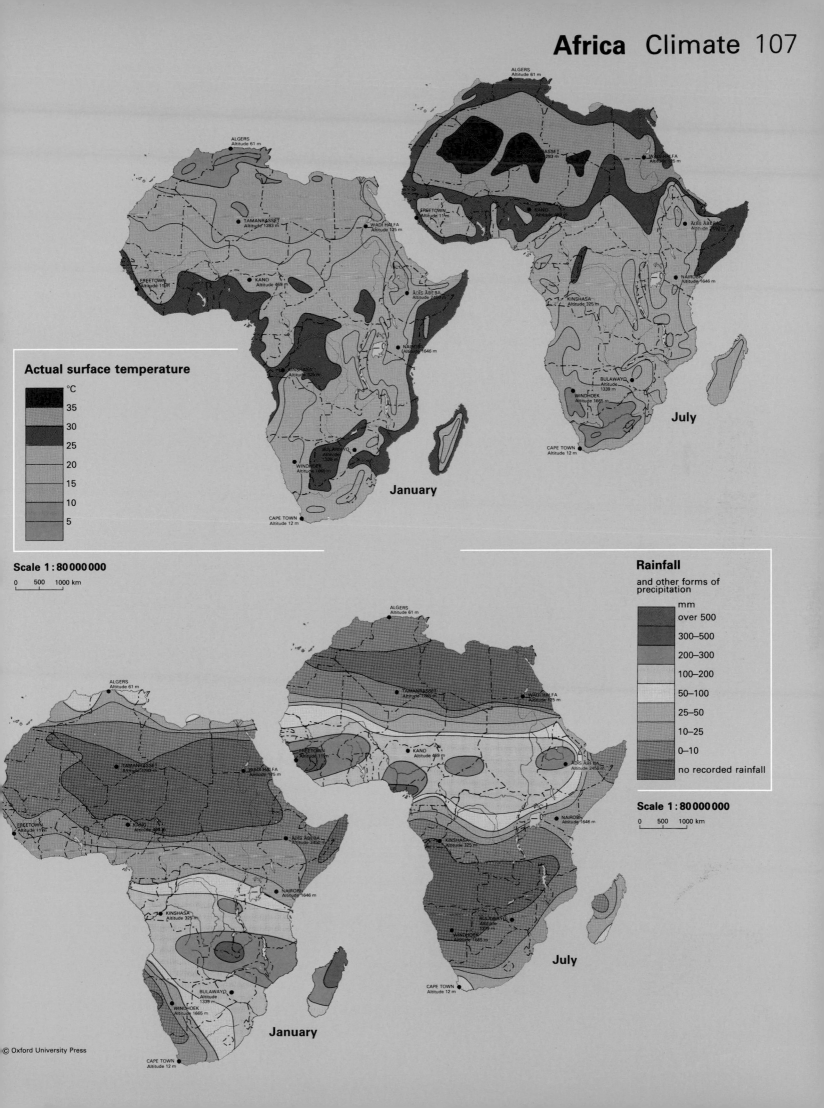

Actual surface temperature

°C
35
30
25
20
15
10
5

January

July

Scale 1:80 000 000

0   500   1000 km

Rainfall

and other forms of precipitation

mm
over 500
300–500
200–300
100–200
50–100
25–50
10–25
0–10
no recorded rainfall

Scale 1:80 000 000

0   500   1000 km

January

July

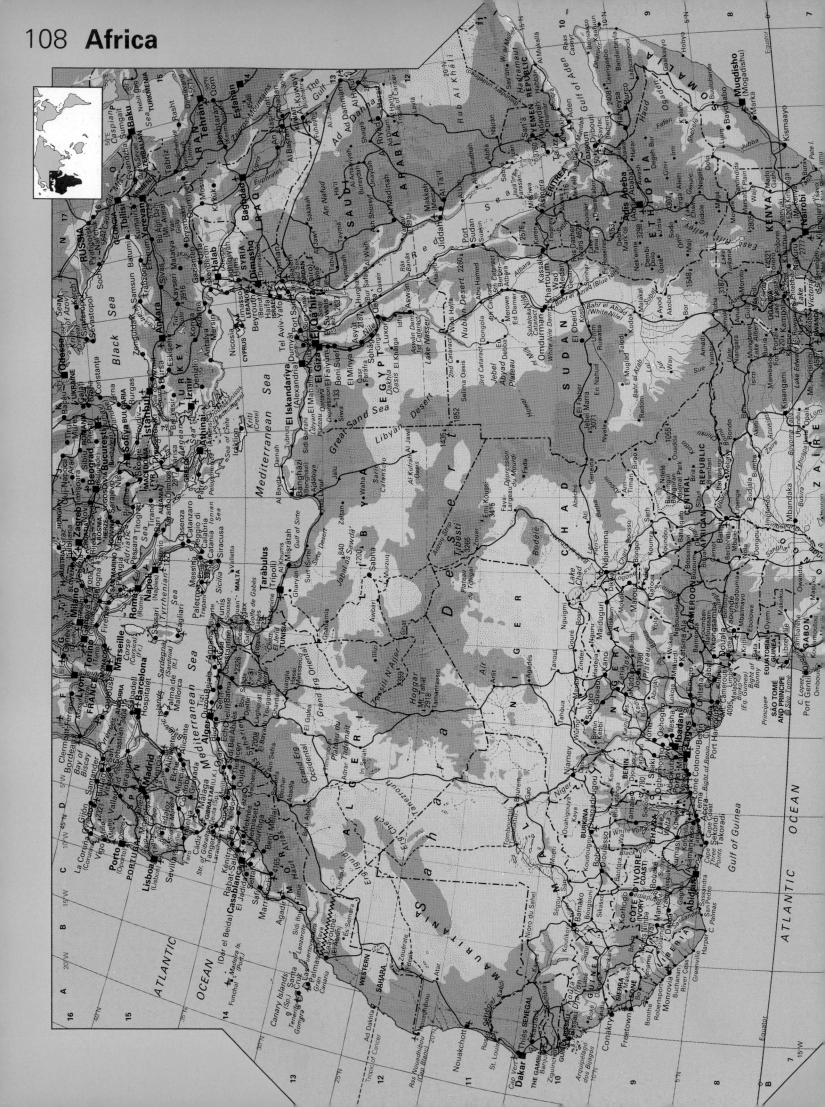

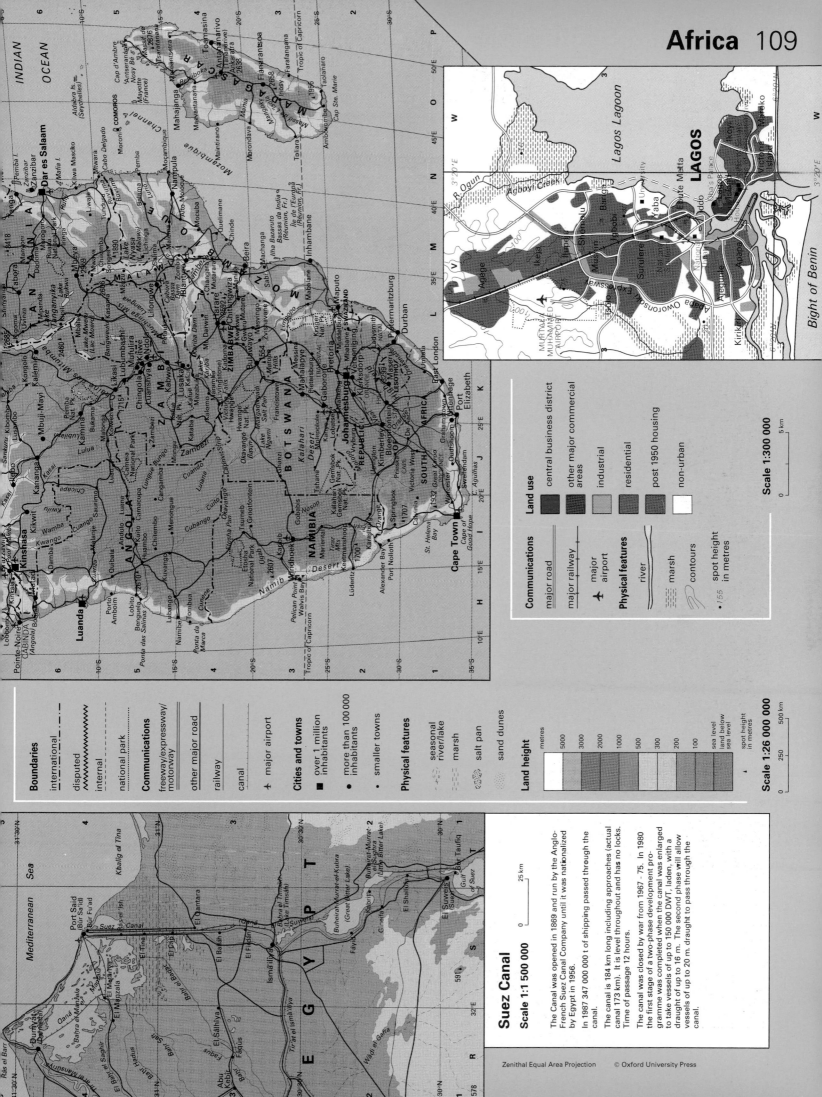

Land use
- central business district
- other major commercial areas
- industrial
- residential
- post 1950 housing
- non-urban

Communications
- major road
- major railway
- ✈ major airport

Physical features
- river
- marsh
- contours
- ·155 spot height in metres

Scale 1:300 000

0   5 km

Boundaries
- international
- disputed
- internal
- national park

Communications
- freeway/expressway/motorway
- other major road
- railway
- canal
- ✈ major airport

Cities and towns
- ■ over 1 million inhabitants
- ● more than 100 000 inhabitants
- • smaller towns

Physical features
- seasonal river/lake
- marsh
- salt pan
- sand dunes

Land height

metres	
5000	
3000	
2000	
1000	
500	
300	
200	
100	
sea level	
land below sea level	

▲ spot height in metres

Scale 1:26 000 000

0   250   500 km

Suez Canal

Scale 1:1 500 000

0   25 km

The Canal was opened in 1869 and run by the Anglo-French Suez Canal Company until it was nationalized by Egypt in 1956.

In 1987 347 000 000 t of shipping passed through the canal.

The canal is 184 km long including approaches (actual canal 173 km). It is level throughout and has no locks. Time of passage 12 hours.

The canal was closed by war from 1967 - 75. In 1980 the first stage of a two-phase development programme was completed when the canal was enlarged to take vessels of up to 150 000 DWT, laden, with a draught of up to 16 m. The second phase will allow vessels of up to 20 m. draught to pass through the canal.

Zenithal Equal Area Projection   © Oxford University Press

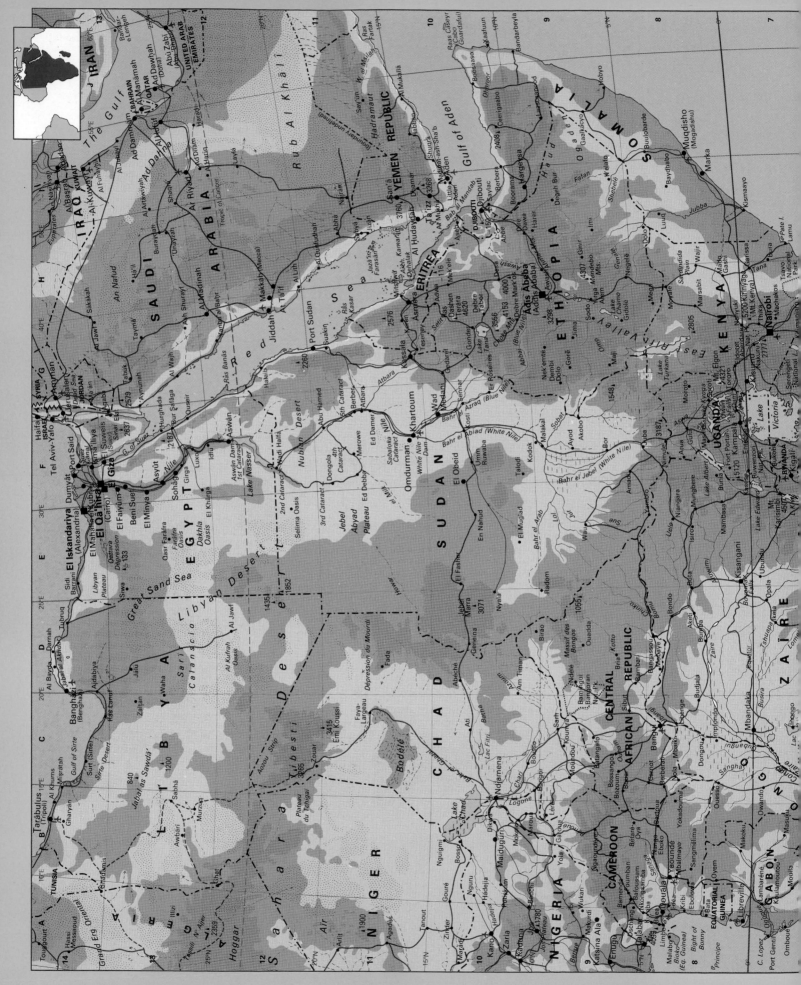

Zenithal Equal Area Projecti

Boundaries

international

disputed

Communications

freeway/expressway/motorway

other major road

track

railway

✈ major airport

Cities and towns

■ over 1 million inhabitants

● more than 100 000 inhabitants

• smaller towns

Physical features

seasonal river/lake

marsh

salt pan

sand dunes

Land height

metres
3000
2000
1000
500
300
200
100
sea level
▲ spot height in metres

Scale 1 : 19 000 000

0   200   400 km

Zenithal Equal Area Projection

© Oxford University Press

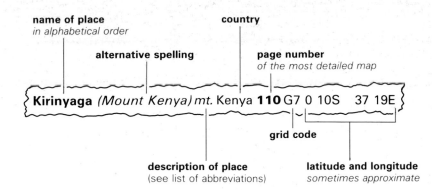

name of place
in alphabetical order

alternative spelling

country

page number
of the most detailed map

Kirinyaga *(Mount Kenya) mt.* Kenya **110** G7 0 10S 37 19E

grid code

description of place
(see list of abbreviations)

latitude and longitude
sometimes approximate

How to use the gazetteer

To find a place on an atlas map
use either the grid code or
latitude and longitude.

Grid code

Latitude and Longitude

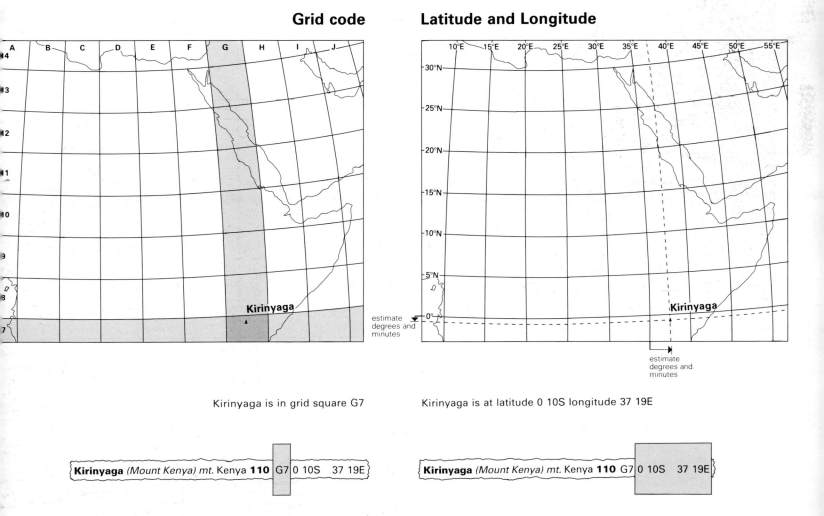

Kirinyaga is in grid square G7

Kirinyaga is at latitude 0 10S longitude 37 19E

estimate
degrees and
minutes

estimate
degrees and
minutes

Kirinyaga *(Mount Kenya) mt.* Kenya **110** G7 0 10S 37 19E

Kirinyaga *(Mount Kenya) mt.* Kenya **110** G7 0 10S 37 19E

A

Amstetten Austria 75 B2 48 08N 14 52E
Am Timan Chad 110 D10 10 59N 20 18E
Amund Ringnes Islands Northwest Territories Canada 89 P8 78 00N 96 00W
Amundsen Gulf Northwest Territories Canada 88 K7 70 30N 125 00W
Amundsen-Scott r.s. South Pole Antarctica 21 90 00S
Amundsen Sea Southern Ocean 21 72 00S 130 00W
Amungen l. Sweden 69 D3 61 10N 15 35E
Amuntai Indonesia 42 E3 2 24S 115 14E
Amur (Heilong Jiang) r. Asia 49 P9 52 30N 126 30E
Amurang Indonesia 43 F4 1 12N 124 37E
Amursk Russia 57 P6 50 16N 136 55E
Amurskiy Zaliv g. Russia 50 E6 42 50N 131 00E
Anabar Nauru 83 M2 0 30S 166 57E
Anabar r. Russia 57 N10 71 30N 113 00E
Anaconda Montana U.S.A. 90 D6 46 09N 112 56W
Anadyr' Russia 57 T8 64 50N 178 00E
Anadyr' r. Russia 57 T9 65 00N 175 00E
Anadyr', Gulf of Russia 57 U8 65 00N 178 00W
Anaheim California U.S.A. 95 C2 33 50N 117 56W
Anai Mudi mt. India 53 D2 10 20N 77 15E
Anan Japan 46 B1 33 54N 134 40E
Ananindeua Brazil 102 H12 1 22S 48 20W
Anantapur India 53 D2 14 42N 77 05E
Anápolis Brazil 102 H9 16 19S 48 58W
Anatolian Plateau Turkey 104 39 00N 39 00E
Anatom i. Vanuatu 78 L5 20 10S 169 50E
An Bien Vietnam 37 C1 9 44N 105 00E
Anchorage Alaska U.S.A. 88 F5 61 10N 150 00W
Ancona Italy 74 B3 43 37N 13 31E
Anda China 49 P8 46 25N 125 20E
Andalsnes Norway 69 B3 62 33N 7 43E
Andaman Islands Indian Ocean 38 A2 12 30N 93 00E
Andaman Sea Indian Ocean 38 A2/B2 12 30N 97 00E
Andenne Belgium 70 E2 50 29N 5 06E
Anderlecht Belgium 70 D2 50 50N 4 20E
Andermatt Switzerland 73 C2 46 38N 8 36E
Anderson r. Northwest Territories Canada 88 J6 69 42N 129 01W
Anderson Indiana U.S.A. 92 C2 40 05N 85 41W
Anderson South Carolina U.S.A. 91 J3 34 30N 82 39W
Andes mts. South America 102/103 B13/C5
Andhra Pradesh admin. India 53 D3 16 00N 79 00E
Andizhan Uzbekistan 59 L3 40 40N 72 12E
Andkhvoy Afghanistan 55 K6 36 58N 65 00E
Andong South Korea 50 D3 36 37N 128 44E
ANDORRA 72 C3
Andorra la Vella Andorra 72 C3 42 30N 1 30E
Andraitx Balearic Islands 72 E4 39 35N 2 25E
Andrésy France 67 A2 48 59N 2 03E
Andreyevka Kazakhstan 48 F8 45 50N 80 34E
Andreyevka Ukraine 58 D4 49 34N 36 38E
Ándros i. Greece 74 D2 37 49N 24 54E
Andros i. The Bahamas 97 I4 24 00N 78 00W
Androscoggin River U.S.A. 93 F2 44 00N 70 00W
Andros Town The Bahamas 97 I4 24 45N 77 50W
Androth Island India 53 C2 10 51N 73 41E
Andújar Spain 72 B2 38 02N 4 03W
Andulo Angola 111 C5 11 29S 16 43E
Aneityum i. Vanuatu 83 J1 20 11S 169 45E
Angamarut Papua New Guinea 45 J3 6 22S 141 00E
Angara r. Russia 57 L7 58 00N 96 00E
Angara Basin Arctic Ocean 20 80 00N
Angarsk Russia 57 M6 52 31N 103 55E
Angel de la Guarda i. Mexico 96 B5 29 00N 113 30W
Angeles The Philippines 40 B4 15 09N 120 33E
Angeles National Forest California U.S.A. 95 B4/C3 34 15N 118 10W
Angemuk mt. Irian Jaya Indonesia 44 H5 3 29S 138 36E
Ångermanälven r. Sweden 69 D3 64 30N 16 15E
Angers France 73 A2 47 29N 0 32W
Angkor hist. site Cambodia 37 B2 13 26N 103 50E
Anglesey i. Wales United Kingdom 68 G5 53 18N 4 25W
Angliers Québec Canada 93 E3 47 33N 79 14W
Ang Mo Kio Singapore 41 D4 1 22N 103 50E
ANGOLA 111 B4/D6
Angola Basin Atlantic Ocean 25 I5 15 00S 3 00E
Angoram Papua New Guinea 45 L4 4 04S 144 04E
Angoulême France 73 B2 45 40N 0 10E
Angren Uzbekistan 59 L3 41 01N 70 10E
Ang Thong Thailand 39 B2 14 35N 100 25E
Anguilla i. Leeward Islands 97 L3 18 14N 63 05W
Anhua China 36 E7 28 27N 111 15E
Anibare Nauru 83 M1 0 31S 166 56E
Anibare Bay Nauru 83 M1 0 31S 166 57E
Aniwa i. Vanuatu 83 J2 18 17S 169 36E
Anjō Japan 46 J1 34 56N 137 05E
Anjŭ North Korea 50 B4 39 36N 125 42E
Ankara Turkey 54 D6 39 55N 32 50E
Ankaratra mt. Madagascar 111 I4 19 25S 47 12E
An Khe (An Tuc) Vietnam 37 C2 13 55N 103 38E
Anklam Germany 71 B2 53 52N 13 42E
An Loc see Hon Quan
Anlong Veng Cambodia 37 B2 14 16N 104 08E
'Annaba Algeria 112 G10 36 55N 7 47E
An Nabk Saudi Arabia 54 E5 31 21N 37 20E
An Nabk Syria 54 E5 34 02N 36 43E
An Nafud d. Saudi Arabia 54 F4 28 20N 40 30E
An Najaf Iraq 54 F5 31 59N 44 19E
Annam Range mts. Laos/Vietnam 37 C2/3 19 00N 104 00E
Annapolis Maryland U.S.A. 93 E1 38 59N 76 30W
Annapurna mt. Nepal 53 E5 28 34N 83 50E
Ann Arbor Michigan U.S.A. 93 D2 42 18N 83 43W
Ann, Cape U.S.A. 93 F2 42 39N 70 37W
Annecy France 73 C2 45 54N 6 07E
Anning China 38 C4 24 54N 102 35E
Anniston Alabama U.S.A. 91 I3 33 38N 85 50W
An Nohn Vietnam 37 C2 13 53N 109 13E
Annotto Bay tn. Jamaica 97 R8 18 16N 76 47W
Anpu China 37 D4 21 29N 110 03E
Anqing China 49 N5 30 46N 119 40E
Ansari Nagar India 52 L4 28 33N 77 12E
Ansbach Germany 71 B1 49 18N 10 36E
Anshan China 49 O7 41 05N 122 58E
Anshun China 49 L4 26 15N 105 51E
Anson Bay Norfolk Island 81 J5/K5 29 00S 167 55E
Anson Bay Reserve Norfolk Island 81 K5 29 00S 167 55E
Anson Point Norfolk Island 81 J5 29 00S 167 54E
Ansudu Irian Jaya Indonesia 44 H5 2 10S 139 19E
Antakya Turkey 54 E6 36 12N 36 10E
Antalya Turkey 54 D6 36 53N 30 42E
Antananarivo (Tananarive) Madagascar 111 I4 18 52S 47 30E
Antarctica 21
Antarctic Peninsula Antarctica 21 68 00S 65 00W
Antequera Spain 72 B2 37 01N 4 34W
Antibes France 73 C1 43 35N 7 07E
Antigua Guatemala 96 F2 14 33N 90 42W
Antigua i. Antigua & Barbuda 97 L3 17 09N 61 49W
ANTIGUA & BARBUDA 97 L3
Antipodes Islands Southern Ocean 80 C1 49 42S 178 50E
Antofagasta Chile 103 C8 23 40S 70 23W
Antrim Mountains Northern Ireland United Kingdom 68 E6 55 00N 6 10W
Antseranana Madagascar 111 I5 12 19S 49 17E
An Tuc see An Khe
Antwerpen admin. Belgium 70 C3 51 20N 4 45E
Antwerpen (Anvers) Belgium 70 D3 51 13N 4 25E
Anuta i. Solomon Islands 83 P2 11 35S 169 50E
Anutu Paina i. Solomon Islands 82 G4 9 10S 161 15E
Anvers see Antwerpen
Anxi China 49 J7 40 32N 95 57E
Anyang China 49 M6 36 04N 114 20E
Anyang South Korea 50 C3 37 23N 126 56E
Anyer-Kidul Indonesia 42 M7 6 02S 105 57E
Anzhero-Sudzhensk Russia 57 K7 56 10N 86 01E
Aoba (Omba) i. Vanuatu 83 G6 15 25S 167 50E
Ao Ban Don b. Thailand 39 A1 9 20N 99 30E
Aoji North Korea 50 E6 42 33N 130 23E
Aola Solomon Islands 82 F4 9 31S 160 30E
Aomori Japan 46 D3 40 50N 140 43E
Aorai, Mount Tahiti 82 T9 17 36S 149 29W
Aosta Italy 74 A4 45 43N 7 19E
Aozou Strip Chad 110 C12 23 00N 17 00E
Apapa Nigeria 109 V3 6 22N 3 25E
Aparri The Philippines 40 B4 18 22N 121 40E
Apatity Russia 56 F9 67 32N 33 21E
Apatzingán Mexico 96 D3 19 05N 102 20W
Apeldoorn Netherlands 70 E4 52 13N 5 57E
Apia Western Samoa 82 B11 13 48S 171 45W
Ap Lei Chau i. Hong Kong U.K. 51 B1 22 10N 114 00E
Apolda Germany 71 B2 51 02N 11 31E
Apolima i. Western Samoa 82 A11 13 48S 172 06W
Apolima Strait Western Samoa 82 A11 13 46S 172 06W
Apo, Mount The Philippines 40 C2 6 58N 125 17E
Apostle Islands Wisconsin U.S.A. 92 B3 47 00N 90 00W
Appalachian Mountains U.S.A. 91 J4 37 00N 82 00W
Appennini (Apennines) mts. Italy 74 A3/C3
Appennino Abruzzese mts. Italy 74 B3 42 00N 14 00E
Appennino Ligure mts. Italy 74 A3 44 00N 9 00E
Appennino Lucano mts. Italy 74 C3 40 00N 15 00E
Appennino Tosco-Emiliano mts. Italy 74 B3 44 00N 12 00E
Appingedam Netherlands 70 F5 53 18N 6 52E
Appleton Wisconsin U.S.A. 92 C2 44 17N 88 24W
Appleton City Missouri U.S.A. 92 B1 38 10N 94 03W
Appomattox Virginia U.S.A. 93 E1 37 12N 78 51W
'Aqaba Jordan 54 O9 29 32N 35 00E
'Aqaba, Gulf of Middle East 54 D4 28 40N 34 40E
Aquidauana Brazil 102 F8 20 27S 55 45W
Aquiles Serdan Mexico 90 E2 28 37N 105 54W
Ara India 53 E5 25 34N 84 40E
Ara r. Japan 47 C3 35 39N 139 51E
Arabian Basin Indian Ocean 24 F7/8 10 00N 65 00E
Arabian Sea Indian Ocean 24 F8 17 00N 60 00E
Aracaju Brazil 102 J10 10 54S 37 07W
Arad Romania 75 D2 46 10N 21 19E
Arafura Sea Australia/Indonesia 78 E8/F8 8 00S 132 00E
Aragats mt. Armenia 58 E3 40 32N 44 11E
Aragón r. Spain 72 B3 42 15N 1 40W
Araguaina Brazil 102 H11 7 16S 48 18W
Araguari Brazil 102 H9 18 38S 48 13W
Arāk Iran 55 G5 34 05N 49 42E
Arakan Yoma mts. Myanmar 38 A3 19 00N 94 00E
Arakawa Japan 46 L2 35 58N 139 03E
Aral Sea Asia 59 H3/J4 45 00N 60 00E
Aral'sk Kazakhstan 59 J4 46 56N 61 43E
Arama New Caledonia 82 T3 20 16S 164 13E
Aramia r. Papua New Guinea 45 K3 7 30S 142 15E
Aranda de Duero Spain 72 B3 41 40N 3 41W
Arandai Irian Jaya Indonesia 44 E5 2 10S 133 00E
Aran Island Irish Republic 68 C6 55 00N 8 30W
Aran Islands Irish Republic 68 B5 53 10N 9 50W
Aranjuez Spain 72 B3 40 02N 3 37W
Aranyaprathet Thailand 39 B2 13 40N 102 30E
Arapiraca Brazil 102 J11 9 45S 36 40W
Ar'ar Saudi Arabia 54 F5 30 58N 41 03E
Araraquara Brazil 103 H8 21 46S 48 08W
Ararat, Mount see Bü Ağri Daği
Aras (Araks, Araxes) r. Turkey 54 F7 40 00N 43 30E
Arauca Colombia 102 C14 7 04N 70 41W
Araure Venezuela 97 K1 9 36N 69 15W
Arawa Papua New Guinea 45 Q3 6 15S 155 35E
Araxá Brazil 102 H9 19 37S 46 50W
Araxes (Araks, Aras) r. Iran 55 G6 38 40N 46 30E
Arbil Iraq 54 F6 36 12N 44 01E
Arbroath Scotland United Kingdom 68 I8 56 34N 2 35W
Arc r. France 73 C2 45 15N 6 10E
Arcachon France 73 A1 44 40N 1 11W
Arcadia California U.S.A. 95 C3 34 09N 118 00W
Arcati Brazil 102 J12 4 32S 37 45W
Archipelago Dehalak is. Ethiopia 110 H11 15 45N 40 12E
Arctic Bay tn. Northwest Territories Canada 89 R7 73 05N 85 20W
Arctic Ocean 20
Arctowski r.s. Antarctica 21 62 09S 58 28W
Ardabil Iran 55 G6 38 15N 48 18E
Ardennes admin. France 70 D1 49 35N 4 35E
Ardennes mts. Belgium 70 E2 50 10N 5 45E
Ardila r. Spain 72 A2 38 15N 6 50W
Ardmore Oklahoma U.S.A. 91 G3 34 11N 97 08W
Ardres France 70 A2 50 51N 1 59E
Arendal Norway 69 B2 58 27N 8 56E
Arequipa Peru 102 C9 16 25S 71 32W
Arezzo Italy 74 B3 43 28N 11 53E
Argao The Philippines 40 B2 9 47N 123 35E
Argentan France 73 A2 48 45N 0 01W
Argenteuil France 67 A2 48 57N 2 14E
ARGENTINA 103 D5
Argentine Basin Atlantic Ocean 25 D2 42 00S 45 00W
Argeş r. Romania 75 E1 44 00N 26 00E
Argun (Ergun He) r. Asia 49 N9 52 00N 120 00E
Argyle, Lake Australia 78 D6 17 00S 128 30E
Århus Denmark 69 C2 56 16N 10 10E
Arica Chile 102 C9 18 30S 70 20W
Ariège r. France 73 B1 42 50N 1 40E
Arima Trinidad and Tobago 96 T10 10 38N 61 17W
Aripuanã r. Brazil 102 E11 7 00S 60 30W
Ariquemes Brazil 102 E11 9 55S 63 06W
Arizona state U.S.A. 90 D3 34 00N 112 00W
Arizpe Mexico 96 B6 30 20N 110 11W
Arjeplog Sweden 69 D4 66 04N 18 00E
Arjona Colombia 102 B15 10 14N 75 22W
Arkalyk Kazakhstan 59 K5 50 17N 66 51E
Arkansas r. U.S.A. 91 H4 35 00N 93 00W
Arkansas state U.S.A. 91 H3 34 00N 93 00W
Arkansas City Kansas U.S.A. 91 G4 37 03N 97 02W
Arkhangel'sk Russia 56 G8 64 32N 40 40E
Arkona, Cape Germany 71 B2 54 41N 13 26E
Arlanza r. Spain 72 B3 42 00N 3 30W
Arlanzón r. Spain 72 B3 42 00N 4 00W
Arles France 73 B1 43 41N 4 38E
Arlit Niger 112 G6 18 50N 7 00E
Arlon Belgium 70 E1 49 41N 5 49E
Armagh Northern Ireland United Kingdom 68 E6 54 21N 6 39W
Armavir Russia 56 G4 44 59N 41 40E
ARMENIA 58 E3/F2
Armenia Colombia 102 B13 4 32N 75 40W
Armentières France 73 B3 50 41N 2 53E
Armidale Australia 78 I3 30 32S 151 40E
Armopa Irian Jaya Indonesia 44 H5 2 18S 139 37E
Armstrong Ontario Canada 92 C4 50 20N 89 02W
Arnhem Netherlands 70 E3 52 00N 5 53E
Arnhem Land geog. reg. Australia 78 E7 13 00S 133 00E
Arno r. Italy 74 B3 43 00N 10 00E
Arnprior Ontario Canada 93 E3 45 26N 76 21W
Arnsberg Germany 71 A2 51 23N 8 03E
Arnstadt Germany 71 B2 50 50N 10 57E
Arona Papua New Guinea 45 L3 6 20S 146 00E
Arquipélago dos Bijagós is. Guinea-Bissau 112 B5 11 20N 16 40W
Ar Ramādī Iraq 54 F5 33 27N 43 19E
Ar Ramlah Jordan 54 O9 29 28N 25 58E
Arran i. Scotland United Kingdom 68 F7 55 35N 5 15W
Ar Raqqah Syria 54 E6 35 57N 39 03E
Arras France 73 B3 50 17N 2 46E
Ar Riyād Saudi Arabia 55 G3 24 39N 46 46E
Arta Greece 74 D2 39 10N 20 59E
Arthur Ontario Canada 93 D2 43 50N 80 32W
Arthur's Pass South Island New Zealand 79 B2 42 55S 171 34E
Artigas Uruguay 103 F6 30 25S 56 28W
Artigas r.s. Antarctica 21 62 11S 58 51W
Arua Uganda 110 F8 3 02N 30 56E
ARUBA 102 D15 12 30N 70 00W
Arué Tahiti 82 S9 17 30S 149 30W
Arun r. England United Kingdom 68 K2 51 00N 0 30W
Arunachal Pradesh admin. India 38 A5 28 00N 95 00E
Arusha Tanzania 110 G7 3 23S 36 40E
Aruwimi r. Zaïre 110 E8 2 00N 25 00E
Arvika Sweden 69 C2 59 41N 12 38E
Arwala Indonesia 43 G2 7 41S 126 49E
Arys' Kazakhstan 59 K3 42 26N 68 49E
Arzamas Russia 58 E6 55 24N 43 48E
Arzew Algeria 72 B2 35 50N 0 19W
Asahi Japan 46 M2 35 43N 140 38E
Asahi-dake mt. Japan 46 D3 43 42N 142 54E
Asahikawa Japan 46 D3 43 46N 142 23E
Asaka Japan 47 B4 35 47N 139 37E
Asamankese Ghana 112 E4 5 45N 0 45W
Asan Man b. South Korea 50 C3 37 00N 126 30E
Asansol India 53 F4 23 40N 86 59E
Åsarna Sweden 69 C3 62 40N 14 20E
Asau Western Samoa 82 A11 13 26S 172 35W
Asbury Park tn. New Jersey U.S.A. 93 F2 40 14N 74 00W
Ascension Island Atlantic Ocean 25 G6 7 57S 14 22W
Aschaffenburg Germany 71 A1 49 58N 9 10E
Aschersleben Germany 71 B2 51 46N 11 28E
Ascoli Piceno Italy 74 B3 42 52N 13 35E
Āseb Eritrea 110 H10 13 01N 42 47E
Asembagus Indonesia 42 R7 7 45S 114 14E
Asenovgrad Bulgaria 74 D3 42 00N 24 53E
Ashburton South Island New Zealand 79 B2 43 54S 171 45E
Ashburton r. Australia 78 B5 22 30S 116 00E
Ashdod Israel 54 O10 31 48N 34 48E
Ashfield Australia 79 G2 33 53S 151 07E
Ashfork Arizona U.S.A. 90 D4 35 13N 112 29W
Ashikaga Japan 46 C2 36 21N 139 26E
Ashina Japan 47 B1 35 13N 139 36E
Ashizuri-misaki c. Japan 46 B1 32 42N 133 00E
Ashkhabad Turkmenistan 59 H2 37 58N 58 24E
Ashland Kentucky U.S.A. 93 D1 38 28N 82 40W
Ashland Oregon U.S.A. 90 B5 42 14N 122 44W
Ashland Wisconsin U.S.A. 92 B3 46 34N 90 54W
Ashok Nagar India 52 L4 28 38N 77 07E
Ashqelon Israel 54 O10 31 40N 34 35E
Ash Shāriqah United Arab Emirates 55 I4 25 20N 55 20E
Ash Shurayf Saudi Arabia 54 E4 25 50N 39 00E
Ashtabula Ohio U.S.A. 93 D2 41 53N 80 47W
Asilah Morocco 72 A2 35 32N 6 04W
Asir Mountains Saudi Arabia 104 18 00N 44 00E
Asmera Eritrea 110 G11 15 20N 38 58E
Åsnen l. Sweden 69 C2 56 45N 14 40E
Asnières France 67 B2 48 55N 2 17E
Asō Japan 46 M3 36 00N 141 29E
Aspiring, Mount South Island New Zealand 79 A2 44 23S 168 44E
Asquith Australia 79 G3 33 41S 151 07E
Assam admin. India 53 G5 26 20N 92 00E
As Samawah Iraq 55 G5 31 18N 45 18E
Asse Belgium 70 D2 50 55N 4 12E
Assen Netherlands 70 F5 53 00N 6 34E
Assinibone River Manitoba Canada 92 A3 49 55N 98 00W
Assis Brazil 103 G8 22 37S 50 25W
Assisi Italy 74 B3 43 04N 12 37E
As Suq Saudi Arabia 54 F3 21 55N 42 02E
As Suwaydā' Syria 54 P11 32 43N 36 33E
Astārā Azerbaijan 58 F2 38 27N 48 53E
Asti Italy 74 A3 44 54N 8 13E
Astipálaia i. Greece 74 E2 36 00N 26 00E
Astoria Oregon U.S.A. 90 B6 46 12N 123 50W
Astrolabe Point Solomon Islands 83 M2 11 40S 166 55E
Asuisui, Cape Western Samoa 82 A11 13 44S 172 29W
Asuka r.s. Antarctica 21 71 32S 24 08E
Asuke Japan 46 J2 35 08N 137 19E
Asunción Paraguay 103 F7 25 15S 57 40W
Aswa r. Uganda 110 F8 3 30N 32 30E
Aswân Egypt 110 F12 24 05N 32 56E
Aswân Dam Egypt 110 F12 23 40N 31 50E
Asyût Egypt 54 D4 27 14N 31 07E
Ata i. Tonga 83 D1 22 35S 176 10W
Ataa Solomon Islands 82 F5 8 32S 161 00E
Atafu Atoll Pacific Ocean 80 D3 8 40S 172 40W
Atambua Indonesia 43 F2 9 06S 124 35E
Atami Japan 46 L2 35 07N 139 04E
Atapupu Indonesia 43 F2 9 02S 124 53E
Atar Mauritania 112 C7 20 32N 13 08W
Atbara Sudan 110 F11 17 42N 34 00E
Atbara r. Sudan 110 G11 17 28N 34 30E
Atbasar Kazakhstan 59 K5 51 49N 68 18E
Atchison Kansas U.S.A. 91 G4 39 33N 95 09W
Ath Belgium 70 C2 50 38N 3 47E
Athabasca Alberta Canada 88 M3 54 44N 113 15W
Athabasca, Lake Alberta/Saskatchewan Canada 88 N4 59 10N 109 30W
Athabasca River Alberta Canada 88 M4 57 30N 111 00W
Athens Greece see Athínai
Athens Georgia U.S.A. 91 J3 33 57N 83 24W
Athens Ohio U.S.A. 93 D1 39 20N 82 06W
Athens Pennsylvania U.S.A. 93 E2 41 57N 76 31W
Athínai (Athens) Greece 74 D2 38 00N 23 44E
Athlone Irish Republic 68 D5 53 25N 7 56W
Áthos mt. Greece 74 D3 40 10N 24 19E
Ati Chad 110 C10 13 11N 18 20E
Atikokan Ontario Canada 92 B3 48 45N 91 38W
Atikonak Lake Newfoundland Canada 89 W3 52 40N 64 35W
Atiu i. Pacific Ocean 81 E2 20 00S 158 07W
Atka Island Alaska U.S.A. 88 A3 52 05N 17440W
Atkri Irian Jaya Indonesia 44 D6 1 45S 130 04E
Atlanta Georgia U.S.A. 91 J3 33 45N 84 23W
Atlantic City New Jersey U.S.A. 93 F1 39 23N 74 27W
Atlantic-Indian Ridge Atlantic Ocean 25 H1/J1 53 00S 3 00E
Atlas Saharien mts. Algeria 112 E9/F9 33 30N 1 00E
Atlin British Columbia Canada 88 I4 59 31N 133 41W
Atlin Lake British Columbia Canada 88 I4 59 31N 133 41W
Atouat Plateau Laos/Vietnam 37 C3 16 00N 107 30E
Astrakhan' Russia 56 G5 46 22N 48 04E
Atsugi Japan 46 L2 35 28N 139 22E
Atsumi Japan 46 J1 34 37N 137 06E
Atsumi-hantō p. Japan 46 J1 34 40N 137 15E
At Tā'if Saudi Arabia 54 F3 21 15N 40 21E
Attapu (Attopeu) Laos 37 C2 14 51N 106 56E
Attawapiskat Ontario Canada 89 S3 53 00N 82 30W
Attawapiskat River Ontario Canada 89 R3 53 00N 86 00W
Attersee l. Austria 71 B1 47 00N 13 00E
Attopeu see Attapu
Auas Mountains Namibia 111 C3 23 00S 17 00E
Aubagne France 73 C1 43 17N 5 35E
Aube r. France 73 B2 48 40N 3 55E
Aubenas France 73 B1 44 37N 4 24E
Aubervilliers France 67 B2 48 55N 2 22E
Auburn Maine U.S.A. 93 F2 44 04N 70 27W
Auburn Nebraska U.S.A. 92 A2 40 22N 95 41W
Auburn New York U.S.A. 93 E2 42 57N 76 34W
Auch France 73 B1 43 40N 0 36E
Auckland North Island New Zealand 79 B3 36 51S 174 46E
Auckland Islands Southern Ocean 80 C1 50 35S 116 00E
Aude r. France 73 B1 43 00N 2 00E
Auden Ontario Canada 92 C4 50 14N 87 54W
Aue Germany 71 B2 50 35N 12 42E
Augsburg Germany 71 B1 48 21N 10 54E
Augusta Australia 78 B3 34 19S 115 09E
Augusta Georgia U.S.A. 91 J3 33 29N 82 00W
Augusta Maine U.S.A. 93 G2 44 17N 69 50W
Auki Solomon Islands 82 F5 8 45S 160 44E
Aulnay-sous-Bois France 67 C2 48 57N 2 31E
Aulne r. France 73 A2 48 10N 4 00W
Aunu'u i. American Samoa 82 E12 14 16S 170 35W
Auponhia Indonesia 44 A6 1 56S 125 30E
Aurangābād India 53 D3 19 52N 75 22E
Aurich Germany 71 A2 53 28N 7 29E
Aurillac France 73 B1 44 56N 2 26E
Auro Papua New Guinea 45 N2 8 30S 148 20E
Aurora Ontario Canada 93 E2 43 00N 79 28W
Aurora Illinois U.S.A. 92 C2 41 45N 88 20W
Aurora Indiana U.S.A. 92 D1 39 03N 84 55W
Au Sable r. Michigan U.S.A. 93 D2 45 00N 84 00W
Austin Minnesota U.S.A. 92 B2 43 40N 92 58W
Austin Texas U.S.A. 91 G3 30 18N 97 47W
AUSTRALIA 78
Australian Capital Territory (A.C.T.) admin. Australia 78 H2 35 00S 144 00E
Austral Islands Pacific Ocean 81 E2 23 23S 149 27W
Austral Ridge Pacific Ocean 23 K5 24 00S 155 30W
AUSTRIA 75 B2/C2
Autlán Mexico 96 D3 19 48N 104 20W
Autun France 73 B2 46 58N 4 18E
Auxerre France 73 B2 47 48N 3 35E
Auyuittuq National Park Northwest Territories Canada 89 V6 67 00N 67 00W
Ava Myanmar 38 B4 21 49N 95 57E
Avallon France 73 B2 47 30N 3 54E
Avea i. Fiji 83 F9 17 10S 178 55W
Aveiro Portugal 72 A3 40 38N 8 40W
Avellaneda Argentina 103 F6 34 40S 58 20W
Avesnes-sur-Helpe France 70 D2 50 08N 3 57E
Avesta Sweden 69 D3 60 09N 16 10E
Aveyron r. France 73 B1 44 30N 2 05E
Avezzano Italy 74 B3 42 02N 13 26E
Avignon France 73 B1 43 56N 4 48E
Avila Spain 72 B3 40 39N 4 42W
Avilés Spain 72 A3 43 33N 5 55W
Avon r. England United Kingdom 68 J3 51 27N 1 40W
Avranches France 73 A2 48 42N 1 21W
Avre r. France 73 B2 49 45N 2 30E
Avuavu Solomon Islands 82 F4 9 51S 160 08E
Awaji Japan 46 G1 34 35N 135 00E
Awaji-shima i. Japan 46 F1 34 30N 135 45E
Awali r. Lebanon 54 O11 33 35N 35 32E
Awar Papua New Guinea 45 L4 4 10S 144 50E
Awash Ethiopia 110 H9 9 01N 41 10E

Awash *r.* Ethiopia **110** H10 10 00N 40 00E
Awa-shima *i.* Japan **46** C2 38 40N 139 15E
Awbārī Libya **110** B13 26 35N 12 46E
Axel Heiberg Island Northwest Territories Canada **89** Q8 80 00N 90 00W
Ayabe Japan **46** G2 35 19N 135 16E
Ayaguz Kazakhstan **59** N4 47 59N 80 27E
Ayamonte Spain **72** A2 37 13N 7 24W
Ayan Russia **57** P7 56 29N 138 07E
Ayaviri Peru **102** C10 14 53S 70 35W
Aydin Turkey **74** E2 37 51N 27 51E
Ayers Rock *mt.* Australia **78** E4 25 18S 131 18E
Ayios Nikólaos Greece **74** E2 35 11N 25 43E
Aylmer Ontario Canada **93** D2 42 47N 80 58W
Aylmer Québec Canada **93** E3 45 23N 75 51W
Ayod Sudan **110** F9 8 08N 31 24E
Ayon *i.* Russia **57** S9 69 55N 169 10E
Ayr Scotland United Kingdom **68** G7 55 28N 4 38W
'Ayūnah Saudi Arabia **54** E4 28 06N 35 08E
AZERBAIJAN **58** F3
Azogues Ecuador **102** B12 2 46S 78 56W
Azores *is.* Atlantic Ocean **25** F10 38 30N 28 00W
Azoum *r.* Chad **110** D10 12 00N 21 00E
Azov, Sea of Asia **58** D4 46 00N 36 00E
Azuero, Peninsula de Panama **97** H1 7 40N 81 00W
Azul Argentina **103** F5 36 46S 59 50W
Azurduy Bolivia **102** E9 20 00S 64 29W
Azusa California U.S.A. **95** C3 34 08N 117 54W
Az Zabadānī Syria **54** P11 33 42N 36 03E
Az Zahrān *(Dhahran)* Saudi Arabia **55** H4 26 13N 50 02E

B

Ba Fiji **83** B9 17 34S 177 40E
Baa Indonesia **43** F1 10 44S 123 06E
Baalbek Lebanon **54** P12 34 00N 36 12E
Baarn Netherlands **70** E4 52 13N 5 16E
Babadag *mt.* Turkey **58** F3 37 49N 28 52E
Babahoyo Ecuador **102** B12 1 53S 79 31W
Bab al Mandab *sd.* Red Sea **110** H10 12 30N 47 00E
Babanakira Solomon Islands **82** E4 9 45S 159 50E
Babat Indonesia **42** P7 7 08S 112 08E
Babelsberg Germany **67** E1 52 23N 13 05E
Babelthuap *i.* Pacific Ocean **80** A4 15 00N 135 00E
Babian Jiang *(Song Da, Hitam) r.* China/Vietnam **38** C4 23 30N 101 20E
Babo Irian Jaya Indonesia **44** E5 2 33S 133 25E
Babushkin Russia **56** M2/N2 55 55N 37 44E
Babuyan *i.* The Philippines **40** B4 19 30N 121 57E
Babuyan Channel The Philippines **40** B4 19 00N 121 00E
Babuyan Islands The Philippines **40** B4 19 00N 122 00E
Babylon *hist. site* Iraq **54** F5 32 33N 44 25E
Bacabal Brazil **102** I12 4 15S 44 45W
Bacău Romania **75** E2 46 33N 26 58E
Bac Can Vietnam **37** C4 22 08N 105 49E
Bac Giang Vietnam **37** C4 21 12N 106 10E
Back *r.* Northwest Territories Canada **89** P6 66 00N 97 00W
Backbone Ranges *mts.* Northwest Territories Canada **88** J5 63 30N 127 50W
Bac Lieu *(Vinh Loi)* Vietnam **37** C1 9 17N 105 44E
Bac Ninh Vietnam **37** C4 21 10N 106 04E
Bacolod The Philippines **40** B3 10 38N 122 58E
Baco, Mount The Philippines **40** B3 12 49N 121 11E
Bac Quang Vietnam **37** B4 22 30N 104 52E
Badajoz Spain **72** A2 38 53N 6 58W
Badalona Spain **72** C3 41 27N 2 15E
Baden Austria **75** C2 48 01N 16 14E
Baden Switzerland **73** C2 47 28N 8 19E
Baden-Baden Germany **71** A1 48 45N 8 15E
Baden-Württemberg *admin.* Germany **71** A1 48 00N 9 00E
Badgastein Austria **71** B1 47 07N 13 09E
Bad Hersfeld Germany **71** A2 50 53N 9 43E
Bad Homburg Germany **71** A2 50 13N 8 37E
Bad Honnef Germany **70** G2 50 38N 7 14E
Bad Ischl Austria **71** B1 47 43N 13 38E
Bad Kissingen Germany **71** B2 50 12N 10 05E
Bad Kreuznach Germany **71** A1 49 51N 7 52E
Badli India **52** L4 28 44N 77 09E
Bad Neuenahr-Ahrweiler Germany **70** G2 50 32N 7 06E
Ba Don Vietnam **37** C3 17 45N 106 25E
Ba Dong Vietnam **37** C1 9 45N 106 40E
Bad Reichenhall **71** B1 47 43N 12 53E
Bad Salzuflen Germany **71** A2 52 06N 8 45E
Bad Tölz Germany **71** B1 47 45N 11 34E
Badu Island Australia **45** K1 10 06S 142 09E
Baffin Bay Canada/Greenland **89** V7 72 00N 65 00W
Baffin Island Northwest Territories Canada **89** S7/V6 68 30N 70 00W
Bafoussam Cameroon **112** H4 5 31N 10 25E
Bāfq Iran **55** I5 31 35N 55 21E
Baga *i.* Solomon Islands **82** B6 7 50S 156 33E
Bagé Brazil **103** G6 31 22S 54 06W
Baghdād Iraq **54** F5 33 20N 44 26E
Baghlān Afghanistan **55** K6 36 11N 68 44E
Bago The Philippines **40** B3 10 34N 122 50E
Baguio The Philippines **40** B4 16 25N 120 37E
Bahamas Bank Atlantic Ocean **84** 24 00N 77 00W
BAHAMAS, THE **97** I4
Baharampur India **53** F4 24 00N 88 30E
Bahau Malaysia **42** B4 2 49N 102 24E
Bahaur Indonesia **42** D3 3 18S 114 02E
Bahawalpur Pakistan **53** C5 29 24N 71 47E
Bahia *admin.* Brazil **102** I10 12 00S 42 30W
Bahía Blanca Argentina **103** E5 38 45S 62 15W
Bahía Blanca *b.* Argentina **103** E5 39 00S 61 00W
Bahia de Campeche *b.* Mexico **96** E4/F4 20 00N 95 00W
Bahía Grande *b.* Argentina **103** D2 51 30S 68 00W
Bahra el Manzala Egypt **109** R4 31 18N 31 54E
Bahra el Timsâh *(Lake Timsâh)* Egypt **109** S3 30 34N 32 18E
Bahraich India **53** E5 27 35N 81 36E
BAHRAIN **55** H4
Bahrain, Gulf of The Gulf **55** H4 25 55N 50 30E
Bahr el Abiad *(White Nile) r.* Sudan **110** F10 14 00N 32 20E
Bahr el Arab *r.* Sudan **110** E9 10 00N 27 30E
Bahr el Azraq *(Blue Nile) r.* Sudan **110** F10 13 30N 33 45E
Bahr el Baqar *r.* Egypt **109** S3 30 54N 32 02E
Bahr el Ghazal *r.* Chad **110** C10 14 00N 16 00E
Bahr Faqus *r.* Egypt **109** R3 30 42N 31 42E
Bahr Hadus *r.* Egypt **109** R4 31 01N 31 43E
Bahr Saft *r.* Egypt **109** R3 30 57N 31 48E
Baia Mare Romania **75** D2 47 39N 23 36E
Baicao Ling *mts.* China **38** C5 26 20N 101 30E
Baicheng China **49** O8 45 37N 122 48E
Baidyabati India **52** K3 22 48N 88 20E
Baie-Comeau *tn.* Québec Canada **93** G3 49 12N 68 10W
Baie de l'Allier *b.* New Caledonia **82** X2 21 05S 168 02E
Baie de la Seine *b.* France **73** A2 49 40N 0 30W
Baie de Taravao *b.* Tahiti **82** T9 17 42S 149 17W
Baie d'Opunohu *b.* Tahiti **82** R10 17 30S 149 52W
Baie-du-Poste *tn.* Québec Canada **93** F4 50 20N 73 50W
Baie du Santal *b.* New Caledonia **82** W3 20 50S 167 05E
Baie St. Paul *tn.* Québec Canada **93** F3 47 27N 70 30W
Baie Trinité *tn.* Québec Canada **93** G3 49 25N 67 20W
Bailleul France **70** B2 50 44N 2 44E
Baimuru Papua New Guinea **45** L3 7 34S 144 49E
Baird Mountains Alaska U.S.A. **88** D6 67 30N 160 00W
Baise *r.* France **73** B1 43 55N 0 25E
Bai Thuong Vietnam **37** C3 19 54N 105 25E
Baiti Nauru **83** L2 0 30S 166 56E
Baiwanzhuang China **47** G1 39 55N 116 18E
Baja Hungary **75** C2 46 11N 18 58E
Baja California *p.* Mexico **96** B5 27 30N 113 00W
Baj Baj India **52** J1 22 28N 88 10E
Baker Oregon U.S.A. **90** C5 44 46N 117 50W
Baker Island Pacific Ocean **80** D4 0 12N 176 28W
Baker Lake Northwest Territories Canada **89** Q5 64 00N 95 00W
Baker Lake *tn.* Northwest Territories Canada **89** P5 64 20N 96 10W
Bakersfield California U.S.A. **90** C4 35 25N 119 00W
Baku Azerbaijan **58** F3 40 22N 49 53E
Balabac *i.* The Philippines **40** A2 8 00N 117 00E
Balabac Strait The Philippines/Malaysia **40** A2 8 00N 117 00E
Balaghat India **53** E4 21 48N 80 16E
Balaghat Range *mts.* India **53** D3 18 45N 77 00E
Balakovo Russia **56** G6 52 04N 47 46E
Balama Mozambique **111** G5 13 19S 38 35E
Bālā Morghāb Afghanistan **55** J6 35 34N 63 20E
Balanga The Philippines **40** B3 14 41N 120 33E
Balashikha Russia **58** D6 55 47N 37 59E
Balashov Russia **58** E5 51 31N 43 10E
Balassagyarmat Hungary **75** C2 48 06N 19 17E
Balaton *l.* Hungary **75** C2 47 00N 17 30E
Balboa Panama **97** I2 8 57N 79 33W
Balclutha South Island New Zealand **79** A1 46 14S 169 44E
Bald Eagle Lake Minnesota U.S.A. **92** B3 47 48N 91 32W
Baldwin Park *tn.* California U.S.A. **95** C3 34 05N 117 59W
Balearic Islands Mediterranean Sea **72** C2/3
Balembangan *i.* Malaysia **42** E5 7 15N 116 55E
Balembangan *p.* Malaysia **40** A2 7 15N 116 55E
Balgowlah Australia **79** H2 33 48S 151 16E
Bali *i.* Indonesia **42** R6 8 30S 115 00E
Balikesir Turkey **54** C6 39 37N 27 51E
Balikpapan Indonesia **42** E3 1 15S 116 50E
Balimo Papua New Guinea **45** K2 8 00S 143 00E
Balingen Germany **71** A1 48 17N 8 52E
Balintang Channel The Philippines **40** B4 20 00N 122 00E
Balkan Mountains Europe **60** 43 00N 25 00E
Balkhash Kazakhstan **59** L4 46 50N 74 57E
Balkhash, Lake *see* Ozero Balkhash
Ballarat Australia **78** G2 37 36S 143 58E
Ball Bay Norfolk Island **81** L4 29 03S 167 59E
Ball Bay Reserve Norfolk Island **81** L4 29 02S 167 58E
Balleny Islands Southern Ocean **22** G1 66 30S 1 64E
Bälly India **52** K2 22 38N 88 20E
Ballygunge India **52** K2 22 31N 88 20E
Ballymena Northern Ireland United Kingdom **68** E6 54 52N 6 17W
Balmain Australia **79** G2 33 51S 151 11E
Balsas Mexico **96** E3 18 00N 99 44W
Baltic Sea Europe **69** D2 55 15N 17 00E
Baltimore Maryland U.S.A. **93** E1 39 18N 76 38W
Baltrum *i.* Germany **71** A2 53 44N 7 23E
Baluchistan *geog. reg.* Pakistan **52** A5/B5 27 30N 65 00E
Balurin Indonesia **43** F2 8 40S 124 00E
Balut *i.* The Philippines **40** C2 5 25N 125 23E
Bam Iran **55** I4 29 07N 58 20E
Bamaga Australia **45** K1 10 50S 142 25E
Bamako Mali **112** D5 12 40N 7 59W
Bambari Central African Republic **110** D9 5 40N 20 37E
Bamberg Germany **71** B1 49 54N 10 54E
Bamenda Cameroon **112** H4 5 55N 10 09E
Bamingui Bangoran National Park Central African Republic **110** C9/D9 8 00N 20 00E
Banam Cambodia **37** C2 11 20N 105 17E
Banas *r.* India **53** D5 26 00N 75 00E
Ban Ban Laos **37** B3 19 38N 103 32E
Banbury England United Kingdom **68** J4 52 04N 1 20W
Bancroft Ontario Canada **93** E3 45 03N 77 52W
Banda India **53** E5 25 28N 80 20E
Banda Aceh Indonesia **42** A5 5 30N 95 20E
Bandama Blanc *r.* Côte d'Ivoire **112** D4 8 00N 5 45W
Bandanaira Indonesia **44** C4 4 13S 129 50E
Ban Dang Khrien Vietnam **37** C2 11 59N 107 29E
Ban Dan Lan Hoi Thailand **39** A3 17 00N 99 36E
Bandar Abbās Iran **55** I4 27 12N 56 15E
Bandarbeyla Somalia **110** J9 9 30N 50 50E
Bandar-e Lengeh Iran **55** H4 26 34N 54 52E
Bandar-e Torkeman Iran **55** H6 36 55N 54 01E
Bandar Khomeynī Iran **55** G5 30 40N 49 08E
Bandar Seri Begawan Brunei Darussalam **42** D4 4 53N 114 57E
Banda Sea Indonesia **43** G2 5 50S 126 00E
Bandeirantes Beach Brazil **103** P1 23 01S 43 23W
Bandel India **52** K3 22 55N 88 23E
Bandirma Turkey **54** C7 40 21N 27 58E
Bandundu Zaïre **111** C7 3 20S 17 24E
Bandung Indonesia **42** N7 6 57S 107 34E
Banff Alberta Canada **88** L3 51 10N 115 34W
Banff National Park Alberta Canada **88** L3 52 00N 116 00W
Banfora Burkina **112** E5 10 36N 4 45W
Bangalore India **53** D2 12 58N 77 35E
Bangassou Central African Republic **110** D8 4 41N 22 48E
Bang Bua Thong Thailand **39** B2 13 55N 100 22E
Banggai Indonesia **43** F3 1 34S 123 33E
Banggi *i.* Malaysia **42** E5 7 15N 117 10E
Banghāzī *(Benghazi)* Libya **110** D14 32 07N 20 04E
Bangil Indonesia **42** Q7 7 34S 112 47E
Bangkalan Indonesia **42** Q7 7 05S 112 44E
Bang Khla Thailand **39** B2 13 43N 101 14E
Bangkinang Indonesia **42** B4 0 21N 101 02E
Bangko Indonesia **42** B3 2 05S 102 20E
Bangkok *(Krung Thep)* Thailand **39** B2 13 44N 100 30E
Bangkok, Bight of Thailand **39** B2 13 00N 100 30E
BANGLADESH **53** F4/G4
Banglang Reservoir Thailand **39** B1 6 00N 101 30E
Bangli Indonesia **42** R6 8 25S 115 25E
Bang Mun Nak Thailand **39** B3 16 02N 100 26E
Bangor Northern Ireland United Kingdom **68** F6 54 40N 5 40W
Bangor Wales United Kingdom **68** G5 53 13N 4 08W
Bangor Maine U.S.A. **93** G2 44 49N 68 47W
Bang Saphan Thailand **39** A2 11 110N 99 33E
Bangued The Philippines **40** B4 17 36N 120 37E
Bangui Central African Republic **110** C8 4 23N 18 37E
Bangweulu, Lake Zambia **111** E5 11 15S 29 45E
Ban Huai Yang Thailand **39** A2 11 38N 99 38E
Baniara Papua New Guinea **45** N2 9 46S 149 51E
Baniyachung Bangladesh **38** A4 24 30N 91 21E
Banja Luka Bosnia-Herzegovina **74** C3 44 47N 17 11E
Banjaran Crocker *mts.* Malaysia **42** E5 5 30N 116 00E
Banjarmasin Indonesia **42** D3 3 22S 114 33E
Banjul The Gambia **112** B5 13 28N 16 39W
Banka India **52** K2 22 36N 88 17E
Banka *i.* Indonesia **42** C3 2 00S 106 00E
Ban Keo Lom Vietnam **37** B4 21 15N 103 14E
Ban Khlung Thailand **39** B2 12 27N 102 12E
Ban Khok Kloi Thailand **39** A1 8 15N 98 18E
Banks Island Vanuatu **83** G8 13 30S 167 30E
Banks Island Northwest Territories Canada **88** K7/L7 72 30N 122 30W
Banks Peninsula South Island New Zealand **79** B2 43 44S 173 00E
Bankstown Australia **79** G2 33 55S 151 02E
Banmauk Myanmar **38** B4 24 26N 95 54E
Ban Me Thuot Vietnam **37** C2 12 41N 108 02E
Ban Mi Thailand **39** B3 15 03N 100 36E
Bann *r.* Northern Ireland United Kingdom **68** E7 54 20N 6 10W
Ban Nang Sata Thailand **39** B1 6 12N 101 12E
Ban Nape Laos **37** C3 18 18N 105 07E
Ban Na San Thailand **39** A1 8 49N 99 20E
Bannu Pakistan **55** L5 33 00N 70 40E
Ban Pak Pat Thailand **39** B3 17 42N 100 37E
Ban Pak Phraek Thailand **39** B1 8 11N 100 10E
Ban Phai Thailand **39** B3 16 03N 102 45E
Ban Phon Laos **37** C3 15 24N 106 43E
Ban Phu Thailand **39** B3 17 41N 102 30E
Ban Pong Thailand **39** A2 13 49N 99 53E
Bansberia India **52** K3 22 57N 88 23E
Banská Bystrica Slovakia **75** C2 48 44N 19 10E
Banstead England United Kingdom **66** C2 51 19N 0 12W
Bantayan *i.* The Philippines **40** B3 11 12N 123 45E
Ban Tha Song Yang Thailand **39** A3 17 33N 97 56E
Bantry Bay Irish Republic **68** B3 51 35N 9 40W
Bantul Indonesia **42** P7 7 56S 110 21E
Ban Xéno Laos **37** C3 16 44N 105 03E
Banyuwangi Indonesia **42** R6 8 12S 114 22E
Baoding China **49** N6 38 54N 115 26E
Baoji China **49** L5 34 23N 107 16E
Bao Loc Vietnam **37** C2 11 33N 107 48E
Baoshan China **38** B5 25 09N 99 11E
Baotou China **49** L7 40 38N 109 59E
Ba'qūbah Iraq **54** F5 33 45N 44 40E
Ba Ra Vietnam **37** C2 11 50N 106 59E
Barabai Indonesia **42** E3 2 38S 115 22E
Barabash Russia **50** E6 43 11N 131 33E
Baraboo Wisconsin U.S.A. **92** C2 43 27N 89 45W
Baracaldo Spain **72** B3 43 17N 2 59W
Barahanagar India **52** K2 22 38N 88 23E
Barahona Dominican Republic **97** J3 18 13N 71 07W
Barail Range India **38** A5 25 20N 93 30E
Barajala Canal India **52** J2 22 35N 88 12E
Barak *r.* India **38** A5 24 50N 93 40E
Bārākpur India **52** K3 22 45N 88 22E
Baral India **52** K1 22 27N 88 22E
Baram *r.* Malaysia **42** D4 3 50N 114 30E
Barangbarang Indonesia **43** F2 6 00S 120 30E
Bārāsat India **52** K2 22 43N 88 26E
Barbacena Brazil **103** I8 21 13S 43 47W
BARBADOS **97** M2
Barbastro Spain **72** C3 42 02N 0 07E
Barbuda *i.* Antigua & Barbuda **97** L3 17 41N 61 48W
Barcaldine Australia **78** H5 23 31S 145 15E
Barcellona Italy **74** B2 38 10N 15 15E
Barcelona Spain **72** C3 41 25N 2 10E
Barcelona Venezuela **102** E15 10 08N 64 43W
Barcelonnette France **73** C1 44 24N 6 40E
Barcelos Brazil **102** E12 0 59S 62 58W
Barcoo *r.* Australia **78** G5 23 30S 144 00E
Barcs Hungary **75** C2 45 58N 17 30E
Barddhamān India **53** F4 23 20N 88 00E
Barduelv *r.* Norway **69** D4 68 48N 18 22E
Bareilly India **53** D5 28 20N 79 24E
Barents Sea Arctic Ocean **20** 75 00N 40 00E
Barga China **53** E6 30 51N 81 20E
Bari Italy **74** C3 41 07N 16 52E
Ba Ria Vietnam **37** C2 10 24N 107 07E
Bariga Nigeria **109** V3 6 32N 3 28E
Barinas Venezuela **102** C14 8 36N 70 15W
Barisal Bangladesh **53** G4 22 41N 90 20E
Bariti, Lake India **52** K3 22 48N 88 26E
Barito *r.* Indonesia **42** D3 2 00S 114 45E
Barking England United Kingdom **66** D3 51 33N 0 06E
Barkly-Tableland *geog. reg.* Australia **78** F6 17 30S 137 00E
Bar-le-Duc France **73** C2 48 46N 5 10E
Barlee, Lake Australia **78** B4 28 30S 120 00E
Barletta Italy **74** C3 41 20N 16 17E
Barnaul Russia **57** K6 53 21N 83 45E
Barnes England United Kingdom **66** C2 51 28N 0 15W
Barnes Ice Cap Northwest Territories Canada **89** U7 70 10N 74 00W
Barnet England United Kingdom **66** C3 51 39N 0 12W
Barneveld Netherlands **70** E4 52 08N 5 35E
Barnstaple England United Kingdom **68** G3 51 05N 4 04W
Barora Fa *i.* Solomon Islands **82** D6 7 30S 158 16E
Barpeta India **36** A7 26 20N 91 02E
Barquisimeto Venezuela **102** D15 10 03N 69 18W
Barra *i.* Scotland United Kingdom **68** D9 57 00N 7 25W
Barra da Tijuca Brazil **103** P1 23 00S 43 20W
Barra do Corba Brazil **102** H11 5 30S 45 12W
Barrancabermeja Colombia **102** C14 7 06N 73 54W
Barrancas Venezuela **102** E14 8 45N 62 13W
Barrancones Point Trinidad and Tobago **96** T10 10 30N 61 28W
Barranjoey Head *c.* Australia **79** H3 33 35S 151 20E
Barranquilla Colombia **102** C15 11 10N 74 50W
Barre Vermont U.S.A. **93** F2 44 13N 72 31W
Barreiras Brazil **102** I10 12 09S 44 58W
Barreiro Portugal **72** A2 38 40N 9 05W
Barrhead Alberta Canada **88** M3 54 10N 114 22W
Barrie Ontario Canada **93** E2 44 22N 79 42W
Barrier Reef Papua New Guinea **45** P1 11 45S 153 00E
Barrow Alaska U.S.A. **88** D7 71 16N 156 50W
Barrow *r.* Irish Republic **68** D4 52 55N 7 00W
Barrow-in-Furness England United Kingdom **68** H6 54 07N 3 14W
Barrow Island Australia **78** B5 21 00S 115 00E
Barrow, Point Alaska U.S.A. **88** D7 71 05N 156 00W
Barry Wales United Kingdom **68** H3 51 24N 3 18W
Barrys Bay *tn.* Ontario Canada **93** E3 45 30N 77 41W
Barstow California U.S.A. **90** C3 34 55N 117 01W
Barthelemy Pass Laos/Vietnam **37** B3 19 50N 104 40E
Bartlesville Oklahoma U.S.A. **91** G4 36 44N 95 59W
Barton Vermont U.S.A. **93** F2 44 44N 72 12W
Barung *i.* Indonesia **42** Q6 8 30S 113 00E
Basalt Island Hong Kong U.K. **51** C1 22 19N 114 21E
Basdorf Germany **67** F2 52 44N 13 27E
Basel Switzerland **73** C2 47 33N 7 36E
Basiano Indonesia **43** F3 1 40S 123 30E
Basilan *i.* The Philippines **40** B2 6 00N 122 00E
Basildon England United Kingdom **68** L3 51 34N 0 25W
Basingstoke England United Kingdom **68** J3 51 16N 1 05W
Baskunchak Russia **58** F4 48 14N 46 44E
Bassas da India *i.* Mozambique Channel **111** G3 22 00S 40 00E
Bassein Myanmar **38** A3 16 46N 94 45E
Bassein *r.* Myanmar **38** A3 16 00N 94 20E
Basse Terre Trinidad and Tobago **96** T9 10 07N 61 17W
Basse Terre *i.* Lesser Antilles **97** L3 16 00N 61 20W
Bass Strait Australia **78** H1/2 40 00S 145 00E
Bastia Corsica France **73** C1 42 14N 9 26E
Bastogne Belgium **70** E2 50 00N 5 43E
Bastrop Louisiana U.S.A. **91** H3 32 49N 91 54W
Bata Equatorial Guinea **112** G3 1 51N 9 49E
Batakan Indonesia **42** D3 4 03S 114 39E
Batala India **53** D6 31 48N 75 17E
Batan *i.* The Philippines **40** B5 20 25N 121 58E
Batanagar India **52** K2 22 30N 88 14E
Batang China **49** J5 30 02N 99 01E
Batangafo Central African Republic **110** C9 7 27N 18 11E
Batangas The Philippines **40** B3 13 46N 121 01E
Batanghari *r.* Indonesia **42** B3 1 20S 103 30E
Batan Islands The Philippines **40** B5 20 00N 122 00E
Batavia New York U.S.A. **93** E2 43 00N 78 11W
Bate Bay Australia **79** G1 34 03S 151 11E
Bates, Mount Norfolk Island **81** K5 29 00S 167 56E
Bath Jamaica **97** R7 17 57N 76 22W
Bath England United Kingdom **68** I3 51 23N 2 22W
Batha *r.* Chad **110** C10 13 00N 19 00E
Bathsheba Barbados **96** V12 13 12N 59 32W
Bathurst Australia **78** H3 33 27S 149 35E
Bathurst New Brunswick Canada **89** V2 47 37N 65 40W
Bathurst, Cape Northwest Territories Canada **88** J7 70 31N 127 53W
Bathurst Inlet Northwest Territories Canada **88** N6 66 49N 108 00W
Bathurst Island Australia **78** E7 12 00S 130 00E
Bathurst Island Northwest Territories Canada **89** P8 76 00N 100 00W
Batiki *i.* Fiji **83** D9 17 47S 179 10E
Batna Algeria **112** G10 35 34N 6 10E
Batnavni Vanuatu **83** H6 15 38S 168 08E
Batong Group Thailand **39** A1 6 30N 99 30E
Baton Rouge Louisiana U.S.A. **91** H3 30 30N 91 10W
Batroûn Lebanon **54** O12 36 16N 35 40E
Battambang Cambodia **37** B2 13 06N 103 13E
Battle Creek *tn.* Michigan U.S.A. **92** C2 42 20N 85 21W
Battle Harbour *tn.* Newfoundland Canada **89** X3 51 16N 55 36W
Batumi Georgia **58** E3 41 37N 41 36E
Batu Pahat Malaysia **42** B4 1 50N 102 56E
Baturaja Indonesia **42** B3 4 10S 104 10E
Baturetno Indonesia **42** P6 8 00S 110 54E
Bat Yam Israel **54** O10 32 01N 34 45E
Baubau Indonesia **43** F2 5 30S 122 37E
Bauchi Nigeria **112** G5 10 16N 9 50E
Bau Island Fiji **83** C9 17 55S 178 37E
Baukau Indonesia **43** G2 8 30S 126 28E
Baulkham Hills Australia **79** F2/G2 33 46S 151 00E
Bauru Brazil **103** H8 22 19S 49 07W
Bautzen Germany **71** B2 51 11N 14 29E
Bavaria *see* Bayern
Bawdwin Myanmar **38** B4 23 06N 97 18E
Bawe Irian Jaya Indonesia **44** F5 2 59S 134 43E
Bawean *i.* Indonesia **42** Q8 5 50S 112 45E
Bayamo Cuba **97** I4 20 23N 76 39W
Bayawan The Philippines **40** B2 9 21N 122 47E
Baybay The Philippines **40** B3 10 40N 124 54E
Bay City Michigan U.S.A. **93** D2 43 35N 83 52W
Bay City Texas U.S.A. **91** G2 28 59N 96 00W
Baydhabo Somalia **110** H8 3 08N 43 34E
Bayerische Alpen *mts.* Germany **71** B1 47 00N 11 00E
Bayerische Wald *geog. reg.* Germany **71** B1 49 00N 13 00E
Bayern *(Bavaria) admin.* Germany **71** B1 49 00N 12 00E
Bayeux France **73** A2 49 16N 0 42W
Bayfield Barbados **96** W12 13 10N 59 25W
Baykal, Lake *see* Ozero Baykal
Baykonyr Kazakhstan **59** K4 47 50N 66 03E
Bay of Plenty North Island New Zealand **79** C3 37 48S 177 12E
Bayombong The Philippines **40** B4 16 27N 121 10E
Bayonne France **73** A1 43 30N 1 28W
Bayonne New Jersey U.S.A. **94** B1 40 39N 74 07W
Bayo Point The Philippines **40** B3 10 24N 121 57E
Bayreuth Germany **71** B1 49 27N 11 35E
Bay Ridge *tn.* New York U.S.A. **94** B1 40 37N 74 02W
Baytown Texas U.S.A. **91** H2 29 43N 94 59W
Bayugan The Philippines **40** C2 8 44N 125 43E
Baza Spain **72** B2 37 30N 2 45W
Bazar-Dyuzi *mt.* Azerbaijan **58** F3 41 14N 47 50E

Bondoc Peninsula The Philippines **40** B3 13 00N 122 00E
Bondowoso Indonesia **42** Q7 7 54S 113 50E
Bongor Chad **110** C10 10 18N 15 20E
Bong Son *(Hoai Nhon)* Vietnam **37** C2 14 24N 109 00E
Bonifacio Corsica **73** C1 41 23N 9 10E
Bonifacio, Strait of Corsica/Sardinia **73** C1 41 20N 8 45E
Bonn Germany **71** A2 50 44N 7 06E
Bonny, Bight of *b.* West Africa **112** G3 2 10N 7 30E
Bonthe Sierra Leone **112** C4 7 32N 12 30W
Bontoc The Philippines **40** B4 17 07N 120 58E
Boorama Somalia **110** H9 9 56N 43 13E
Boosaaso Somalia **110** I10 11 18N 49 10E
Boothia, Gulf of Northwest Territories Canada **89** R6 69 00N 88 00W
Boothia Peninsula Northwest Territories Canada **89** Q7 70 30N 94 30W
Boot Reefs Papua New Guinea **45** L1 10 00S 144 45E
Bor Sudan **110** F9 6 18N 31 34E
Borås Sweden **56** C2 57 44N 12 55E
Bordeaux France **73** A1 44 50N 0 34W
Borden Peninsula Northwest Territories Canada **89** S7 73 00N 82 30W
Borehamwood England United Kingdom **66** B3 51 40N 0 16W
Borgholm Sweden **69** D2 56 51N 16 40E
Borgsdorf Germany **67** F2 52 44N 13 17E
Borikhan Laos **37** B3 18 35N 103 44E
Borisoglebsk Russia **58** E5 51 23N 42 02E
Borisov Belarus **75** E3 54 09N 28 30E
Borken Germany **70** F3 51 50N 6 52E
Borkum Germany **71** A2 53 35N 6 40E
Borkum *i.* Germany **71** A2 53 00N 6 00E
Borlänge Sweden **69** D3 60 29N 15 25E
Bormida di Spigno *r.* Italy **73** C1 44 17N 8 14E
Borneo *i.* Indonesia/Malaysia **42** D4 1 00N 113 00E
Bornholm *i.* Denmark **69** C2 55 02N 15 00E
Borongan The Philippines **40** C3 11 38N 125 27E
Borough Green England United Kingdom **66** D2 51 17N 0 19E
Borūjerd Iran **55** G5 33 55N 48 48E
Borzya Russia **57** N6 50 24N 116 35E
Bose China **36** D6 24 00N 106 30E
Bosna *r.* Bosnia-Herzegovina **74** C3 45 00N 18 00E
BOSNIA-HERZEGOVINA 74 C3/4
Bosnik Irian Jaya Indonesia **44** G6 1 09S 136 14E
Bōsō-hantō Japan **46** M2
Bosphorous *sd.* Europe/Asia **60** 41 00N 29 00E
Bossangoa Central African Republic **110** C9 6 27N 17 21E
Bosso Niger **112** H5 13 43N 13 19E
Boston England United Kingdom **68** K4 52 29N 0 01W
Boston Massachusetts U.S.A. **93** F2 42 20N 71 05W
Boston Mountains Arkansas U.S.A. **91** H4 36 00N 94 00W
Botafogo Brazil **103** Q2 22 57S 43 11W
Botany Australia **79** G2 33 58S 151 12E
Botany Bay Australia **79** G2 34 04S 151 08E
Bothnia, Gulf of Finland/Sweden **69** D3 61 00N 19 10E
Botoșani Romania **75** E2 47 44N 26 41E
Botrange *sum.* Belgium **70** F2 50 30N 6 05E
BOTSWANA 111 D3/E3
Bottrop Germany **71** A2 51 31N 6 55E
Bötzow Germany **67** E2 52 40N 13 07E
Bouaké Côte d'Ivoire **112** E4 7 42N 5 00W
Bouar Central African Republic **110** C9 5 58N 15 35E
Bouârfa Morocco **112** E9 32 30N 1 59W
Boucherville Québec Canada **93** F3 45 00N 73 00W
Boufarik Algeria **72** C2 36 36N 2 54E
Bougainville Island Papua New Guinea **45** Q3 6 15S 155 00E
Bougainville Strait Papua New Guinea **82** B6 8 00S 156 00E
Bougouni Mali **112** D5 11 25N 7 28W
Bougzoul Algeria **72** C2 35 42N 2 51E
Bouillon Belgium **70** E1 49 47N 5 04E
Boulder Colorado U.S.A. **90** E5 40 02N 105 16W
Boulogne-Billancourt France **67** A2/B2 48 50N 2 15E
Boulogne-sur-Mer France **73** B3 50 43N 1 37E
Bouloupari New Caledonia **82** V2 21 50S 166 04E
Bouma Fiji **83** E10 16 50S 179 56W
Boung Long Cambodia **37** C2 13 45N 107 00E
Boun Tai Laos **37** B4 21 26N 102 00E
Bounty Islands Pacific Ocean **80** C1 7 45S 179 05E
Bourail New Caledonia **82** U2 21 34S 165 29E
Bourem Mali **112** E6 16 59N 0 20W
Bourg-en-Bresse France **73** C2 46 12N 5 13E
Bourges France **73** B2 47 05N 2 23E
Bourke Australia **78** H3 30 09S 145 59E
Bournemouth England United Kingdom **68** J2 50 43N 1 54W
Bouroumba Vanuatu **83** H5 16 42S 168 08E
Bou Saâda Algeria **112** F10 35 10N 4 09E
Bousso Chad **110** C10 10 32N 16 45E
Bouvet Island Southern Ocean **25** I1 54 26S 3 24E
Bowen Australia **78** H5 20 00S 148 10E
Bowling Green Kentucky U.S.A. **92** C1 37 00N 86 29W
Bowling Green Missouri U.S.A. **92** B1 39 21N 91 11W
Bowling Green Ohio U.S.A. **93** D2 41 22N 83 40W
Bowman North Dakota U.S.A. **90** F6 46 11N 103 26W
Bowutu Mountains Papua New Guinea **45** M3 7 45S 147 00E
Box Hill England United Kingdom **66** B2 51 16N 0 13W
Boxmeer Netherlands **70** E3 51 39N 5 57E
Boxtel Netherlands **70** E3 51 36N 5 20E
Boyne *r.* Irish Republic **68** E5 53 40N 6 35W
Boyoma Falls Zaïre **110** E8 0 18N 25 30E
Bozeman Montana U.S.A. **90** D6 45 40N 111 00W
Bozoum Central African Republic **110** C9 6 16N 16 22E
Brabant *admin.* Belgium **70** D2 50 45N 4 30E
Brač *i.* Croatia **74** C3 43 00N 16 00E
Braddell Heights *tn.* Singapore **41** D4 1 21N 103 53E
Bradenton Florida U.S.A. **91** J2 27 29N 82 33W
Bradford England United Kingdom **68** J5 53 48N 1 45W
Bradford Pennsylvania U.S.A. **93** E2 41 57N 78 39W
Brady Texas U.S.A. **90** G3 31 08N 99 22W
Braga Portugal **72** A3 41 32N 8 26W
Bragança Brazil **102** H12 1 02S 46 46W
Bragança Portugal **72** A3 41 47N 6 46W
Brahmapur India **53** E3 19 21N 84 51E
Brahmaputra *r.* Asia **53** G5 26 40N 93 00E
Brăila Romania **75** E2 45 17N 27 58E
Braine l'Alleud Belgium **70** D2 50 41N 4 22E
Brainerd Minnesota U.S.A. **92** B3 46 20N 94 10W
Brampton Ontario Canada **93** E2 43 42N 79 46W
Brandenburg Germany **71** B2 52 25N 12 34E
Brandenburg *admin.* Germany **71** B2 53 00N 13 00E
Brandon Manitoba Canada **89** P2 49 50N 99 57W
Brandon Vermont U.S.A. **93** F2 43 47N 73 05W
Brantford Ontario Canada **93** D2 43 09N 80 17W
Brasileia Brazil **102** D10 10 59S 68 45W
Brásilia Brazil **102** H9 15 45S 47 57W
Brașov Romania **75** E2 45 39N 25 35E
Brasschaat Belgium **70** D3 51 17N 4 30E
Brassey Range *mts.* Malaysia **40** A2 5 40N 117 50E
Bratislava Slovakia **75** C2 48 10N 17 10E
Bratsk Russia **57** M7 56 20N 101 50E
Bratsk Vodokhranilishche *res.* Russia **57** M7 56 00N 102 00E
Brattleboro Vermont U.S.A. **93** F2 42 51N 75 36W
Braunau Austria **71** B1 48 16N 13 03E
Braunschweig Germany **71** B2 52 15N 10 30E
Brawley California U.S.A. **90** C3 32 59N 115 30W
Bray Irish Republic **68** E5 53 12N 6 06W
BRAZIL 102 G10
Brazil Basin Atlantic Ocean **25** F5/6 10 00S 26 00W
Brazilian Highlands Brazil **98** 10 00S 50 00W
Brazil Plateau Brazil **98** 20 00S 45 00W
Brazos *r.* Texas U.S.A. **91** G3 32 00N 97 00W
Brazzaville Congo **112** I2 4 14S 15 14E
Brdy *mts.* Czech Republic **71** B1 49 00N 14 00E
Brea Reservoir California U.S.A. **95** C2 33 54N 117 56W
Brebes Indonesia **42** O7 6 54S 109 00E
Breckenridge Minnesota U.S.A. **92** A3 46 14N 96 35W
Brecon Beacons *mts.* Wales United Kingdom **68** H3 51 53N 3 30W
Breda Netherlands **70** D3 51 35N 4 46E
Bredy Russia **59** J5 52 23N 60 16E
Bregenz Austria **71** A1 47 31N 9 46E
Breidha Fjördur *b.* Iceland **69** H7 65 15N 23 00W
Brekstad Norway **69** B3 63 50N 9 50E
Bremen Germany **71** A2 53 05N 8 48E
Bremen *admin.* Germany **71** A2 53 00N 9 00E
Bremerhaven Germany **71** A2 53 33N 8 35E
Bremerton Washington U.S.A. **90** B6 47 34N 122 40W
Brenham Texas U.S.A. **91** G3 30 09N 96 24W
Brenner Pass Austria/Italy **75** B2 47 02N 11 32E
Brent *bor.* England United Kingdom **66** B3 51 34N 0 17W
Brentwood England United Kingdom **66** E3 51 38N 0 18E
Brescia Italy **74** B4 45 33N 10 13E
Brest Belarus **75** D3 52 08N 23 40E
Brest France **73** A2 48 23N 4 30W
Brewerton New York U.S.A. **93** E2 43 15N 76 09W
Brezhnev *see* Neberezhnyye Chelny
Bria Central African Republic **110** D9 67 32N 22 00E
Briançon France **73** C1 44 53N 6 39E
Brickfield Trinidad and Tobago **96** T9 10 20N 61 16W
Bridgeport Connecticut U.S.A. **93** F2 41 12N 73 12W
Bridgeton New Jersey U.S.A. **93** E1 39 26N 75 14W
Bridgetown Barbados **96** V12 13 06N 59 37W
Bridgwater England United Kingdom **68** H3 51 08N 3 00W
Brie-Comte-Robert France **67** C1 48 41N 2 37E
Brienz Switzerland **73** C2 46 46N 8 02E
Brieselang Germany **67** E2 52 36N 13 00E
Briey France **73** C2 49 15N 5 57E
Brig Switzerland **73** C2 46 19N 8 00E
Brigham City Utah U.S.A. **90** D5 41 30N 112 02W
Brighton England United Kingdom **68** K2 50 50N 0 10W
Brighton Beach *tn.* New York U.S.A. **94** C1 40 34N 73 58W
Brignoles France **73** C1 43 25N 6 03E
Brindisi Italy **74** C3 40 37N 17 57E
Brisbane Australia **78** I4 27 30S 153 00E
Bristol England United Kingdom **68** I3 51 27N 2 35W
Bristol Bay Alaska U.S.A. **88** D4 57 30N 159 00W
Bristol Channel United Kingdom **68** H3 51 20N 3 50W
British Columbia *province* Canada **88** J4 56 50N 125 30W
British Mountains U.S.A./Canada **88** G6 65 40N 142 30W
Britt Ontario Canada **93** D3 45 46N 80 35W
Brittany Peninsula France **60** 48 00N 4 00W
Brive-la-Gailliarde France **73** B2 45 09N 1 32E
Brno Czech Republic **75** C2 49 13N 16 40E
Brockton Massachusetts U.S.A. **93** F2 42 06N 71 01W
Brockville Ontario Canada **93** E2 44 35N 75 44W
Brodeur Peninsula Northwest Territories Canada **89** R7 72 00N 87 30W
Brody Ukraine **58** B5 50 05N 25 08E
Broer Ruys, Cape Greenland **20** 73 30N 20 20W
Broken Bridge Creek Norfolk Island **81** L5 29 01S 167 57E
Broken Hill *tn.* Australia **78** G3 31 57S 141 30E
Broken Ridge Indian Ocean **24** I3 30 00S 93 00E
Bromley *bor.* England United Kingdom **66** D2 51 31N 0 01W
Brønnøysund Norway **69** C4 65 38N 12 15E
Brooke's Point *tn.* The Philippines **40** A2 8 50N 117 52E
Brookings South Dakota U.S.A. **92** A2 44 19N 96 47W
Brooklyn New York U.S.A. **94** C1 40 41N 73 57W
Brooks Alberta Canada **88** M3 50 35N 111 54W
Brooks Range *mts.* Alaska U.S.A. **88** E6/G6 67 55N 155 00W
Brookvale Australia **79** H2 33 46S 151 16E
Brookville Pennsylvania U.S.A. **93** E2 41 10N 79 06W
Broome Australia **78** C6 17 58S 122 15E
Browning Montana U.S.A. **90** D6 48 33N 113 00W
Brown's Town Jamaica **97** Q8 18 28N 77 22W
Browns Valley *tn.* Minnesota U.S.A. **92** A3 45 35N 96 50W
Brownsville Texas U.S.A. **91** G2 25 54N 97 30W
Brownwood Texas U.S.A. **90** G3 31 42N 98 59W
Bruay-en-Artois France **73** B3 50 29N 2 33E
Bruce Mines *tn.* Ontario Canada **93** D3 46 19N 83 48W
Bruce Peninsula Ontario Canada **93** D2/3 45 00N 81 20W
Bruchsal Germany **71** A1 49 07N 8 35E
Bruges *see* Brugges
Brugg Switzerland **73** C2 47 29N 8 13E
Brugge *(Bruges)* Belgium **70** C3 51 13N 3 14E
Brühl Germany **70** F2 50 50N 6 55E
Brunei Bay Brunei Darussalam/Malaysia **40** A2 5 05N 115 20E
BRUNEI DARUSSALAM 42 D4
Brunoy France **67** C1 48 40N 2 31E
Brunssum Netherlands **70** E2 50 57N 5 59E
Brunswick Georgia U.S.A. **91** J3 31 09N 81 30W
Brunswick Maine U.S.A. **93** G2 43 55N 69 59W
Brussel *see* Bruxelles
Brussels *see* Bruxelles
Bruxelles *(Brussel, Brussels)* Belgium **70** D2 50 50N 4 21E
Bryan Texas U.S.A. **91** G3 30 41N 96 24W
Bryansk Russia **56** F6 53 15N 34 09E
Brzeg Poland **75** C3 50 52N 17 27E
Bua Fiji **83** C10 16 49S 178 39E
Buada Lagoon Nauru **83** L1 0 31S 166 55E
Bü Ağri Daği *(Mt. Ararat) mt.* Turkey **54** F6 39 44N 44 15E
Buala Solomon Islands **82** E5 8 11S 159 37E
Bua Yai Thailand **39** B3 15 35N 102 25E
Buca Fiji **83** D10 16 39S 179 51E
Bucaramanga Colombia **102** C14 7 08N 73 10W
Bucas Grande *i.* The Philippines **40** C2 9 38N 125 58E
Buchanan Liberia **112** C4 5 57N 10 02W
Bucharest *see* București
Bucholz Germany **67** F2 51 25N 6 45E
Buckingham Québec Canada **93** E3 45 35N 75 25W
Buckinghamshire *co.* England United Kingdom **66** A3 51 50N 0 50W
Buckow Germany **67** F1 52 24N 1324E
Bucks Point Reserve Norfolk Island **81** L4 29 02S 167 59E
Bucksport Maine U.S.A. **93** G2 44 35N 68 47W
București *(Bucharest)* Romania **75** E1 44 25N 26 07E
Budapest Hungary **75** C2 47 30N 19 03E
Budjala Zaïre **110** C8 2 38N 19 48E
Buea Cameroon **112** G3 4 09N 9 13E
Buena Park *tn.* California U.S.A. **95** B2 33 52N 118 02W
Buenaventura Colombia **102** B13 3 54N 77 02W
Buenaventura Mexico **96** C5 29 50N 107 30W
Buenos Aires Argentina **103** F6 34 40S 58 30W
Buenos Aires, Lake Argentina/Chile **103** C3 47 00S 72 00W
Buffalo New York U.S.A. **93** E2 42 52N 78 55W
Buffalo Wyoming U.S.A. **90** E5 44 21N 106 40W
Buffalo Lake Northwest Territories Canada **88** L5 60 40N 115 30W
Buffalo Narrows *tn.* Saskatchewan Canada **88** N4 55 52N 108 28W
Buff Bay *tn.* Jamaica **97** R8 18 18N 76 40W
Bugsuk *i.* The Philippines **40** A2 8 15N 117 17E
Bugul'ma Russia **59** G5 54 32N 52 46E
Buheirat-Murrat-el-Kubra *(Great Bitter Lake) l.* Egypt **109** S2 30 22N 32 22E
Buheirat-Murrat-el-Sughra *(Little Bitter Lake) l.* Egypt **109** T2 30 14N 32 33E
Buin Papua New Guinea **45** Q3 6 52S 155 42E
Bujumbura Burundi **111** E7 3 22S 29 19E
Bukachacha Russia **57** N6 53 00N 116 58E
Buka Island Papua New Guinea **45** Q4 5 15S 154 35E
Bukama Zaïre **111** E6 9 13S 25 52E
Bukatatonoa Reefs Fiji **83** F8 18 15S 178 25W
Bukavu Zaïre **110** E7 2 30S 28 50E
Bukhara Uzbekistan **59** J2 39 47N 64 26E
Bukit Batok Singapore **41** B4 1 21N 103 45E
Bukit Gombak *hill* Singapore **41** C4 1 22N 103 45E
Bukit Liangpran *hill* Indonesia **42** D4 1 04N 114 22E
Bukit Mandai Singapore **41** C4 1 25N 103 46E
Bukit Mertajam Malaysia **39** B1 5 21N 100 27E
Bukit Panjang Singapore **41** C4 1 23N 103 46E
Bukit Panjang Singapore **41** C4 1 23N 103 46E
Bukit Paya *mt.* Indonesia **42** D3 0 31S 112 37E
Bukit Timah Singapore **41** B4 1 22N 103 44E
Bukit Timah *hill* Singapore **41** C4 1 21N 103 47E
Bukittinggi Indonesia **42** B3 0 18S 100 20E
Bukoba Tanzania **110** F7 1 19S 31 49E
Bula Indonesia **43** H3 3 07S 130 27E
Bula Papua New Guinea **45** J2 9 15S 141 15E
Bulan The Philippines **40** B3 12 40N 123 53E
Bulandshahr India **53** D5 28 30N 77 49E
Bulawayo Zimbabwe **111** E3 20 10S 28 43E
BULGARIA 74 D3/E3
Bulileka Fiji **83** D10 16 27S 179 29E
Bulim Singapore **41** B4 1 22N 103 43E
Buliya *i.* Fiji **83** C8 18 50S 178 33E
Buller *r.* South Island New Zealand **79** B2 41 50S 171 35E
Bull Shoals Lake U.S.A. **91** H4 36 00N 93 00W
Bulolo Papua New Guinea **45** M3 7 13S 146 35E
Buluan, Lake The Philippines **40** B2 6 40N 124 50E
Bulukumba Indonesia **43** F2 5 35N 120 13E
Bulun Russia **57** O10 70 45N 127 20E
Bumba Zaïre **110** D8 2 10N 22 30E
Bumba Bum *mt.* Myanmar **38** B5 26 45N 97 16E
Bumbora Reserve Norfolk Island **81** K4 29 03S 167 56E
Bumbulan Indonesia **43** F4 0 31N 122 04E
Bunabufi Papua New Guinea **45** L4 4 36S 145 32E
Bunama Papua New Guinea **45** O1 10 10S 151 05E
Bunbury Australia **78** B3 33 20S 115 34E
Bundaberg Australia **78** I5 24 50S 152 21E
Bundeena Australia **79** G1 34 05S 151 07E
Bung Boraphet *l.* Thailand **39** B3 15 45N 100 30E
Bung Kan Thailand **39** B3 18 20N 103 41E
Bungo-suidō *sd.* Japan **46** B1 33 00N 132 30E
Bunia Zaïre **110** F8 1 33N 30 13E
Buntok Indonesia **42** D3 1 45S 114 47E
Buol Indonesia **43** F4 0 50N 121 30E
Buona Vista Singapore **41** C3 1 17N 103 47E
Bura Kenya **110** G7 1 06S 39 58E
Buran Darat *i.* Singapore **41** D2 1 15N 103 51E
Burauen The Philippines **40** B3 10 58N 124 56E
Buraydah Saudi Arabia **54** F4 26 20N 43 59E
Burbank California U.S.A. **95** A3 34 10N 118 25W
Burco Somalia **108** O9 9 31N 45 33E
Burdur Turkey **54** D6 37 44N 30 17E
Bure *r.* England United Kingdom **68** M4 52 47N 1 20E
Bureya *r.* Russia **57** P6 52 00N 133 00E
Bûr Fu'ad Egypt **109** S4 31 50N 32 19E
Burg Germany **71** B2 52 17N 11 51E
Burgas Bulgaria **74** E3 42 30N 27 29E
Burgos Spain **72** B3 42 21N 3 41W
Burhanpur India **53** D4 21 18N 76 08E
Burias *i.* The Philippines **40** B3 13 00N 123 00E
Buri Khali India **52** J1 22 30N 88 10E
Buri Ram Thailand **39** B2 14 59N 103 09E
BURKINA 112 E5
Burk's Falls *tn.* Ontario Canada **93** E3 45 37N 79 25W
Burlington Ontario Canada **93** E2 43 19N 79 48W
Burlington Colorado U.S.A. **90** F4 39 17N 102 17W
Burlington Iowa U.S.A. **92** B2 40 50N 91 07W
Burlington Vermont U.S.A. **93** F2 44 28N 73 14W
Burlington West Virginia U.S.A. **93** E1 39 20N 78 56W
Burlington Wisconsin U.S.A. **92** C2 42 41N 88 17W
BURMA *see* MYANMAR
Burnie Australia **78** H1 41 03S 145 55E
Burnt Pine Norfolk Island **81** K4 29 02S 167 57E
Burquin China **59** O4 47 44N 86 55E
Bursa Turkey **54** C7 40 12N 29 04E
Bûr Safâga Egypt **110** F13 25 43N 33 55E
Bûr Taufiq Egypt **109** T1 29 57N 32 34E
BURUNDI 111 E7
Burwell Nebraska U.S.A. **90** G5 41 48N 99 09W
Busa, Mount The Philippines **40** B2 6 07N 124 41E
Būshehr Iran **55** H4 28 57N 50 52E
Bushey England United Kingdom **66** B3 51 39N 0 22W
Busira *r.* Zaïre **110** C7 1 00S 20 00E
Bussum Netherlands **70** E4 52 16N 5 09E
Busto Arsizio Italy **74** A4 45 37N 8 51E
Busuanga *i.* The Philippines **40** B3 12 00N 120 00E
Buta Zaïre **110** D8 2 49N 24 50E
Butare Rwanda **110** E7 2 35S 29 44E
Butaritari *i.* Pacific Ocean **80** C4 3 10N 172 45E
Bute *i.* Scotland United Kingdom **68** F7 55 50N 5 05W
Buthidaung Myanmar **38** A4 20 50N 92 35E
Butler Pennsylvania U.S.A. **93** E2 40 51N 79 55W
Butovo Russia **56** M1 55 30N 37 32E
Butte Montana U.S.A. **90** D6 46 00N 112 31W
Butterworth Malaysia **42** B5 5 24N 100 22E
Butt of Lewis *c.* Scotland United Kingdom **68** E10 58 30N 6 20W
Butuan The Philippines **40** C2 8 56N 125 31E
Buulobarde Somalia **110** I8 3 50N 45 33E
Buxtehude Germany **71** A2 53 29N 9 42E
Buzău Romania **75** E2 45 10N 26 49E
Bwagaoia Papua New Guinea **45** P1 10 39S 152 48E
Bydgoszcz Poland **75** C3 53 16N 18 00E
Byelorussia *see* BELARUS
Byfleet England United Kingdom **66** B2 51 21N 0 29W
Bygland Norway **69** B2 58 50N 7 49E
Bylot Island Northwest Territories Canada **89** T7 73 30N 79 00W
Byron, Cape Solomon Islands **83** M3 10 40S 166 09E
Byrranga Mountains Russia **57** L10 75 00N 100 00E
Bytom Poland **75** C3 50 21N 18 51E

C
Cabanatuan The Philippines **40** B4 15 30N 120 58E
Cabano Québec Canada **93** G3 47 40N 68 56W
Cabimas Venezuela **102** C15 10 26N 71 27W
Cabinda *admin.* Angola **111** B6 5 30S 12 20E
Cabo Brazil **102** J11 8 16S 35 00W
Cabo Blanco *c.* Costa Rica **97** G1 9 36N 85 06W
Cabo Caballeria *c.* Balearic Islands **72** F5 40 05N 4 05E
Cabo Catoche *c.* Mexico **97** G4 21 38N 87 08W
Cabo Corrientes *c.* Colombia **102** B14 5 29N 77 36W
Cabo Corrientes *c.* Mexico **96** C4 20 25N 105 42W
Cabo d'Artrutx *c.* Balearic Islands **72** E4 39 55N 3 49E
Cabo de Barberia *c.* Balearic Islands **72** D4 38 40N 1 20E
Cabo de Cala Figuera *c.* Balearic Islands **72** E4 39 27N 2 31E
Cabo de Creus *c.* Spain **72** C3 42 19N 3 19E
Cabo de Formentor *c.* Balearic Islands **72** E4 39 58N 3 13E
Cabo de Gata *c.* Spain **72** B2 36 44N 2 10W
Cabo de Hornos *(Cape Horn) c.* Chile **103** D1 56 00S 67 15W
Cabo de la Nao *c.* Spain **72** C2 38 44N 0 14E
Cabo Delgado *c.* Mozambique **111** H5 10 45S 40 45E
Cabo de Palos *c.* Spain **72** B2 37 38N 0 40W
Cabo de Peñas *c.* Spain **72** A3 43 39N 5 50W
Cabo de Salinas *c.* Balearic Islands **72** E4 39 16N 3 04E
Cabo de São Vicente *c.* Portugal **72** A2 37 01N 8 59W
Cabo de Tortosa *c.* Spain **72** C3 40 44N 0 54E
Cabo Dos Bahías *c.* Argentina **103** D4 45 00S 65 30W
Cabo Espichel *c.* Portugal **72** A2 38 24N 9 13W
Cabo Falso *c.* Mexico **96** B4 22 50N 110 00W
Cabo Finisterre *c.* Spain **72** A3 42 52N 9 16W
Cabo Freu *c.* Balearic Islands **72** E4 39 45N 3 27E
Cabo Gracias á Dios *c.* Nicaragua **97** H3 15 00N 83 10W
Cabo Guardafui *see* Raas Caseyr
Cabo Orange *c.* Brazil **102** G13 4 25N 51 32W
Cabo Ortegal *c.* Spain **72** A3 43 46N 7 54W
Cabora Bassa Dam Mozambique **111** F4 16 00S 33 00E
Caborca Mexico **96** B6 30 42N 112 10W
Cabo San Juan *c.* Argentina **103** E2 54 45S 63 46W
Cabo Santa Elena *c.* Costa Rica **97** G2 10 54N 85 56W
Cabot Strait Nova Scotia/Newfoundland Canada **89** W2 47 10N 59 30W
Cabo Vírgenes *c.* Argentina **103** D2 52 20S 68 00W
Cabrera *i.* Balearic Islands **72** E4 39 00N 2 59E
Cabriel *r.* Spain **72** B2 39 20N 1 15W
Čačak Serbia Yugoslavia **74** D3 43 54N 20 22E
Cáceres Brazil **102** F9 16 05S 57 40W
Cáceres Spain **72** A2 39 29N 6 23W
Cachoeira Brazil **102** J10 12 35S 38 59W
Cachoeira do Sol Brazil **103** G7 30 03S 52 52W
Cachoeiro de Itapemirim Brazil **103** I8 20 51N 41 07W
Cadig Mountains The Philippines **40** B3 14 00N 122 00E
Cádiz Spain **72** A2 36 32N 6 18W
Cadiz The Philippines **40** B3 10 57N 123 18E
Cádiz, Gulf of Spain **72** A2 36 30N 7 15W
Caen France **73** A2 49 11N 0 22W
Caernarfon Wales United Kingdom **68** G5 53 08N 4 16W
Cagayan *r.* The Philippines **40** B4 17 00N 123 00E
Cagayan de Oro The Philippines **40** B2 8 29N 124 40E
Cagayan Islands The Philippines **40** B2 9 00N 121 00E
Cagayan Sulu The Philippines **42** E5 6 00N 119 00E
Cagayan Sulu *(Pulau Mapin) i.* The Philippines **40** A2 7 00N 118 28E
Cágliari Italy **74** A2 39 13N 9 08E
Caguas Puerto Rico **97** K3 18 41N 66 04W
Caha Mountains Irish Republic **68** B3 51 40N 9 40W
Cahors France **73** B1 44 28N 0 26E
Caicos Passage *sd.* West Indies **97** J4 22 20N 72 30W
Cairngorms *mts.* Scotland United Kingdom **68** H9 57 10N 3 30W
Cairns Australia **78** H6 16 51S 145 43E
Cairo Illinois U.S.A. **92** C1 37 01N 89 09W
Cairo *see* El Qâ'hira
Cajamarca Peru **102** B11 7 09S 78 32W
Cajàzeiras Brazil **102** J11 6 52S 38 31W
Caju Brazil **103** Q2 22 53S 43 13W
Cakau Matacucu *reef* Fiji **83** E10 16 06S 179 38W

Cakau Vucovuco *reef* Fiji 83 E10 16 03S 179 31E
Çakirgöl Daği Turkey 58 D3 40 33N 39 40E
Cakovec Croatia 74 C4 46 24N 16 26E
Calabar Nigeria 112 G3 4 56N 8 22E
Calabozo Venezuela 97 K1 8 58N 67 28W
Calagua Islands The Philippines 40 B3 14 00N 123 00E
Calahorra Spain 72 B3 46 19N 1 58W
Calais France 73 B2 50 57N 1 52E
Calama Chile 103 D8 22 30S 68 55W
Calamar Colombia 102 C15 10 16N 74 55W
Calamba The Philippines 40 B3 14 12N 121 10E
Calamian Group *is.* The Philippines 40 A3/B3 12 00N 120 00E
Calang Indonesia 42 A4 4 37N 95 37E
Calapan The Philippines 40 B3 13 23N 121 10E
Calatayud Spain 72 B3 41 21N 1 39W
Calauag The Philippines 40 B3 13 58N 122 17E
Calayan *i.* The Philippines 40 B4 19 20N 121 30E
Calbayog The Philippines 40 B3 12 04N 124 38E
Calçoene Brazil 102 G13 20 30N 50 55W
Calcutta India 53 F4 22 30N 88 20E
Caldas da Rainha Portugal 72 A2 39 24N 9 08W
Caldwell Idaho U.S.A. 90 C5 43 39N 116 40W
Caldwell New Jersey U.S.A. 94 A2 40 49N 74 16W
Calgary Alberta Canada 88 M3 51 05N 11 05W
Cali Colombia 102 B13 3 24N 76 30W
Calicut India 53 D2 11 15N 75 45E
Caliente Nevada U.S.A. 90 D4 37 36N 114 31W
California Trinidad and Tobago 96 T9 10 24N 61 28W
California *state* U.S.A. 90 C4 35 00N 119 00W
Callao Peru 102 B10 12 05S 77 08W
Caltanissetta Italy 74 B2 37 29N 14 04E
Calvi Corsica 73 C1 42 34N 8 44E
Calvia Balearic Islands 72 E4 39 33N 2 29E
Calvinia Republic of South Africa 111 C1 31 25S 19 47E
Camaçari Brazil 102 J10 12 44S 38 16W
Camacupa Angola 111 C5 12 03S 17 50E
Camagüey Cuba 97 I4 21 25N 77 55W
Ca Mau *(Quan Long)* Vietnam 37 C1 9 15N 105 10E
Ca Mau Peninsula Vietnam 37 B1/C1 9 00N 105 10E
CAMBODIA 37 B2/C2
Cambrai France 73 B3 50 10N 3 14E
Cambrian Mountains Wales United Kingdom 68 H4 52 15N 3 45W
Cambridge Ontario Canada 93 D2 43 22N 80 20W
Cambridge Jamaica 97 Q8 18 18N 77 54W
Cambridge North Island New Zealand 79 C3 37 53S 175 28E
Cambridge England United Kingdom 68 L4 52 12N 0 07E
Cambridge Maryland U.S.A. 91 K4 38 34N 76 04W
Cambridge Ohio U.S.A. 93 D2 40 02N 81 36W
Cambridge Bay *tn.* Northwest Territories Canada 89 N6 69 09N 105 00W
Camden New Jersey U.S.A. 93 E1 39 57N 75 06W
Cameia National Park Angola 111 D5 12 00S 22 00E
CAMEROON 112 H3/4
Cametá Brazil 102 H12 2 12S 49 30W
Camiguin *i.* The Philippines 40 B2 9 00N 124 00E
Camiguin *i.* The Philippines 40 B4 18 55N 121 55E
Camiri Bolivia 102 E8 20 08S 63 33W
Cammon Plateau Laos 37 C3 17 50N 105 20E
Camocin Brazil 102 I12 2 55S 40 50W
Camorta *i.* Nicobar Islands 53 G1 7 30N 93 30E
Camotes Islands The Philippines 40 B3 10 00N 124 00E
Campbell Islands Pacific Ocean 80 C1 52 30S 169 02E
Campbell River *tn.* British Columbia Canada 88 J2 50 00N 125 18W
Campbellsville Kentucky U.S.A. 92 C1 37 20N 85 21W
Campbellton New Brunswick Canada 89 V2 48 00N 66 30W
Campbeltown Scotland United Kingdom 68 F7 55 26N 5 36W
Campeche Mexico 96 F3 19 50N 90 30W
Campina Grande Brazil 102 J11 7 15S 35 50W
Campinas Brazil 103 H8 22 54S 47 06W
Campines *see* Kempenland
Camplong Indonesia 43 F1 10 00S 123 55E
Campoalegre Colombia 102 B13 2 49N 75 19W
Campobasso Italy 74 B3 41 33N 14 39E
Campo Grande Brazil 102 G8 20 24S 54 35W
Campo Maior Brazil 102 I12 4 50S 42 12W
Campo Mourão Brazil 103 G8 24 01S 52 24W
Campos Brazil 103 I8 21 46S 41 21W
Campos del Puerto Balearic Islands 72 E4 39 26N 3 01E
Campos Elyseos Brazil 103 P3 22 42S 43 16W
Cam Rahn Vietnam 37 C2 11 54N 109 14E
Ca Na Vietnam 37 C2 11 21N 108 53E
Canada Basin Arctic Ocean 20 80 00N 140 00W
Canadian *r.* U.S.A. 90 F4 35 00N 104 00W
Canakkale Turkey 54 C7 40 09N 26 25E
Canala New Caledonia 82 U2 21 30S 165 58E
Canal de la Havannah *sd.* New Caledonia 82 V1 22 25S 167 00E
Canal de l'Ourcq France 67 C2 48 55N 2 32E
Canal des Ardennes France 70 D1 49 50N 4 30E
Canal du Midi France 73 B1 43 20N 2 00E
Cananea Mexico 96 B6 30 59N 110 20W
Canary Basin Atlantic Ocean 25 E9/F9 26 20N 30 00W
Canary Islands Spain 112 B8/C8 28 30N 15 10W
Canaveral, Cape Florida U.S.A. 91 J2 28 28N 80 28W
Canberra Australia 78 H2 35 18S 149 08E
Cangamba Angola 111 C5 13 40S 19 47E
Cangrejos Point Trinidad and Tobago 96 T9 10 25N 61 29W
Cangyuan China 38 B4 23 09N 99 19E
Cangzhou China 49 N6 38 19N 116 54E
Caniapiscau *r.* Québec Canada 89 V4 57 30N 68 40W
Canmore Alberta Canada 88 L3 51 07N 115 18W
Cannanore India 53 D2 11 53N 75 23 E
Cannes France 73 C1 43 33N 7 00E
Canõas Brazil 103 G7 28 55S 51 10W
Canso Nova Scotia Canada 89 W2 45 20N 61 00W
Cantabrian Mountains *see* Cordillera Cantabrica
Cantaro Trinidad and Tobago 96 T10 10 42N 61 28W
Canterbury Australia 79 G2 33 55S 151 07E
Canterbury England United Kingdom 68 M3 51 17N 1 05E
Canterbury Bight South Island New Zealand 79 B2 44 00S 172 00E
Canterbury Plains South Island New Zealand 79 B2 43 45S 171 56E
Can Tho Vietnam 37 C2 10 03N 105 46E
Canto de Rio Brazil 103 Q2 22 55S 43 06W
Canton Ohio U.S.A. 93 D2 40 48N 81 23W
Canton *see* Guangzhou
Canton Island Pacific Ocean 80 D3 2 50S 171 40W
Cao Bang Vietnam 37 C4 22 40N 106 16E
Cao Hai *l.* China 38 C5 26 55N 104 15E
Caojian China 38 B5 25 40N 99 10E
Caparo Trinidad and Tobago 96 T9 10 27N 61 19W
Caparo *r.* Trinidad and Tobago 96 T9 10 31N 61 25W
Cap Blanc *see* Ras Nouadhibou
Cap Bocage *c.* New Caledonia 82 U2 21 10S 165 38E
Cap Bon *c.* Tunisia 74 B2 37 08N 11 00E
Cap Boyer *c.* New Caledonia 82 X2 21 37S 168 10E
Cap Corse *c.* Corsica 73 C1 43 00N 9 21E
Cap d'Ambre *c.* Madagascar 111 I5 12 00S 49 15E
Cap de Flotte *c.* New Caledonia 82 W2 21 10S 167 25E
Cap de la Hague *c.* France 73 A2 49 44N 1 56W
Cap de la Madeleine *tn.* Québec Canada 93 F3 46 22N 72 31W
Cap des Pins *c.* New Caledonia 82 W2 21 05S 167 28E
Cap des Trois Fourches *c.* Morocco 72 B2 35 26N 2 57W
Cap Dumoulin *c.* New Caledonia 82 U2 21 25S 165 57E
Cape Basin Atlantic Ocean 25 I3 36 00S 6 00E
Cape Breton Island Nova Scotia Canada 89 W2 46 45N 60 00W
Cape Charles *tn.* Virginia U.S.A. 93 E1 37 17N 76 01W
Cape Coast *tn.* Ghana 112 E4 5 10N 1 13W
Cape Cod Bay U.S.A. 93 F2 41 00N 70 00W
Cape Dorset *tn.* Northwest Territories Canada 89 T5 64 10N 76 40W
Cape Dyer *tn.* Northwest Territories Canada 89 W6 66 30N 61 20W
Cape Girardeau *tn.* Missouri U.S.A. 92 C1 37 19N 89 31W
Cape Horn *see* Cabo de Hornos
Capelle aan den IJssel Netherlands 70 D3 51 56N 4 36E
Cape May *tn.* New Jersey U.S.A. 93 F1 38 56N 74 54W
Cape Province *admin.* Republic of South Africa 111 D1 31 00S 22 00E
Cape Rise Atlantic Ocean 25 J2 42 00S 11 00E
Cape Rodney *tn.* Papua New Guinea 45 N1 10 15S 148 25E
Cap Escarpé *c.* New Caledonia 82 W3 20 41S 167 13E
Cape Town Republic of South Africa 111 C1 33 56S 18 28E
Cape Verde Basin Atlantic Ocean 25 E8 11 00N 35 00W
Cape Verde Islands Atlantic Ocean 25 F8 16 00N 24 00W
Cape York Peninsula Australia 78 G7 12 30S 142 30E
Cap Ferret *c.* France 73 A1 44 42N 1 16W
Cap Gris Nez *c.* France 70 A2 50 52N 1 35E
Cap-Haïtien Haiti 97 J3 19 47N 72 17W
Capitán Arturo Prat *r.s.* Antarctica 21 62 30S 59 41W
Cap Nahoi *c.* Vanuatu 83 F7 14 38S 166 36E
Cap Ndoua *c.* New Caledonia 82 V1 22 25S 166 55E
Capo Carbonara *c.* Italy 74 A2 39 07N 9 33E
Capo Passero *c.* Italy 74 C2 36 42N 15 09E
Capo Santa Maria di Leuca *c.* Italy 74 C2 39 47N 18 22E
Capo San Vito *c.* Italy 74 B2 38 12N 12 43E
Capri *i.* Italy 74 B3 40 33N 14 15E
Capricorn Channel Australia 78 I5 23 00S 152 30E
Caprivi Strip Namibia 111 D4 17 30S 27 50E
Cap Rossel *c.* New Caledonia 82 V3 20 23S 166 37E
Cap Roussin *c.* New Caledonia 82 W2 21 20S 167 59E
Cap Ste. Marie *c.* Madagascar 111 I2 25 34S 45 10E
Cap St-Hilaire *c.* New Caledonia 82 V3 20 38S 166 38E
Cap Vert *c.* Senegal 112 B5 14 43N 17 33W
Cap Wabao *c.* New Caledonia 82 W2 21 35S 167 56E
Caracal Romania 75 D1 44 07N 24 18E
Caraoas Venezuela 102 D15 10 35N 66 56W
Caramoan Peninsula The Philippines 40 B3 14 00N 123 00E
Caratinga Brazil 102 I9 19 50S 42 06W
Caravelas Brazil 102 J9 17 45S 39 15W
Carbondale Pennsylvania U.S.A. 93 E2 41 35N 75 31W
Carcassonne France 73 B1 43 13N 2 21E
Carcross Yukon Territory Canada 88 I5 60 11N 134 41W
Cardamom Hills India 53 D1 9 50N 77 00E
Cárdenas Mexico 96 E4 22 00N 99 41W
Cardiff Wales United Kingdom 68 H3 51 30N 3 13W
Cardigan Bay Wales United Kingdom 68 G4 52 30N 4 30W
Carei Romania 75 D2 47 40N 22 28E
Cargados Carajos Shoals Indian Ocean 24 E5 16 00S 60 00E
Cariacica Brazil 102 I9 20 15S 40 23W
Caribbean Sea Central America 97 I3 15 00N 75 00W
Caribou Mountains Alberta Canada 88 L4 59 00N 115 30W
Caringbah Australia 79 G1 34 03S 151 07E
Caripito Venezuela 102 E15 10 07N 63 07W
Carleton Place Ontario Canada 93 E3 45 08N 76 09W
Carlisle England United Kingdom 68 I6 54 54N 2 55W
Carlisle Bay Barbados 96 V12 13 05N 59 37W
Carlsbad New Mexico U.S.A. 90 F3 32 25N 104 14W
Carlsberg Ridge Indian Ocean 24 E7/F6 5 00N 65 00E
Carmacks Yukon Territory Canada 88 H5 62 04N 136 21W
Carman Manitoba Canada 92 A3 49 32N 97 59W
Carmarthen Wales United Kingdom 68 G3 51 51N 4 20W
Carmel Church *tn.* Virginia U.S.A. 93 E1 37 54N 77 25W
Carmen Colombia 102 B14 9 46N 75 06W
Carnarvon Australia 78 A5 24 51S 113 45E
Carnegie, Lake Australia 78 C4 27 00S 124 00E
Carnegie Ridge Pacific Ocean 23 R7 1 30S 95 00W
Car Nicobar *i.* Nicobar Islands 53 G1 9 00N 93 00E
Carnot Central African Republic 110 C8 4 59N 15 56E
Carnsore Point Irish Republic 68 E4 52 10N 6 22W
Carolina Brazil 102 H11 7 20S 47 25W
Caroline Island Pacific Ocean 81 E3 10 00S 150 00W
Caroline Islands Pacific Ocean 22 E8/F8 8 00N 148 00E
Caroni Trinidad and Tobago 96 T10 10 36N 61 22W
Caroni *r.* Trinidad and Tobago 96 T10 10 35N 61 20W
Carpathians *mts.* Europe 75 C2/E2 49 00N 22 00E
Carpaţii Meridionali *mts.* Romania 75 D2/E2 45 00N 24 00E
Carpentaria, Gulf of Australia 78 F7/G7 13 30S 138 00E
Carpentras France 73 C1 44 03N 5 03E
Carrauntoohill *mt.* Irish Republic 68 B3 52 00N 9 45W
Carrion *r.* Spain 72 B3 42 30N 4 45W
Carson California U.S.A. 95 A2 33 49N 118 16W
Carson City Nevada U.S.A. 90 C4 39 10N 119 46W
Cartagena Colombia 102 B15 10 24N 75 33W
Cartagena Spain 72 B2 37 36N 0 59W
Cartago Costa Rica 97 H1 9 50N 83 52W
Carteret New Jersey U.S.A. 94 B1 40 34N 74 13W
Carteret Islands *(Tulun Islands)* Papua New Guinea 45 Q4 4 40S 155 30E
Cartwright Newfoundland Canada 89 X3 53 40N 57 00W
Caruarú Brazil 102 J11 8 15S 35 55W
Carúpano Venezuela 102 E15 10 39N 63 14W
Casablanca *(Dar el Beida)* Morocco 112 D9 33 39N 7 35W
Casa Grande Arizona U.S.A. 90 D3 32 52N 111 46W
Cascade *tn.* Norfolk Island 81 L5 29 01S 167 58E
Cascade Bay Norfolk Island 81 L5 29 01S 167 57E
Cascade Creek Norfolk Island 81 L4 29 02S 167 57E
Cascade Range *mts.* North America 90 B5/6 48 00N 121 00W
Cascade Reserve Norfolk Island 81 L5 29 01S 167 58E
Cascadura Brazil 103 P2 22 53S 43 21W
Cascais Portugal 72 A2 38 41N 9 25W
Cascavel Brazil 102 J12 4 10S 38 15W
Caserta Italy 74 B3 41 04N 14 20E
Casey *r.s.* Antarctica 21 66 18S 110 32E
Casper Wyoming U.S.A. 90 E5 42 50N 106 20W
Caspian Lowlands Kirgyzstan 58 F4/G4 48 00N 50 00E
Cassiar Mountains British Columbia Canada 88 I4/J4 59 15N 129 49W
Cassino Italy 74 B3 41 29N 13 50E
Castellane France 73 C1 43 50N 6 30E
Castellón de la Plana Spain 72 B2 39 59N 0 03W
Castelnaudary France 73 B1 43 18N 1 57E
Castelo Branco Portugal 72 A2 39 50N 7 30W
Castlebar Irish Republic 68 B5 53 52N 9 17W
Castle Hill *tn.* Australia 79 F3 33 44S 150 59E
Castle Peak Hong Kong U.K. 51 A2 22 23N 113 57E
Castres France 73 B1 43 36N 2 14E
Castricum Netherlands 70 D4 52 33N 4 40E
Castries St. Lucia 97 L2 14 02N 60 59W
Castrovillari Italy 74 C2 39 48N 16 12E
Catamarca Argentina 103 D7 28 28S 65 46W
Catanduanes *i.* The Philippines 40 B3 14 00N 124 00E
Catánia Italy 74 C2 37 31N 15 06E
Catanzaro Italy 74 C2 38 54N 16 36E
Cataract, 1st *(R. Nile)* Egypt 110 F12 24 00N 32 45E
Cataract, 2nd *(R. Nile)* Sudan 110 F12 21 40N 31 12E
Cataract, 3rd *(R. Nile)* Sudan 110 F11 19 45N 30 25E
Cataract, 4th *(R. Nile)* Sudan 110 F11 18 40N 32 10E
Cataract, 5th *(R. Nile)* Sudan 110 F11 18 25N 33 52E
Catarman The Philippines 40 B3 12 29N 124 35E
Catbalogan The Philippines 40 B3 11 46N 124 55E
Cateel Bay The Philippines 40 C2 8 00N 126 00E
Caterham England United Kingdom 66 C2 51 17N 0 04W
Cat Island The Bahamas 97 I4 24 30N 75 30W
Catskill Mountains New York U.S.A. 93 E2 42 10N 74 20W
Caucaia Brazil 102 J12 3 44S 38 45W
Caucasus Mountains Asia 58 E3 43 00N 43 00E
Cavite The Philippines 40 B3 14 29N 120 54E
Caxias Brazil 102 I12 4 53N 43 20W
Caxias do Sul Brazil 103 G7 29 14S 51 10W
Cayenne French Guiana 102 G13 4 55N 52 18W
Cayuga Lake New York U.S.A. 93 E2 43 00N 77 00W
Cea *r.* Spain 72 A3 42 40N 5 10W
Ceara *admin.* Brazil 102 I11/J11 5 30S 40 00W
Cebu The Philippines 40 B3 10 17N 123 56E
Cebu *i.* The Philippines 40 B3 10 00N 124 00E
Cedar *r.* Iowa U.S.A. 91 H5 42 00N 92 00W
Cedar City Utah U.S.A. 90 D4 37 40N 113 04W
Cedar Creek *r.* North Dakota U.S.A. 90 F6 46 00N 102 00W
Cedar Falls *tn.* Iowa U.S.A. 92 B2 42 34N 92 26W
Cedar Grove New Jersey U.S.A. 94 B2 40 51N 74 14W
Cedar Lake Manitoba Canada 89 O3 53 40N 100 30W
Cedar Rapids *tn.* Iowa U.S.A. 92 B2 41 59N 91 39W
Cedros *i.* Mexico 96 A5 28 00N 115 00W
Cedros Bay Trinidad and Tobago 96 S9 10 08N 61 50W
Cedros Point Trinidad and Tobago 96 S9 10 07N 61 49W
Ceduna Australia 78 E3 32 07S 133 42E
Ceerigaabo Somalia 110 I10 10 40N 47 20E
Cegléd Hungary 75 C2 47 10N 19 47E
Celaya Mexico 96 D4 20 32N 100 48W
Celebes Sea Indonesia 43 F4 3 00N 122 00E
Celje Slovenia 74 C4 46 15N 15 16E
Celle Germany 71 B2 52 37N 10 05E
Celtic Sea British Isles 68 E3 51 00N 7 00W
Cemetry Bay Norfolk Island 81 L4 29 03S 167 58E
CENTRAL AFRICAN REPUBLIC 110 C9/D9
Central Cordilleras *hills* Spain 60 41 00N 5 00W
Centralia Illinois U.S.A. 92 C1 38 32N 89 08W
Central Pacific Basin Pacific Ocean 22 I9 10 00N 177 00W
Central Plain Ireland 60 53 30N 8 00W
Central Siberian Plateau Russia 57 M9/N8 65 00N 110 00E
Centro Brazil 103 Q2 22 53S 43 07W
Cepu Indonesia 42 P7 7 07S 111 35E
Cergy-Pontoise France 73 B2 49 02N 2 04E
Cerro de Pasco Peru 102 B10 10 43S 76 15W
České Budějovice Czech Republic 75 B2 48 58N 14 29E
Český Les Sumava *mts.* Czech Republic 71 B1 49 00N 12 00E
Ceuta *territory* Spain 72 A2 35 53N 5 19W
Cévennes *mts.* France 73 B1 44 20N 3 30E
Ceyhan *r.* Turkey 54 E6 37 45N 36 45E
Cèze *r.* France 73 B1 44 30N 4 00E
Cha-am Thailand 39 A2 12 46N 99 56E
Chacachacaré *i.* Trinidad and Tobago 96 S10 10 41N 61 45W
Chachapoyas Peru 102 B11 6 13S 77 54W
Chachoengsao Thailand 39 B2 13 39N 101 03E
CHAD 110 C10/D11
Chad, Lake West Africa 110 B10 13 50N 14 00E
Chae Hom Thailand 39 A3 18 44N 99 35E
Chaeryŏng North Korea 50 B4 38 20N 125 37E
Chagai Hills Afghanistan/Pakistan 55 J5 29 30N 63 00E
Chaghcharān Afghanistan 55 K5 34 31N 65 15E
Chagos Archipelago *(British Indian Ocean Territory)* Indian Ocean 24 G6 6 00S 73 00E
Chagos-Laccadive Ridge Indian Ocean 24 G6/G7 0 00 75 00E
Chaguanas Trinidad and Tobago 96 T10 10 31N 61 25W
Chaguaramas Trinidad and Tobago 96 S10 10 41N 61 38W
Chai Badan Thailand 39 B3 15 08N 101 03E
Chai Nat Thailand 39 B3 15 12N 100 10E
Chaîne des Albères *mts.* France 73 B1 42 30N 2 45E
Chaîne des Mitumba *(Mitumba Mountains) mts.* Zaïre 111 E6 7 30S 27 30E
Chai Wan Hong Kong U.K. 51 C1 22 15N 114 14E
Chai Wan Kok Hong Kong U.K. 51 B2 22 23N 114 06E
Chaiya Thailand 39 A1 9 25N 99 13E
Chaiyaphum Thailand 39 B3 15 46N 102 05E
Chalfont St. Peter England United Kingdom 66 A3 51 37N 0 33W
Challenger Fracture Zone Pacific Ocean 23 P4/R4 33 30S 100 00W
Châlons-sur-Marne France 73 B2 48 58N 4 22E
Chalon-sur-Saône France 73 B2 46 47N 4 51E
Cham Germany 71 B1 49 13N 12 41E
Chaman Pakistan 52 B6 30 55N 66 27E
Chambal *r.* India 53 D5 26 00N 77 00E
Chamberlain Lake Maine U.S.A. 93 G3 46 00N 69 00W
Chambersburg Pennsylvania U.S.A. 93 E1 39 57N 77 40W
Chambéry France 73 C2 45 34N 5 55E
Chambri Lake Papua New Guinea 45 K4 4 30S 143 30E
Chamo, Lake Ethiopia 110 G9 5 55N 37 35E
Chamonix France 73 C2 45 55N 6 52E
Champaign Illinois U.S.A. 92 C2 40 07N 88 14W
Champasak Laos 37 C2 14 56N 105 57E
Champdani India 52 K3 22 48N 88 21E
Champhon *r.* Laos 37 C3 16 50N 105 30E
Champigny France 67 C2 48 49N 2 32E
Champlain, Lake U.S.A. 93 F2 45 00N 73 00W
Champotón Mexico 96 F3 19 20N 90 43W
Champs-sur-Marne France 67 C2 48 51N 2 35E
Chana Thailand 39 B1 6 55N 100 46E
Chañaral Chile 103 C7 26 23S 70 40W
Chandigarh India 53 D6 30 44N 76 54E
Chandler Québec Canada 89 W2 48 21N 64 41W
Chandnagar India 52 K3 22 52N 88 22E
Chandrapur India 53 D3 19 58N 79 21E
Changara Mozambique 111 F4 16 50S 33 17E
Changbai China 50 D5 41 29N 128 12E
Changbai Shan *mts.* China 50 C5/D6 42 00N 128 00E
Chang Cheng *see* Great Wall
Changchun China P7 43 50N 125 20E
Changde China 49 M4 29 03N 111 35E
Chang-hua Taiwan 51 G7 24 06N 120 31E
Changi Singapore 41 E4 1 23N 103 59E
Changi Point Singapore 41 E4 1 23N 104 00E
Changjiang China 37 C3 19 23N 109 05E
Chang Jiang *(Yangtze) r.* China 49 L5 31 00N 110 00E
Changjin *r.* North Korea 50 C5 41 00N 127 00E
Changning China 38 B4 24 49N 99 39E
Changsan-got *c.* North Korea 50 B4 38 05N 124 38E
Changsha China 49 M4 28 10N 113 00E
Ch'angwŏn South Korea 50 D2 35 14N 128 37E
Changxindian China 47 F1 39 50N 116 12E
Changzhi China 49 M6 36 05N 113 12E
Changzhou China 49 O5 31 39N 120 45E
Channel Islands British Isles 68 I1 49 30N 2 30W
Channel-Port aux Basques Newfoundland Canada 89 X2 47 30N 58 50W
Chanthaburi Thailand 39 B2 12 35N 102 08E
Chanute Kansas U.S.A. 92 A1 37 41N 95 26W
Chaoyang China 49 O7 41 36N 120 25E
Chaozhou China 49 N3 23 42N 116 36E
Cha Pa Vietnam 37 B4 22 20N 103 50E
Chapada Diamantina *mts.* Brazil 102 I10 12 30S 42 30W
Chapecó Brazil 103 G7 27 14S 52 41W
Chapelton Jamaica 97 Q8 18 05N 77 16W
Chapleau Ontario Canada 93 D3 47 50N 83 24W
Chār Bahār Iran 55 J4 25 16N 60 41E
Chardzhou Turkmenistan 59 J2 39 09N 63 34E
Charente *r.* France 73 B2 46 00N 0 20E
Chari *r.* Chad 110 C10 11 00N 16 00E
Chārīkār Afghanistan 55 K5 35 01N 69 11E
Chariton Iowa U.S.A. 92 B2 41 00N 93 18W
Chariton *r.* U.S.A. 92 B1 40 00N 93 00W
Charleroi Belgium 70 D2 50 25N 4 27E
Charles Manitoba Canada 89 O4 55 33N 101 01W
Charlesbourg Québec Canada 93 F3 46 53N 71 16W
Charles City Iowa U.S.A. 92 B2 43 05N 92 40W
Charleston South Carolina U.S.A. 91 K3 32 48N 79 58W
Charleston West Virginia U.S.A. 93 D1 38 23N 81 40W
Charlestown Rhode Island U.S.A. 93 F2 41 24N 71 38W
Charleville Australia 78 H4 26 25S 146 13E
Charleville-Mézières France 73 B2 49 46N 4 43E
Charlevoix Michigan U.S.A. 92 C3 45 19N 85 16W
Charlotte North Carolina U.S.A. 91 J4 35 03N 80 50W
Charlottenburg Germany 67 E2 52 32N 13 18E
Charlottesville Virginia U.S.A. 93 E1 38 02N 78 29W
Charlottetown Prince Edward Island Canada 89 W2 46 14N 63 09W
Charters Towers Australia 78 H5 20 02S 146 20E
Chartres France 73 B2 48 27N 1 30E
Charybdis Reef Fiji 83 C9 17 13S 178 00E
Chasŏng North Korea 50 C5 41 24N 126 40E
Châteaubriant France 73 A2 47 43N 1 22W
Châteaudun France 73 B2 48 04N 1 20E
Châteauroux France 73 B2 46 49N 1 41E
Château-Thierry France 73 B2 49 03N 3 24E
Châtelet Belgium 70 D2 50 24N 4 32E
Châtellerault France 73 B2 46 49N 0 33E
Chatham New Brunswick Canada 89 V2 47 02N 65 30W
Chatham Ontario Canada 93 D2 42 24N 82 11W
Chatham Islands Pacific Ocean 80 D1 44 00S 176 30W
Chatham Rise Pacific Ocean 22 H3 45 00S 175 00E
Châtillon-sur-Seine France 73 B2 47 52N 4 35E
Chatou France 67 A2 48 54N 2 10E
Chatswood Australia 79 G2 33 48S 151 11E
Chattanooga Tennessee U.S.A. 91 I4 35 02N 85 18W
Chau Doc *(Chau Phu)* Vietnam 37 C2 10 42N 105 03E
Chauk Myanmar 38 A4 20 52N 94 50E
Chaumont France 73 C2 48 07N 5 08E
Chau Phu *see* Chau Doc
Cheb Czech Republic 75 B3 50 08N 12 28E
Cheboksary Russia 56 G7 56 08N 47 12E
Cheboygan Michigan U.S.A. 93 D3 45 40N 84 28W
Chech'ŏn South Korea 50 D3 37 05N 128 09E
Cheduba *i.* Myanmar 38 A3 18 50N 93 40E
Cheduba Strait Myanmar 38 A3 18 55N 93 35E
Cheju South Korea 50 C1 33 31N 126 29E
Cheju do *(Quelpart) i.* South Korea 50 C1 33 00N 126 30E
Cheju haehyŏp *sd.* South Korea 50 C1 33 45N 126 45E

Conecuh *r.* Alabama U.S.A. **91** I3 31 00N 87 00W
Conejara *i.* Balearic Islands **72** E4 39 11N 2 58E
Coney Island New York U.S.A. **94** C1 40 34N 74 00W
Conflans-Ste. Honorine France **67** A3 49 01N 2 09E
CONGO 112 H2/I1
Congo *(Zaïre) r.* Congo **112** I3 2 00S 17 00E
Coniston Ontario Canada **93** D3 46 29N 80 51W
Connecticut *state* U.S.A. **93** F2 41 00N 73 00W
Conset Bay Barbados **96** W12 13 10N 59 25W
Con Son *i.* Vietnam **37** C1 8 50N 106 00E
Constanța Romania **75** E1 44 12N 28 40E
Constantine Algeria **112** G10 36 22N 6 40E
Constitución Chile **103** C5 31 05S 57 51W
Contanama Peru **102** B11 7 19S 75 04W
Cook Inlet Alaska U.S.A. **88** E5 60 00N 152 30W
Cook Islands Pacific Ocean **80/81** D3 19 30S 159 50W
Cook, Mount South Island New Zealand **79** B2 43 36S 170 09E
Cook Strait New Zealand **79** B2 41 24S 174 36E
Cooktown Australia **78** H6 15 29S 145 15E
Coolgardie Australia **78** C3 31 01S 121 12E
Cooper Creek Australia **78** F4 28 00S 138 00E
Coosa *r.* U.S.A. **91** I3 33 00N 86 00W
Coos Bay *tn.* Oregon U.S.A. **90** B5 43 23N 124 12W
Copacabana Brazil **103** Q2 22 58S 43 11W
Copacabana Beach Brazil **103** Q2 22 59S 43 11W
Copenhagen *see* København
Copiapó Chile **103** C7 27 20S 70 23W
Copper *r.* Alaska U.S.A. **88** F5 60 30N 144 50W
Copper Cliff *tn.* Ontario Canada **93** D3 46 28N 81 05W
Copper Harbor Michigan U.S.A. **92** C3 47 28N 87 54W
Coppermine Northwest Territories Canada **88** L6 67 49N 115 12W
Coppermine *r.* Northwest Territories Canada **88** M6 67 00N 114 50W
Coquet *r.* England United Kingdom **68** J7 55 20N 1 50W
Coquimbo Chile **103** C7 29 57S 71 25W
Coral Ontario Canada **93** D4 50 13N 81 41W
Coral Harbour *tn.* Northwest Territories Canada **89** S5 64 10N 83 15W
Coral Sea Pacific Ocean **78** I6/J7 15 00S 154 00E
Coral Sea Islands Territory *admin.* Australia **78** I6 17 00S 150 00E
Corantijn *(Courantyne) r.* Surinam **102** F13 4 30N 57 30W
Corbeil-Essonnes France **73** B2 48 36N 2 29E
Cordillera Cantabrica *(Cantabrian Mountains) mts.* Spain **72** A3/B3 43 00N 5 30W
Cordillera Central *mts.* The Philippines **40** B4 17 00N 121 00E
Cordillera de Mérida *mts.* Venezuela **97** J1 8 00N 72 00W
Cordilleras Range The Philippines **40** B3 11 00N 122 00E
Córdoba Argentina **103** E6 31 25S 64 11W
Córdoba Mexico **96** E3 18 55N 96 55W
Córdoba Spain **72** B2 37 53N 4 46W
Cordova Alaska U.S.A. **88** F5 60 29N 145 52W
Corfu *see* Kérkira
Corinth Mississippi U.S.A. **91** I3 34 58N 88 30W
Cork Irish Republic **68** C3 51 54N 8 28W
Çorlu Turkey **74** E3 41 11N 27 48E
Cormeilles-en-Paris France **67** A2 48 58N 2 11E
Corner Brook *tn.* Newfoundland Canada **89** X2 48 58N 57 58W
Corning New York U.S.A. **93** E2 42 10N 77 04W
Cornwall Ontario Canada **93** F3 45 02N 74 45W
Cornwallis Island Northwest Territories Canada **89** Q7 74 40N 97 30W
Coro Venezuela **102** D15 11 20N 70 00W
Coroico Bolivia **102** D9 16 19S 67 45W
Coromandel Coast India **53** E2 12 30N 81 30E
Coromandel Peninsula North Island New Zealand **79** C3 37 00S 175 42E
Coron The Philippines **40** B3 12 02N 120 12E
Coron *i.* The Philippines **40** B3 11 56N 120 14E
Coronation Gulf Northwest Territories Canada **88** M6 68 15N 112 30W
Coronel Pringles Argentina **103** E5 37 56S 61 25W
Corpus Christi Texas U.S.A. **91** G2 27 47N 97 26W
Corrientes Argentina **103** F7 27 30S 58 48W
Corrieverton Guyana **102** F14 5 53N 57 10W
Corse *(Corsica) i.* France **73** C1 42 00N 9 00E
Corsica *see* Corse
Corte Corsica **73** C1 41 18N 9 08E
Cortland New York U.S.A. **93** E2 42 36N 76 10W
Çoruh *r.* Turkey **54** F7 40 45N 40 45E
Corumbá Brazil **102** F9 19 00S 57 35W
Corunna *see* La Coruña
Corvallis Oregon U.S.A. **90** B5 44 34N 123 16W
Corydon Indiana U.S.A. **92** C1 38 12N 86 09W
Cosenza Italy **74** C2 39 17N 16 16E
Cossipore India **52** K2 22 37N 88 23E
Costa Blanca *geog. reg.* Spain **72** B2/C2 38 15N 0 20W
Costa Brava *geog. reg.* Spain **72** C3 41 40N 3 50E
Costa del Sol *geog. reg.* Spain **72** B2 36 40N 4 40W
COSTA RICA 97 H1/2
Cotabato The Philippines **40** B2 7 14N 124 15E
Cotagaita Bolivia **102** D8 20 47S 65 40W
Côteau Québec Canada **93** F3 45 16N 74 16W
Côte D'Azur *geog. reg.* France **73** C1 43 00N 7 00E
CÔTE D'IVOIRE *(IVORY COAST)* **112** D4/E4
Côte d'Or *hills* France **73** B2 47 00N 4 30E
Cotentin *p.* France **60** 49 30N 1 30W
Côtes du Nivernais *plat.* France **73** B2 47 15N 3 20E
Cotonou Benin **112** F4 6 24N 2 31E
Cotopaxi *mt.* Ecuador **102** B12 0 40S 78 28W
Cotswold Hills England United Kingdom **68** I3 51 40N 2 10W
Cottbus Germany **71** B2 51 43N 14 21E
Couesnon *r.* France **73** A2 48 30N 1 40W
Coulommiers France **73** B2 48 49N 3 05E
Council Bluffs Iowa U.S.A. **92** A2 41 14N 95 54W
Courtrai *see* Kortrijk
Couva Trinidad and Tobago **96** T9 10 25N 61 27W
Couva *r.* Trinidad and Tobago **96** T9 10 25N 61 24W
Couvin Belgium **70** D2 50 03N 4 30E
Coventry England United Kingdom **68** J4 52 25N 1 30W
Covilhã Portugal **72** A3 40 17N 7 30W
Covina California U.S.A. **95** C3 34 04N 117 53W
Covington Indiana U.S.A. **92** C2 40 10N 87 23W
Covington Kentucky U.S.A. **93** D1 39 04N 84 30W
Cowan Creek Australia **79** G3 33 36S 151 13E
Cow Bay Phillip Island **81** K2 49 07S 167 56E
Cox's Bazar Bangladesh **53** G4 21 25N 91 59E
Coyote Creek California U.S.A. **95** B2 33 50N 118 05W
Crailsheim Germany **71** B1 49 09N 10 06E
Craiova Romania **75** D1 44 18N 23 47E
Crawfordsville Indiana U.S.A. **92** C2 40 03N 86 54W
Crawley England United Kingdom **68** K3 51 07N 0 12W
Cree *r.* Saskatchewan Canada **88** N4 58 00N 106 30W
Cree Lake Saskatchewan Canada **88** N4 57 30N 106 30W
Creil France **73** B2 49 16N 2 29E
Cremona Italy **74** B4 45 08N 10 01E
Crepeta Vanuatu **83** G8 13 53S 167 30E
Cres *i.* Croatia **74** B3 45 00N 14 00E
Crescent City California U.S.A. **90** B5 41 46N 124 13W
Crescent Island Hong Kong U.K. **51** C3 22 32N 114 19E
Creston Iowa U.S.A. **92** B2 41 04N 94 20W
Crestview Florida U.S.A. **91** I3 30 44N 86 34W
Crete *see* Kriti
Créteil France **67** B2 48 47N 2 28E
Crete, Sea of Mediterranean Sea **74** D2/E2 35 00N 20 00E
Cretin, Cape Papua New Guinea **45** M3 6 40S 147 53E
Creuse *r.* France **73** B2 46 45N 0 45E
Crewe England United Kingdom **68** I5 53 05N 2 27W
Criciúma Brazil **103** H7 28 45S 49 25W
Crimea *see* Krim
CROATIA 74 C3/4
Croker, Cape Australia **44** E1 10 58S 132 36E
Croker Island Australia **44** E1 11 08S 132 33E
Cromwell South Island New Zealand **79** A1 45 03S 169 12E
Cronulla Australia **79** G1 34 04S 151 09E
Crooked Island Hong Kong U.K. **51** C3 22 33N 114 18E
Crooked Island The Bahamas **97** J4 22 45N 74 10W
Crookston Minnesota U.S.A. **92** A3 47 47N 96 36W
Crotone Italy **74** C2 39 05N 17 08E
Crow Peak *mt.* Montana U.S.A. **90** D6 46 19N 111 56W
Crows Nest Australia **79** G2 33 50S 151 12E
Croydon Australia **78** G6 18 10S 142 15E
Croydon *bor.* Greater London England United Kingdom **66** C2 51 23N 0 06W
Crozet Basin Indian Ocean **24** E3/F3 40 00S 55 00E
Cruzeiro do Sul Brazil **102** C11 7 40S 72 39W
Crystal Falls *tn.* Michigan U.S.A. **92** C3 46 06N 88 11W
Cuando *r.* Southern Africa **111** D4 16 00S 21 30E
Cuango *r.* Angola **111** C6 9 00S 18 30E
Cuanza *r.* Angola **111** C6 9 40S 16 00E
CUBA 97 I4
Cubango *r.* Angola **111** C4 17 00S 18 00E
Cúcuta Colombia **102** C14 7 55N 73 31W
Cuddalore India **53** D2 11 43N 79 46E
Cuddapah India **53** D2 14 30N 78 50E
Cuenca Ecuador **102** B12 2 54S 79 00W
Cuenca Spain **72** B3 40 04N 2 07W
Cuernavaca Mexico **96** E3 18 57N 99 15W
Cuiabá Brazil **102** F9 15 32S 56 05W
Cuito *r.* Angola **111** C4 17 30S 19 30E
Cu Lao Thu *i.* Vietnam **37** C2 10 30N 108 59E
Culemborg Netherlands **70** E3 51 58N 5 14E
Culiacán Mexico **96** C4 24 50N 107 23W
Culion *i.* The Philippines **40** A3/B3 12 00N 120 00E
Culver City California U.S.A. **95** A3 34 01N 118 24W
Cumaná Venezuela **102** E15 10 29N 64 12W
Cumberland Maryland U.S.A. **93** E1 39 40N 78 47W
Cumberland *r.* U.S.A. **91** I4 37 00N 86 00W
Cumberland Peninsula Northwest Territories Canada **89** W6 67 00N 65 00W
Cumberland Plateau U.S.A. **91** I4 36 00N 85 00W
Cumberland Sound Northwest Territories Canada **89** V6 65 30N 66 00W
Cumbernauld Scotland United Kingdom **68** H7 55 57N 4 00W
Cumbrian Mountains England United Kingdom **68** H6 54 30N 3 00W
Cumuto Trinidad and Tobago **96** T10 10 25N 61 12W
Cunene *r.* Angola/Namibia **111** B4 17 00S 13 30E
Cuneo Italy **74** A3 44 24N 7 33E
Cung Son Vietnam **37** C2 13 03N 108 59E
Cunnamulla Australia **78** H4 28 04S 145 40E
Cunupia Trinidad and Tobago **96** T10 10 32N 61 22W
Curacautin Chile **103** C5 38 28S 71 52W
Curaçao *i.* Lesser Antilles **97** K2 12 20N 68 20W
Cure *r.* France **73** B2 47 40N 3 40E
Curicó Chile **103** C5 35 00S 71 15W
Curitiba Brazil **103** H7 25 25S 49 25W
Curvelo Brazil **102** I9 18 45S 44 27W
Cuttack India **53** F4 20 26N 85 56E
Cuxhaven Germany **71** A2 53 52N 8 42E
Cuyahoga Falls *tn.* Ohio U.S.A. **93** D2 41 08N 81 27W
Cuyo *i.* The Philippines **40** B3 10 50N 121 02E
Cuyo Islands The Philippines **40** B3 11 00N 121 00E
Cuzco Peru **102** C10 13 32S 1 57W
Cwmbran Wales United Kingdom **68** H3 51 39N 3 00W
Cyclades *see* Kikládes
Cypress Hills Alberta/Saskatchewan Canada **88** N2 48 40N 108 00W
CYPRUS 54 D5
CZECHOSLOVAKIA *now*: CZECH REPUBLIC, SLOVAKIA
CZECH REPUBLIC 75 B2/C2
Częstochowa Poland **75** C3 50 49N 19 07E

D

Daanbantayan The Philippines **40** B3 11 12N 124 00E
Dabola Guinea **112** C5 10 48N 11 02W
Dachau Germany **71** B1 48 15N 11 26E
Dadra & Nagar Haveli *admin.* India **53** C4 20 00N 73 00E
Da Dung *r.* Vietnam **37** C2 11 30N 107 30E
Daet The Philippines **40** B3 14 07N 122 58E
Dafang China **36** D7 26 50N 105 30E
Dafla Hills India **38** A5 27 25N 93 30E
Dagenham England United Kingdom **66** D3 51 33N 0 08E
Dagua Papua New Guinea **45** K5 3 25S 143 20E
Daguan China **38** C5 27 42N 103 59E
Dagupan The Philippines **40** B4 16 02N 120 21E
Da Hinggan Ling *(Greater Khingan Range) mts.* China **49** N8/O9 50 00N 122 00E
Dahlewitz Germany **67** F1 52 19N 13 27E
Dāhod India **53** C4 22 48N 74 18E
Dahongliutan Kashmir **53** D7 35 55N 79 10E
Dahua China **36** D6 23 45N 108 06E
Dahuk Iraq **54** F6 36 52N 43 00E
Dahuni Papua New Guinea **45** N1 10 35S 149 59E
Dai *i.* Solomon Islands **82** F6 7 50S 160 35E
Dai Loc Vietnam **37** C3 16 00N 108 20E
Daiō-zaki *c.* Japan **46** H1 34 16N 136 55E
Dairût Egypt **54** D4 27 34N 30 48E
Dai-sen *mt.* Japan **46** B2 35 23N 133 34E
Dakar Senegal **112** B5 14 38N 17 27W
Dakhla Oasis Egypt **110** E13 26 00N 28 00E
Dala Solomon Islands **82** F5 8 36S 160 41E
Da Lat Vietnam **37** C2 11 56N 108 25E
Dalbandin Pakistan **52** A5 28 56N 64 30E
Dalby Australia **78** I4 27 11S 151 12E
Dalhart Texas U.S.A. **90** F4 36 05N 102 32W
Dali China **38** C5 25 42N 100 12E
Dalian China **49** O6 38 53N 121 37E
Dallas Texas U.S.A. **91** G3 32 47N 96 48W
Dallgow Germany **67** E2 52 32N 13 03E
Daloa Côte d'Ivoire **112** D4 6 56N 6 28W
Dalton Georgia U.S.A. **91** J3 34 46N 84 59W
Dalupiri *i.* The Philippines **40** B4 19 07N 121 14E
Daly *r.* Australia **78** E7 14 00S 132 00E
Daly Waters *tn.* Australia **78** E6 16 13S 133 20E
Daman India **53** C4 20 15N 72 58E
Damanhûr Egypt **54** D5 31 03N 30 28E
Damascus *see* Dimashq
Damāvand Iran **55** H6 35 47N 52 04E
Damāvand *mt.* Iran **55** H6 35 56N 52 08E
Damba Angola **111** C6 6 44S 15 20E
Damietta *see* Dumyât
Damoh India **53** D4 23 50N 79 30E
Dampier Australia **78** B5 20 45S 116 48E
Dampier, Cape Papua New Guinea **45** O3 6 00S 151 00E
Danakil *geog. reg.* Africa **104** 14 00N 40 00E
Da Nang Vietnam **37** C3 16 04N 108 14E
Danao The Philippines **40** B3 10 33N 124 01E
Danau Paniai *i.* Irian Jaya Indonesia **44** G5 3 50S 136 15E
Danau Toba *l.* Indonesia **42** A4 2 30N 98 30E
Danbury Connecticut U.S.A. **93** F2 41 24N 73 26W
Dandong China **49** O7 40 08N 124 24E
Dangori India **53** H5 27 40N 95 35E
Dangrek Range *mts.* Cambodia/Thailand **37** B2 14 00N 103 00E
Danli Honduras **97** G2 14 02N 86 30W
Dannevirke North Island New Zealand **79** C2 40 12S 176 06E
Dansal Papua New Guinea **45** L4 4 42S 145 52E
Danubyu Myanmar **38** B3 17 15N 95 35E
Danville Illinois U.S.A. **92** C2 40 09N 87 37W
Danville Indiana U.S.A. **92** C1 39 44N 86 31W
Danville Kentucky U.S.A. **92** D1 37 40N 84 49W
Danville Pennsylvania U.S.A. **93** E2 40 58N 76 37W
Danville Virginia U.S.A. **91** K4 36 34N 79 25W
Dan Xian China **37** C3 19 34N 109 35E
Dao Cac Ba *i.* Vietnam **37** C4 20 47N 107 00E
Dao Cai Bau *i.* Vietnam **37** C4 21 45N 107 30E
Dao Xian China **36** E7 25 34N 111 26E
Dapitan The Philippines **40** B2 8 39N 123 26E
Dar'ā Syria **54** P11 32 37N 36 06E
Darai Hills Papua New Guinea **45** K3 7 15S 143 45E
Daram *i.* The Philippines **40** B3 11 38N 124 46E
Darap Indonesia **42** D3 2 00S 112 00E
Darapap Papua New Guinea **45** L5 3 49S 144 19E
Darbhanga India **53** F5 26 10N 85 54E
Dardanelles *sd.* Turkey **54** C6 40 08N 26 10E
Dar el Beida *see* Casablanca
Dar es Salaam Tanzania **111** G6 6 51S 39 18E
Dargaville North Island New Zealand **79** B3 35 56S 173 52E
Darjiling India **53** F5 27 02N 88 20E
Darlac Plateau Vietnam **37** C2 13 00N 108 15E
Darling *r.* Australia **78** G3 31 30S 144 00E
Darling Downs *mts.* Australia **78** H4 28 00S 148 30E
Darlington England United Kingdom **68** J6 54 31N 1 34W
Dar Moo-oo Bay Phillip Island **81** L2 29 07S 167 57E
Darmstadt Germany **71** A1 49 52N 8 39E
Darnah Libya **110** D14 32 46N 22 39E
Darnley, Cape Antarctica **21** 67 16S 69 53E
Daroca Spain **72** B3 41 07N 1 25W
Dartford England United Kingdom **66** D2 51 27N 0 13E
Dartmoor *moor* England United Kingdom **68** H2 50 35N 3 50W
Dartmouth Nova Scotia Canada **89** W1 44 40N 63 35W
Dar Tomato Bay Phillip Island **81** K1 29 07S 167 56E
Daru Papua New Guinea **45** K2 9 05S 143 10E
Darwin Australia **78** E7 12 23S 130 44E
Daryācheh-ye Orūmīyeh *(L. Urmia) l.* Iran **55** G6 37 20N 45 55E
Dasht-e-Kavir *geog. reg.* Iran **55** H5/I5 34 30N 54 30E
Dasht-e-Lut *geog. reg.* Iran **55** I5 32 00N 57 00E
Dasht-i-Margo *d.* Afghanistan **55** J5 30 30N 62 30E
Datang China **37** C4 22 22N 108 22E
Datchet England United Kingdom **66** A2 51 30N 0 35W
Datong China **49** M7 40 02N 113 33E
Datong Shan *mts.* China **49** J6/K6 38 00N 99 00E
Datong He *r.* China **49** K6 37 30N 102 00E
Datu Piang The Philippines **40** B2 7 02N 124 30E
Daugavpils Latvia **69** F2 55 52N 26 31E
Daun Germany **70** F2 50 11N 6 50E
Daung Kyun *i.* Myanmar **38** B2 12 14N 98 00E
Dauphin Manitoba Canada **89** P3 51 09N 100 05W
Davangere India **53** D2 14 30N 75 52E
Davao The Philippines **40** C2 7 05N 125 38E
Davao Gulf The Philippines **40** C2 6 00N 126 00E
Davenport Iowa U.S.A. **92** B2 41 32N 90 36W
David Panama **97** H1 8 26N 82 26W
Davis *r.s* Antarctica **21** 68 36S 77 58E
Davis Inlet *tn.* Newfoundland Canada **89** W4 55 51N 60 52W
Davis Sea Antarctica **21** 65 00S 90 00E
Davis Strait Canada/Greenland **89** X6 69 00N 60 00W
Davos Switzerland **73** C2 46 47N 9 50E
Dawna Range *mts.* Myanmar **38** B3 17 10N 98 00E
Dawson Yukon Territory Canada **88** H5 64 04N 139 24W
Dawson Creek *tn.* British Columbia Canada **88** K4 55 44N 120 15W
Dax France **73** A1 43 43N 1 03W
Daxin China **37** C4 22 50N 107 22E
Dayao China **38** C5 25 45N 101 23E
Daying Jiang *r.* China **38** B4 24 45N 98 00E
Dayr az Zawr Syria **54** F6 35 20N 40 02E
Dayton Ohio U.S.A. **93** D1 39 45N 84 10W
Daytona Beach *tn.* Florida U.S.A. **91** J2 29 11N 81 01W
Dazhang Xi *r.* China **51** E8 25 00N 118 00E
De Aar Republic of South Africa **111** D1 30 40S 24 01E
Dead Sea Israel/Jordan **54** O10 31 35N 35 30E
Dean Funes Argentina **103** E6 30 25S 64 22W
Dease *r.* British Columbia Canada **88** J4 58 30N 129 00W
Dease Lake *tn.* British Columbia Canada **88** J4 58 05N 130 04W
Death Valley California U.S.A. **90** C4 36 00N 117 00W
Debao China **37** C4 23 24N 106 44E
Débé Trinidad and Tobago **96** T9 10 12N 61 27W
Debrecen Hungary **75** D2 47 30N 21 37E
Debre Mark'os Ethiopia **110** G10 10 19N 37 41E
Debre Tabor Ethiopia **110** G10 11 50N 38 06E
De Burg Netherlands **70** D5 53 04N 4 46E
Decatur Alabama U.S.A. **91** I3 34 36N 87 00W
Decatur Illinois U.S.A. **92** C1 39 51N 88 57W
Deccan *plat.* India **53** D3 18 00N 78 00E
Déception Québec Canada **89** U5 62 10N 74 45W
Dechang China **38** C5 27 25N 102 17E
Děčín Czech Republic **71** B2 50 48N 14 15E
Dee *r.* England/Wales United Kingdom **68** I4 53 16N 3 10W
Dee *r.* Dumfries & Galloway Scotland United Kingdom **68** G7 54 55N 4 00W
Dee *r.* Grampian Scotland United Kingdom **68** I9 57 05N 2 10W
Deep Bay Hong Kong U.K. **51** A3 22 30N 113 55E
Deep River *tn.* Ontario Canada **93** E3 46 04N 77 29W
Deer Lake *tn.* Newfoundland Canada **89** X2 49 11N 57 27W
Dee Why Australia **79** H2 33 45S 151 17E
Degeh Bur Ethiopia **110** H9 8 11N 43 31E
Dêgên China **38** B5 28 30N 98 59E
Dehra Dun India **53** D6 30 19N 78 03E
Deinze Belgium **70** C2 50 59N 3 32E
Dej Romania **75** D2 47 08N 23 55E
Dekese Zaïre **111** D7 3 28S 21 24E
Delaware Ohio U.S.A. **93** D2 40 18N 83 06W
Delaware *state* U.S.A. **93** E1 39 00N 75 00W
Delaware Bay U.S.A. **93** E1 39 10N 75 10W
Delft Netherlands **70** D4 52 00N 4 22E
Delfzijl Netherlands **70** F5 53 19N 6 56E
Delhi India **53** D5 28 40N 77 14E
Delhi Cantonment India **52** L4 28 35N 77 08E
Delicias Mexico **90** E2 28 10N 105 30W
Delitzsch Germany **71** B2 51 32N 12 20E
Dellen *l.* Sweden **69** D3 61 50N 16 45E
Dellys Algeria **72** C2 36 57N 3 55E
Delmenhorst Germany **71** A2 53 03N 8 37E
De Long Mountains Alaska U.S.A. **88** C6 68 30N 162 00W
Del Rio Texas U.S.A. **90** F2 29 23N 100 56W
Delta Colorado U.S.A. **90** E4 38 42N 108 04W
Dembī Dolo Ethiopia **110** F9 8 34N 34 50E
Demer *r.* Belgium **70** D3 51 02N 4 52E
Deming New Mexico U.S.A. **90** E3 32 17N 107 46W
Demta Irian Jaya Indonesia **44** J5 2 22S 140 06E
Denain France **73** B3 50 19N 3 24E
Den Chai Thailand **39** B3 18 00N 100 06E
Dendang Indonesia **42** C3 3 06S 107 52E
Dender *r.* Belgium **70** C2 50 50N 3 55E
Dendermonde Belgium **70** D3 51 02N 4 06E
Dengchuan China **38** C5 25 59N 100 09E
Den Haag *(The Hague) see* 's-Gravenhage
Den Helder Netherlands **70** D4 52 58N 4 46E
Denigomodu Nauru **83** L2 0 31S 166 54E
Denison Iowa U.S.A. **92** A2 42 01N 95 20W
Denison Texas U.S.A. **91** G3 33 47N 96 34W
Denizli Turkey **54** C6 37 46N 29 05E
Denman Glacier Antarctica **21** 67 00S 100 00E
DENMARK 69 B2
Denmark Strait Greenland/Iceland **89** DD6 67 00N 26 00W
Denpasar Indonesia **42** R6 8 40S 115 14E
Denton Texas U.S.A. **91** G3 33 14N 97 18W
D'Entrecasteaux Islands Papua New Guinea **45** O2 9 15S 150 45E
Denver Colorado U.S.A. **90** E4 39 45N 105 00W
Deodora Brazil **103** P2 22 51S 43 22W
De Panne Belgium **70** B3 51 06N 2 35E
Dépression du Mourdi *dep.* Chad **110** D11 17 00N 22 41E
Deputatskiy Russia **57** P9 69 15N 139 59E
Dera Ghazi Khan Pakistan **53** C6 30 05N 70 44E
Dera Ismail Khan Pakistan **53** C6 31 51N 70 56E
Derbent Russia **58** F3 42 03N 48 18E
Derby Australia **78** C6 17 19S 123 38E
Derby England United Kingdom **68** J4 52 55N 1 30W
Desē Ethiopia **110** G10 11 05N 39 40E
Deseado Argentina **103** D3 47 44S 65 56W
Desierto de Atacama *(Atacama Desert) d.* Chile **102/103** C8 22 30S 70 00W
Des Moines Iowa U.S.A. **92** B2 41 35N 93 35W
Des Moines *r.* Iowa U.S.A. **92** B2 41 00N 92 00W
Desna *r.* Europe **56** F6 52 00N 32 30E
Dessau Germany **71** B2 51 51N 12 15E
Desvres France **70** A2 50 40N 1 50E
Detmold Germany **71** A2 51 55N 8 52E
Detroit Michigan U.S.A. **93** D2 42 23N 83 05W
Detroit Lakes *tn.* Minnesota U.S.A. **92** A3 46 49N 95 49W
Detroit River North America **93** D2 42 00N 83 00W
Det Udom Thailand **39** C2 14 54N 105 05E
Deurne Netherlands **70** E3 51 28N 5 47E
Deva Romania **75** D2 45 53N 22 55E
Deventer Netherlands **70** F4 52 15N 6 10E
Deveron *r.* Scotland United Kingdom **68** I9 57 25N 3 03W
Devils Gate Reservoir California U.S.A. **95** B3 34 11N 118 10W
Devil's Lake *tn.* North Dakota U.S.A. **92** A3 48 03N 98 57W
Devon Island Northwest Territories Canada **89** R8 75 10N 85 00W
Devonport Australia **78** H1 41 09S 146 16E
Dezfūl Iran **55** G5 32 23N 48 28E
Dezhou China **49** N6 37 29N 116 11E
Dhaka Bangladesh **53** G4 23 42N 90 22E
Dhamār Yemen Republic **54** F1 14 33N 44 30E
Dhanbad India **53** F4 23 47N 86 32E
Dharoor *r.* Somalia **110** I10 10 00N 54 00E
Dhārwād India **53** D3 15 30N 75 04E
Dhodhekánisos *(Dodecanese) is.* Greece **74** E2 37 00N 26 00E
Dhoraji India **52** C4 21 42N 70 32E
Dhule India **53** C4 20 52N 74 50E

Golfo del Darién g. Colombia/Panama 97 I1 9 00N 77 00W
Golfo de Panamá g. Panama 97 I1 8 00N 79 00W
Golfo de San Jorge g. Argentina 103 D3 47 00S 66 00W
Golfo de Tehuantepec g. Mexico 96 E3/F3 15 30N 95 00W
Golfo de Venezuela g. Venezuela 102 C15 12 00N 71 30W
Golfo di Cágliari g. Italy 74 A2 39 00N 9 00E
Golfo di Catania g. Italy 74 C2 37 30N 15 20E
Golfo di Gaeta g. Italy 74 B3 41 00N 13 00E
Golfo di Genova g. Italy 74 A3 44 00N 9 00E
Golfo di Squillace g. Italy 74 C2 38 30N 17 00E
Golfo di Taranto g. Italy 74 C2/3 40 00N 17 00E
Golfo di Venezia Adriatic Sea 74 B4 45 00N 13 00E
Golfo San Matías g. Argentina 103 E4 42 00S 64 00W
Golmud China 48 H6 36 22N 94 55E
Golo r. Corsica 73 C1 42 30N 9 10E
Golok Thailand 39 B1 6 00N 101 56E
Gomel' Belarus 75 F3 52 25N 31 00E
Gomera i. Canary Islands 112 B8 28 08N 17 14W
Gómez Palacio Mexico 96 D5 25 39N 103 30W
Gonder Ethiopia 110 G10 12 39N 37 29E
Gondia India 53 E4 21 23N 80 14E
Gonesse France 67 B2 48 59N 2 27E
Gongshan China 38 B5 27 46N 98 42E
Gongwan Shan mts. China 38 C5 25 30N 103 00E
Goodenough Island Papua New Guinea 45 O2 9 15S 150 30E
Good Hope, Cape of Republic of South Africa 111 C1 34 30S 19 00E
Goodland Kansas U.S.A. 90 F4 39 20N 101 43W
Goondiwindi Australia 78 I4 28 30S 150 17E
Goose Green tn. Falkland Islands 25 M16 51 52S 59 00W
Göppingen Germany 71 A1 48 43N 9 39E
Gora Kamen' mt. Russia 57 L9 69 06N 94 59E
Gorakhpur India 53 E5 26 45N 83 23E
Gora Narodnaya mt. Russia 57 I9 65 02N 60 01E
Gora Pobeda mt. Russia 57 Q9 65 10N 146 00E
Gora Telposiz mt. Russia 59 H7 63 59N 59 02E
Gorda Rise Pacific Ocean 23 M12/N12 43 00N 130 00W
Gordon Australia 79 G2 33 46S 151 09E
Gordon Landing tn. Yukon Territory Canada 88 H5 63 38N 135 27W
Gorē Ethiopia 110 G9 8 10N 35 29E
Gore South Island New Zealand 79 A1 46 06S 168 56E
Gore Bay tn. Ontario Canada 93 D3 45 54N 82 28W
Gorgān Iran 55 H6 36 50N 54 29E
Gorinchem Netherlands 70 D3 51 50N 4 59E
Gorizia Italy 74 B4 45 57N 13 37E
Gorkiy Park Russia 56 M1 55 44N 37 37E
Görlitz Germany 71 B2 51 09N 15 00E
Gorlovka Ukraine 58 D4 48 17N 38 05E
Gorno-Altaysk Russia 59 O5 51 59N 85 56E
Goroka Papua New Guinea 45 L3 6 02S 145 22E
Gorong i. Indonesia 43 H3 4 15S 131 20E
Gorontalo Indonesia 43 F4 0 33N 123 05E
Gorzów Wielkopolski Poland 75 C3 52 42N 15 12E
Goslar Germany 71 B2 51 55N 10 25E
Gostivar Macedonia (Former Yugoslav Republic) 74 D3 41 47N 20 55E
Göta älv r. Sweden 69 C2 58 00N 12 00E
Göteborg Sweden 69 C2 57 45N 12 00E
Gotemba Japan 46 K2 35 20N 138 58E
Gotha Germany 71 B2 50 57N 10 43E
Gotland i. Sweden 69 D2 57 30N 18 40E
Gotō-rettō i. Japan 50 D1 32 45N 128 45E
Göttingen Germany 71 A2 51 32N 9 57E
Gottwaldov see Zlúi
Gouda Netherlands 70 D4 52 00N 4 42E
Gough Island Atlantic Ocean 25 H2 40 20S 10 00W
Goulburn Australia 78 H3 34 47S 149 43E
Gourde, Point Trinidad and Tobago 96 S10 10 40N 61 36W
Gouré Niger 112 H5 13 59N 10 15E
Goussainville France 67 B3 49 02N 2 28E
Governador Valadares Brazil 102 I9 18 51S 41 57W
Governor's Harbour The Bahamas 91 K2 25 20N 76 20W
Gozo i. Malta 74 B2 35 00N 14 00E
Gracefield Québec Canada 93 E3 46 05N 76 05W
Grafton Australia 78 I4 29 40S 152 56E
Grafton West Virginia U.S.A. 93 D1 39 21N 80 03W
Graham Texas U.S.A. 90 G3 33 07N 98 36W
Graham Island British Columbia Canada 88 I3 53 50N 133 00W
Graham Land geog. reg. Antarctica 21 67 00S 64 00W
Grahamstown Republic of South Africa 111 E1 33 18S 26 32E
Grampian Mountains Scotland United Kingdom 68 G8/H8 56 45N 4 00W
Granada Nicaragua 97 G2 11 58N 85 59W
Granada Spain 72 B2 37 10N 3 35W
Granby Québec Canada 93 F3 45 23N 72 44W
Gran Canaria i. Canary Islands 112 B8 28 00N 15 35W
Gran Chaco geog. reg. Argentina 103 E8 25 00S 62 30W
Gran Couva Trinidad and Tobago 96 T9 10 24N 61 23W
Grand r. U.S.A. 92 B1 40 00N 94 00W
Grand r. South Dakota U.S.A. 90 F6 46 00N 102 00W
Grand Bahama i. The Bahamas 97 I5 27 00N 78 00W
Grand Banks Atlantic Ocean 84 47 00N 47 00W
Grand Beach tn. Manitoba Canada 92 A4 50 34N 96 38W
Grand Canal see Yun
Grand Canyon U.S.A. 90 D4 36 04N 112 07W
Grand Canyon National Park Arizona/Nevada U.S.A. 90 D4 34 00N 114 00W
Grand Canyon Village Arizona U.S.A. 90 D4 36 02N 112 09W
Grand Cayman i. Caribbean Sea 97 H3 19 20N 81 15W
Grand Coulee Dam Washington U.S.A. 90 C6 47 59N 118 58W
Grande Cache Alberta Canada 88 L3 53 50N 118 30W
Grande Prairie tn. Alberta Canada 88 L4 55 10N 118 52W
Grand Erg Occidental geog. reg. Algeria 112 F9 30 35N 0 30E
Grand Erg Oriental geog. reg. Algeria 112 G9 30 15N 6 45E
Grande Rivière tn. Trinidad and Tobago 96 T10 10 50N 61 03W
Grande Rivière de la Balein r. Québec Canada 89 T4 55 15N 77 00W
Grande Terre i. Lesser Antilles 97 L3 17 00N 61 40W
Grand Falls tn. New Brunswick Canada 89 V2 47 02N 67 46W
Grand Forks North Dakota U.S.A. 92 A3 47 57N 97 05W
Grand Haven Michigan U.S.A. 92 C2 43 04N 86 13W
Grand Island tn. Nebraska U.S.A. 91 G5 40 56N 98 21W
Grand Junction tn. Colorado U.S.A. 90 E4 39 04N 108 33W
Grand Lake Newfoundland Canada 89 X2 49 00N 57 20W
Grand Marias Minnesota U.S.A. 92 B3 47 45N 90 20W
Grand Passage New Caledonia 82 S5 18 45S 163 20E
Grand Rapids tn. Manitoba Canada 89 P3 53 12N 99 19W
Grand Rapids tn. Michigan U.S.A. 92 C2 42 57N 86 40W
Grand Rapids tn. Minnesota U.S.A. 92 B3 47 13N 93 31W
Grand Récif de Cook reef New Caledonia 82 S4 19 30S 163 50E
Grand Récif de Koumac reef New Caledonia 82 S3 20 30S 164 00E
Grand Récif Mathieu reef New Caledonia 82 T3 20 50S 164 15E
Grand Récif Mengalia reef New Caledonia 82 U3 20 40S 165 15E
Grand Récif Sud reef New Caledonia 82 V1 22 45S 166 50E
Grand Traverse Bay Michigan U.S.A. 92 C2 45 00N 85 00W
Grand Union Canal England United Kingdom 66 B3 51 37N 0 29W
Grane Norway 69 C4 65 35N 13 25E
Grange Hill tn. Jamaica 97 P8 18 19N 78 11W
Granite City Illinois U.S.A. 92 B1 38 43N 90 04W
Granite Falls tn. Minnesota U.S.A. 92 A2 44 49N 95 31W
Granite Peak Montana U.S.A. 90 E6 45 10N 109 50W
Grants Pass tn. Oregon U.S.A. 90 B5 42 26N 123 20W
Granville France 73 A2 48 50N 1 35W
Granville Lake Manitoba Canada 89 O4 56 00N 101 00W
Grasse France 73 C1 43 40N 5 56E
Grass Island Hong Kong U.K. 51 D2 22 29N 114 22E
Grassy Hill mt. Hong Kong U.K. 51 B2 22 25N 114 10E
Gravelbourg Saskatchewan Canada 88 N2 49 53N 106 33W
Gravelines France 70 B2 50 59N 2 08E
Gravenhurst Ontario Canada 93 E2 44 55N 79 22W
Gravesend New York U.S.A. 94 C1 40 36N 73 58W
Gray France 73 C2 47 27N 5 35E
Grayling Michigan U.S.A. 93 D2 44 40N 84 43W
Grays Thurrock England United Kingdom 66 D2 51 29N 0 20E
Graz Austria 75 C2 47 05N 15 22E
Great Abaco i. The Bahamas 97 I5 26 40N 77 00W
Great Astrolabe Reef Fiji 83 C8 18 45S 178 30E
Great Australian Bight b. Australia 78 D3/E3 33 00S 130 00E
Great Barrier Island North Island New Zealand 79 C3 36 13S 175 24E
Great Barrier Reef Australia 78 G7/I5 15 00S 146 00E
Great Basin Nevada U.S.A. 90 C4 40 00N 117 00W
Great Bear Lake Northwest Territories Canada 88 K6 66 00N 120 00W
Great Bend Kansas U.S.A. 90 G4 38 22N 98 47W
Great Bitter Lake see Buheirat-Murrat-el-Kubra
Great Bookham England United Kingdom 66 B2 51 16N 0 21W
Great Coco Island Myanmar 38 A2 14 10N 93 25E
Great Dividing Range mts. Australia 78 G7/H2
Greater Antilles is. West Indies 97 H4/K3
Greater Khingan Range see Da Hinggan Ling
Greater London admin. England United Kingdom 66 C3 51 30N 0 10W
Great Exuma i. The Bahamas 97 I4 23 30N 76 00W
Great Falls tn. Montana U.S.A. 90 D6 47 30N 111 16W
Great Inagua i. The Bahamas 97 J4 21 40N 73 00W
Great Karoo mts. Republic of South Africa 111 D1 32 30S 22 30E
Great Lakes North America 84 45 00N 90 00W
Great Nicobar i. Nicobar Islands 53 G1 6 30N 94 00E
Great North East Channel Australia 45 K2 9 50S 143 00E
Great Oasis, The geog. reg. Egypt 54 D3 25 00N 30 30E
Great Ouse r. England United Kingdom 68 K4 52 30N 0 20E
Great Pedro Bluff c. Jamaica 97 Q7 17 51N 77 45W
Great Salt Lake Utah U.S.A. 90 D5 41 10N 112 40W
Great Sand Sea Sahara Desert 110 D13/E13 27 00N 25 00E
Great Sandy Desert Australia 78 C5/D5 21 00S 124 00E
Great Sea Reef Fiji 83 C10/D10 16 10S 179 00E
Great Slave Lake Northwest Territories Canada 88 M5 62 00N 114 00W
Great Victoria Desert Australia 78 D4/E4 28 00S 130 00E
Great Wall China 49 M6 40 00N 111 00E
Great Wall (Chang Cheng) r.s. Antarctica 21 62 13S 58 58W
Great Yarmouth England United Kingdom 68 M4 52 37N 1 44E
Great Zab r. Iraq 58 E2 36 00N 44 00E
GREECE 74 D2/E3
Greeley Colorado U.S.A. 90 F5 40 26N 104 43W
Green r. U.S.A. 90 D5 42 00N 110 00W
Green r. Kentucky U.S.A. 92 C1 37 00N 87 00W
Green Bay Wisconsin U.S.A. 92 C2/3 45 00N 87 00W
Green Bay tn. Wisconsin U.S.A. 92 C2 44 32N 88 00W
Greenbrier r. West Virginia U.S.A. 93 E1 38 00N 80 00W
Greenfield Massachusetts U.S.A. 93 F2 42 36N 72 37W
Green Island Hong Kong U.K. 51 B1 22 17N 114 06E
Green Islands Papua New Guinea 45 Q4 4 30S 154 15E
GREENLAND 89 AA6
Greenland Basin Atlantic Ocean 25 H13 72 00N 0 00
Greenland Sea Arctic Ocean 20 76 00N 5 00W
Green Mountains Vermont U.S.A. 93 F2 43 00N 73 00W
Greenock Scotland United Kingdom 68 G7 55 57N 4 45W
Greensboro North Carolina U.S.A. 91 K4 36 03N 79 50W
Greenville Liberia 112 D3 5 01N 9 03W
Greenville Maine U.S.A. 93 G3 45 28N 69 36W
Greenville Mississippi U.S.A. 91 H3 33 23N 91 03W
Greenville Ohio U.S.A. 93 D2 40 06N 84 37W
Greenville South Carolina U.S.A. 91 J3 34 52N 82 25W
Greenville Texas U.S.A. 91 G3 33 09N 97 06W
Greenwich bor. England United Kingdom 66 C2 51 29N 0 00
Greenwood Mississippi U.S.A. 91 H3 33 31N 90 10W
Greifswald Germany 71 B2 54 06N 13 24E
Greiz Germany 71 B2 50 40N 12 11E
GRENADA 97 L2
Grenchen Switzerland 73 C2 47 13N 7 24E
Grenoble France 73 C2 45 11N 5 43E
Gresik Indonesia 42 Q7 7 12S 112 38E
Grevenbroich Germany 71 A2 51 06N 6 36E
Greymouth South Island New Zealand 79 B2 42 27S 171 12E
Grey Range mts. Australia 78 G4 27 00S 144 00E
Griffin Georgia U.S.A. 91 J3 33 15N 84 17W
Grimsby England United Kingdom 68 K5 53 35N 0 05W
Grimsey i. Iceland 69 I7 66 33N 18 00W
Grodno Belarus 75 D3 53 40N 23 50E
Gronau Germany 70 G4 52 13N 7 02E
Groningen Netherlands 70 F5 53 13N 6 35E
Groningen admin. Netherlands 70 F5 53 30N 6 45E
Grønnedal Greenland 89 Z5 61 20N 48 00W
Groote Eylandt i. Australia 78 F7 14 00S 137 00E
Grootfontein Namibia 111 C4 19 32S 18 05E
Grossbeeren Germany 67 F1 52 20N 13 19E
Grosser Müggelsee l. Germany 67 G1 52 26N 13 39E
Grosser Zernsee l. Germany 67 D1 52 22N 12 57E
Grosseto Italy 74 B3 42 46N 11 07E
Groß Glockner mt. Austria 75 B2 47 05N 12 44E
Groundhog r. Ontario Canada 93 D3 49 00N 82 00W
Groznyy Russia 56 G4 43 21N 45 42E
Grudziądz Poland 75 C3 53 29N 18 45E
Guadalajara Mexico 96 D4 20 40N 103 20W
Guadalajara Spain 72 B3 40 37N 3 10W
Guadalcanal Solomon Islands 82 E4/F4 9 30S 160 00E
Guadalhorce r. Spain 72 B2 36 45N 4 45W
Guadalope r. Spain 72 B3 40 50N 0 30W
Guadalquivir r. Spain 72 A2 37 45N 5 30W
Guadalupe Brazil 103 P2 22 50S 43 23W
Guadalupe i. Mexico 96 A5 29 00N 118 24W
Guadeloupe i. Lesser Antilles 97 L3 16 30N 61 30W
Guadiana r. Portugal 72 A2 38 30N 7 30W
Guadix Spain 72 B2 37 19N 3 08W
Guaico Trinidad and Tobago 96 T10 10 35N 61 09W
Guajará Mirim Brazil 102 D10 10 50S 65 21W
GUAM 80 B4
Guamúchil Mexico 96 C5 25 28N 108 10W
Guanabara Bay Brazil 103 Q2/3 22 45S 43 10W
Guanare Venezuela 97 K1 9 04N 69 45W
Guang'anmen China 47 G1 39 40N 116 20E
Guangdong admin. China 37 C4 20 00N 110 00E
Guangxi admin. China 37 C4 23 00N 108 00E
Guangzhou (Canton) China 49 M3 23 08N 113 20E
Guantánamo Cuba 97 I4 20 09N 75 14W
Guapo Bay Trinidad and Tobago 96 S9 10 12N 61 40W
Guaqui Bolivia 102 D9 16 38S 68 50W
Guarapuava Brazil 103 G7 25 22S 51 28W
Guarda Portugal 72 A3 40 32N 7 17W
Guardiana r. Spain 72 B2 39 00N 4 00W
Guari Papua New Guinea 45 M2 8 06S 146 53E
Guasave Mexico 90 E2 25 33N 108 30W
Guasdualito Venezuela 102 C14 7 15N 70 40W
Guasopa Papua New Guinea 45 P2 9 15S 152 59E
GUATEMALA 96 F3
Guatemala Guatemala 96 F2 14 38N 90 22W
Guatemala Basin Pacific Ocean 23 Q9 12 00N 95 00W
Guatuaro Point Trinidad and Tobago 96 U9 10 20N 60 58W
Guayaguayare Trinidad and Tobago 96 T9 10 09N 61 01W
Guayaguayare Bay Trinidad and Tobago 96 T9 10 07N 61 03W
Guayaquil Ecuador 102 A12 2 13S 79 54W
Guaymas Mexico 96 B5 27 59W 110 54W
Gubin Poland 71 B2 51 59N 14 43E
Gudbrandsdalen v. Norway 69 B3 62 00N 58 50E
Gudong China 38 B5 25 20N 98 20E
Gudri r. Pakistan 52 A5 26 00N 64 00E
Guelph Ontario Canada 93 D2 43 34N 80 16W
Guéret France 73 B2 46 10N 1 52E
Guernsey i. Channel Isles British Isles 68 I1 46 27N 2 35W
Guia de Pacobaiba Brazil 103 Q3 22 42S 43 10W
Guiana Highlands South America 98 4 00N 60 00W
Guildford England United Kingdom 66 A1 51 14N 0 35W
Guilin China 49 M4 25 21N 110 11E
Guimarães Portugal 72 A3 41 26N 8 19W
Guimaras i. The Philippines 40 B3 10 00N 122 00E
GUINEA 112 C5
Guinea Basin Atlantic Ocean 25 H6/7 1 00N 8 00W
GUINEA-BISSAU 112 B5/C5
Guinea, Gulf of 108 E8 3 50N 3 00W
Güines Cuba 97 H4 22 50N 82 02W
Guînes France 70 A2 50 51N 1 52E
Guiping China 36 E6 23 40N 105 10E
Güiria Venezuela 102 E15 10 37N 62 21W
Guiuan The Philippines 40 C3 11 02N 125 44E
Gui Xian China 36 D6 24 00N 109 45E
Guiyang China 49 L4 26 35N 106 40E
Gujarat admin. India 53 C4 23 20N 72 00E
Gujing China 38 C5 25 29N 103 51E
Gujranwala Pakistan 53 C6 32 06N 74 11E
Gulang China 38 B5 26 02N 98 39E
Gulbarga India 53 D3 17 22N 76 47E
Gul Basin Singapore 41 B3 1 18N 103 40E
Gulfport Mississippi U.S.A. 91 I3 30 21N 80 08W
Gulf, The Middle East 55 H4 27 20N 51 00E
Gullivare Sweden 69 E4 67 08N 20 25E
Gulu Uganda 110 F8 2 46N 32 21E
Gumma pref. Japan 46 K3 36 10N 138 27E
Gummersbach Germany 71 A2 51 02N 7 34E
Gunnison r. Colorado U.S.A. 90 E4 38 00N 107 00W
Guntersville, Lake Alabama U.S.A. 91 I3 34 00N 86 00W
Guntur India 53 E3 16 20N 80 27E
Gunung Agung mt. Indonesia 42 8 25S 115 28E
Gunungapi i. Indonesia 44 B3 6 37S 126 38E
Gunung Argopuro mt. Indonesia 42 Q7 7 58S 113 33E
Gunung Binaija mt. Indonesia 44 C5 3 15S 129 25E
Gunung Kerinci mt. Indonesia 42 B3 1 43S 101 15E
Gunung Kinabalu mt. Malaysia 42 E5 6 03N 116 32E
Gunung Lawu mt. Indonesia 42 P7 7 40S 111 13E
Gunung Leuser mt. Indonesia 42 A4 3 46N 97 12E
Gunung Liman mt. Indonesia 42 P7 7 48S 111 5E
Gunung Mekongga mt. Indonesia 43 F3 4 00S 122 00E
Gunung Merapi mt. Indonesia 42 B3 0 20S 100 26E
Gunung Nokilalaki mt. Indonesia 43 F3 1 16S 120 18E
Gunung Ogoamas mt. Indonesia 43 F4 0 39N 120 16E
Gunung Patuha mt. Indonesia 42 N7 7 12S 101 17E
Gunung Raung mt. Indonesia 42 R6 8 07S 114 03E
Gunung Semeru mt. Indonesia 42 Q6 8 05S 112 50E
Gunungsitoli Indonesia 42 A4 1 16N 97 34E
Gunung Slamet mt. Indonesia 42 O7 7 14S 109 10E
Gunung Sumbing mt. Indonesia 42 P7 7 23S 110 02E
Gunung Tahan mt. Malaysia 42 B4 4 38N 102 14E
Gunung Trus Madi mt. Malaysia 40 A2 5 34N 116 29E
Gurig National Park Australia 44 E1 11 20S 132 00E
Gusau Nigeria 108 G10 12 12N 6 40E
Güstrow Germany 71 B2 53 48N 12 11E
Gütersloh Germany 71 A2 51 54N 8 22E
Guthrie Oklahoma U.S.A. 91 G4 35 53N 97 26W
GUYANA 102 F13
Guyandotte r. West Virginia U.S.A. 93 D1 38 00N 82 00W
Gwalior India 53 D5 26 12N 78 09E
Gweru Zimbabwe 111 E4 19 27S 29 49E
Gyandzha (Kirovabad) Azerbaijan 58 F3 40 39N 46 20E
Gyangze China 53 F5 28 53N 89 35E
Gyaring Co l. China 53 F6 31 05N 88 00E
Gyda Peninsula Russia 57 J10 70 00N 77 30E
Gympie Australia 78 I4 26 10S 152 35E
Gyōda Japan 46 L3 36 10N 139 27E
Gyöngyös Hungary 75 D2 47 46N 20 00E
Györ Hungary 75 C2 47 41N 17 40E

H

Ha'afeva l. Tonga 83 B3 19 55S 174 44W
Haaksbergen Netherlands 70 F4 52 09N 6 45E
Ha'ano i. Tonga 83 B3 19 40S 174 16W
Ha'apai Group is. Pacific Ocean 80 D3 19 58S 176 00W
Haapiti Tahiti 82 R9 17 33S 149 52W
Haapsalu Estonia 69 E2 58 58N 23 32E
Haarlem Netherlands 70 D4 52 23N 4 39E
Haast Pass South Island New Zealand 79 A2 44 06S 169 21E
Hab r. Pakistan 52 B5 25 00N 67 00E
Habbān Yemen Republic 55 G1 14 21N 47 04E
Haboro Japan 46 D3 44 23N 141 43E
Hachinohe Japan 46 D3 40 30N 141 30E
Hachioji Japan 46 L2 35 40N 139 20E
Hackensack New Jersey U.S.A. 94 B2/C2 40 53N 74 01W
Hackensack River New Jersey U.S.A. 94 B2 40 47N 74 06W
Hackney bor. Greater London England United Kingdom 66 C3 51 33N 0 03W
Ha Coi Vietnam 37 C4 21 25N 107 45E
Hadano Japan 46 L2 35 25N 139 10E
Hadejia Nigeria 112 H5 12 30N 10 03E
Hadejia r. Nigeria 112 G5 4 10N 9 30E
Hadera Israel 54 O11 32 26N 34 55E
Hadhramaut geog. reg. Yemen Republic 55 G2 15 40N 47 30E
Hadīboh Yemen Republic 55 H1 12 36N 53 59E
Ha Dong Vietnam 37 C4 20 58N 105 46E
Haeju North Korea 50 B4 38 04N 125 40E
Haenam South Korea 50 C2 34 35N 126 35E
Hafnafjördur Iceland 69 H6 64 04N 21 58W
Hagen Germany 71 A2 51 22N 7 27E
Hagerstown Maryland U.S.A. 93 E1 39 39N 77 44W
Hagi Japan 50 E2 34 25N 131 22E
Ha Giang Vietnam 37 B4 22 50N 104 58E
Hagondange France 73 C2 49 16N 6 11E
Haguenau France 73 C2 48 49N 7 47E
Haidian China 47 G1 39 59N 116 21E
Hai Duong Vietnam 37 C4 20 56N 106 21E
Haifa Israel 54 O11 32 49N 34 59E
Haikou China 49 M3 20 05N 110 25E
Hā'il Saudi Arabia 54 F4 27 31N 41 45E
Hailar China 49 N8 49 15N 119 41E
Hailuoto i. Finland 69 E3 65 01N 24 45E
Hainan admin. China 37 C3 18 50N 110 00E
Hainan Dao i. China 49 L2/M2 18 50N 109 50E
Hainan Strait see Qiongzhou Haixia
Hainaut admin. Belgium 70 C2/D2 50 30N 4 00E
Haines Alaska U.S.A. 88 H4 59 11N 135 23W
Haines Junction Yukon Territory Canada 88 H5 60 45N 137 21W
Haiphong Vietnam 37 C4 20 50N 106 41E
HAITI 97 J3
Haitou China 37 C3 19 34N 109 03E
Haiyuan China 37 C4 22 10N 107 35E
Haka Myanmar 38 A4 22 42N 93 41E
Hakodate Japan 46 D3 41 46N 140 44E
Hakusan Japan 46 H1 34 38N 136 20E
Halab (Aleppo) Syria 54 E6 36 14N 37 10E
Halaib Sudan 110 G12 22 12N 36 35E
Halawa, Cape Hawaiian Islands 23 Y18 21 09N 157 15W
Halba Lebanon 54 P12 34 33N 36 04E
Halberstadt Germany 71 B2 51 54N 11 04E
Halcon, Mount The Philippines 40 B3 13 16N 120 59E
Halifax Nova Scotia Canada 89 W1 44 38N 63 35W
Halishahar India 52 K3 22 55N 88 25E
Halla San mt. South Korea 50 C1 33 25N 126 30E
Halle Belgium 70 D2 50 44N 4 14E
Halle Germany 71 B2 51 28N 11 58E
Halley r.s. Antarctica 21 75 35S 26 15W
Hall Peninsula Northwest Territories Canada 89 V5 68 40N 66 00W
Halls Creek tn. Australia 78 D6 18 17S 127 38E
Halmahera i. Indonesia 43 G4 0 30S 127 00E
Halmahera Sea Indonesia 43 G3 0 15S 128 30E
Halmstad Sweden 56 C2 56 41N 12 55E
Haltern Germany 70 G3 51 45N 7 10E
Halvø (Hayes) p. Greenland 89 V8 76 00N 67 30W
Hamada Japan 46 B1 34 56N 132 04E
Hamadān Iran 55 G5 34 46N 48 35E
Hamāh Syria 54 E6 35 10N 36 45E
Hamamatsu Japan 46 C1 34 42N 137 42E
Hamar Norway 56 C3 60 57N 10 55E
Hamburg Germany 71 B2 53 33N 10 00E
Hamburg Iowa U.S.A. 92 A2 40 36N 95 40W
Hamburg Pennsylvania U.S.A. 93 E2 40 33N 75 59W
Hamburg admin. Germany 71 A2/B2 53 00N 10 00E
Hamden Connecticut U.S.A. 93 F2 41 23N 72 55W
Hämeenlinna Finland 69 E3 61 00N 24 25E
Hameln Germany 71 A2 52 07N 9 22E
Hamersley Range mts. Australia 78 B5 22 00S 117 00E
Hamgyŏng-Sanmaek mts. North Korea 50 D5 41 00N 129 00E
Hamhŭng North Korea 50 C4 39 54N 127 35E
Hami (Kumul) China 48 H7 42 37N 93 32E

Hamilton Ontario Canada 93 E2 43 15N 79 50W
Hamilton North Island New Zealand 79 C3 37 47S 175 17E
Hamilton Ohio U.S.A. 93 D1 39 23N 84 33W
Hamilton Inlet Newfoundland Canada 89 X3 54 18N 57 42W
Hamm Germany 71 A2 51 40N 7 49E
Hammerdal Sweden 69 D3 63 35N 15 20E
Hammerfest Norway 69 E5 70 40N 23 44E
Hammersmith bor. England United Kingdom 66 C2 51 30N 0 14W
Hamminkeln Germany 70 F3 51 43N 6 36E
Hammond Indiana U.S.A. 92 C2 41 36N 87 30W
Hampstead Heath England United Kingdom 66 C3 51 34N 0 10W
Hampton Virginia U.S.A. 93 E1 37 02N 76 23W
Ham Tan Vietnam 37 C2 10 39N 107 47E
Hamuku Irian Jaya Indonesia 44 F5 3 23S 135 09E
Hanazono Japan 46 G1 34 09N 135 31E
Hancock New York U.S.A. 93 E2 41 58N 75 17W
Handa Japan 46 H1 34 52N 136 57E
Handan China 49 M6 36 35N 114 31E
Hang Ha Po Hong Kong U.K. 51 B2 22 27N 114 08E
Hang Hau Hong Kong U.K. 51 C1 22 18N 114 16E
Hang Hau Tsuen Hong Kong U.K. 51 A2 22 28N 113 59E
Hango Finland 69 E2 50 50N 23 00E
Hangzhou China 49 O5 30 18N 120 07E
Hanna Alberta Canada 88 M3 51 38N 111 56W
Hannibal Missouri U.S.A. 92 B1 39 41N 91 20W
Hanno Japan 46 L2 35 52N 139 19E
Hannover Germany 71 A2 52 23N 9 44E
Hannut Belgium 70 E2 50 40N 5 05E
Hanöbukten b. Sweden 69 C2 55 50N 14 30E
Hanoi Vietnam 37 C4 21 01N 105 52E
Hanover Ontario Canada 93 D2 44 10N 81 03W
Hanover New Hampshire U.S.A. 93 F2 43 42N 71 17W
Hanover Pennsylvania U.S.A. 93 E1 39 47N 76 59W
Hao i. Pacific Ocean 81 E3 18 04S 141 00W
Haora India 52 K2 22 35N 88 19E
Happy Land tn. Vanuatu 83 J3 18 55S 169 05E
Happy Valley Hong Kong U.K. 51 C1 22 16N 114 11E
Happy Valley-Goose Bay tn. Newfoundland Canada 89 W3 53 15N 60 20W
Hapsu North Korea 50 D5 41 12N 128 48E
Haql Saudi Arabia 54 D4 29 14N 34 56E
Harad Saudi Arabia 55 G3 24 12N 49 12E
Harare Zimbabwe 111 F4 17 50S 31 03E
Harbin China 49 P8 45 45N 126 41E
Harbor Beach tn. Michigan U.S.A. 93 D2 43 51N 83 40W
Harbour Breton tn. Newfoundland Canada 89 X2 47 29N 55 50W
Harbours, Bay of Falkland Islands 25 M15 52 30S 59 30W
Hardangerfjorden fj. Norway 69 B2 59 45N 5 20E
Hardangervidda plat. Norway 69 B3 60 10N 7 00E
Hardenberg Netherlands 70 F4 52 34N 6 38E
Harderwijk Netherlands 70 E4 52 21N 5 37E
Harefield England United Kingdom 66 B3 51 36N 0 28W
Härer Ethiopia 110 H9 9 20N 42 10E
Hargeysa Somalia 110 H9 9 31N 44 02E
Haridwar India 53 D5 29 58N 78 09E
Harima-nada sea Japan 46 B1 34 30N 134 30E
Haringey bor. England United Kingdom 66 C3 51 35N 0 07W
Hari Rud r. Afghanistan 55 J5 34 00N 64 00E
Harlem New York U.S.A. 94 B2 40 48N 73 56W
Harlingen Netherlands 70 E5 53 10N 5 25E
Harlingen Texas U.S.A. 91 G2 26 12N 97 43W
Härnösand Sweden 69 D3 62 37N 17 55E
Harper Liberia 112 D3 4 25N 7 43W
Harricanaw River Québec Canada 93 E4 50 00N 79 50W
Harrington Harbour tn. Québec Canada 89 X3 50 31N 59 30W
Harris i. Scotland United Kingdom 68 D9 57 50N 6 55W
Harrisburg Illinois U.S.A. 92 C1 37 40N 88 10W
Harrisburg Pennsylvania U.S.A. 93 E2 40 17N 76 54W
Harrisonburg Virginia U.S.A. 93 E1 38 27N 78 54W
Harrisonville Missouri U.S.A. 92 B1 38 04N 94 21W
Harrisville Michigan U.S.A. 93 D2 44 41N 83 19W
Harrogate England United Kingdom 68 J6 54 00N 1 33W
Harrow bor. Greater London England United Kingdom 66 B3 51 34N 0 20W
Hart Michigan U.S.A. 92 C2 43 43N 86 22W
Hartford Connecticut U.S.A. 93 F2 41 00N 72 00W
Hartland Point England United Kingdom 68 G3 51 02N 4 31W
Hartlepool England United Kingdom 68 J6 54 41N 1 13W
Harwich England United Kingdom 68 M3 51 57N 1 17E
Haryana admin. India 53 D5 29 20N 75 30E
Harz mts. Europe 71 B2 52 00N 10 00E
Hasaki Japan 46 M2 35 46N 140 50E
Hase r. Germany 71 A2 52 00N 8 00E
Hashima Japan 46 H2 35 19N 136 43E
Hashimoto Japan 46 G1 34 19N 135 33E
Hassan India 53 D2 13 01N 76 03E
Hasselt Belgium 70 E2 50 56N 5 20E
Hassi Messaoud Algeria 112 G9 31 52N 5 43E
Hastings Barbados 96 V12 13 05N 59 36W
Hastings England United Kingdom 68 L2 50 51N 0 36E
Hastings Minnesota U.S.A. 92 B2 44 43N 92 50W
Hastings Nebraska U.S.A. 91 G5 40 37N 98 22W
Ha Tien Vietnam 37 B2 10 24N 104 30E
Ha Tinh Vietnam 37 C3 18 21N 105 55E
Hat Lek Thailand 39 B2 11 38N 102 54E
Ha Tsuen Hong Kong U.K. 51 A2 22 26N 113 59E
Hattiesburg Mississippi U.S.A. 91 I3 31 20N 89 19W
Hat Yai Thailand 39 B1 7 00N 100 25E
Hatzfeldhafen Papua New Guinea 45 L4 4 26S 145 11E
Haud geog. reg. Africa 110 H9/I9 8 00N 50 00E
Haugesund Norway 69 B2 59 25N 5 16E
Hauhui Solomon Islands 82 F4 9 18S 161 06E
Haung (Haung) r. Laos/Thailand 37 B3 17 45N 101 20E
Haukivesi l. Finland 69 F3 62 10N 28 30E
Hauraha Solomon Islands 82 G3 10 47S 161 55E
Hauraki Gulf North Island New Zealand 79 B3/C3 36 38S 175 04E
Hausruck mts. Austria 71 B1 47 00N 14 00E
Haut Atlas mts. Morocco 112 D9 30 45N 6 50W
Hautes Fagnes moor Belgium 70 F2 50 29N 6 08E
Hauteurs de Gatine hills France 73 A2 46 38N 0 38W
Hauts de Meuse hills France 73 C2 49 15N 5 20E
Hauz Khas India 52 L4 28 34N 77 11E
Havana see La Habana
Havel r. Germany 71 B2 52 00N 12 00E
Havelkanal can. Germany 67 E2 52 38N 13 02E
Havelock Ontario Canada 93 E2 44 26N 77 53W
Haveluloto Tonga 83 D1 21 08S 175 14W
Haverhill Massachusetts U.S.A. 93 F2 42 47N 71 07W
Havering bor. England United Kingdom 66 D3 51 34N 0 14E
Havre Montana U.S.A. 90 E6 48 34N 109 40W
Hawaii i. Hawaiian Islands 23 Z17 19 50N 157 50W
Hawaiian Islands Pacific Ocean 22/23 I10/K10 25 00N 166 00W
Hawaiian Ridge Pacific Ocean 23 J10 23 00N 166 00W
Hawea, Lake South Island New Zealand 79 A2 44 28S 169 17E
Hawera North Island New Zealand 79 B3 39 35S 174 17E
Hawick England United Kingdom 68 I7 55 25N 2 47W
Hawke Bay North Island New Zealand 79 C3 39 23S 177 12E
Hawkesbury Ontario Canada 89 U2 45 36N 74 38W
Hawthorne California U.S.A. 95 A2 33 54N 118 21W
Hawthorne New Jersey U.S.A. 94 B2 40 57N 74 10W
Hay r. Alberta/Northwest Territories Canada 88 L5 61 00N 115 30W
Hayama Japan 47 B2 35 16N 139 35E
Haycock i. Solomon Islands 82 C6 7 30S 157 40E
Hayes England United Kingdom 66 B3 51 31N 0 25W
Hayes r. Manitoba Canada 89 Q4 56 00N 94 00W
Hayes see Halvø
Hay River tn. Northwest Territories Canada 88 L5 60 51N 115 42W
Hayward Wisconsin U.S.A. 92 B3 46 02N 91 26W
Hazard Kentucky U.S.A. 93 D1 37 14N 83 11W
Hazebrouck France 70 B2 50 43N 2 32E
Hazelton British Columbia Canada 88 J4 55 16N 127 18W
Headstone Point Norfolk Island 81 K4 29 02S 167 55E
Headstone Reserve Norfolk Island 81 K4 29 02S 167 55E
Heard Island Indian Ocean 24 G1 53 07S 73 20E
Hearst Ontario Canada 93 D3 49 42N 83 40W
Heart r. North Dakota U.S.A. 90 F6 47 00N 102 00W
Heathcote Australia 79 G1 34 05S 151 00E
Hebi China 49 M6 35 57N 114 08E
Hebron Jordan 54 O10 31 32N 35 06E
Hecate Strait British Columbia Canada 88 I3 53 00N 131 00W
Hechi China 36 D6 24 39N 108 02E
Hechuan China 49 L5 30 02N 106 5E
Heda Japan 46 K1 34 58N 138 46E
Hedesundafjärdarna l. Sweden 69 D3 60 20N 17 00E
Heemstede Netherlands 70 D4 52 21N 4 37E
Heerenveen Netherlands 70 E4 52 57N 5 55E
Heerhugowaard Netherlands 70 D4 52 40N 4 50E
Heerlen Netherlands 70 E2 50 53N 5 59E
Hefei China 49 N5 31 55N 117 18E
Hegang China 49 Q8 47 36N 130 30E
Hegura-jima i. Japan 46 C2 37 52N 136 56E
Heidelberg Germany 71 A1 49 25N 8 42E
Heidenheim Germany 71 B1 48 41N 10 10E
Heilbronn Germany 71 A1 49 08N 9 14E
Hei Ling Chau i. Hong Kong U.K. 51 B1 22 15N 114 02E
Heilong Jiang see Amur
Heiloo Netherlands 70 D4 52 36N 4 43E
Heinze Chaung b. Myanmar 38 B2 14 45N 97 00E
Heist op den Berg Belgium 70 D3 51 05N 4 44E
Hekla mt. Iceland 69 I6 64 00N 19 41W
Hekou China 49 K3 22 30N 104 00E
Helan Shan mts. China 49 L6 38 00N 106 00E
Helchteren Belgium 70 E3 51 03N 5 23E
Helena Montana U.S.A. 90 D6 46 35N 112 00W
Helen Reef Caroline Islands 43 H4 2 43N 131 46E
Helgeland geog. reg. Norway 69 C4 64 45N 13 00E
Heligoland Bight b. Germany 71 A2 54 00N 8 00E
Hellendoorn Netherlands 70 F4 52 23N 6 27E
Hellersdorf Germany 67 G2 52 32N 13 35E
Hellevoetsluis Netherlands 70 D3 51 49N 4 08E
Hellín Spain 72 B2 38 31N 1 43W
Helmand r. Afghanistan 55 J5 30 00N 62 30E
Helmond Netherlands 70 E3 51 28N 5 40E
Helong China 50 D6 42 38N 128 58E
Helsingborg Sweden 69 C2 56 03N 12 43E
Helsinki (Helsingfors) Finland 69 E3 60 08N 25 00E
Hempstead New York U.S.A. 94 D1 40 41N 73 39W
Henares r. Spain 72 B3 40 45N 3 10W
Henderson Kentucky U.S.A. 92 C1 37 49N 87 35W
Henderson Nevada U.S.A. 90 D4 36 01N 115 00W
Hendon England United Kingdom 66 C3 51 35N 0 14W
Heng-ch'un Taiwan 51 G5 22 03N 120 45E
Hengduan Shan mts. China 38 B5 28 00N 98 30E
Hengelo Netherlands 70 F4 52 16N 6 46E
Hengyang China 49 M4 26 58N 112 31E
Henningsdorf admin. Germany 67 E2 52 39N 13 08E
Henrietta Maria, Cape Ontario Canada 89 S4 55 00N 82 30W
Henryetta Oklahoma U.S.A. 91 G4 35 27N 96 00W
Henzada Myanmar 38 B3 17 36N 95 26E
Hepu China 37 C4 21 37N 109 11E
Heqing China 38 C5 26 35N 100 13E
Herāt Afghanistan 55 J5 34 20N 62 12E
Hérault r. France 73 B1 43 50N 3 30E
Herblay France 67 A2 48 59N 2 10E
Hereford England United Kingdom 68 I4 52 04N 2 43W
Herentals Belgium 70 D3 51 11N 4 50E
Herford Germany 71 A2 52 07N 8 40E
Herisau Switzerland 71 A1 47 23N 9 17E
Hermel Lebanon 54 P12 34 25N 36 23E
Hermit Islands Papua New Guinea 45 L6 1 30S 145 15E
Hermon, Mount Lebanon/Syria 54 O11 33 24N 35 50E
Hermosillo Mexico 96 B5 29 15N 110 59W
Herne Germany 70 G3 51 32N 7 12E
Herning Denmark 69 B2 56 08N 8 59E
Hernodorf Germany 67 F2 52 38N 13 18E
Herstal Belgium 70 E2 50 40N 5 38E
Hertfordshire co. England United Kingdom 66 C3 51 50N 0 05W
Hervey i. Pacific Ocean 81 E3 19 21S 158 58W
Hessen admin. Germany 71 A2 50 00N 9 00E
Heung (Haung) r. Laos/Thailand 37 B3 17 45N 101 20E
Hezhang China 38 C5 27 08N 104 48E
Hibbing Minnesota U.S.A. 92 B3 47 25N 92 55W
Hickory North Carolina U.S.A. 91 J4 35 44N 81 23W
Hidaka Japan 46 F2 35 29N 134 44E
Hidalgo Mexico 96 E4 24 16N 99 28W
Hidalgo del Parral Mexico 96 C5 26 58N 105 40W
Hienghène New Caledonia 82 T3 20 40S 164 54E
Higashi-Matsuyama Japan 46 L3 36 02N 139 25E
Higashi-Murayama Japan 47 A4 35 46N 139 28E
Higashi-Ōsaka Japan 46 G1 34 40N 135 35E
Higashi-suidō sd. Japan 46 A1 34 10N 130 00E
Highgate Jamaica 97 R8 18 16N 76 53W
High Island Hong Kong U.K. 51 D2 22 21N 114 21E
High Island Reservoir Hong Kong U.K. 51 D2 22 22N 114 20E
High Level tn. Alberta Canada 88 L4 58 10N 117 20W
High Point tn. North Carolina U.S.A. 91 K4 35 58N 80 00W
High Veld mts. Republic of South Africa 111 E2 28 00S 28 00E
Hiiumaa i. Estonia 69 E2 58 55N 22 30E
Hikami Japan 46 F2 35 12N 135 00E
Hikone Japan 46 H2 35 17N 136 13E
Hila Indonesia 43 G2 7 36S 127 25E
Hildesheim Germany 71 A2 52 09N 9 58E
Hillaby, Mount Barbados 96 V12 13 12N 59 35W
Hillingdon bor. England United Kingdom 66 B3 51 32N 0 27W
Hillsboro Ohio U.S.A. 93 D1 39 12N 83 37W
Hilo Hawaiian Islands 23 Z17 19 42N 155 04W
Hilversum Netherlands 70 E4 52 14N 5 10E
Himachal Pradesh admin. India 53 D6 32 00N 77 30E
Himalaya mts. Asia 53 D6/G5
Himeji Japan 46 B1 34 50N 134 40E
Hims Syria 54 E5 34 42N 36 40E
Hindu Kush mts. Afghanistan 55 K6 35 00N 70 00E
Hinigaran The Philippines 40 B3 10 17N 122 51E
Hinnøya i. Norway 69 D4 68 35N 15 50E
Hirado i. Japan 50 D1 33 20N 129 30E
Hirakata Japan 46 G1 34 45N 135 35E
Hirakud Reservoir India 53 E4 21 40N 83 40E
Hiratsuka Japan 46 L2 35 20N 139 19E
Hirosaki Japan 46 D3 40 34N 140 28E
Hirson France 73 B2 49 56N 4 05E
Hiroshima Japan 46 B1 34 23N 132 27E
Hisai Japan 46 H1 34 42N 136 28E
Hisar India 53 D5 29 10N 75 45E
Hisiu Papua New Guinea 45 M2 9 02S 146 48E
Hispaniola i. West Indies 97 J3 18 00N 70 00W
Hitachi Japan 46 D2 36 35N 140 40E
Hitiaa Tahiti 82 T9 17 35S 149 17W
Hitra i. Norway 69 B3 63 37N 8 46E
Hiu i. Vanuatu 83 F8 13 07S 166 34E
Hiva Hoa i. Pacific Ocean 81 F3 9 45S 139 00W
Hjørring Denmark 69 B2 57 28N 9 59E
Hkakabo Razi mt. Myanmar 38 B5 28 17N 97 46E
Hnathalo New Caledonia 82 W3 20 48S 167 18E
Ho Ghana 112 F4 6 38N 0 38E
Hoa Binh Vietnam 37 C4 20 49N 105 20E
Hoa Da Vietnam 37 C2 11 13N 108 34E
Hoai Nhon see Bong Son
Hobart Australia 78 H1 42 54S 147 18E
Hoboken New Jersey U.S.A. 94 B1 40 44N 74 02W
Hobyo Somalia 110 I9 5 20N 48 30E
Ho Chi Minh (Saigon) Vietnam 37 C2 10 46N 106 43E
Ho Chung Hong Kong U.K. 51 C2 22 22N 114 14E
Hódmezovásárhely Hungary 75 D2 46 26N 20 21E
Hodogaya Japan 47 B2 35 26N 139 36E
Hoek van Holland Netherlands 70 D4 51 59N 4 08E
Hoeryŏng North Korea 50 D6 42 29N 129 45E
Hof Germany 71 B2 50 19N 11 56E
Höfn Iceland 69 I6 64 16N 15 10W
Hofsjökull ice cap Iceland 69 I6 64 45N 18 45W
Hofu Japan 46 B1 34 02N 131 34E
Hoggar mts. Algeria 112 G7 23 45N 6 00E
Hog Harbour tn. Vanuatu 83 G6 15 10S 167 08E
Hohe Acht mt. Germany 70 G2 50 22N 7 00E
Hohe Rhön hills Germany 71 A2/B2 50 00N 10 00E
Hohe Tauern mts. Austria 71 B1 47 00N 13 00E
Hohhot China 49 M7 40 49N 117 37E
Hoi An Vietnam 37 C3 15 55N 108 29E
Hoi Ha Hong Kong U.K. 51 C2 22 28N 114 20E
Hokitika South Island New Zealand 79 B2 42 43S 170 58E
Hokkaidō i. Japan 46 D3 43 30N 143 00E
Hokota Japan 46 M3 36 10N 141 30E
Holetown Barbados 96 V12 13 11N 59 38W
Holguín Cuba 97 I4 20 54N 76 15W
Holland tn. Michigan U.S.A. 92 C2 42 46N 86 06W
Holland Village Singapore 41 C3 1 19N 103 48E
Hollick-Kenyon Plateau Antarctica 21 77 00S 100 00W
Hollis Reservoir Trinidad and Tobago 96 T10 10 42N 61 11W
Hollywood California U.S.A. 95 A3 34 05N 118 21W
Hollywood Reservoir California U.S.A. 95 A3 34 07N 118 20W
Holsteinborg Greenland 89 Y6 66 55N 53 30W
Holston r. U.S.A. 91 J4 37 00N 82 00W
Ho-lung Taiwan 51 G7 24 37N 120 46E
Holy Cross Alaska U.S.A. 88 D5 62 10N 159 53W
Holyhead Wales United Kingdom 68 G5 53 19N 4 38W
Holy Island England United Kingdom 68 J7 55 41N 1 48W
Holy Island Wales United Kingdom 68 G5 53 16N 4 39W
Holyoke Massachusetts U.S.A. 93 F2 42 12N 72 37W
Ho Man Tin Hong Kong U.K. 51 B1 22 19N 114 10E
Homburg Germany 71 A1 49 20N 7 20E
Home Bay Northwest Territories Canada 89 V6 69 00N 67 00W
Homer Alaska U.S.A. 88 E4 59 40N 151 37W
Homestead Florida U.S.A. 91 J2 25 29N 80 29W
Homonhon i. The Philippines 40 C3 10 45N 125 41E
Hon Chong Vietnam 37 B2 10 25N 104 30E
Honda Colombia 102 C14 5 15N 74 50W
Honda Bay The Philippines 40 A2 10 00N 119 00E
HONDURAS 96/97 G2
Hone Manitoba Canada 89 O4 56 20N 101 15W
Hon Gai Vietnam 37 C4 20 57N 107 06E
Hong Kah Singapore 41 B4 1 21N 103 43E
Hong Kong i. Hong Kong U.K. 51 B1/C1 22 10N 114 10E
Hong Kong territory U.K. 49 M3 23 00N 114 00E
Hong Lok Yuen Hong Kong U.K. 51 B2 22 27N 114 09E
Hongsŏng South Korea 50 C3 36 36N 126 41E
Honguedo Passage (Détroit d'Honguedo) sd. Québec Canada 89 W2 49 30N 64 20W
Hongwŏn North Korea 50 C5 40 00N 127 56E
Honiara Solomon Islands 82 E4 9 28S 159 57E
Honjō Japan 46 L3 36 16N 139 09E
Hon Lon i. Vietnam 37 C2 12 36N 109 22E
Honokaa Hawaiian Islands 23 Z18 20 04N 155 27W
Honolulu Hawaiian Islands 23 Y18 21 19N 157 50W
Hon Quan (An Loc) Vietnam 37 C2 11 40N 106 35E
Hon Rai i. Vietnam 37 B1 9 47N 104 33E
Honshū i. Japan 46 C2 37 15N 139 00E
Hon Tre i. Vietnam 37 C2 12 12N 109 19E
Hood, Mount Oregon U.S.A. 90 B6 45 24N 121 41W
Hood Point Papua New Guinea 45 M1 10 10S 145 45E
Hoofdorp Netherlands 70 D4 52 18N 4 41E
Hoogeveen Netherlands 70 F4 52 43N 6 29E
Hoogezand Netherlands 70 F5 53 10N 6 45E
Hook England United Kingdom 66 B2 51 17N 0 58W
Hoolehua Hawaiian Islands 23 Y18 21 11N 157 06W
Hooper Bay tn. Alaska U.S.A. 88 B5 61 29N 166 10W
Hoorn Netherlands 70 E4 52 38N 5 03E
Ho-pang Myanmar 38 B4 23 20N 98 40E
Hope Barbados 96 V13 13 20N 59 36W
Hope British Columbia Canada 88 K2 49 21N 121 28W
Hopes Advance, Cape Québec Canada 89 V5 61 00N 69 40W
Hopkinsville Kentucky U.S.A. 91 I4 36 50N 87 30W
Ho Pui Hong Kong U.K. 51 B2 22 24N 114 04E
Hormuz, Strait of The Gulf 55 I4 26 35N 56 30E
Hornavan l. Sweden 69 D4 66 15N 17 40E
Hornchurch England United Kingdom 66 D3 51 34N 0 13E
Hornsby Australia 79 G3 33 42S 151 06E
Horsens Denmark 69 B2 55 53N 9 53E
Horsham Australia 78 G2 36 45S 142 15E
Hoskins Papua New Guinea 45 O4 5 30S 150 27E
Hospet India 53 D3 15 16N 76 20E
Hospitalet Spain 72 C3 41 21N 2 06E
Hotan China 48 E6 37 07N 79 57E
Hotan He r. China 48 F6 37 07N 79 57E
Hoting Sweden 69 D3 64 08N 16 15E
Hot Springs tn. Arkansas U.S.A. 91 H3 34 30N 93 02W
Houaïlou New Caledonia 82 U2 21 18S 165 33E
Houamuang Laos 37 B4 20 00N 104 00E
Houayxay Laos 37 B4 20 15N 100 29E
Hougang Singapore 41 D4 1 22N 103 54E
Houghton Michigan U.S.A. 92 C3 47 06N 88 34W
Houma China 49 M6 35 36N 111 15E
Houma Tonga 83 D1 21 10S 175 18W
Houma Louisiana U.S.A. 91 H2 29 35N 90 44W
Houma Toloa c. Tonga 83 D1 21 16S 175 08W
Hounslow bor. England United Kingdom 66 B2 51 28N 0 21W
Houston Texas U.S.A. 91 G2 29 45N 95 25W
Hovd Mongolia 48 H8 48 00N 91 43E
Hövsgöl Nuur l. Mongolia 49 K9 51 00N 100 30E
Howar r. Sudan 110 E11 17 00N 25 00E
Howe, Cape Australia 78 H2 37 20S 149 59E
Howe, Point Norfolk Island 81 K6 28 59S 167 55E
Howland Island Pacific Ocean 80 D4 0 48N 176 38W
Höxter Germany 71 A2 51 47N 9 22E
Hoy i. Scotland United Kingdom 68 H10 58 48N 3 20W
Hoya Japan 47 B3 35 44N 139 34E
Hoyerswerda Germany 71 B2 51 28N 14 17E
Hradec Králové Czech Republic 75 C3 50 13N 15 50E
Hron r. Slovakia 75 C2 48 00N 18 00E
Hsenwi Myanmar 38 B4 23 16N 97 59E
Hsi-hseng Myanmar 38 B4 20 07N 97 17E
Hsin-tien Taiwan 51 H7 24 57N 121 32E
Hsin-ying Taiwan 51 G6 23 18N 120 18E
Hsipaw Myanmar 38 B4 22 32N 97 12E
Hua Bon see Cheo Reo
Huacho Peru 102 B10 11 05S 77 36W
Hua Hin Thailand 39 A2 12 56N 99 58E
Huaide China 49 O7 43 30N 124 48E
Huai Luang Reservoir Thailand 39 B3 17 20N 102 35E
Huainan China 49 N5 32 41N 117 06E
Huai Yot Thailand 39 A1 7 49N 99 49E
Huaiji China 36 E6 24 03N 112 06E
Huajuápan de León Mexico 96 E3 17 50N 97 48W
Hua-lien Taiwan 51 H6 23 58N 121 35E
Huambo Angola 111 C5 12 44S 15 47E
Huamuang Laos 37 B4 20 02N 104 00E
Huancayo Peru 102 B10 12 05S 75 12W
Huang Hai see Yellow Sea
Huang He r. China 49 M6 38 00N 111 00E
Huangshi China 49 N5 30 13N 115 05E
Huanuco Peru 102 B11 9 55S 76 11W
Hua-p'ing Hsü i. Taiwan 51 H8 25 26N 121 57E
Huaráz Peru 102 B11 9 33S 77 31W
Huascaran mt. Peru 102 B11 9 08S 77 36W
Huashixia China 49 J6 35 13N 99 12E
Huatabampo Mexico 90 E2 26 49N 109 40W
Huat Choe Singapore 41 B4 1 20N 103 41E
Huch'ang North Korea 50 C5 41 23N 127 04E
Huddersfield England United Kingdom 68 J5 53 39N 1 47W
Hudson Bay Canada 89 R5 60 00N 89 00W
Hudson Bay tn. Saskatchewan Canada 89 O3 52 45N 102 45W
Hudson Strait Northwest Territories/Québec Canada 89 U5 62 00N 70 00W
Hue Vietnam 37 C3 16 28N 107 35E
Huelva Spain 72 A2 37 15N 6 56W
Huelva r. Spain 72 A2 37 50N 6 30W
Huesca Spain 72 B3 42 08N 0 25W
Huevos i. Trinidad and Tobago 96 S10 10 47N 61 11W
Hughenden Australia 78 G5 20 50S 144 10E
Hugli r. India 52 J2 22 30N 88 14E
Hugli-Chinsurah India 52 K3 22 54N 88 23E
Hugo Oklahoma U.S.A. 91 G3 34 01N 95 31W
Hŭich'ŏn North Korea 50 C5 40 06N 126 20E
Huili China 38 C5 26 40N 102 20E
Huisne r. France 73 B2 48 15N 0 40E
Huixtla Mexico 96 F3 15 09N 92 30W
Huize China 38 C5 26 26N 103 22E
Huizen Netherlands 70 E4 52 17N 5 15E
Huizhou China 49 M3 23 08N 114 28E
Hukawng Valley Myanmar 38 B5 26 35N 96 45E
Hula Papua New Guinea 45 M1 10 05S 147 45E
Hull Québec Canada 93 E3 45 26N 75 45W
Hull Island see Orona
Hulst Netherlands 70 D3 51 17N 4 03E
Humaitá Brazil 102 E11 7 33S 63 01W
Humber r. England United Kingdom 68 K5 53 40N 0 10W
Humboldt Saskatchewan Canada 88 N3 52 12N 105 07W
Humboldt mt. New Caledonia 82 V2 21 55S 166 29E
Humboldt r. Nevada U.S.A. 90 C5 41 00N 118 00W

Kasaragod India 53 C2 12 30N 74 59E
Kasavu Fiji 83 C9 17 58S 178 31E
Kasempa Zambia 111 E5 13 28S 25 48E
Kasese Uganda 110 F8 0 10N 30 06E
Kaset Wisai Thailand 39 B3 15 40N 103 38E
Kāshān Iran 55 H5 33 59N 51 35E
Kashi China 48 E6 39 29N 76 02E
Kashihara Japan 46 G1 34 28N 135 46E
Kashima Japan 46 M2 35 58N 140 39E
Kashiwa Japan 46 L2 35 51N 139 58E
Kashiwazaki Japan 46 C2 37 22N 138 33E
Kashmir *see* Jammu & Kashmir
Kaskö Finland 69 E3 62 23N 21 10E
Kas Kong Cambodia 37 B2 11 29N 103 10E
Kasli Russia 59 J6 55 54N 60 45E
Kásos Greece 74 E2 35 00N 28 00E
Kassala Sudan 110 G11 15 24N 36 30E
Kassel Germany 71 A2 51 18N 9 30E
Kasserine Tunisia 74 A2 35 13N 8 43E
Kastamonu Turkey 58 C3 41 22N 33 47E
Kastoria Greece 74 D3 40 33N 21 15E
Kasugai Japan 46 H2 35 15N 136 57E
Kasukabe Japan 46 L3 35 59N 139 45E
Kasumiga-ura *l.* Japan 46 M3 36 03N 140 20E
Kasur Pakistan 53 C6 31 07N 74 30E
Kataba Zambia 111 E4 16 02S 25 03E
Katafaga *i.* Fiji 83 F9 17 31S 178 42W
Katase Japan 47 A2 35 18N 139 30E
Katchall *i.* Nicobar Islands 36 A3 7 30N 93 30E
Katerini Greece 74 D3 40 15N 22 30E
Katha Myanmar 38 B4 24 11N 96 20E
Katherine Australia 78 E7 14 29S 132 20E
Kathiawar *p.* India 52 C4 21 10N 71 00E
Kat Hing Wai Hong Kong U.K. 51 B2 22 26N 114 03E
Kathmandu Nepal 53 F5 27 42N 85 19E
Katihar India 53 F5 25 33N 87 34E
Katong Singapore 41 D3 1 19N 103 55E
Katowice Poland 75 C3 50 15N 18 59E
Katrineholm Sweden 69 D2 58 59N 16 15E
Katsina Ala Nigeria 112 G4 7 10N 9 30E
Katsuura Japan 46 M2 35 10N 140 20E
Kattakurgan Uzbekistan 59 K2 39 54N 66 13E
Kattegat *sd.* Denmark/Sweden 69 C2 57 00N 11 00E
Katun' *r.* Russia 59 O5 51 30N 86 00E
Katwijk aan Zee Netherlands 70 D4 52 12N 4 24E
Kau Indonesia 43 G4 1 15N 127 50E
Kauai *i.* Hawaiian Islands 23 X18-19 22 00N 159 30W
Kauai Channel *sd.* Hawaiian Islands 23 X18 21 45N 158 50W
Kaufbeuren Germany 71 B1 47 53N 10 37E
Kaukkwe Hills Myanmar 38 B4 24 45N 97 20E
Kaula *i.* Hawaiian Islands 23 W18 21 35N 160 40W
Kaulakahi Channel *sd.* Hawaiian Islands 23 X18 21 58N 159 50W
Kaulsdorf Germany 67 G1 52 29N 13 34E
Kaunas Lithuania 69 E1 54 52N 23 55E
Kaura Namoda Nigeria 112 G5 12 39N 6 38E
Kau Sai Chau *i.* Hong Kong U.K. 51 C2 22 22N 114 19E
Kau-ye Kyun *i.* Myanmar 38 B2 11 00N 98 30E
Kau Yi Chau Hong Kong U.K. 51 B1 22 17N 114 04E
Kavajë Albania 74 C3 41 11N 19 33E
Kavála Greece 74 D3 40 56N 24 25E
Kavaratti Island India 53 C2 10 32N 72 43E
Kavieng Papua New Guinea 45 O5 2 34S 150 48E
Kawa Myanmar 38 B3 17 04N 96 30E
Kawachi-Nagano Japan 46 G1 34 24N 135 32E
Kawagoe Japan 46 L2 35 55N 139 30E
Kawaguchi Japan 46 L2 35 47N 139 44E
Kawaihae Hawaiian Islands 23 Z18 20 02N 155 05W
Kawang Myanmar 38 B5 27 45N 97 42E
Kawasaki Japan 47 C3 35 30N 139 45E
Kawawa Japan 47 B3 35 31N 139 33E
Kawawachikamach *see* Schefferville
Kawerau North Island New Zealand 79 C3 38 05S 176 42E
Kawkareik Myanmar 38 B3 16 33N 98 18E
Kawlin Myanmar 38 B4 23 48N 95 41E
Kawthaung Myanmar 38 B1 10 01N 98 32E
Kaya Burkina 112 E5 13 04N 1 09W
Kayah State *admin.* Myanmar 38 B3 19 15N 97 30E
Kayan Myanmar 38 B3 16 54N 96 35E
Kayan *r.* Indonesia 42 E4 2 50N 116 20E
Kayeli Indonesia 44 B5 3 25S 127 07E
Kayes Mali 112 C5 14 26N 11 28W
Kayseri Turkey 54 E6 38 42N 35 28E
Kayuagung Indonesia 42 B3 3 18S 104 53E
Kazach'ye Russia 57 P10 70 46N 136 15E
KAZAKHSTAN 59 H4/O4
Kazakh Upland Kazakhstan 59 L5 47 00N 75 00E
Kazan' Russia 56 G7 55 45N 49 10E
Kazanlŭk Bulgaria 74 E3 42 37N 25 23E
Kazbek *mt.* Georgia 58 E3 42 42N 44 30E
Kāzerūn Iran 55 H4 29 35N 51 40E
Kazym *r.* Russia 57 I8 63 00N 67 30E
Kéa *i.* Greece 74 D2 37 00N 24 00E
Kearney Nebraska U.S.A. 90 G5 40 42N 99 04W
Kearny New Jersey U.S.A. 94 B2 40 45N 74 07W
Kebumen Indonesia 42 O7 7 40S 109 41E
Kecskemét Hungary 75 C2 46 56N 19 43E
Kediri Indonesia 42 Q7 7 45S 112 01E
Keele *r.* Northwest Territories Canada 88 J5 64 15N 126 00W
Keene New Hampshire U.S.A. 93 F2 42 55N 72 17W
Keetmanshoop Namibia 111 C2 26 36S 18 08E
Keewatin Ontario Canada 92 B3 49 47N 94 30W
Kefallinia *i.* Greece 74 D2 38 00N 20 00E
Kefamenanu Indonesia 43 F2 9 31S 124 29E
Keflavik Iceland 69 H6 64 01N 22 35W
Kehl Germany 71 A1 48 35N 7 50E
Keihoku Japan 46 G2 35 09N 135 37E
Kei Ling Ha Lo Wai Hong Kong U.K. 51 C2 22 25N 114 16E
Kei Lun Wai Hong Kong U.K. 51 A2 22 24N 113 58E
Keitele *l.* Finland 69 F3 63 10N 26 24E
Keiyasi Fiji 83 B9 17 55S 177 45E
Keketa Papua New Guinea 45 K3 6 48S 143 38E
K'elafo Ethiopia 110 H9 5 37N 44 10E
Kelefesia *i.* Tonga 83 B2 20 30S 174 45W
Kelkit *r.* Turkey 54 E7 40 20N 37 40E
Kells Irish Republic 68 E5 53 44N 6 53W
Kelowna British Columbia Canada 88 L2 49 50N 119 29W
Kelsey Bay *tn.* British Columbia Canada 88 J3 50 22N 125 29W
Kemerovo Russia 57 K7 55 25N 86 05E
Kemi Finland 69 E4 65 46N 24 34E
Kemijärvi *l.* Finland 69 F4 66 42N 27 30E
Kemijöki *r.* Finland 69 F4 66 00N 25 00
Kempenland *(Campines) admin.* Belgium 70 E3 51 08N 5 22E
Kemp Land *geog. reg.* Antarctica 21 65 00S 60 00E
Kempten Germany 71 B1 47 44N 10 19E
Kemptville Ontario Canada 93 E3 45 01N 75 39W
Kemsing England United Kingdom 66 D2 51 18N 0 14E
Kenai Alaska U.S.A. 88 E5 60 35N 151 19W
Kendal England United Kingdom 68 I6 54 20N 2 45W
Kendari Indonesia 43 F3 3 57S 122 36E
Kendawangan Indonesia 42 D3 2 32S 110 13E
Kenema Sierra Leone 112 C4 7 57N 11 11W
Kengtung Myanmar 38 B4 21 15N 99 40E
Keningau Malaysia 42 E5 5 21N 116 11E
Kénitra Morocco 112 D9 34 20N 6 34W
Kennebunk Maine U.S.A. 93 F2 43 24N 70 33W
Kennedy Peak Myanmar 38 A4 23 35N 93 48E
Kennedy Town Hong Kong U.K. 51 B1 22 17N 114 07E
Kenora Ontario Canada 92 B3 49 47N 94 26W
Kenosha Wisconsin U.S.A. 92 C2 42 34N 87 50W
Kensington *bor.* England United Kingdom 66 C3 51 29N 0 10W
Kent England United Kingdom 66 D2 51 15N 0 09E
Kenthurst Australia 79 F3 33 40S 151 01E
Kenting National Park Taiwan 51 G5 22 00N 120 50E
Kenton Ohio U.S.A. 93 D2 40 38N 83 38W
Kent Peninsula Northwest Territories Canada 89 N6 68 30N 106 00W
Kentucky *r.* Kentucky U.S.A. 92 D1 38 00N 85 00W
Kentucky *state* U.S.A. 91 I4 37 00N 85 00W
Kentucky Lake Kentucky U.S.A. 92 C1 37 00N 88 00W
KENYA 110 G7/G8
Kenya, Mount *see* Kirinyaga
Keokuk Iowa U.S.A. 92 B2 40 23N 91 25W
Keo Nua Pass Laos/Vietnam 37 C3 18 00N 105 00E
Kepi Irian Jaya Indonesia 44 H3 6 34S 139 22E
Keppel Harbour Singapore 41 C3 1 16N 103 50E
Kepulauan Alor *is.* Indonesia 44 A2 8 15S 124 30E
Kepulauan Anambas *is.* Indonesia 42 C4 3 00N 106 20E
Kepulauan Aru *is.* Indonesia 43 H2 6 00S 134 30E
Kepulauan Asia *is.* Indonesia 43 H4 1 15N 131 15E
Kepulauan Ayu *is.* Indonesia 43 H4 0 45N 131 15E
Kepulauan Babar *is.* Indonesia 43 G2 7 50S 129 30E
Kepulauan Banda *is.* Indonesia 43 G3 4 45S 129 45E
Kepulauan Banggai *is.* Indonesia 43 F3 1 30S 123 00E
Kepulauan Banyak *is.* Indonesia 42 A4 2 00N 97 20E
Kepulauan Barat Daya *is.* Indonesia 43 G2 7 15S 127 00E
Kepulauan Batu *is.* Indonesia 42 A3 0 18S 98 29E
Kepulauan Gorong *i.* Indonesia 44 D4 4 00S 131 25E
Kepulauan Kai *is.* Indonesia 43 H2 5 30S 132 30E
Kepulauan Kangean *is.* Indonesia 42 R7 7 00S 115 30T
Kepulauan Karimata *is.* Indonesia 42 C3 1 25S 108 50E
Kepulauan Karimunjawa *is.* Indonesia 42 P8 5 50S 110 30E
Kepulauan Laut Kecil *is.* Indonesia 42 E3 4 50S 116 00E
Kepulauan Leti *is.* Indonesia 43 G2 8 15S 127 45E
Kepulauan Lingga *is.* Indonesia 42 B3 0 10S 104 30E
Kepulauan Lucipara *is.* Indonesia 44 B4 5 15S 127 45E
Kepulauan Maluku *(Moluccas)* Indonesia 43 G3 4 00S 127 00E
Kepulauan Mapia *is.* Indonesia 43 H4 1 10N 134 25E
Kepulauan Masalembu *is.* Indonesia 42 R8 5 30S 114 20E
Kepulauan Mentawai *is.* Indonesia 42 A3 2 00S 99 00E
Kepulauan Natuna Selatan *is.* Indonesia 42 C4 2 50N 109 00E
Kepulauan Obi *is.* Indonesia 44 B6 1 30S 127 30E
Kepulauan Riau *is.* Indonesia 42 B4 0 30N -4 30E
Kepulauan Sabalana *is.* Indonesia 42 E2 6 40S 119 00E
Kepulauan Sangir *is.* Indonesia 43 G4 3 00N 125 30E
Kepulauan Sermata *i.* Indonesia 43 G2 8 13S 128 55E
Kepulauan Sula *is.* Indonesia 43 G3 1 50S 124 50E
Kepulauan Talaud *is.* Indonesia 43 G4 4 00N 127 00E
Kepulauan Tambelan *is.* Indonesia 42 C4 1 00N 107 25E
Kepulauan Tanimbar *is.* Indonesia 43 H2 7 30S 131 30E
Kepulauan Tayandu *is.* Indonesia 43 H2 5 30S 132 00E
Kepulauan Tengah *is.* Indonesia 42 E2 7 20S 118 00E
Kepulauan Tongian *is.* Indonesia 43 F3 0 30S 122 00E
Kepulauan Tukangbesi *is.* Indonesia 43 F2 5 30S 123 30E
Kepulauan Watubela *is.* Indonesia 44 D4 4 45S 131 30E
Kerala *admin.* India 53 D2 10 10N 76 30E
Keravat Papua New Guinea 45 P4 4 20S 152 00E
Kerch' Ukraine 58 D4 45 22N 36 27E
Kerema Papua New Guinea 45 L3 7 59S 145 46E
Keren Eritrea 110 G11 15 46N 38 30E
Kerguelen Plateau Indian Ocean 24 G1/H1 55 00S 80 00E
Kerikeri North Island New Zealand 79 B3 35 14S 173 57E
Kerki Turkmenistan 59 K2 37 53N 65 10E
Kérkira Greece 74 C2 39 00N 19 00E
Kérkira *(Corfu) i.* Greece 74 C2 39 00N 19 00E
Kerkrade Netherlands 70 F2 50 52N 6 04E
Kermadec Islands Pacific Ocean 80 D2 30 00S 178 30W
Kermadec Trench Pacific Ocean 22 I4 33 00S 177 00W
Kermān Iran 55 I5 30 18N 57 05E
Kermānshāh Iran 55 G5 34 19N 47 04E
Kerme Körfezi *b.* Turkey 74 E2 37 00N 27 00E
Kerpen Germany 70 F2 50 52N 6 42E
Kerrville Texas U.S.A. 90 G3 30 03N 99 09W
Kerulen *r.* Mongolia 49 M8 47 30N 112 30E
Kesagami Lake Ontario Canada 93 D4 50 00N 80 00W
Keşan Turkey 74 E3 40 52N 26 37E
Ket' Russia 59 O6 58 30N 86 30E
Ket' *r.* Russia 57 K7 58 30N 86 30E
Ketam Channel Singapore 41 E4 1 24N 103 57E
Ketapang Indonesia 42 C3 1 50S 109 59E
Ketchikan Alaska U.S.A. 88 I4 55 25N 131 40W
Ketrzyn Poland 75 D3 54 05N 21 24E
Kettering Ohio U.S.A. 93 D1 39 42N 84 11W
Kewanee Illinois U.S.A. 92 C2 41 14N 89 56W
Kewaunee Wisconsin U.S.A. 92 C2 44 27N 87 31W
Keweenaw Bay Wisconsin U.S.A. 92 C3 47 00N 88 00W
Keweenaw Peninsula Michigan U.S.A. 92 C3 47 00N 88 00W
Key West Florida U.S.A. 91 J1 24 34N 81 48W
Khabarovsk Russia 57 P5 48 32N 135 08E
Khalîg el Tîna Egypt 109 T4 31 08N 32 36E
Khalkidhikí *p.* Greece 74 D3 40 30N 23 00E
Khalkis Greece 74 D2 38 28N 23 36E
Khambhat India 53 C4 22 19N 72 39E
Khambhat, Gulf of India 53 C4 20 30N 72 00E
Khammam India 53 E3 17 16N 80 13E
Khammouan *(Thakhek)* Laos 37 B3 17 22N 104 50E
Khānābād Afghanistan 55 K6 36 42N 69 08E
Khānaqīn Iraq 55 G5 34 22N 45 22E
Khandwa India 53 D4 21 49N 76 23E
Khanh Hung *see* Soc Trang
Khaniá Greece 74 D2 35 31N 24 01E
Khanty-Mansiysk Russia 57 I8 61 01N 69 00E
Khān Yūnis Israel 54 O10 31 21N 34 18E
Khao Laem Reservoir Thailand 39 A2/A3 14 50N 98 30E
Khao Luang *mt.* Thailand 39 A1 8 28N 99 40E
Khao Soi Dao Tai *mt.* Thailand 39 B2 12 53N 102 11E
Khao Yai National Park Thailand 39 B2 14 20N 101 30E
Kharagpur India 53 F4 22 23N 87 22E
Kharan Pakistan 52 B5 28 32N 65 26E
Khardah India 52 K2 22 43N 88 20E
Khārg Island Iran 55 H4 29 14N 50 20E
Khar'kov Ukraine 58 D4 50 00N 36 15E
Khartoum Sudan 110 F11 15 33N 32 35E
Khasan Russia 50 E6 42 28N 130 48E
Khāsh Iran 55 J4 28 14N 61 15E
Khash *r.* Afghanistan 55 J5 31 30N 62 30E
Khashm el Girba Sudan 54 E1 14 59N 35 59E
Khasi Hills India 38 A5 25 30N 92 20E
Khaskovo Bulgaria 74 E3 41 57N 25 32E
Khatanga Russia 57 M10 71 59N 102 31E
Khatanga *r.* Russia 57 M10 72 30N 102 30E
Khatib Bongsu River Singapore 41 D5 1 26N 103 51E
Khemisset Morocco 112 D9 33 50N 6 03W
Khemmarat Thailand 39 C3 16 03N 105 16E
Khe Sanh Vietnam 37 C3 16 37N 106 50E
Kheta *r.* Russia 57 L10 71 30N 95 00E
Khilok *r.* Russia 57 M6 51 00N 107 30E
Khimki Russia 56 L2 55 51N 37 28E
Khimki-Khovrino Russia 56 L2 55 51N 37 30E
Khimki Reservoir Russia 56 L2 55 49N 37 29E
Khíos Greece 74 E2 38 23N 26 07E
Khíos *i.* Greece 74 E2 38 00N 26 00E
Khiva Uzbekistan 59 J3 41 25N 60 49E
Khlong Thom Thailand 39 A1 7 52N 99 05E
Khmel'nitsky Ukraine 58 B4 49 25N 26 59E
Khodzheyli Uzbekistan 59 H3 42 25N 59 25E
Khok Samrong Thailand 39 B3 15 06N 100 45E
Kholayarvi Russia 69 F4 67 07N 28 50E
Kholmsk Russia 57 Q5 47 02N 142 03E
Không Laos 37 C2 14 08N 105 50E
Khôngxédôn Laos 37 C3 15 35N 105 57E
Khon Kaen Thailand 39 B3 16 25N 102 50E
Khoper Russia 58 E5 50 20N 42 00E
Khorat *see* Nakhon Ratchasima
Khorat Plateau Thailand 39 B3 16 00N 103 30E
Khorochevo Russia 56 L2 55 46N 37 30E
Khorog Tajikistan 59 L2 37 22N 71 32E
Khorramābad Iran 55 G5 33 29N 48 21E
Khorramshahr Iran 55 G5 30 25N 48 09E
Khouribga Morocco 112 D9 32 54N 6 57W
Khrebet Kopat Dag *canal* Turkmenistan 59 H2 39 50N 56 00E
Khrishnapur Canal India 52 K2 22 34N 88 23E
Khujand *(Leninabad)* Kirgyzstan 59 K3 40 20N 69 55E
Khu Khan Thailand 39 B2 14 37N 104 12E
Khulna Bangladesh 53 F4 22 49N 89 34E
Khwae Noi *r.* Thailand 39 A2 14 30N 99 00E
Khwae Yai *r.* Thailand 39 A2 14 20N 99 20E
Khyber Pass Afghanistan/Pakistan 55 L5 34 06N 71 05E
Kiantajärvi *l.* Finland 69 F4 65 02N 29 00E
Kibobo Islets Fiji 83 E9 17 01S 179 00W
Kibombo Zaïre 111 E7 3 58S 25 54E
Kiel Germany 71 B2 54 20N 10 08E
Kiel Bay Europe 71 B2 54 00N 10 00E
Kielce Poland 75 D3 50 51N 20 39E
Kieta Papua New Guinea 45 Q3 6 15S 155 37E
Kiev *see* Kiyev
Kigali Rwanda 110 F7 1 56S 30 04E
Kigoma Tanzania 111 E7 4 52S 29 36E
Kii-Nagashima Japan 46 H1 34 11N 136 19E
Kii-sanchi *mts.* Japan 46 G1 34 15N 135 50E
Kii-suidō *sd.* Japan 46 B1 34 00N 134 45E
Kikinda Serbia Yugoslavia 74 D4 45 50N 20 30E
Kikladhes *(Cyclades) is.* Greece 74 D2/E2 37 00N 25 00E
Kikori Papua New Guinea 45 L3 7 25S 144 13E
Kikori *r.* Papua New Guinea 45 K3 6 50S 143 55E
Kikwit Zaïre 111 C6 5 02S 18 51E
Kila Kila Papua New Guinea 45 M2 9 31S 147 10E
Kilanea Hawaiian Islands 23 W19 22 05N 159 35W
Kilchu North Korea 50 D5 40 55N 129 21E
Kilimanjaro *mt.* Tanzania 110 G7 3 04S 37 22E
Kilkenny Irish Republic 68 D4 52 39N 7 15W
Kilkís Greece 74 D3 40 59N 22 52E
Killarney Irish Republic 68 B4 52 03N 9 30W
Killarney Manitoba Canada 89 P2 49 12N 99 40W
Killeen Texas U.S.A. 91 G3 31 08N 97 44W
Kilmarnock Scotland United Kingdom 68 G7 55 36N 4 30W
Kiltan Island India 53 C2 11 30N 73 00E
Kilwa Masoko Tanzania 111 G6 8 55S 39 31E
Kilyos Turkey 74 E3 41 14N 29 02E
Kimbe Papua New Guinea 45 O4 5 36S 150 10E
Kimbe Bay Papua New Guinea 45 O4 5 15S 150 30E
Kimberley British Columbia Canada 88 L2 49 40N 115 58W
Kimberley Republic of South Africa 111 D2 28 45S 24 46E
Kimberley Plateau Australia 78 D6 17 30S 126 00E
Kimberling City Missouri U.S.A. 92 B1 36 40N 93 25W
Kimch'aek *see* Sŏngjin
Kimch'ŏn South Korea 50 D3 36 07N 128 08E
Kimitsu Japan 46 L2 35 19N 139 53E
Kinabatangan *r.* Malaysia 40 A2 5 20N 118 00E
Kinbasket Lake British Columbia Canada 88 L3 51 57N 118 02W
Kincardine Ontario Canada 93 D2 44 11N 81 38W
Kindersley Saskatchewan Canada 88 N3 51 27N 109 08W
Kindia Guinea 112 C5 10 03N 12 49W
Kindu Zaïre 111 E7 3 00S 25 56E
Kineshma Russia 58 E6 57 28N 42 08E
King George Bay Falkland Islands 25 L16 51 50S 61 00W
King George Island Antarctica 21 60 00S 60 00W
King George Island South Shetland Islands 103 F0 62 00S 58 00W
King George's Reservoir England United Kingdom 66 C3 51 41N 0 05W
King Island Australia 78 G2 40 00S 144 00E
Kingissepp *see* Kuressaare
Kingman Arizona U.S.A. 90 D4 35 12N 114 02W
Kingman Reef Pacific Ocean 81 D3 6 27N 162 24W
King Sejong *r.s.* Antarctica 21 62 13S 58 47W
Kingsgrove Australia 79 G2 33 58S 151 09E
Kings Langley England United Kingdom 66 B3 51 43N 0 28W
King's Lynn Norfolk England United Kingdom 68 L4 52 45N 0 24E
King Sound Australia 78 C6 16 00S 123 00E
Kings Point *tn.* New York U.S.A. 94 C2 40 49N 73 45W
Kingsport Tennessee U.S.A. 91 J4 36 33N 82 34W
Kingston Ontario Canada 93 E2 44 14N 76 30W
Kingston Jamaica 97 R7 17 58N 76 48W
Kingston Norfolk Island 81 L4 29 03S 167 57E
Kingston New York U.S.A. 93 F2 41 55N 74 00W
Kingston Common Reserve Norfolk Island 81 K4 29 03S 167 57E
Kingston upon Hull England United Kingdom 68 K5 53 45N 0 20W
Kingston-upon-Thames England United Kingdom 66 B2 51 25N 0 18W
Kingstown St. Vincent and The Grenadines 97 L2 13 12N 61 14W
Kingsville Ontario Canada 93 D2 42 02N 82 44W
Kingsville Texas U.S.A. 91 G2 27 32N 97 53W
King William Island Northwest Territories Canada 89 P6 69 00N 97 30W
Kinkala Congo 112 G2 4 18S 14 49E
Kino *r.* Japan 46 G1 34 15N 135 30E
Kinshasa Zaïre 111 C7 4 18S 15 18E
Kinu Myanmar 38 B4 22 47N 95 36E
Kinzig *r.* Germany 71 A2 50 00N 9 00E
Kioa Fiji 83 D10 16 14S 179 07E
Kiparissiakós Kólpos *g.* Greece 74 D2 37 00N 21 00E
Kipili Tanzania 111 F6 7 30S 30 39E
Kirakira Solomon Islands 82 G3 10 30S 161 55E
Kirensk Russia 57 M7 57 45N 108 02E
KIRGHIZIA *see* KIRGYZSTAN
Kirghiz Step *geog. reg.* Kazakhstan 58/59 F4/K4
KIRGYZSTAN *(KIRGHIZIA)* 59 L3/M3
KIRIBATI 80 D3
Kirikiri Nigeria 109 V3 6 22N 3 22E
Kirikkale Turkey 54 D6 39 51N 33 32E
Kirinyaga *(Mount Kenya) mt.* Kenya 110 G7 0 10S 37 19E
Kirkağaç Turkey 74 E2 39 06N 27 40E
Kirkcaldy Fife Scotland United Kingdom 68 H8 56 07N 3 10W
Kirkcudbright Scotland United Kingdom 68 G6 54 50N 4 03W
Kirkland Lake *tn.* Ontario Canada 93 D3 48 10N 80 02W
Kirklareli Turkey 74 E3 41 45N 27 12E
Kirksville Missouri U.S.A. 92 B2 40 12N 92 35W
Kirkūk Iraq 54 F6 35 28N 44 26E
Kirkwall Orkney Islands Scotland United Kingdom 68 I10 58 59N 2 58W
Kirov Russia 56 G7 58 00N 49 38E
Kirov *r.* Russia 58 G6 58 00N 50 50E
Kirovabad *see* Gyandzha
Kirovakan Armenia 58 E3 40 49N 44 30E
Kirovograd Ukraine 58 C4 48 31N 32 15E
Kirti Nagar India 52 L4 28 39N 77 09E
Kiruna Sweden 69 E4 67 53N 20 15E
Kiryū Japan 46 C2 36 26N 139 18E
Kisangani Zaïre 110 E8 0 33N 25 14E
Kisar *i.* Indonesia 44 B2 8 05S 127 12E
Kisarazu Japan 47 C2 35 22N 139 55E
Kiselevsk' Russia 59 O5 54 01N 86 41E
Kishiwada Japan 46 G1 34 28N 135 22E
Kiskunfélegyháza Hungary 75 C2 46 42N 19 52E
Kiskunhalas Hungary 75 C2 46 26N 19 29E
Kislovodsk Russia 58 E3 43 56N 42 44E
Kismaayo Somalia 110 H7 0 25S 42 31E
Kisumu Kenya 110 F7 0 08S 34 47E
Kita Japan 47 B4 35 46N 139 43E
Kita-Kyūshū Japan 46 B1 33 52N 130 49E
Kitami Japan 46 D3 43 51N 143 54E
Kita-ura Japan 46 M3 36 02N 140 33E
Kitchener Ontario Canada 93 D2 43 27N 80 30W
Kithira *i.* Greece 74 D2 36 00N 23 00E
Kíthnos *i.* Greece 74 D2 37 00N 24 20E
Kitimat British Columbia Canada 88 J3 54 06N 128 38W
Kitridge Point Barbados 96 W12 13 08N 59 22W
Kittanning Pennsylvania U.S.A. 93 E2 40 49N 79 31W
Kittery Maine U.S.A. 93 F2 43 05N 70 45W
Kitwe Zambia 111 E5 0 08S 30 30E
Kitzbühel Austria 75 B2 47 27N 12 23E
Kitzbühler Alpen *mts.* Austria 71 B1 47 00N 12 00E
Kitzingen Germany 71 B1 49 45N 10 11E
Kiu Lom Reservoir Thailand 39 A3 18 35N 99 35E
Kiunga Papua New Guinea 45 J3 6 10S 141 15E
Kivu, Lake Zaïre/Rwanda 110 E7 2 00S 29 00E
Kiwai Island Papua New Guinea 45 K2 8 35S 143 25E
Kiyev *(Kiev)* Ukraine 58 C5 50 25N 30 30E
Kiyose Japan 47 B4 35 46N 139 32E
Kızıl Irmak *r.* Turkey 54 D7 40 30N 34 00E
Kizlyar Russia 58 F3 43 51N 46 43E
Kizu-gawa *r.* Japan 46 G1 34 50N 135 55E
Kizyl Arvat Turkmenistan 59 H2 39 00N 56 23E
Kladar Irian Jaya Indonesia 44 G2 8 24S 137 48E
Kladno Czech Republic 75 B3 50 10N 14 07E
Kladow Germany 67 E1 52 27N 13 08E
Klaeng Thailand 39 B2 12 46N 101 39E
Klagenfurt Austria 75 B2 46 38N 14 20E
Klaipėda Lithuania 69 E2 55 43N 21 07E
Klamath *r.* U.S.A. 90 B5 42 00N 123 00W
Klamath Falls *tn.* Oregon U.S.A. 90 B5 42 14N 121 47W
Klamono Irian Jaya Indonesia 44 D6 1 08S 131 28E
Klang Malaysia 42 B4 3 03N 101 25E
Klarälven *r.* Sweden 69 C3 60 45N 13 00E
Klaten Indonesia 42 P7 7 40S 110 32E
Klatovy Czech Republic 75 B2 49 24N 13 17E
Kleinmachnow Germany 67 E1/F1 52 24N 13 13E
Klerksdorp Republic of South Africa 111 E2 26 52S 26 39E
Kleve Germany 71 A2 51 47N 6 11E
Kłodzko Poland 75 C3 50 28N 16 40E
Klöfta Norway 69 C3 60 04N 11 06E
Kluane National Park Yukon Territory Canada 88 H5 60 30N 139 00W
Kluang Malaysia 42 B4 2 01N 103 19E
Klyazma *r.* Russia 58 E6 56 00N 42 00E
Klyuchevskaya Sopka *mt.* Russia 57 S7 56 03N 160 38E
Kmagha Solomon Islands 82 E5 8 20S 159 44E
Knokke-Heist Belgium 70 C3 51 21N 3 19E
Knossós *hist. site* Greece 74 E2 35 18N 25 10E
Knox Indiana U.S.A. 92 C2 41 17N 86 37W
Knoxville Iowa U.S.A. 92 B2 41 26N 93 05W

Ladysmith British Columbia Canada **88** K2 48 57N 123 50W
Ladysmith Republic of South Africa **111** E2 28 34S 29 47E
Ladysmith Wisconsin U.S.A. **92** B3 45 27N 91 07W
Lae Papua New Guinea **45** M3 6 45S 147 00E
Laedalsøyri Norway **69** B3 61 05N 7 15E
Laena *i.* Solomon Islands **82** C6 7 20S 157 35E
La Esmeralda Venezuela **102** D13 3 11N 65 33W
Lafayette Indiana U.S.A. **92** C2 40 25N 86 54W
Lafayette Louisiana U.S.A. **91** H3 30 12N 92 18W
La Fé Cuba **97** H4 22 02N 84 15W
la Flèche France **73** A2 47 42N 0 04W
la'Foa New Caledonia **82** U2 21 40S 165 52E
Lågen *r.* Norway **69** B3 61 40N 9 45E
Laghouat Algeria **112** F9 33 49N 2 55E
Lago Argentino *l.* Argentina **103** C2 50 10S 72 30W
Lago da Tijuca *l.* Brazil **103** P2 22 59S 43 22W
Lago de Chapala *l.* Mexico **96** D4 20 05N 103 00W
Lago de Maracaibo *l.* Venezuela **102** C14 9 50N 71 30W
Lago de Marapendi *l.* Brazil **103** Q2 23 00S 43 20W
Lago de Nicaragua *l.* Nicaragua **97** G2 11 50N 86 00W
Lago de Piratininga *l.* Brazil **103** Q2 22 57S 43 05W
Lago de Poopó *l.* Bolivia **102** D9 18 30S 67 20W
Lago di Bolsena *l.* Italy **74** B3 42 00N 12 00E
Lago di Como *l.* Italy **74** A4 46 00N 9 00E
Lago di Garda *l.* Italy **74** B4 45 00N 10 00E
Lago do Jacarepaguá *l.* Brazil **103** P2 22 58S 43 23W
Lago Maggiore *l.* Italy **74** A4 46 00N 8 00E
Lagonoy Gulf The Philippines **40** B3 13 00N 124 00E
Lago Rodrigo de Freitas *l.* Brazil **103** Q2 22 58S 43 13W
Lagos Nigeria **112** F4 6 27N 3 28E
Lagos Portugal **72** A2 37 05N 8 40W
Lagos Island *tn.* Nigeria **109** V3 6 24N 3 28E
Lagos Lagoon Nigeria **109** W3 6 30N 3 33E
Lago Titicaca *l.* Peru/Bolivia **102** C9/D9 16 00S 69 30W
La Grande Oregon U.S.A. **90** C6 45 21N 118 05W
La Grande 2, Réservoir Québec Canada **89** T3 54 00N 77 00W
La Grande 3, Réservoir Québec Canada **89** U3 54 10N 72 30W
La Grande Rivière *r.* Québec Canada **89** U3 54 00N 74 00W
La Grange Georgia U.S.A. **91** I3 33 02N 85 02W
La Guaira Venezuela **102** D15 10 38N 66 55W
Laguna Brazil **103** H7 28 29S 48 45W
Laguna Caratasca *l.* Honduras **97** H3 15 05N 84 00W
Laguna de Bay *l.* The Philippines **40** B3 14 00N 121 00E
Laguna de Perlas *l.* Nicaragua **97** H2 12 30N 83 30W
Laguna Madre *l.* Mexico **96** E4 25 00N 98 00W
Laguna Mar Chiquita *l.* Argentina **103** E6 30 30S 62 30W
Lagunillas Venezuela **102** C15 10 07N 71 16W
La Habana *(Havana)* Cuba **97** H4 23 07N 82 25W
La Habra California U.S.A. **95** C2 33 56N 117 59W
Lahad Datu Malaysia **42** E5 5 01N 118 20E
Lahaina Hawaiian Islands **23** Y18 20 23N 156 40W
Lahn *r.* Germany **71** A2 50 00N 8 00E
Lahore Pakistan **53** C6 31 34N 74 22E
Lahr Germany **71** A1 48 21N 7 52E
Lahti Finland **69** F3 61 00N 25 40E
Lai Chau Vietnam **37** B4 22 04N 103 10E
Lai Chi Chong Hong Kong U.K. **51** C2 22 27N 114 17E
Lai Chi Wo Hong Kong U.K. **51** C3 22 32N 114 15E
Lais Indonesia **42** B3 3 30S 102 02E
Lajes Brazil **103** G7 27 48S 50 20W
Lajpat Nagar India **52** M4 28 34N 77 15E
La Junta Colorado U.S.A. **90** F4 37 59N 103 34W
Lakao *i.* Solomon Islands **83** N4 9 55S 167 10E
Lakeba *i.* Fiji **83** F8 18 10S 178 49W
Lakeba Passage Fiji **83** F9 18 00S 178 40W
Lake Charles *tn.* Louisiana U.S.A. **91** H3 30 13N 93 13W
Lake City Michigan U.S.A. **92** C2 44 22N 85 12W
Lake Harbour *tn.* Northwest Territories Canada **89** V5 62 50N 69 50W
Lakeland *tn.* Florida U.S.A. **91** J2 28 02N 81 59W
Lake Murray *tn.* Papua New Guinea **45** J3 6 35S 141 28E
Lakeport California U.S.A. **90** B4 39 04N 122 56W
Lake River *tn.* Ontario Canada **89** S3 54 30N 82 30W
Lakeview Oregon U.S.A. **90** B5 42 13N 120 21W
Lakewood California U.S.A. **95** B2 33 49N 118 08W
Lakewood Ohio U.S.A. **93** D2 41 29N 81 50W
Lakor *i.* Indonesia **44** C2 8 18S 128 09E
Lakota North Dakota U.S.A. **92** A3 48 02N 98 20W
Lak Sao Laos **37** B3 18 12N 104 59E
Laksefjord *fj.* Norway **69** F5 70 40N 26 30E
Lakselv Norway **69** E5 70 03N 24 55E
Lakshadweep *admin.* India **53** C1 9 30N 73 00E
Laliki Indonesia **43** G2 7 41S 126 22E
Lalinda Vanuatu **83** H5 16 20S 168 05E
La Línea de la Concepción Spain **72** A2 36 10N 5 21W
Lalitpur India **53** D4 24 42N 78 24E
Lalona *i.* Tonga **83** B2 20 21S 174 32W
la Louvrière Belgium **70** D2 50 29N 4 12E
La Mancha *admin.* Spain **72** B2 39 10N 2 45W
Lamap *(Port Sandwich)* Vanuatu **83** G5 16 25S 167 48E
Lamar Colorado U.S.A. **90** F4 38 04N 102 37W
Lamari *r.* Papua New Guinea **45** L3 6 45S 145 30E
Lambaréné Gabon **112** H2 0 41S 10 13E
Lambert Glacier Antarctica **21** 73 00S 70 00E
Lambeth *bor.* England United Kingdom **66** C2 51 30N 0 07W
Lamboukouti Vanuatu **83** H5 16 53S 168 34E
Lam Chi *r.* Thailand **39** B3 16 15N 102 40E
Lamdesar Indonesia **44** D3 7 15S 131 57E
Lamego Portugal **72** A3 41 05N 7 49W
Lamen Vanuatu **83** H5 16 37S 168 09E
Lami Fiji **83** C8 18 06S 178 25E
Lamía Greece **74** D2 38 55N 22 26E
Lamitan The Philippines **40** B2 6 39N 122 09E
Lamlam Irian Jaya Indonesia **44** D6 0 05S 130 44E
Lamma Island Hong Kong U.K. **51** B1 22 12N 114 08E
Lammermuir Hills Scotland United Kingdom **68** I7 55 50N 2 45W
Lam Nam Chi *r.* Thailand **39** B2 14 50N 103 20E
Lamon Bay The Philippines **40** B3 14 00N 122 00E
Lamongan Indonesia **42** Q7 7 05S 112 26E
Lampang Thailand **39** A3 18 16N 99 30E
Lam Pao Reservoir Thailand **39** B3 16 40N 103 25E
Lampazos Mexico **96** D5 27 00N 100 30W
Lampedusa *i.* Italy **74** B2 35 00N 12 00E
Lamphun Thailand **39** A3 18 36N 99 02E
Lampung *admin.* Indonesia **42** B2/C2 4 30S 105 00E
Lam San Singapore **41** B4 1 22N 103 43E
Lam Si Bai *r.* Thailand **39** B3 15 30N 104 40E
Lam Tei Hong Kong U.K. **51** A2 22 25N 113 59E
Lamu Kenya **110** H7 2 17S 40 54E
Lanai *i.* Hawaiian Islands **23** Y18 20 50N 156 55W
Lanai City Hawaiian Islands **23** Y18 20 50N 156 56W
Lanao, Lake The Philippines **40** B2 8 00N 124 00E
Lanbi Kyun *i.* Myanmar **38** B2 10 58N 98 10E
Lancang Jiang *r.* China **49** J5 30 00N 98 00E
Lancaster England United Kingdom **68** I6 54 03N 2 48W
Lancaster California U.S.A. **90** C3 34 42N 118 09W
Lancaster New Hampshire U.S.A. **93** F2 44 29N 71 34W
Lancaster Ohio U.S.A. **93** D1 39 43N 82 37W
Lancaster Pennsylvania U.S.A. **93** E2 40 01N 76 19W
Lancaster Sound Northwest Territories Canada **89** R7 74 00N 87 30W
Landau Germany **71** A1 49 12N 8 07E
Landerneau France **73** A2 48 27N 4 16W
Landes *geog. reg.* France **73** A1 44 15N 1 00E
Landfall Island Andaman Islands **38** A2 13 40N 93 00E
Landgraaf Netherlands **70** F2 50 55N 6 02E
Landianchang China **47** F1 39 58N 116 17E
Land's End *c.* England United Kingdom **68** F2 50 03N 5 44W
Landshut Germany **71** B1 48 31N 12 10E
Landskrona Sweden **69** C2 55 53N 12 50E
La Nga *r.* Vietnam **37** C2 11 20N 107 50E
Langdon North Dakota U.S.A. **92** A3 48 46N 98 21W
Langeland *i.* Denmark **71** B2 55 00N 10 00E
Langeoog *i.* Germany **71** A2 53 00N 7 00E
Langer See *l.* Germany **67** G1 52 24N 13 36E
Langjökull *ice cap* Iceland **69** H6 64 45N 20 00W
Langkawi *i.* Myanmar **39** A1 6 25N 99 40E
Langon France **73** A1 44 33N 0 14W
Langøy *i.* Norway **69** C4 68 45N 15 00E
Langres France **73** C2 47 53N 5 20E
Langsa Indonesia **42** A4 4 28N 97 59E
Lang Son Vietnam **37** C4 21 50N 106 45E
Lang Suan Thailand **39** A1 9 55N 99 01E
Langtao Myanmar **38** B5 27 16N 97 39E
Lan Hsü *i.* Taiwan **51** H5 22 04N 121 32E
Lannion France **73** A2 48 44N 3 27W
L'Annociation Québec Canada **93** F3 46 24N 74 52W
Lanping China **38** B5 26 19N 99 20E
Lansdowne House *tn.* Ontario Canada **89** R3 52 05N 88 00W
L'Anse Michigan U.S.A. **92** C3 46 45N 88 27W
Lansing Michigan U.S.A. **93** D2 42 44N 85 34W
Lantau Channel Hong Kong U.K. **51** A1 22 11N 113 52E
Lantau Island Hong Kong U.K. **51** A1 22 15N 113 56E
Lantau Peak Hong Kong U.K. **51** A1 22 15N 113 55E
Lanzarote *i.* Canary Islands **112** C8 29 00N 13 38W
Lanzhou China **49** K6 36 01N 103 45E
Laoag The Philippines **40** B4 18 14N 120 36E
Laoang The Philippines **40** C3 12 35N 125 02E
Laobie Shan *mts.* China **38** B4 24 00N 99 30E
Lao Cai Vietnam **37** B4 22 30N 103 57E
Laon France **73** B2 49 34N 3 37E
La Oroya Peru **102** B10 11 36S 75 54W
LAOS **37** B3/C2
La Paz Bolivia **102** D9 16 30S 68 10W
La Paz Mexico **96** B4 24 10N 110 17W
La Perouse Australia **79** G2/H2 33 59S 151 14E
La Pesca Mexico **96** E4 23 46N 97 47W
La Plata Argentina **103** F5 34 52S 57 55W
Lappajärvi *l.* Finland **69** E3 63 13N 23 40E
Lappland *geog. reg.* Finland/Sweden **69** E4 67 30N 20 05E
Laprairie Québec Canada **93** F3 45 24N 73 30W
Laptev Sea Arctic Ocean **20** O10 76 00N 125 00E
Laptev Strait Russia **57** Q10 73 00N 141 00E
Lapua Finland **69** E3 62 57N 23 00E
La Puebla Balearic Islands **72** E4 39 46N 3 01E
La Puente California U.S.A. **95** C3 34 01N 117 58W
Lapu-Lapu The Philippines **40** B3 10 18N 123 58E
L'Aquila Italy **74** B3 42 22N 13 24E
Lār Iran **55** H4 27 42N 54 19E
Larache Morocco **112** D10 35 12N 6 10W
Laramie Wyoming U.S.A. **90** E5 41 20N 105 38W
Larantuka Indonesia **43** F2 8 20S 123 00E
Laredo Texas U.S.A. **90** G2 27 32N 99 22W
La Rioja Argentina **103** D7 29 26S 66 50W
Lárisa Greece **74** D2 39 38N 22 25E
Larkana Pakistan **52** B5 27 32N 68 18E
Larnaca Cyprus **54** D5 34 54N 33 29E
Larne Northern Ireland United Kingdom **68** F6 54 51N 5 49W
la Roche New Caledonia **82** X2 21 27S 168 05E
la Roche-en-Ardenne Belgium **70** E2 50 11N 5 35E
La Rochelle France **73** A2 46 10N 1 10W
la Roche-sur-Yon France **73** A2 46 40N 1 25W
La Romana Dominican Republic **97** K3 18 27N 68 57W
Larsen Ice Shelf Antarctica **21** 67 00S 62 00W
La Salle Illinois U.S.A. **92** C2 41 20N 89 06W
Las Cruces New Mexico U.S.A. **90** E3 32 18N 106 47W
Lasem Indonesia **42** P7 6 42S 111 30E
La Serena Chile **103** C7 29 54S 71 18W
la Seyne-sur-Mer France **73** C1 43 06N 5 53E
Lashio Myanmar **38** B4 22 58N 97 48E
Las Marismas *geog. reg.* Spain **72** A2 36 55N 6 00W
Las Palmas Canary Islands **112** B8 28 08N 15 27W
La Spezia Italy **74** A3 44 07N 9 48E
L'Assomption Québec Canada **93** F3 45 48N 73 27W
Last Mountain Lake Saskatchewan Canada **88** N3 51 40N 106 55W
Las Vegas Nevada U.S.A. **90** C4 36 10N 115 10W
Las Vegas New Mexico U.S.A. **90** E4 35 36N 105 15W
Latacunga Ecuador **102** B12 0 58S 78 36W
Late *i.* Tonga **83** B4 18 49S 174 40W
Latina Italy **74** B3 41 28N 12 53E
la Tontouta New Caledonia **82** V1 22 00S 166 15E
La Tuque Québec Canada **93** F3 47 26N 72 47W
Latur India **53** D3 18 24N 76 34E
LATVIA **69** F2
Lau Papua New Guinea **45** O4 5 51S 151 20E
Laucala *i.* Fiji **83** E10 16 46S 179 42W
Lauf Germany **71** B1 49 30N 11 16E
Launceston Australia **78** H1 41 25S 147 07E
Launglon Myanmar **38** B2 13 59N 98 08E
Laurel Mississippi U.S.A. **91** I3 31 41N 89 09W
Lausanne Switzerland **73** C2 46 32N 6 39E
Laut *i.* Indonesia **42** C4 4 40N 107 50E
Laut *i.* Indonesia **42** E3 3 30S 116 20E
Lautem Indonesia **44** B2 8 24S 126 56E
Lautoka Fiji **83** B9 17 36S 177 28E
Lauzon Québec Canada **93** F3 46 49N 71 10W
Laval France **73** A2 48 04N 0 45W
Lavanggu Solomon Islands **82** F2 11 42S 160 15E
La Vega Dominican Republic **97** J3 19 15N 70 33W
Laverton Australia **78** C4 28 49S 122 25E
La Victoria Venezuela **102** D15 10 16N 67 21W
Lawang Indonesia **42** Q7 7 50S 112 40E
Lawksawk Myanmar **38** B4 21 13N 96 50E
Lawndale California U.S.A. **95** A2 33 52N 118 21W
Lawrence Kansas U.S.A. **91** G4 38 58N 95 15W
Lawrence Massachusetts U.S.A. **93** F2 42 41N 71 12W
Lawton Oklahoma U.S.A. **90** G3 34 36N 98 25W
Lay *r.* France **73** A2 46 32N 1 15W
Laylá Saudi Arabia **55** G3 22 16N 46 45E
Laysan *i.* Hawaiian Islands **22** I10 25 46N 171 44W
Lea *r.* England United Kingdom **66** C3 51 40N 0 05W
Leach Cambodia **37** B2 12 18N 103 51E
Leamington Ontario Canada **93** D2 42 03N 82 35W
Lear *i.* Vanuatu **83** G8 13 31S 167 20E
Leatherhead England United Kingdom **66** B2 51 18N 0 20W
Lebak The Philippines **40** B2 6 30N 124 02E
LEBANON **54** O11/P12
Lebanon Missouri U.S.A. **91** H4 37 40N 92 40W
Lebanon New Hampshire U.S.A. **93** F2 43 39N 72 17W
Lebanon Pennsylvania U.S.A. **93** E2 40 21N 76 25W
le Blanc France **73** B2 46 38N 1 04E
le Blanc-Mesnil France **67** B2 48 56N 2 28E
Lebu Chile **103** C5 37 38S 73 43W
Lecce Italy **74** C3 40 21N 18 11E
Lech *r.* Europe **71** B1 48 00N 11 00E
Lechtaler Alpen *mts.* Austria **71** B1 47 00N 10 00E
le Creusot France **73** B2 46 48N 4 27E
Ledong China **37** C3 18 43N 109 09E
Leduc Alberta Canada **88** M3 53 17N 113 30W
Lee *r.* Irish Republic **68** C3 51 50N 8 50W
Leech Lake Minnesota U.S.A. **92** B3 47 00N 94 00W
Leeds England United Kingdom **68** J5 53 50N 1 35W
Leer Germany **71** A2 53 14N 7 27E
Leerdam Netherlands **70** E3 51 53N 5 05E
Leeuwarden Netherlands **70** E5 53 12N 5 48E
Leeuwin, Cape Australia **78** B3 34 24S 115 09E
Leeward Islands Lesser Antilles **97** L3 17 30N 64 00W
Leganés Spain **72** B3 40 20N 3 4WE
Legaspi The Philippines **40** B3 13 10N 123 45E
Legnica Poland **75** C3 51 12N 16 10E
Leh Kashmir **53** D6 34 09N 77 35E
le Havre France **73** B2 49 30N 0 06E
Leicester England United Kingdom **68** J4 52 38N 1 05W
Leichhardt Australia **79** G2 33 53S 151 09E
Leiden Netherlands **70** D4 52 10N 4 30E
Leidschendam Netherlands **70** D4 52 05N 4 24E
Leie *r.* Belgium **70** C2 50 50N 3 20E
Leine *r.* Germany **71** A2 52 00N 10 00E
Leipzig Germany **71** B2 51 20N 12 25E
Leiria Portugal **72** A2 39 45N 8 49W
Leitre Papua New Guinea **45** J5 2 52S 141 42E
Leizhou Bandao *p.* China **49** M3 21 00N 110 00E
Lek *r.* Netherlands **70** D3 51 48N 4 47E
Lekkous *r.* Morocco **72** A1 35 00N 5 40W
Leksula Indonesia **44** B5 3 46S 126 35E
Leli *i.* Solomon Islands **82** G5 8 45S 161 04E
Lelystad Netherlands **70** E4 52 32N 5 29E
le Mans France **73** B2 48 00N 0 12E
Lemgo Germany **71** A2 52 02N 8 54E
Lemmer Netherlands **70** E4 52 50N 5 43E
Lemyethna Myanmar **38** B3 17 36N 95 08E
Lena *r.* Russia **57** O9 70 00N 125 00E
Lengshuijiang China **36** E7 27 40N 111 26E
Leninabad *see* Khojand
Leninakan *see* Kumairi
Leningrad *see* St. Petersburg
Lenino Russia **56** M1 55 35N 37 10E
Leninogorsk Kazakhstan **59** N5 50 23N 83 32E
Leninsk-Kuznetskiy Russia **57** K6 54 44N 86 13E
Lenkoran' Azerbaijan **58** F2 38 45N 48 50E
Lennoxville Québec Canada **93** F3 45 22N 71 51W
Lens France **73** B3 50 26N 2 50E
Lensk Russia **57** N8 60 48N 114 55E
Lenya *r.* Myanmar **38** B2 11 00N 98 55E
Leoben Austria **75** C2 47 23N 15 06E
León Mexico **96** D4 21 10N 101 42W
León Spain **72** A3 42 35N 5 34W
Leon *r.* Texas U.S.A. **91** G3 32 00N 98 00W
Leonard Murray Mountains Papua New Guinea **45** K3 7 00S 143 30E
Leone American Samoa **82** 14 21S 170 47W
Leonora Australia **78** C4 28 54S 121 20E
Lepel' Belarus **75** E3 54 48N 28 40E
le Puy France **73** B2 45 03N 3 53E
le Raincy France **67** C2 48 54N 2 32E
Léré Chad **110** B9 9 41N 14 17E
Lérida *(Lleida)* Spain **72** C3 41 37N 0 38E
Lerwick Scotland United Kingdom **68** J12 60 09N 1 09W
Les Cayes Haiti **97** J3 18 15N 73 46W
Les Coudreaux France **67** C2 48 54N 2 36E
Lesiaceva Point Fiji **83** D10 16 50S 179 17E
Les Îles Belcher *is.* Northwest Territories Canada **89** T4 56 00N 79 30W
Leskovac Serbia Yugoslavia **74** D3 43 00N 21 57E
LESOTHO **111** E2
les Pétroglyphes New Caledonia **82** V2 21 38S 166 01E
les Sables-d'Olonne France **73** A2 46 30N 1 47W
Lesse Belgium **70** E2 50 10N 5 10E
Lesser Antilles *is.* West Indies **97** K2/L3
Lesser Slave Lake Alberta Canada **88** L4 55 25N 115 30W
Lessines Belgium **70** C2 50 43N 3 50E
les Ulis France **67** A1 48 41N 2 11E
Lésvos *i.* Greece **74** E2 39 00N 26 00E
Leszno Poland **75** C3 51 51N 16 35E
Letha Range Myanmar **38** A4 23 30N 93 30E
Lethbridge Alberta Canada **88** M2 49 43N 112 48W
Leti *i.* Indonesia **44** B2 8 10S 127 40E
Leticia Colombia **102** C12 4 09S 69 57W
le Touquet-Paris-Plage France **73** B3 50 13N 1 36E
Letpadan Myanmar **38** B3 17 46N 95 45E
le Tréport France **73** B3 50 04N 1 22E
Letsok-aw Kyun *i.* Myanmar **38** B2 11 30N 98 15E
Leulumoega Western Samoa **82** B11 13 49S 171 53W
Leuven *(Louvain)* Belgium **70** D2 50 53N 4 42E
Levádhia Greece **74** D2 38 26N 22 53E
Lévêque, Cape Australia **78** C6 16 25S 122 55E
Leverkusen Germany **71** A2 51 02N 6 59E
Levice Slovakia **75** C2 48 14N 18 35E
Levin North Island New Zealand **79** C2 40 37S 175 17E
Lévis Québec Canada **93** F3 46 47N 71 12W
Levkás *i.* Greece **74** D2 38 00N 20 00E
Levuka Fiji **83** C9 17 42S 178 50E
Lewe Myanmar **38** B3 19 40N 96 04E
Lewes Delaware U.S.A. **93** E1 38 47N 75 09W
Lewis *i.* Scotland United Kingdom **68** E10 58 15N 6 30W
Lewisburg Pennsylvania U.S.A. **93** E2 40 58N 76 55W
Lewisham *bor.* England United Kingdom **66** C2 51 27N 0 00
Lewis Pass South Island New Zealand **79** B2 42 23S 172 24E
Lewiston Idaho U.S.A. **90** C6 46 25N 117 00W
Lewiston Maine U.S.A. **93** F2 44 08N 70 14W
Lewiston New York U.S.A. **93** E2 43 11N 79 03W
Lewistown Montana U.S.A. **90** E6 47 04N 109 26W
Lewistown Pennsylvania U.S.A. **93** E2 40 37N 77 36W
Lexington Kentucky U.S.A. **93** D1 38 03N 84 30W
Lexington Virginia U.S.A. **93** E1 37 47N 79 27W
Lexington Park Maryland U.S.A. **93** E1 38 15N 76 28W
Leyte *i.* The Philippines **40** B3/C3 11 00N 125 00E
Leyte Gulf The Philippines **40** C3 11 00N 125 00E
Lezhë Albania **74** C3 41 47N 19 39E
Lhasa China **48** H4 29 41N 91 10E
Lhazê China **48** G4 29 08N 87 43E
Lhokseumawe Indonesia **42** A5 5 09N 97 09E
Li Thailand **39** A3 17 48N 98 58E
Lianga The Philippines **40** C2 8 38N 126 05E
Liangwang Shan *mts.* China **38** C5 25 30N 103 20E
Lian Xian China **36** E6 24 48N 112 26E
Lianyungang China **49** N5 34 37N 119 10E
Liaoyang China **49** O7 41 16N 123 12E
Liaoyuan China **49** P7 42 53N 125 10E
Liard *r.* British Columbia/Northwest Territories Canada **88** J4 61 55N 122 30W
Libenge Zaïre **110** C8 3 39N 18 39E
Liberal Kansas U.S.A. **90** F4 37 03N 100 56W
Liberec Czech Republic **75** C3 50 48N 15 05E
LIBERIA **112** C4/D4
Liberty New York U.S.A. **93** F2 41 47N 74 46W
Libourne France **73** A1 44 55N 0 14W
Libreville Gabon **112** G3 0 30N 9 25E
LIBYA **110** B13/D13
Libyan Desert North Africa **110** E12/D13 25 00N 25 00E
Libyan Plateau Egypt **110** E14 31 00N 26 00E
Lichinga Mozambique **111** G5 13 19S 35 13E
Lichtenberg Germany **67** G2 52 32N 13 30E
Lichtenrade Germany **67** F1 52 23N 13 22E
Licking *r.* Kentucky U.S.A. **93** D1 38 00N 84 00W
Lida Belarus **75** E3 53 50N 25 19E
Lidcombe Australia **79** G2 33 52S 151 03E
LIECHTENSTEIN **73** C2
Liège Belgium **70** E2 50 38N 5 35E
Liège *admin.* Belgium **70** E2 50 30N 5 45E
Lienz Austria **75** B2 46 51N 12 50E
Liepāja Latvia **69** E2 56 30N 21 00E
Lier Belgium **70** D3 51 08N 4 35E
Liestal Switzerland **73** C2 47 29N 7 43E
Lifou *i.* New Caledonia **82** W3 21 00S 167 10E
Lifuka *i.* Tonga **83** B3 19 50S 174 22W
Ligao The Philippines **40** B3 13 14N 123 33E
Ligurian Sea Mediterranean Sea **74** A3 44 00N 9 00E
Lihir Group *is.* Papua New Guinea **45** P5 3 10S 152 30E
Lihue Hawaiian Islands **23** X18 21 59N 159 23W
Lijiang China **38** C5 26 51N 100 18E
Likasi Zaïre **111** E5 10 58S 26 47E
Liku Indonesia **32** D4 1 47N 109 19E
Likupang Indonesia **43** G4 1 40N 125 05E
Lille France **73** B3 50 39N 3 05E
Lillehammer Norway **69** C3 61 06N 10 27E
Lilongwe Malawi **111** F5 13 58S 33 49E
Liluah India **52** K2 22 37N 88 20E
Lima Peru **102** B10 12 06S 8 40W
Lima Ohio U.S.A. **93** D2 40 43N 84 06W
Lima *r.* Portugal **72** A3 42 00N 8 30W
Limassol Cyprus **54** D5 34 04N 33 03E
Limburg Germany **71** A2 50 23N 8 04E
Limburg *admin.* Belgium **70** E2 50 55N 5 20E
Limburg *admin.* Netherlands **70** E3 51 32N 5 45E
Lim Chu Kang Singapore **41** B4 1 24N 103 41E
Limeira Brazil **103** H8 22 34S 47 25W
Limerick Irish Republic **68** C4 52 04N 8 38W
Limfjorden *sd.* Denmark **69** B2 57 00N 8 50E
Límnos *i.* Greece **74** E2 39 00N 25 00E
Limoges France **73** B2 45 50N 1 15E
Limón Costa Rica **97** H2 10 00N 83 01W
Limoux France **73** B1 43 03N 2 13E
Limpopo *r.* Southern Africa **111** F3 22 30S 32 00E
Limu *i.* Tonga **83** B2 20 02S 174 29W
Linapacan *i.* The Philippines **40** A3 11 00N 120 00E
Linares Mexico **96** E4 24 54N 99 38W
Linares Spain **72** B2 38 05N 3 38W
Lincang China **38** C4 23 56N 100 16E
Lincoln England United Kingdom **68** K5 53 14N 0 33W
Lincoln Maine U.S.A. **93** G3 45 23N 68 30W
Lincoln Nebraska U.S.A. **92** A2 40 49N 96 41W
Lincoln Wolds *hills* England United Kingdom **68** K5 53 25N 0 05W
Linden Guyana **102** F14 5 59N 58 19W
Linden New Jersey U.S.A. **94** B1 40 37N 74 13W
Lindenberg Germany **67** G2 52 37N 13 31E
Lindfield Australia **79** G2 33 47S 151 10E
Lindis Pass South Island New Zealand **79** A2 44 35S 169 39E
Lindsay Ontario Canada **93** E2 44 21N 78 44W
Line Islands Kiribati **81** D3/E2 0 00 160 00W
Lingao China **37** C3 19 59N 109 41E
Lingayen The Philippines **40** B4 16 02N 120 14E
Lingayen Gulf The Philippines **40** B4 16 00N 120 00E
Lingen Germany **71** A2 52 32N 7 19E
Lingga *i.* Indonesia **42** B3 0 10S 104 40E
Ling Tong Mei Hong Kong U.K. **51** B2 22 29N 114 06E
Linhares Brazil **102** J9 19 22S 40 04W
Linh Cam Vietnam **37** C3 18 31N 105 35E
Linjiang China **50** C5 41 45N 126 56E
Linköping Sweden **69** D2 58 25N 15 35E
Linsell Sweden **69** C3 62 10N 13 50E
Linstead Jamaica **97** Q8 18 08N 77 02W
Linton North Dakota U.S.A. **90** F6 46 17N 100 14W
Linxia China **49** K6 35 31N 103 08E
Linz Austria **75** B2 48 19N 14 18E
Lion Rock *mt.* Hong Kong U.K. **51** C2 22 21N 114 11E
Lioppa Indonesia **44** B3 7 41S 126 01E
Lipa The Philippines **40** B3 13 57N 121 10E
Lipe Solomon Islands **83** M3 10 20S 166 15E
Lipetsk Russia **56** F6 52 37N 39 36E
Lippe *r.* Germany **70** G3 51 00N 7 00E
Lippstadt Germany **71** A2 51 41N 8 20E
Lisas, Point Trinidad and Tobago **96** T9 10 22N 61 37W
Lisboa *(Lisbon)* Portugal **72** A2 38 44N 9 08W
Lisbon Portugal *see* Lisboa
Lisbon North Dakota U.S.A. **92** A3 46 28N 97 30W

Mahalapye Botswana **109** K3 23 05S 26 52E
Mahanadi *r.* India **53** E4 21 00N 84 00E
Maharashtra *admin.* India **53** C3/D3 19 30N 75 00E
Maharepa Tahiti **82** R10 17 28S 149 47W
Maha Sarakham Thailand **39** B3 16 08N 103 21E
Mahaxai Laos **37** C3 17 28N 105 18E
Mahdia Tunisia **74** B2 35 29N 11 03E
Mahia Peninsula North Island New Zealand **79** C3 39 10S 177 53E
Mahina Tahiti **82** T9 17 29S 149 27W
Mahlow Germany **67** F1 52 22N 13 24E
Mahón Balearic Islands **72** F4 39 54N 4 15E
Mahrauli India **52** L4 28 30N 77 11E
Mala American Samoa **82** F12 14 14S 169 26W
Maibang Indonesia **43** F2 8 08S 124 33E
Maidstone England United Kingdom **68** L3 51 17N 0 32E
Maiduguri Nigeria **112** H5 11 53N 13 16E
Maikala Range *mts.* India **53** E4 22 30N 81 30E
Main *r.* Germany **71** A2 50 00N 8 00E
Main Channel Ontario Canada **93** D3 45 00N 82 00W
Maingkwan Myanmar **38** B5 26 20N 96 37E
Mainit, Lake The Philippines **40** C2 9 00N 125 00E
Mainland *i.* Orkney Islands Scotland United Kingdom **68** H11 59 00N 3 15W
Mainland *i.* Shetland Islands Scotland United Kingdom **68** J12 60 15N 1 20W
Maintirano Madagascar **111** H4 18 01S 44 03E
Mainz Germany **71** A1 50 00N 8 16E
Mai Po Lo Wai Hong Kong U.K. **51** B2 22 29N 114 03E
Maiquetía Venezuela **102** D15 10 38N 66 59W
Maiskhal *i.* Bangladesh **38** A4 21 36N 91 53E
Maisons-Lafitte France **67** A2 48 57N 2 09E
Maitland Australia **78** I3 32 33S 151 33E
Maitland Range Malaysia **40** A1-2 5 00N 116 40E
Maitri *r.s.* Antarctica **21** 70 37S 8 22E
Maizuru Japan **46** G2 35 30N 135 20E
Majene Indonesia **42** E3 3 33S 118 59E
Maji Ethiopia **110** G9 6 12N 35 32E
Majiuqiao China **47** H1 39 45N 116 33E
Majorca *see* Mallorca
Majuro Pacific Ocean **80** C4 7 05N 171 08E
Makabe Japan **46** M3 36 15N 140 06E
Makale Indonesia **43** E3 3 06S 119 53E
Makassar Strait *sd.* Indonesia **42** E3 0 00 119 00E
Makaw Myanmar **38** B5 26 28N 96 40E
Makeni Sierra Leone **112** C4 8 57N 12 02W
Makeyevka Ukraine **58** D4 48 01N 38 00E
Makgadikgadi Salt Pan Botswana **111** E3 21 00S 26 00E
Makhachkala Russia **56** G4 42 59N 47 30E
Maki Irian Jaya Indonesia **44** F5 3 18S 134 13E
Makkah *(Mecca)* Saudi Arabia **54** E3 21 26N 39 49E
Makkovik Newfoundland Canada **89** X4 55 09N 59 10W
Makó Hungary **75** D2 46 11N 20 30E
Makodroga *i.* Fiji **83** C9 17 24S 179 01E
Makogai *i.* Fiji **83** C9 17 26S 178 59E
Makoku Gabon **112** H3 0 38N 12 47E
Makran *geog. reg.* Iran/Pakistan **55** J4 25 55N 61 30E
Makung *(Penghu)* Taiwan **51** F6 23 35N 119 33E
Makurdi Nigeria **112** G4 7 44N 8 35E
Malabar Coast India **53** C2/D1 12 00N 74 00E
Malabo Equatorial Guinea **112** G3 3 45N 8 48E
Malacca, Strait of *(Selat Melaka)* Indonesia **42** B4 4 00N 100 00E
Málaga Spain **72** B2 36 43N 4 25W
Malaita Solomon Islands **82** F5/G4 9 00S 161 00E
Malakal Sudan **110** F9 9 31N 31 40E
Malake Fiji **83** C9 17 20S 178 09E
Malakobi *i.* Solomon Islands **82** D6 7 20S 158 00E
Malakula Vanuatu **83** G5 16 20S 167 30E
Malam Papua New Guinea **45** K2 8 45S 142 46E
Malalamai Papua New Guinea **45** M4 5 49S 146 44E
Malang Indonesia **42** Q7 7 59S 112 45E
Malanje Angola **111** C6 9 32S 16 20E
Malao Vanuatu **83** F6 15 10S 166 49E
Mälaren *(Lake Mälar) l.* Sweden **69** D2 59 30N 17 00E
Malartic Québec Canada **93** E3 48 09N 78 09W
Malatya Turkey **54** E6 38 22N 38 18E
Malau Fiji **83** D10 16 24S 179 23E
MALAWI 111 F5
Malawi, Lake *see* Nyasa Lake
Malaya *see* Peninsular Malaysia
Malaybalay The Philippines **40** C2 8 09N 125 07E
MALAYSIA 42 B5-E5
Malbork Poland **75** C3 54 02N 19 01E
Maldegem Belgium **70** C3 51 12N 3 27E
Malden Island Pacific Ocean **81** E3 4 03S 154 59W
MALDIVES 24 G7
Maldonado Uruguay **103** G6 34 57S 54 59W
Malegaon India **53** C4 20 32N 74 38E
Malema Mozambique **111** G5 14 57S 37 25E
Malevangga Solomon Islands **82** B7 6 40S 156 28E
MALI 112 D5/F6
Mali *i.* Fiji **83** D10 16 28S 179 21E
Mali Hka *r.* Myanmar **38** B5 26 00N 97 40E
Mali Kyun *i.* Myanmar **38** B2 13 10N 98 10E
Malili Indonesia **43** F3 2 38S 121 06E
Malima *i.* Fiji **83** E9 17 07S 179 13W
Malindang, Mount The Philippines **40** B2 8 12N 123 40E
Malines *see* Mechelen
Malin Head *c.* Irish Republic **68** D7 55 30N 7 20W
Malipo China **37** B4 23 09N 104 45E
Mallaig Scotland United Kingdom **68** F9 57 00N 5 50W
Mallawi Egypt **54** D4 27 44N 30 50E
Mallorca *(Majorca) i.* Balearic Islands **72** E4 39 50N 2 30E
Malmédy Belgium **70** F2 50 26N 6 02E
Malmesbury Republic of South Africa **111** C1 33 28S 18 43E
Malmö Sweden **69** C2 55 35N 13 00E
Malo Solomon Islands **8** L3 10 40S 165 45E
Malo *i.* Vanuatu **83** G6 15 40S 167 10E
Maloelap Atoll Pacific Ocean **80** C4 8 45N 171 00E
Malolo *i.* Fiji **83** B9 17 45S 177 10E
Malolo Barrier Reef Fiji **83** B9 17 49S 177 09E
Malolos The Philippines **40** B3 14 51N 120 49E
Malom Papua New Guinea **45** O5 3 15S 151 55E
Malone New York U.S.A. **93** F2 44 52N 74 19W
Malonga Zaïre **111** D5 10 26S 23 10E
Måløy Norway **69** B3 61 57N 5 06E
Malpelo *i.* Colombia **102** A13 4 00N 81 35W
MALTA 74 B2
Malta Montana U.S.A. **90** E6 48 22N 107 51W
Malta *i.* Mediterranean Sea **74** B2 35 00N 14 00E
Ma Lui Shui Hong Kong U.K. **51** C2 22 25N 114 12E
Maluku *(Moluccas) admin.* Indonesia **43** G3 2 00S 127 00E
Malu'u Solomon Islands **82** F5 8 20S 160 40E
Malviya Nagar India **52** L4 28 32N 77 12E
Mamanuku-i-cake Group Fiji **83** B9 17 30S 177 05E
Mamaroneck New York U.S.A. **94** D2 40 57N 73 43W
Mamba Japan **46** K3 36 07N 138 54E
Mambasa Zaïre **110** E8 1 20N 29 05E
Mamberamo *r.* Indonesia **33** 2 00S 138 00E
Mamburao The Philippines **40** B3 13 13N 120 39E
Mamié New Caledonia **82** V1 22 02S 166 55E
Mamonovo Russia **58** A5 54 30N 19 59E
Mamuju Indonesia **42** E3 2 41S 118 55E
Man Côte d'Ivoire **112** D4 7 31N 7 37W
Mana *i.* Fiji **83** B9 17 40S 177 09E
Manacapuru Brazil **102** E12 3 16S 60 37W
Manacor Balearic Islands **72** E4 39 35N 3 12E
Manado Indonesia **43** F4 1 32N 124 55E
Managua Nicaragua **97** G2 12 06N 86 18W
Manali India **53** D6 32 12N 77 06E
Manam Island Papua New Guinea **45** L4 4 15S 144 15E
Manatuto Indonesia **44** A2 8 31S 126 00E
Manau Papua New Guinea **45** M2 8 02S 148 00E
Manaus Brazil **102** F12 3 06S 60 00W
Manchester England United Kingdom **68** I5 53 30N 2 15W
Manchester Kentucky U.S.A. **93** D1 37 09N 83 46W
Manchester New Hampshire U.S.A. **93** F2 42 59N 71 28W
Manchester Tennessee U.S.A. **91** I4 35 29N 86 04W
Mandal Norway **69** B2 58 02N 7 30E
Mandalay Myanmar **38** B4 21 57N 96 04E
Mandalay *admin.* Myanmar **38** B4 21 10N 95 30E
Mandaue The Philippines **40** B3 10 21N 123 57E
Mandeville Jamaica **97** Q8 18 02N 77 31W
Mandvi India **52** B4 22 50N 69 25E
Mandya India **53** D2 12 34N 76 55E
Manfredonia Italy **74** C3 41 37N 15 55E
Mangai Papua New Guinea **45** O5 2 49S 151 09E
Mangaia *i.* Pacific Ocean **81** E2 21 56S 157 56W
Mangalore India **53** C2 12 54N 74 51E
Manggar Indonesia **42** C3 2 52S 108 13E
Manggautu Solomon Islands **82** E1 11 38S 159 58E
Manggawitu Irian Jaya Indonesia **44** E4 4 13S 133 30E
Mangin Range Myanmar **38** B4 24 30N 95 50E
Mango *i.* Tonga **83** B2 20 20S 174 53W
Mangoky *r.* Madagascar **111** H3 22 00S 45 00E
Mangui China **49** O9 52 05N 122 17E
Manhasset New York U.S.A. **94** D2 40 48N 73 41W
Manhattan Kansas U.S.A. **92** A1 39 11N 96 35W
Manhattan New York U.S.A. **94** C2 40 48N 73 58W
Manhattan Beach *tn.* California U.S.A. **95** A2 33 53N 118 24W
Mania *r.* Madagascar **111** I4 19 30S 50 30E
Manica Mozambique **111** F4 18 56S 32 52E
Manicoré Brazil **102** E11 5 48S 61 16W
Manicouagan Québec Canada **89** V3 50 40N 68 45W
Manicouagan *r.* Québec Canada **93** G3/4 50 00N 69 00W
Manihiki *i.* Pacific Ocean **81** D3 10 24S 161 01W
Manikpur India **52** J2 22 32N 88 12E
Manila The Philippines **40** B3 14 37N 120 58E
Manila Bay The Philippines **40** B3 14 00N 121 00E
Manipur *admin.* India **53** G4 24 30N 94 00E
Manipur *r.* India/Myanmar **38** A4 23 55N 93 35E
Manisa Turkey **74** E2 38 36N 27 29E
Manistee Michigan U.S.A. **92** C2 44 14N 86 20W
Manistee *r.* Michigan U.S.A. **92** C2 45 00N 85 00W
Manistique Michigan U.S.A. **92** C3 45 58N 86 17W
Manitoba *province* Canada **89** P4 55 15N 100 00W
Manitoba, Lake Manitoba Canada **89** P3 50 30N 98 15W
Manitoulin Island Ontario Canada **93** D3 46 00N 82 00W
Manitowoc Wisconsin U.S.A. **92** C2 44 04N 87 40W
Maniwaki Québec Canada **93** E3 46 22N 75 58W
Manizales Colombia **102** B14 5 03N 75 32W
Manjra *r.* India **53** D3 18 30N 76 00E
Man Kam To Hong Kong U.K. **51** B3 22 32N 114 07E
Mankato Minnesota U.S.A. **92** B2 44 10N 94 00W
Manly Australia **79** H2 33 48S 151 17E
Manna Indonesia **42** B3 4 29S 102 55E
Mannar, Gulf of India/Sri Lanka **53** D1 8 30N 79 00E
Mannheim Germany **71** A1 49 30N 8 28E
Manning Alberta Canada **88** L4 56 53N 117 39W
Manning Strait Solomon Islands **82** C6 7 20S 158 00E
Manokwari Irian Jaya Indonesia **44** F6 0 53S 134 05E
Manono *i.* Western Samoa **82** A11 13 50S 172 06W
Manoron Myanmar **38** B2 11 36N 99 02E
Manotick Ontario Canada **93** E3 45 10N 75 45W
Manpojin North Korea **50** C5 41 06N 126 24E
Manra *(Sydney Island) i.* Pacific Ocean **80** D3 4 30S 171 30W
Manresa Spain **72** C3 41 43N 1 50E
Mansa Zambia **111** E5 11 10S 28 52E
Mansel Island Northwest Territories Canada **89** T5 62 00N 80 00W
Mansfield Ohio U.S.A. **93** D2 40 46N 82 31W
Mansfield Pennsylvania U.S.A. **93** E2 41 47N 77 05W
Manta Ecuador **102** A12 0 59S 80 44W
Mantalingajan, Mount The Philippines **40** A2 8 50N 117 43E
Mantarara Indonesia **44** A6 1 50S 125 03E
Mantes-la-Jolie France **73** B2 48 59N 1 43E
Mantova Italy **74** B4 45 10N 10 47E
Manua Islands American Samoa **82** F12 14 14S 169 28W
Manukau North Island New Zealand **79** B3 37 00S 174 52E
Manukau Harbour North Island New Zealand **79** B3 37 02S 174 43E
Manus Island Papua New Guinea **45** M6 2 00S 147 00E
Manyoni Tanzania **111** F6 5 46S 34 50E
Manzanares Spain **72** B2 39 00N 3 23W
Manzanilla Bay Trinidad and Tobago **96** T9/10 10 40N 61 55W
Manzanilla Point Trinidad and Tobago **96** T10 10 31N 61 01W
Manzanillo Cuba **97** I4 20 21N 77 21W
Manzanillo Mexico **96** D3 19 00N 104 20W
Manzhouli China **49** N8 46 36N 117 28E
Maoming China **49** M3 21 50N 110 56E
Ma On Shan Hong Kong U.K. **51** C2 22 26N 114 13E
Ma On Shan *mt.* Hong Kong U.K. **51** C2 22 24N 114 16E
Maotou Shan *mt.* China **38** C4 24 22N 100 46E
Mapi Irian Jaya Indonesia **44** H3 7 06S 139 23E
Mapi *r.* Irian Jaya Indonesia **44** H3 6 30S 139 35E
Maple Creek *tn.* Saskatchewan Canada **88** N2 49 55N 109 28W
Maprik Papua New Guinea **45** K5 3 38S 143 02E
Maputo Mozambique **111** F2 25 58S 32 35E
Marabá Brazil **102** H11 5 23S 49 10W
Marabo *i.* Fiji **83** F8 18 59S 178 50W
Maracaibo Venezuela **102** C15 10 44N 71 37W
Maracay Venezuela **102** D15 10 20N 67 28W
Maradi Niger **112** G5 13 29N 7 10E
Marais Poitevin *marsh* France **73** A2 46 22N 1 06W
Marakei *i.* Pacific Ocean **80** C4 2 00N 173 25E
Maramasike *(Small Malaita) i.* Solomon Islands **82** G4 9 30S 161 30E
Maramba *(Livingstone)* Zambia **111** E4 17 50S 25 53E
Marang Malaysia **42** B5 5 12N 103 12E
Maranhão *admin.* Brazil **102** H11 5 20S 46 00W
Marapa *i.* Solomon Islands **82** F4 9 50S 160 50E
Marathon Ontario Canada **92** C3 48 44N 86 23W
Maraval Trinidad and Tobago **96** T10 10 42N 61 31W
Maravovo Solomon Islands **82** E4 9 21S 159 37E
Marawi The Philippines **40** B2 7 59N 124 16E
Marbella Spain **72** B2 36 31N 4 53W
Marble Bar *tn.* Australia **78** B5 21 16S 119 45E
Marble Canyon *tn.* Arizona U.S.A. **90** D4 36 50N 111 38W
Marburg Germany **71** A2 50 49N 8 36E
Marche-en-Famenne Belgium **70** E2 50 13N 5 21E
Marchfield Barbados **96** W12 13 07N 59 29W
Marcus Island Pacific Ocean **22** F10 24 30N 157 30E
Mardan Pakistan **53** C6 34 14N 72 05E
Mar del Plata Argentina **103** F5 38 00S 57 32W
Mardin Turkey **54** F6 37 19N 40 43E
Maré *i.* New Caledonia **82** W2/X2 21 30S 168 00E
Margai Caka *l.* China **53** F7 35 00N 87 00E
Margat *r.* The Philippines **40** B4 17 00N 121 00E
Margate England United Kingdom **68** M3 51 24N 1 24E
Margilan Uzbekistan **59** L3 40 30N 71 45E
Maria *i.* Pacific Ocean **81** E2 23 00S 155 00W
Maria Elena Chile **103** D8 22 18S 69 40W
Marianas Trench Pacific Ocean **22** E9 16 00N 147 30E
Mariani India **38** A5 26 39N 94 18E
Marian Lake *tn.* Northwest Territories Canada **88** L5 62 55N 115 55W
Mariánské Lázně Czech Republic **71** B1 49 48N 12 45E
Maria van Diemen, Cape North Island New Zealand **79** B4 34 29S 172 39E
Maribor Slovenia **74** C4 46 34N 15 38E
Marie Byrd Land *geog. reg.* Antarctica **21** 77 00S 130 00W
Mariehamn Finland **69** D3 60 05N 19 55E
Mariental Namibia **111** C3 24 36S 17 59E
Marietta Ohio U.S.A. **93** D1 39 26N 81 27W
Marignane France **73** C1 43 25N 5 12E
Marijampole *(Kapsukas)* Lithuania **69** E1 54 31N 23 20E
Marília Brazil **103** G8 22 13S 49 58W
Marina del Rey California U.S.A. **95** A2 33 58N 118 28W
Marina East Singapore **41** D3 1 17N 103 53E
Marina South Singapore **41** D3 1 17N 103 52E
Marinduque *i.* The Philippines **40** B3 13 20N 122 00E
Marinette Wisconsin U.S.A. **92** C3 45 06N 87 38W
Maringá Brazil **103** G8 23 26S 52 02W
Marion Illinois U.S.A. **92** C1 37 42N 88 58W
Marion Indiana U.S.A. **92** C2 40 33N 85 40W
Marion Ohio U.S.A. **93** D2 40 35N 83 08W
Marion, Lake South Carolina U.S.A. **91** J3 33 00N 80 00W
Mariscal Estigarribia Paraguay **103** E8 22 03S 60 35W
Mariu Indonesia **45** J2 8 40S 140 37E
Mariupol *(Zhdanov)* Ukraine **58** D4 47 05N 37 34E
Mariveles The Philippines **40** B3 14 26N 120 29E
Marjayoun Lebanon **54** O11 33 22N 35 34E
Mark *r.* Belgium **70** D3 51 45N 4 45E
Marka Somalia **110** H8 1 42N 44 47E
Markerwaard Netherlands **70** E4 52 35N 5 15E
Markha *r.* Russia **57** N8 64 00N 12 30E
Markham *r.* Papua New Guinea **45** M3 6 30S 146 15E
Markovo Russia **57** T8 64 40N 170 24E
Marl Germany **71** A2 51 38N 7 06E
Marly-le-Roi France **67** A2 48 52N 2 05E
Marmande France **73** B1 44 30N 0 10E
Marmara, Sea of Turkey **54** C7 15 40N 28 10E
Marne *r.* France **73** B2 49 00N 5 00E
Maroantsetra Madagascar **111** I4 15 23S 49 44E
Maroko Nigeria **109** W3 6 21N 3 32E
Maroni *r.* Surinam **102** G13 4 00N 54 30W
Maros Indonesia **43** E3 4 59S 119 35E
Maroua Cameroon **112** H5 10 35N 14 20E
Maroubra Australia **79** G2/H2 33 57S 151 15E
Marquesas Islands Pacific Ocean **81** E3 10 00S 137 00W
Marquette Michigan U.S.A. **92** C3 46 33N 87 23W
Marrakech Morocco **112** D9 31 49N 8 00W
Marrickville Australia **79** G2 33 55S 151 09E
Marsabit Kenya **110** G8 2 20N 37 59E
Marsala Italy **74** B2 37 48N 12 27E
Marseille France **73** C1 43 18N 5 22E
Marshall Missouri U.S.A. **92** B1 39 06N 93 11W
MARSHALL ISLANDS 80 C4
Marshalltown Iowa U.S.A. **92** B2 42 05N 92 54W
Marshfield Wisconsin U.S.A. **92** B2 44 40N 90 11W
Marsh Harbour The Bahamas **91** K2 26 31N 77 05W
Martaban Myanmar **38** B3 16 32N 97 35E
Martaban, Gulf of Myanmar **38** B3 16 15N 96 40E
Martapura Indonesia **42** D3 3 25S 114 45E
Martha's Vineyard *i.* Massachusetts U.S.A. **93** F2 41 00N 70 00W
Martigny Switzerland **73** C2 46 07N 7 05E
Martigues France **73** C1 43 24N 5 03E
Martinique *i.* Lesser Antilles **97** L2 14 30N 61 00W
Martin Lake Alabama U.S.A. **91** I3 33 00N 86 00W
Martinsburg West Virginia U.S.A. **93** E1 39 28N 77 59W
Martinsville Indiana U.S.A. **92** C1 39 25N 86 25W
Martinsville Virginia U.S.A. **91** K4 36 43N 79 53W
Martin Vaz *i.* Atlantic Ocean **25** F4 21 00S 27 30W
Marton North Island New Zealand **79** C2 40 05S 175 23E
Marum, Mount Vanuatu **83** H5 16 15S 168 08E
Marunga Papua New Guinea **45** P4 4 58S 152 13E
Marutea *i.* Pacific Ocean **81** E3 17 00S 143 10W
Marvejols France **73** B1 44 33N 3 18E
Marwitz Germany **67** E2 52 44N 13 08E
Mary Turkmenistan **59** J2 37 42N 61 54E
Maryborough Australia **78** I4 25 32S 152 36E
Maryland *state* U.S.A. **93** E1 39 00N 77 00W
Marysville California U.S.A. **90** B4 39 10N 121 34W
Marysville Ohio U.S.A. **93** D2 40 13N 83 22W
Masada *see* Mezada
Masamasa *i.* Solomon Islands **82** B7 6 50S 156 10E
Masan South Korea **50** D2 35 10N 128 35E
Masapun Indonesia **44** B3 7 46S 126 39E
Masaya Nicaragua **97** G2 11 59N 86 03W
Masbate The Philippines **40** B3 12 21N 123 36E
Mascara Algeria **72** C2 35 20N 0 09E
Mascarene Basin Indian Ocean **24** E5 15 00S 55 00E
Mascot Australia **79** G2 33 56S 151 12E
Masela *i.* Indonesia **44** C2 8 07S 129 51E
Maseru Lesotho **111** E2 29 19S 27 29E
Mashhad Iran **55** I6 36 16N 59 34E
Masin Irian Jaya Indonesia **44** H3 6 09S 139 25E
Masindi Uganda **110** F8 1 41N 31 45E
Masirah *i.* Oman **55** I3 20 25N 58 40E
Mason City Iowa U.S.A. **92** B2 43 10N 93 10W
Masqat Oman **55** I3 23 37N 58 38E
Massachusetts *state* U.S.A. **93** F2 42 00N 72 00W
Massachusetts Bay U.S.A. **93** F2 42 00N 70 00W
Masseik Belgium **70** E3 51 08N 5 48E
Massena New York U.S.A. **93** F2 44 56N 74 57W
Massey Ontario Canada **93** D3 46 13N 82 06W
Massif Central *mts.* France **73** B1/2 45 00N 3 30E
Massif de la Vanoise *mts.* France **73** C2 45 20N 6 20E
Massif de L'Isola *mts.* Madagascar **111** H3/I3 23 00S 45 00E
Massif de l'Ouarsenis *mts.* Algeria **72** C2 36 00N 2 00E
Massif des Bongos *mts.* Central African Republic **110** D9 9 00N 23 00E
Massif des Ecrins *mts.* France **73** C1 45 00N 6 00E
Massif de Tsaratanana *mts.* Madagascar **111** I5 14 00S 49 00E
Massy France **67** B1 48 44N 2 17E
Masterton North Island New Zealand **79** C2 40 57S 175 39E
Masuda Japan **46** B1 34 42N 131 51E
Masuku Gabon **112** H2 1 40S 13 31E
Masvingo Zimbabwe **111** F3 20 05S 30 50E
Matacawa Levu *i.* Fiji **83** B10 16 59S 177 20E
Matachel *r.* Spain **72** A2 38 40N 6 00W
Matadi Zaïre **111** B6 5 50S 13 32E
Matagalpa Nicaragua **97** G2 12 52N 85 58W
Matagami Québec Canada **93** E3 49 45N 77 45W
Mataiéa Tahiti **82** T8 17 47S 149 24W
Matamoros Mexico **96** D5 25 33N 103 51W
Matamoros Mexico **96** E5 25 50N 97 31W
Matane Québec Canada **93** F3 48 50N 67 31W
Matanzas Cuba **97** H4 23 04N 81 35W
Mataram Indonesia **42** E2 8 36S 116 07E
Mataró Spain **72** C3 41 32N 2 27E
Mataura South Island New Zealand **79** A1 46 12S 168 52E
Mataura *r.* South Island New Zealand **79** A1 45 45S 168 50E
Matautu Western Samoa **82** B11 13 57S 171 55W
Matehuala Mexico **96** D4 23 40N 100 40W
Matelot Trinidad and Tobago **96** T10 10 49N 61 07W
Matera Italy **74** C3 40 40N 16 37E
Mateur Tunisia **74** A2 37 03N 9 40E
Mathura India **53** D5 27 30N 77 42E
Mati The Philippines **40** C2 6 59N 126 12E
Mato Grosso *admin.* Brazil **102** F10 14 00S 56 00W
Mato Grosso *tn.* Brazil **102** F9 15 05S 59 57W
Mato Grosso do Sul *admin.* Brazil **102** F8/9 20 00S 55 00W
Matong Papua New Guinea **45** O4 5 35S 151 46E
Matopo Hills Zimbabwe **111** E3 21 00S 28 30E
Matosinhos Portugal **72** A3 41 08N 8 45W
Matrah Oman **55** I3 23 31N 58 18E
Matsudo Japan **47** C4 35 46N 139 54E
Matsue Japan **46** B2 35 29N 133 04E
Matsumoto Japan **46** C2 36 18N 137 58E
Matsusaka Japan **46** H1 34 33N 136 31E
Matsuyama Japan **46** B1 33 50N 132 47E
Mattagami River Ontario Canada **93** D3 50 00N 82 00W
Mattawa Ontario Canada **93** E3 46 19N 78 42W
Matterhorn *mt.* Switzerland **73** C2 45 59N 7 39E
Mattice Ontario Canada **93** D3 49 36N 83 16W
Mattoon Illinois U.S.A. **92** C1 39 29N 88 21W
Matu Solomon Islands **82** L3 10 40S 166 00E
Matua Indonesia **42** D3 3 30S 111 00E
Matuku *i.* Fiji **83** D7 19 11S 179 45E
Matura Trinidad and Tobago **96** T10 10 40N 61 04W
Matura Bay Trinidad and Tobago **96** T10 10 40N 61 04W
Maturín Venezuela **102** E14 9 45N 63 10W
Matveyevskoye Russia **56** L1 55 42N 37 30E
Maubara Indonesia **43** G2 8 39S 125 19E
Maubeuge France **73** B3 50 17N 3 58E
Ma-ubin Myanmar **38** B3 16 44N 95 37E
Maués Brazil **102** F12 3 22S 57 38W
Maui *i.* Hawaiian Islands **23** Y18 21 00N 156 30W
Maulvi Bazar Bangladesh **38** A4 24 30N 91 48E
Maumere Indonesia **43** F2 8 35S 122 13E
Mauna Kea *mt.* Hawaiian Islands **23** Z17 19 50N 155 25W
Mauna Loa *vol.* Hawaiian Islands **23** Z17 19 28N 155 35W
Mauriche National Park Québec Canada **93** F3 46 30N 74 00W
MAURITANIA 112 C6/D7
MAURITIUS 24 E4
Ma Wan *i.* Hong Kong U.K. **51** B2 22 21N 114 03E
Ma Wan Chung Hong Kong U.K. **51** A1 22 17N 113 56E
Mawchi Myanmar **38** B3 19 00N 96 30E
Mawlaik Myanmar **38** A4 23 40N 94 26E
Mawson *r.s.* Antarctica **21** 67 36S 62 52E
Maya *i.* Indonesia **42** C3 0 50S 109 40E
Mayaguana *i.* The Bahamas **97** J4 22 30N 72 40W
Mayagüez Puerto Rico **97** K3 18 13N 67 09W
Mayaro Bay Trinidad and Tobago **96** U9 10 07N 61 00W
Mayen Germany **70** G2 50 19N 7 14E
Mayenne France **73** A2 48 18N 0 37W
Mayenne *r.* France **73** A2 47 45N 0 50W
Maykop Russia **56** G4 44 37N 40 48E
Maymyo Myanmar **38** B4 22 05N 96 33E
Mayo Yukon Territory Canada **88** H5 63 34N 135 52W
Mayo *i.* Indonesia **42** E2 8 00S 117 30E
Mayon *mt.* The Philippines **40** B3 13 15N 123 42E
Mayotte *i.* Indian Ocean **111** I5 13 00S 45 00E
May Pen Jamaica **97** Q7 17 58N 77 15W
Mayraira Point The Philippines **40** B4 18 37N 120 52E
Maysville Kentucky U.S.A. **93** D1 38 38N 83 46W
Mayu *r.* Myanmar **38** A4 20 45N 92 40E
Mayumba Gabon **112** H2 3 23S 10 38E
Mayville North Dakota U.S.A. **92** A3 47 30N 97 20W
Mazabuka Zambia **111** E4 15 50S 27 47E
Mazamet France **73** B1 43 29N 2 22E
Mazār-e Sharīf Afghanistan **55** K6 36 42N 67 06E
Mazatenango Guatemala **96** F2 14 31N 91 30W
Mazatlán Mexico **96** C4 23 11N 106 25W

Mazirbe Latvia **69** E2 57 40N 22 21E
Mbaiki Central African Republic **110** C8 3 53N 18 01E
Mbala Zambia **111** F6 8 50S 31 24E
Mbalmayo Cameroon **112** H3 3 30N 11 31E
Mbandaka Zaïre **110** C8 0 03N 18 28E
Mbita'ama Solomon Islands **82** F5 8 20S 160 42E
Mbokonumbeta *i.* Solomon Islands **82** F5 9 00S 160 10E
Mborokua *i.* Solomon Islands **82** D4 9 02S 158 44E
Mbuji-Mayi Zaïre **111** D6 6 10S 23 39E
Mbulo *i.* Solomon Islands **82** D5 8 46S 158 21E
Mbuma Solomon Islands **82** F5 9 00S 160 45E
Mdrak Vietnam **37** C2 12 40N 108 48E
Mead, Lake U.S.A. **90** D4 36 10N 114 25W
Meadville Pennsylvania U.S.A. **93** D2 41 38N 80 10W
Meaford Ontario Canada **93** D2 44 36N 80 35W
Meama *i.* Tonga **83** B3 19 45S 174 35W
Meaux France **73** B2 48 58N 2 54E
Mechelen *(Malines)* Belgium **70** D3 51 02N 4 29E
Mecheria Algeria **112** E9 33 31N 0 20W
Mechernich Germany **70** F2 50 35N 6 39E
Mecklenburg Bay Europe **71** B2 54 00N 12 00E
Mecklenburg-Vorpommern *admin.* Germany **71** B2 53 30N 12 30E
Medan Indonesia **42** A4 3 35N 98 39E
Médéa Algeria **112** F10 36 15N 2 48E
Medellín Colombia **102** B14 6 15N 75 36W
Medemblik Netherlands **70** E4 52 47N 5 06E
Medenine Tunisia **112** H9 33 24N 10 25E
Medford Oregon U.S.A. **90** B5 42 20N 122 52W
Medicine Hat Alberta Canada **88** M3 50 03N 110 41W
Medina del Campo Spain **72** B3 41 18N 4 55W
Medinīpur India **53** F4 22 25N 87 24E
Medvedkovo Russia **56** M2 55 55N 37 08E
Medvezh'yegorsk Russia **56** F8 62 56N 34 28E
Medway *r.* England United Kingdom **68** L3 51 24N 0 40E
Medwin Point Christmas Island **81** R1 10 34S 105 40E
Meekatharra Australia **78** B4 26 30S 118 30E
Meerut India **53** D5 29 00N 77 42E
Mēga Ethiopia **110** G8 4 02N 38 19E
Mega Irian Jaya Indonesia **44** D6 0 41S 131 53E
Mégantic Québec Canada **93** F3 46 10N 71 40W
Meghalaya *admin.* India **53** G5 25 30N 91 00E
Meguro Japan **47** B3 35 36N 139 43E
Meiktila Myanmar **38** B4 20 53N 95 54E
Meiningen Germany **71** B2 50 34N 10 25E
Mei Xian China **49** N3 24 19N 116 13E
Mejerda *r.* Tunisia **74** A2 36 30N 9 00E
Mek'elē Ethiopia **110** G10 13 32N 39 33E
Meknès Morocco **112** D9 33 53N 5 37W
Mekong *(Lancang Jiang, Mae Nam Khong) r.* Asia **37** C2 11 00N 105 00E
Mekong, Mouths of the *est.* Vietnam **37** C1 9 30N 106 45E
Melaka Malaysia **42** B4 2 11N 102 14E
Melalap Malaysia **40** A2 5 15N 115 59E
Melanesia *geog. reg.* Pacific Ocean **22** F7
Melawi *r.* Indonesia **42** D3 1 00S 112 30E
Melbourne Australia **78** H2 37 45S 144 58E
Melbourne Florida U.S.A. **91** J2 28 04N 80 38W
Melfort Saskatchewan Canada **88** O3 52 52N 104 38W
Melilla *territory* Spain **72** B2 35 17N 2 57W
Melitopol' Ukraine **58** D4 46 51N 35 22E
Mellègue *r.* Tunisia **74** A2 36 00N 8 00E
Melo Uruguay **103** G6 32 22S 54 10W
Melouprey Cambodia **37** C2 13 14N 105 28E
Melun France **73** B2 48 32N 2 40E
Melville Saskatchewan Canada **89** O3 50 57N 102 49W
Melville Bugt *b.* Greenland **89** W8 75 30N 62 30W
Melville, Cape Australia **78** G7 14 08S 144 31E
Melville Hills Northwest Territories Canada **88** K6 69 00N 121 00W
Melville Island Australia **78** E7 11 30S 131 00E
Melville Island Northwest Territories Canada **88** M8 75 30N 112 00W
Melville, Lake Newfoundland Canada **89** X3 53 45N 59 00W
Melville Peninsula Northwest Territories Canada **89** S6 68 00N 84 00W
Mé Maoya *mt.* New Caledonia **82** U2 21 20S 165 20E
Memberama *r.* Irian Jaya Indonesia **44** H5 2 15S 138 05E
Memboro Indonesia **43** E2 9 25S 119 34E
Memmingen Germany **71** B1 47 59N 10 11E
Mempawah Indonesia **42** C4 0 23N 108 56E
Memphis Tennessee U.S.A. **91** I4 35 10N 90 00W
Memphis *hist. site* Egypt **54** D4 29 52N 31 12E
Menai Australia **79** G1 34 01S 151 01E
Menanga Indonesia **43** F3 1 41S 124 52E
Mendawai *r.* Indonesia **42** D3 1 20S 113 00E
Mende France **73** B1 44 32N 3 30E
Mendebo Mountains Ethiopia **110** G9/H9 7 00N 40 00E
Menderes *r.* Turkey **54** C6 37 50N 28 10E
Mendi Papua New Guinea **45** K3 6 13S 143 39E
Mendip Hills England United Kingdom **68** I3 51 18N 2 45W
Mendocino Seascarp Pacific Ocean **23** L12 41 00N 145 00W
Mendota Illinois U.S.A. **92** C2 41 33N 89 09W
Mendoza Argentina **103** D6 32 48S 68 52W
Menen Belgium **70** C2 50 48N 3 07E
Meneng Nauru **83** M1 0 32S 166 56E
Meneng Point Nauru **83** M1 0 32S 166 57E
Menes Indonesia **42** M7 6 27S 105 57E
Mengdingjie China **49** J3 23 03N 99 03E
Menggala Indonesia **42** C3 4 30S 105 19E
Menglian China **37** A4 22 19N 99 39E
Mengsa China **38** B4 23 41N 99 39E
Mengxing China **37** B4 21 51N 101 31E
Mengzi China **36** C6 23 22N 103 28E
Menominee Michigan U.S.A. **92** C3 45 07N 87 37W
Menongue Angola **111** C5 14 36S 17 48E
Menorca *(Minorca) i.* Balearic Islands **72** E4/F4 39 45N 4 15E
Mentakab Malaysia **42** B4 3 29N 102 20E
Menton France **73** C1 43 47N 7 30E
Menyamya Papua New Guinea **45** L3 7 07S 145 59E
Meoqui Mexico **90** E2 28 18N 105 30W
Meppel Netherlands **70** F4 52 42N 6 12E
Meppen Germany **71** A2 52 41N 7 18E
Mera Japan **46** L1 34 56N 139 50E
Merak Indonesia **42** N8 5 55S 106 00E
Merauke Indonesia **45** J2 8 30S 140 22E
Merauke *r.* Indonesia **45** J3 7 59S 140 55E
Merced California U.S.A. **90** B4 37 17N 120 29W
Mercedes Argentina **103** D6 33 41S 65 28W
Mercedes Uruguay **103** F6 34 15S 58 02W
Meredith, Cape Falkland Islands **25** L15 52 15S 60 40W
Méré Lava *i.* Vanuatu **83** H7 14 28S 168 00E
Mergui Myanmar **38** B2 12 26N 98 34E
Mergui Archipelago Myanmar **38** B2 11 00N 97 40E
Meriani Papua New Guinea **45** M2 9 27S 147 27E
Mérida Mexico **96** G4 20 59N 89 39W
Mérida Spain **72** A2 38 55N 6 20W
Mérida Venezuela **102** C14 8 24N 71 08W
Meriden Connecticut U.S.A. **93** F2 41 32N 72 48W
Meridian Mississippi U.S.A. **91** I3 32 21N 88 42W
Mérig *i.* Vanuatu **83** G7 14 17S 167 48E
Mérignac France **73** A1 44 50N 0 36W
Merir *i.* Caroline Islands **43** H4 4 19N 132 18E
Merowe Sudan **110** F11 18 30N 31 49E
Merrill Wisconsin U.S.A. **92** C3 45 12N 89 43W
Merritt British Columbia Canada **88** K3 50 09N 120 49W
Merrylands Australia **79** F2/G2 33 50S 150 59E
Merseburg Germany **71** B2 51 22N 12 00E
Mersey *r.* England United Kingdom **68** I5 53 20N 2 53W
Mersin Turkey **54** D6 36 47N 34 37E
Mersing Malaysia **42** B4 2 26N 103 50E
Merthyr Tydfil Wales United Kingdom **68** H3 51 46N 3 23W
Merton *bor.* England United Kingdom **66** C2 51 25N 0 12W
Mertz Glacier Antarctica **21** 68 00S 145 00E
Merzig Germany **71** A1 49 26N 6 39E
Mesa Arizona U.S.A. **90** D3 33 25N 115 50W
Mesolóngion Greece **74** D2 38 21N 21 26E
Mesopotamia *geog. reg.* Middle East **58** C2/D1 35 00N 40 00E
Messina Italy **74** C2 38 13N 15 33E
Messina Republic of South Africa **111** E3 22 23S 30 00E
Meta Icognita Peninsula Northwest Territories Canada **89** U5 63 30N 70 00W
Metz France **73** C2 49 07N 6 11E
Meu *r.* France **73** A2 48 05N 2 07W
Meudon France **67** A2/B2 48 48N 2 15E
Meulaboh Indonesia **42** A4 4 10N 96 09E
Meurthe-Moselle *admin.* France **70** E1 49 15N 5 50E
Meuse *admin.* France **70** E1 49 15N 5 30E
Meuse *r.* Belgium/France **70** E2 50 03N 4 40E
Mexicali Mexico **96** A6 32 36N 115 30W
MEXICO **96** D4
México Mexico **96** E3 19 25N 99 10W
Mexico, Gulf of Mexico **96/97** F4/G4 25 00N 90 00W
Meycauayan *see* Valenzuela
Meymaneh Afghanistan **55** J6 35 55N 64 47E
Mezada *(Masada) hist. site* Israel **54** O10 31 17N 35 20E
Mezaligon Myanmar **38** B3 17 58N 95 14E
Mezen' Russia **56** G9 65 50N 44 20E
Mezhdurechensk Russia **59** O5 53 43N 88 11E
Miagao The Philippines **40** B3 10 39N 122 14E
Miami Florida U.S.A. **91** J2 25 45N 80 15W
Miami Oklahoma U.S.A. **92** A1 36 53N 94 54W
Mīāneh Iran **55** G6 37 23N 47 45E
Mianmian Shan *mts.* China **38** C5 27 30N 100 40E
Mianwali Pakistan **53** C6 32 32N 71 33E
Miao-li Taiwan **51** G7 24 37N 120 49E
Miass Russia **56** I6 55 00N 60 08E
Michigan *state* U.S.A. **92/93** C3/D2 45 00N 85 00W
Michigan City Indiana U.S.A. **92** C2 41 43N 86 54W
Michigan, Lake Canada/U.S.A. **92** C2 45 00N 87 00W
Michipicoten Ontario Canada **89** S2 47 57N 84 55W
Michipicoten Island Ontario Canada **92** C3 48 00N 86 00W
Michurinsk Russia **58** E5 52 54N 40 30E
Micronesia *geog. reg.* Pacific Ocean **22** G8
Midai *i.* Indonesia **42** C4 2 40N 107 45E
Mid-Atlantic Ridge Atlantic Ocean **25** D8/F11
Middelburg Netherlands **70** C3 51 30N 3 36E
Middle America Trench Pacific Ocean **23** P9/Q9 16 30N 99 00W
Middle Andaman *i.* Andaman Islands **38** A2 12 30N 92 45E
Middleburg Republic of South Africa **111** E2 31 28S 25 01E
Middlebury Vermont U.S.A. **93** F2 44 02N 73 11W
Middlegate Norfolk Island **81** L4 29 02S 167 57E
Middle Harbour Australia **79** G2 33 48S 151 14E
Middle Loup *r.* Nebraska U.S.A. **90** F5 42 00N 101 00W
Middle Point Christmas Island **81** Q1 10 31S 105 55E
Middlesborough England United Kingdom **68** J6 54 35N 1 14W
Middletown Connecticut U.S.A. **93** F2 41 34N 72 39W
Middletown New York U.S.A. **93** F2 41 26N 74 26W
Middletown Ohio U.S.A. **93** D1 39 31N 84 13W
Mid-Indian Basin Indian Ocean **24** H6 10 00S 80 00E
Mid-Indian Ridge Indian Ocean **24** F3/G3
Midland Michigan U.S.A. **93** D2 43 38N 84 14W
Midland Ontario Canada **93** E2 44 45N 79 53W
Midland Texas U.S.A. **90** F3 32 00N 102 09W
Midland Beach New York U.S.A. **94** B1 40 33N 74 07W
Midori Japan **47** B3 35 33N 139 39E
Midouze *r.* France **73** A1 44 00N 0 45E
Mid-Pacific Mountains Pacific Ocean **22** F10/H10 21 00N 160 00E
Midsayap The Philippines **40** B2 7 14N 124 33E
Midu China **38** C5 25 20N 100 31E
Midway Islands Pacific Ocean **22** I10 28 15N 177 25W
Mie *pref.* Japan **46** H1 34 35N 136 20E
Mien Hsü *i.* Taiwan **51** I8 25 31N 122 07E
Mieres Spain **72** A3 43 15N 5 46W
Mijares *r.* Spain **72** B3 40 03N 0 30W
Mikhaylovgrad Bulgaria **74** D3 43 25N 23 11E
Miki Japan **46** F1 34 50N 134 59E
Mikir Hills India **38** A5 26 30N 93 00E
Mikiwa-wan *b.* Japan **46** J1 34 42N 137 10E
Mikkeli Finland **69** F3 61 44N 27 15E
Milagro Ecuador **102** B12 2 11S 79 36W
Milan *see* Milano
Milano *(Milan)* Italy **74** A4 45 28N 9 12E
Milâs Turkey **74** E2 37 19N 27 48E
Mildura Australia **78** G3 34 14S 142 13E
Mile China **38** C4 24 21N 103 31E
Miles City Montana U.S.A. **90** E6 46 24N 105 48W
Milford Pennsylvania U.S.A. **93** F2 41 19N 74 48W
Milford Utah U.S.A. **90** D4 38 22N 113 00W
Milford Haven Wales United Kingdom **68** F3 51 44N 5 02W
Milford Sound *tn.* South Island New Zealand **79** A2 44 36S 167 49E
Milian *r.* Malaysia **40** A2 5 20N 116 00E
Miliana Algeria **72** C2 36 20N 2 15E
Mili Atoll Pacific Ocean **80** C4 6 08N 171 59E
Millau France **73** B1 44 06N 3 05E
Millbank South Dakota U.S.A. **92** A3 45 14N 96 38W
Mille Lacs *l.* Minnesota U.S.A. **92** B3 46 00N 94 00W
Millinocket Maine U.S.A. **93** G3 45 42N 68 43W
Milne Bay Papua New Guinea **45** O1 10 25S 150 35E
Milos *i.* Greece **74** D2 36 00N 24 00E
Milton Ontario Canada **93** E2 43 31N 79 53W
Milton South Island New Zealand **79** A1 46 07S 169 58E
Milton Pennsylvania U.S.A. **93** E2 41 01N 76 52W
Milton Keynes England United Kingdom **68** K4 52 02N 0 42W
Milwaukee Wisconsin U.S.A. **92** C2 43 03N 87 56W
Mimizan France **73** A1 44 12N 1 14W
Mimot Cambodia **37** C2 11 49N 106 11E
Mina *r.* Algeria **72** C2 35 30N 1 00E
Minahassa Peninsula Indonesia **43** F4 0 30N 123 00E
Minaki Ontario Canada **92** B3 50 00N 94 40W
Minamata Japan **46** B1 32 13N 130 23E
Minami-Ashigara Japan **46** L2 35 20N 139 06E
Minas Uruguay **103** F6 34 20S 55 15W
Minas Gerais *admin.* Brazil **102** I9 17 30S 45 00W
Minatitlán Mexico **96** F3 17 59N 94 32W
Minbu Myanmar **38** A4 20 09N 94 52E
Minch, The *sd.* Scotland United Kingdom **68** F10 58 00N 6 00W
Mindanao *i.* The Philippines **40** B2 8 00N 125 00E
Mindanao *r.* The Philippines **40** B2 7 00N 124 00E
Mindanao Sea The Philippines **40** B2 9 00N 125 00E
Mindel *r.* Germany **71** B1 48 00N 10 00E
Minden Ontario Canada **93** E2 44 56N 78 44W
Minden Germany **71** A2 52 18N 8 54E
Minden Louisiana U.S.A. **91** H3 32 26N 93 17W
Mindoro *i.* The Philippines **40** B3 13 00N 121 00E
Mindoro Strait The Philippines **40** B3 12 00N 120 00E
Mingan Québec Canada **89** W3 50 19N 64 02W
Mingechaur Azerbaijan **58** F3 40 45N 47 03E
Mingin Myanmar **38** A4 22 51N 94 30E
Minhla Myanmar **38** B3 19 58N 95 03E
Minho *see* Miño
Minicoy Island India **53** C1 8 29N 73 01E
Minneapolis Minnesota U.S.A. **92** B2 45 00N 93 15W
Minnedosa Manitoba Canada **89** P3 50 14N 99 50W
Minnesota *r.* Minnesota U.S.A. **91** G5 44 00N 95 00W
Minnesota *state* U.S.A. **92** A3/B3 47 00N 95 00W
Minnitaki Lake Ontario Canada **92** B3 50 00N 92 00W
Mino Japan **46** H2 35 43N 136 56E
Miño *(Minho) r.* Spain/Portugal **72** A3 42 00N 8 40W
Mino-Kamo Japan **46** J2 35 29N 137 01E
Minorca *see* Menorca
Minot North Dakota U.S.A. **90** F6 48 16N 101 19W
Minsk Belarus **75** E3 53 51N 27 30E
Minusinsk Russia **57** L6 53 43N 91 45E
Miraflores Locks Panama **97** Y1 8 59N 79 36W
Miraj India **53** C3 16 51N 74 42E
Miram Shah Pakistan **55** L5 33 00N 70 05E
Miranda de Ebro Spain **72** B3 42 41N 2 57W
Miri Malaysia **42** D4 4 23N 114 00E
Miri Hills India **38** A5 27 55N 93 30E
Mirimiri Irian Jaya Indonesia **44** E6 1 58S 132 05E
Mirnyy Russia **57** N8 62 30N 113 58E
Mirnyy *r.s.* Antarctica **21** 66 33S 93 01E
Mirpur Khas Pakistan **52** B5 25 33N 69 05E
Mirs Bay Hong Kong U.K. **51** D3 22 33N 114 24E
Mirtoan Sea Greece **74** D2 37 00N 23 00E
Miryang South Korea **50** D2 35 31N 128 45E
Mirzapur India **53** E5 25 09N 82 34E
Misaki Japan **46** G1 34 19N 135 09E
Misawa Japan **46** D3 40 42N 141 26E
Misfaq Egypt **54** N10 31 01N 33 11E
Mishima Japan **46** K2 35 08N 138 54E
Mishmi Hills India **38** B5 28 30N 96 30E
Misima Island Papua New Guinea **45** P1 10 38S 152 45E
Miskolc Hungary **75** D2 48 07N 20 47E
Miṣrātah Libya **110** C14 32 23N 15 06E
Missinaibi River Ontario Canada **93** D4 49 30N 83 20W
Mississauga Ontario Canada **93** E2 43 38N 79 36W
Mississippi *r.* U.S.A. **91** H3 35 00N 90 00W
Mississippi *state* U.S.A. **91** H3 32 00N 90 00W
Mississippi Delta Louisiana U.S.A. **91** I2 30 00N 90 00W
Missoula Montana U.S.A. **90** D6 46 52N 114 00W
Missouri *r.* U.S.A. **91** H4 39 00N 93 00W
Missouri *state* U.S.A. **91** H4 38 00N 93 00W
Mistassini Québec Canada **93** F3 48 54N 72 13W
Mitaka Japan **46** L2 35 41N 139 35E
Mitcham England United Kingdom **66** C2 51 24N 0 09W
Mitchell Australia **78** H4 26 30S 147 56E
Mitchell South Dakota U.S.A. **92** A2 43 40N 98 01W
Mitchell *r.* Australia **78** G6 17 00S 142 30E
Mitiaro *i.* Pacific Ocean **81** E3 20 00S 157 00W
Mitilíni Greece **74** E2 39 06N 26 34E
Mitino Russia **56** L2 55 53N 37 24E
Mito Japan **46** D2 36 22N 140 29E
Mitry-Mory France **67** C2 48 58N 2 38E
Mits'iwa Eritrea **110** G11 15 42N 39 25E
Mitsukaidō Japan **46** L3 36 03N 139 59E
Mitú Colombia **102** C13 1 07N 70 05W
Mitumba Mountains *see* Chaine des Mitumba
Miura Japan **46** L2 35 08N 139 37E
Miura-hantō *p.* Japan **46** L2 35 14N 139 40E
Miya-gawa *r.* Japan **46** H1 34 20N 136 16E
Miyako Japan **46** D2 39 38N 141 59E
Miyakonojō Japan **46** B1 31 43N 131 02E
Miyama Japan **46** G2 35 17N 135 32E
Miyazaki Japan **46** B1 31 56N 131 27E
Miyazu Japan **46** G2 35 33N 135 12E
Mizen Head *c.* Irish Republic **68** B3 51 30N 9 50W
Mizo Hills India **38** A4 28 30N 96 30E
Mizunami Japan **46** J2 35 25N 137 16E
Mjøsa *l.* Norway **69** C3 60 40N 10 40E
Mladá Boleslav Czech Republic **75** B3 50 26N 14 55E
Mława Poland **75** D3 53 08N 20 20E
Mnevniki Russia **56** L2 55 46N 37 29E
Moa Island Australia **45** K1 10 10S 142 16E
Moala *i.* Fiji **83** D8 18 34S 179 56E
Moala Group Fiji **83** D8 18 40S 179 58E
Mobara Japan **46** M2 35 26N 140 20E
Mobaye Central African Republic **110** D8 4 19N 21 11E
Mobile Alabama U.S.A. **91** I3 30 40N 88 05W
Moçambique Mozambique **111** H4 15 03S 40 45E
Moce *i.* Fiji **83** F8 18 39S 178 32W
Moc Hoa Vietnam **37** C2 10 46N 105 56E
Mocuba Mozambique **111** G4 16 52S 36 57E
Modan Irian Jaya Indonesia **44** E5 2 23S 133 55E
Módena Italy **74** B3 44 39N 10 55E
Modesto California U.S.A. **90** B4 37 37N 121 00W
Modowi Irian Jaya Indonesia **44** F4 4 06S 134 38E
Moers Germany **70** F3 51 27N 6 36E
Moe-Yallourn Australia **78** H2 38 09S 146 22E
Mogadishu *see* Muqdisho
Mogaung Myanmar **38** B5 25 20N 96 54E
Mogaung *r.* Myanmar **38** B5 25 10N 97 05E
Mogilev Belarus **75** F3 53 54N 30 20E
Mogilev-Podol'skiy Ukraine **58** B4 48 29N 27 49E
Mogocha Russia **57** N6 53 44N 119 45E
Mogok Myanmar **38** B4 22 55N 96 29E
Mogollon Rim *plat.* Arizona U.S.A. **90** D3 34 00N 111 00W
Mohammadia Algeria **72** C2 35 35N 0 05E
Mohe China **49** O9 52 55N 122 20E
Moindou New Caledonia **82** U2 21 40S 165 35E
Mo-i-Rana Norway **69** C4 66 18N 14 00E
Mojave California U.S.A. **90** C4 35 02N 118 11W
Mojokerto Indonesia **42** Q7 7 25S 112 31E
Mokokchung India **38** A5 26 20N 94 30E
Mokolo Cameroon **112** H5 10 49N 13 54E
Mokp'o South Korea **50** C2 34 50N 126 25E
Moksha *r.* Russia **58** E5 50 00N 43 00E
Mol Belgium **70** E3 51 11N 5 07E
Molango Mexico **96** E4 20 48N 98 44W
MOLDAVIA *see* MOLDOVA
MOLDOVA **75** E2
Moldova *r.* Romania **75** E2 47 00N 26 00E
Mole *r.* England United Kingdom **66** B2 51 15N 0 20W
Molepolole Botswana **111** E3 24 25S 25 30E
Moline Illinois U.S.A. **92** B2 41 31N 90 26W
Mollendo Peru **102** C9 17 00S 72 00W
Mölndal Sweden **69** C2 57 40N 12 00E
Molodechno Belarus **75** E3 54 16N 26 50E
Molodezhnaya *r.s.* Antarctica **21** 67 40S 45 51E
Molokai *i.* Hawaiian Islands **23** Y18 21 40N 155 55W
Molopo *r.* Southern Africa **111** D2 26 30S 22 30E
Moluccas *see* Kepulauan Maluku
Molucca Sea Indonesia **43** G4 0 30S 125 30E
Mombasa Kenya **111** G7 4 04S 39 40E
Mombetsu Japan **46** D3 42 28N 142 10E
Momi Fiji **83** B9 17 55S 177 18E
Møn *i.* Denmark **71** B2 55 00N 12 00E
MONACO **73** C1
Monadhliath Mountains Scotland United Kingdom **68** G9 57 10N 4 00W
Monahans Texas U.S.A. **90** F3 31 35N 102 54W
Monastir Tunisia **74** B2 35 46N 10 59E
Mona Vale Australia **79** H3 33 41S 151 18E
Monbetsu Japan **46** D3 44 23N 143 22E
Monçaó Brazil **102** H12 3 30S 45 15W
Monchegorsk Russia **69** G4 67 55N 33 01E
Mönchengladbach Germany **71** A2 51 12N 6 25E
Monclova Mexico **96** D5 26 55N 101 25W
Moncton New Brunswick Canada **89** V2 46 04N 64 50W
Mondego *r.* Portugal **72** A3 40 30N 8 15W
Mondovi Italy **74** A3 44 23N 7 49E
Monemvasia Greece **74** D2 36 41N 23 03E
Mong Cai Vietnam **37** C4 21 31N 108 00E
Mongga Solomon Islands **82** C6 7 52S 157 00E
Möng Hpayak Myanmar **38** B4 20 32N 99 57E
Mong Kok Hong Kong U.K. **51** B1 22 09N 114 09E
Mongkol Borey Cambodia **37** B2 13 29N 103 04E
Möng Kung Myanmar **38** B4 21 37N 97 31E
Möng Mit Myanmar **38** B4 23 05N 96 45E
MONGOLIA **48/49** H8/M8
Möng Ping Myanmar **38** B4 21 26N 99 01E
Mong Tong Hang Hong Kong U.K. **51** B1 22 20N 114 02E
Mongu Zambia **111** D4 15 13S 23 09E
Möng Yai Myanmar **38** B4 22 21N 98 02E
Möng Yang Myanmar **38** B4 21 50N 99 42E
Möng Yawng Myanmar **38** C4 21 07N 100 24E
Möng Yu Myanmar **38** B4 24 00N 97 59E
Mono *i.* Solomon Islands **82** A6 7 20S 155 30E
Mono *r.* Togo **112** F4 7 30N 1 30E
Monopoli Italy **74** C3 40 57N 17 18E
Monos *i.* Trinidad and Tobago **96** S10 10 42N 61 42W
Monroe Louisiana U.S.A. **91** H3 32 31N 92 06W
Monroe Michigan U.S.A. **93** D2 41 56N 83 21W
Monroe Reservoir Indiana U.S.A. **92** C1 39 00N 86 00W
Monrovia Liberia **112** C4 6 20N 10 46W
Mons Belgium **70** C2 50 28N 3 58E
Mon State *admin.* Myanmar **38** B3 16 45N 97 10E
Montagnes de la Margeride *mts.* France **73** B1 44 50N 3 15E
Montagnes Noires *mts.* France **73** A2 48 00N 3 30W
Montana *state* U.S.A. **90** E6 47 00N 111 00W
Montañas de León *mts.* Spain **72** A3 42 30N 6 15E
Montargis France **73** B2 48 00N 2 44E
Montauban France **73** B1 44 01N 1 20E
Montauk Point New York U.S.A. **93** F2 41 04N 71 51W
Montbéliard France **73** C2 47 31N 6 48E
Mont Blanc *mt.* France/Italy **73** C2 45 50N 6 52E
Mont Cameroun *mt.* Cameroon **112** G3 4 13N 9 10E
Montceau-les-Mines France **73** B2 46 40N 4 23E
Montclair New Jersey U.S.A. **94** B2 40 48N 74 12W
Mont-de-Marsan France **73** A1 43 54N 0 30W
Montdidier France **73** B2 49 39N 2 35E
Mont-Dore New Caledonia **82** V1 22 15S 166 37E
Montebello California U.S.A. **95** B3 34 01N 118 07W
Monte Binga *mt.* Zimbabwe/Mozambique **111** F4 19 47S 33 03E
Monte Carlo Monaco **73** C1 43 44N 7 25E
Monte Cinto *mt.* Corsica **73** C1 42 23N 8 57E
Montego Bay *tn.* Jamaica **97** Q8 18 27N 77 56W
Montélimar France **73** B1 44 33N 4 45E
Montenegro *admin.* Yugoslavia **74** C3
Monterey California U.S.A. **90** B4 36 35N 121 55W
Monterey Park *tn.* California U.S.A. **95** B3 34 03N 118 08W
Montería Colombia **102** B14 8 45N 75 54W
Montero Bolivia **102** E9 17 20S 63 15W
Monte Roraima *mt.* Guyana **102** E14 5 14N 60 44W
Monterrey Mexico **96** D5 25 40N 100 20W
Montes Claros *tn.* Brazil **102** I9 16 45S 43 52W
Montes de Toledo *mts.* Spain **72** B2 39 35N 4 30W
Montevideo Uruguay **103** F6 34 55S 56 10W
Mont Forel *mt.* Greenland **89** BB6 67 00N 37 00W
Montgeron France **67** B1 48 42N 2 27E
Montgomery Alabama U.S.A. **91** I3 32 22N 86 20W
Monti del Gennargentu *mts.* Sardinia Italy **74** A2/3 40 00N 9 30E
Monti Nebrodi *mts.* Italy **74** B2/C2 37 00N 14 00E
Mont-Joli Québec Canada **93** G3 48 36N 68 14W
Mont-Laurier *tn.* Québec Canada **93** E3 46 33N 75 31W
Montluçon France **73** B2 46 20N 2 36E
Montmagny Québec Canada **93** F3 46 50N 70 33W

Nanyang China 49 M5 33 06N 112 31E
Nanyuan China 47 G1 39 48N 116 23E
Nanyuki Kenya 110 G8 0 01N 37 05E
Naone Vanuatu 83 H6 15 02S 168 08E
Napanee Ontario Canada 93 E2 44 15N 74 57W
Napido Irian Jaya Indonesia 44 F6 0 39S 135 27E
Napier North Island New Zealand 79 C3 39 30S 176 54E
Naples Italy see Napoli
Naples Florida U.S.A. 91 J2 26 09N 81 48W
Napo China 37 C4 23 26N 105 50E
Napoli (Naples) Italy 74 B3 40 50N 14 15E
Napoopoo Hawaiian Islands 23 Z17 19 29N 155 55W
Nappanee Indiana U.S.A. 92 C2 41 27N 86 01W
Nara Japan 46 G1 34 41N 135 49E
Nara pref. Japan 46 G1 34 25N 135 50E
Narathiwat Thailand 39 B1 6 30N 101 50E
Narayanganj Bangladesh 53 G4 23 36N 90 28E
Narbonne France 73 B1 43 11N 3 00E
Nares Deep Atlantic Ocean 25 B9 26 00N 61 10W
Nares Strait Canada/Greenland 89 U8 78 30N 72 30W
Narita Japan 46 M2 35 46N 140 20E
Narmada r. India 53 C4/D4 22 00N 75 00E
Naroi Fiji 83 D8 18 32S 179 55E
Narra The Philippines 40 A2 9 20N 118 29E
Narrabeen Australia 79 H3 33 43S 151 18E
Narrogin Australia 78 B3 32 57S 117 07E
Narsaq Greenland 89 Z5 61 00N 46 00W
Narsarsuaq Greenland 89 Z5 61 10N 45 20W
Narutō Japan 46 M2 35 37N 140 20E
Narva Estonia 69 F2 59 22N 28 17E
Narvik Norway 69 D4 68 26N 17 25E
Nar'yan Mar Russia 56 H9 67 37N 53 02E
Nasau Fiji 83 F8 18 40S 178 30W
Nasawa Vanuatu 83 H6 15 14S 168 09E
Nasca Ridge Pacific Ocean 23 R5/S6 20 00S 81 00W
Nashua New Hampshire U.S.A. 93 F2 42 44N 71 28W
Nashville Tennessee U.S.A. 91 I4 36 10N 86 50W
Näsijärvi l. Finland 69 E3 61 45N 24 00E
Nasik India 53 C3 20 00N 73 52E
Nasorolevu mt. Fiji 83 D10 16 44S 179 23E
Nassau The Bahamas 97 I5 25 05N 77 20W
Nassau Island Pacific Ocean 80 D3 11 33S 165 25W
Nasser, Lake Egypt 110 F12 22 35N 31 40E
Nässjö Sweden 69 C2 57 40N 14 40E
Nasugbu The Philippines 40 B3 14 04N 120 37E
Natal Brazil 102 J11 5 46S 35 15W
Natal Indonesia 42 A4 0 32N 99 07E
Natal province Republic of South Africa 111 F2 29 00S 31 00E
Natasho Japan 46 G2 35 23N 135 39E
Natashquan Québec Canada 89 W3 50 10N 61 50W
Natchez Mississippi U.S.A. 91 H3 31 32N 91 24W
Natewa Bay Fiji 83 D10 16 30S 179 43E
Na Thap r. Thailand 39 B1 6 50N 100 40E
Natron, Lake Tanzania 110 G7 2 00S 36 00E
Nattaung mt. Myanmar 38 B3 18 49N 97 01E
Natuna Besar i. Indonesia 42 C4 3 40N 108 00E
Naturaliste, Cape Australia 78 B3 33 32S 115 01E
Naujan The Philippines 40 B3 13 21N 121 15E
Naumburg Germany 71 B2 51 09N 11 48E
NAURU 83
Nausori Fiji 83 C8 18 01S 178 32E
Navadwip India 53 F4 23 24N 88 23E
Navala Fiji 83 B9 17 40S 177 49E
Navet Trinidad and Tobago 96 T9 10 15N 61 10W
Navet r. Trinidad and Tobago 96 T9 10 16N 61 10W
Navet Dam Trinidad and Tobago 96 T9 10 26N 61 12W
Navia r. Spain 72 A3 43 10N 7 05W
Naviti i. Fiji 83 B9 17 08S 177 15E
Navoalavu Fiji 83 D10 16 18S 179 34E
Navoi Uzbekistan 59 K3 40 04N 65 02E
Navojoa Mexico 96 C5 7 04N 109 28W
Návplion Greece 74 D2 37 34N 22 48E
Navsari India 53 C4 20 58N 73 01E
Navua Fiji 83 C8 18 15S 178 10E
Navutu-i-loma i. Fiji 83 F8 19 00S 178 30W
Navutu-i-ra i. Fiji 83 F8 18 55S 178 31W
Nawi Fiji 83 D10 16 42S 179 56E
Nawin r. Myanmar 38 B3 18 58N 95 30E
Nawng-awn Myanmar 38 B4 21 00N 99 00E
Nawngkio Myanmar 38 B4 22 17N 96 50E
Náxos i. Greece 74 E2 37 00N 25 00E
Nayau i. Fiji 83 E9 18 00S 179 05W
Nayoro Japan 46 D3 44 21N 142 30E
Nazareth Israel 54 O11 32 41N 35 16E
Nazca Peru 102 C9 14 53S 74 54W
Nazili Turkey 74 E2 37 55N 28 20E
Nazwá Oman 55 I3 22 56N 57 33E
Ndélé Central African Republic 110 D9 8 25N 20 38E
Ndende i. Solomon Islands 83 L3/M3 10 42S 165 50E
Ndjamena Chad 110 C10 12 10N 14 59E
Ndola Zambia 111 E5 13 00S 28 39E
Néapolis Greece 74 D2 36 31N 23 03E
Neath Wales United Kingdom 68 H3 51 40N 3 48W
Nebit-Dag mt Turkmenistan 59 G2 39 31N 54 24E
Nebraska state U.S.A. 90 F5 42 00N 102 00W
Nebraska City Nebraska U.S.A. 92 A2 40 41N 95 50W
Nece New Caledonia 82 W2 21 29S 167 50E
Neckar r. Germany 71 A1 48 00N 9 00E
Neckei i. Hawaiian Islands 23 J10 23 25N 164 42W
Necochea Argentina 103 F5 38 31S 58 46W
Nederrijn r. Netherlands 70 E3 51 58N 5 35E
Needles California U.S.A. 90 D3 34 51N 114 36W
Neepawa Manitoba Canada 92 A4 50 14N 99 29W
Nee Soon Singapore 41 C4 1 24N 103 49E
Nefta Tunisia 112 G9 33 53N 7 50E
Negev d. Israel 54 O10 30 50N 30 45E
Negrais, Cape Myanmar 38 B3 15 57N 94 12E
Negritos Peru 102 A12 4 42S 81 18W
Negros i. The Philippines 40 B2/B3 10 00N 123 00E
Neiafu Tonga 83 C4 18 44S 174 00W
Neijiang China 49 L4 29 32N 105 03E
Nei Mongol Zizhiqu (Inner Mongolia Autonomous Region) admin. China 49 M7 42 30N 112 30E
Neisse (Nysa) r. Germany 71 B2 52 00N 14 00E
Neiva Colombia 102 B13 2 58N 75 15W
Nek'emtē Ethiopia 110 G9 9 04N 36 30E
Nellore India 53 D2 14 29N 80 00E
Nelson Manitoba Canada 88 L2 49 29N 117 17W
Nelson admin. South Island New Zealand 79 B2 41 30S 172 30E
Nelson Forks British Columbia Canada 88 K4 59 30N 124 00W
Nelson River Manitoba Canada 89 Q4 57 00N 94 00W
Neman r. Eurasia 69 E2 55 00N 22 00E
Nembao Solomon Islands 83 M2 11 20S 166 30E
Nemboi Solomon Islands 82 L3 10 50S 165 50E
Nemuro Japan 46 E3 43 22N 145 36E
Nemuro-Kaikyō sd. Japan 46 E3 44 00N 146 00E
Nenana Alaska U.S.A. 88 F5 64 35N 149 20W
Nenas Channel Singapore/Malaysia 41 E5 1 25N 103 59E
Nene r. England United Kingdom 68 K4 52 25N 0 05E
Nenjiang China 49 O8 49 10N 125 15E
Nen Jiang r. China 49 P9 50 00N 125 00E
Neosho r. U.S.A. 92 A1 37 00N 95 00W
NEPAL 53 E5
Nepean Ontario Canada 93 E3 45 16N 75 48W
Nepean Island Norfolk Island 81 L3 29 05S 167 58E
Nepoui New Caledonia 82 T2 21 19S 164 59E
Nerchinsk Russia 57 N6 52 02N 116 38E
Neretva r. Bosnia-Herzegovina 74 C3 43 30N 15 18E
Nerva Spain 72 A2 37 41N 6 33W
Neryungri Russia 57 O7 56 39N 124 38E
Nes Netherlands 70 E5 53 27N 5 46E
Neskaupstadur Iceland 69 J7 65 10N 13 43W
Neste r. France 73 B1 43 00N 0 15E
Nestor Trinidad and Tobago 96 T10 10 31N 61 09W
Nestor Falls tn. Ontario Canada 92 B3 49 06N 93 55W
Netanya Israel 54 O11 32 20N 34 51E
NETHERLANDS 70 C3/F5
Nettetal Germany 70 F3 51 20N 6 14E
Nettilling Lake Northwest Territories Canada 89 U6 66 30N 71 10W
Netzahualcóyotl Mexico 96 E3 19 24N 99 02W
Neubrandenburg Germany 71 B2 53 33N 13 16E
Neuburg Germany 71 B1 48 44N 11 12E
Neuchâtel Switzerland 73 C2 46 55N 6 56E
Neuenhagen Germany 67 G2 52 32N 13 41E
Neufchâteau Belgium 70 E1 49 51N 5 26E
Neufchâteau France 73 C2 48 21N 5 42E
Neufchâtel-en-Bray France 73 B2 49 44N 1 26E
Neufchâtel-sur-Aisne France 70 D1 49 27N 4 02E
Neuilly France 67 B2 48 53N 2 17E
Neuilly Plaisance France 67 C2 48 51N 2 31E
Neukölln Germany 67 F1 52 29N 13 28E
Neumarkt Germany 71 B1 49 17N 11 29E
Neumünster Germany 71 A2 54 05N 9 59E
Neunkirchen Germany 71 A1 49 21N 7 12E
Neuquén Argentina 103 D5 38 55N 68 05W
Neuruppin Germany 71 B2 52 56N 12 49E
Neusiedler See l. Austria 75 C2 48 00N 16 00E
Neuss Germany 71 A2 51 12N 6 42E
Neustadt Germany 71 A1 49 21N 8 09E
Neustrelitz Germany 71 B2 53 22N 13 05E
Neu-Ulm Germany 71 B1 48 23N 10 01E
Neuwied Germany 71 A2 50 26N 7 28E
Nevada Missouri U.S.A. 92 B1 37 51N 94 22W
Nevada state U.S.A. 90 C4 39 00N 118 00W
Nevers France 73 B2 47 00N 3 09E
Neves Brazil 103 Q2 22 51S 43 05W
Nevinnomyssk Russia 58 E3 44 38N 41 59E
Neviot Egypt 54 O9 28 58N 34 38E
New r. U.S.A. 93 D1 37 00N 81 00W
New Addington England United Kingdom 66 D2 51 21N 0 01E
New Albany Indiana U.S.A. 92 C1 38 17N 85 50W
New Amsterdam Guyana 102 F14 6 18N 57 30W
Newark New Jersey U.S.A. 94 B2 40 43N 74 11W
Newark Ohio U.S.A. 93 D2 40 03N 82 25W
Newark Bay New Jersey U.S.A. 94 B1 40 40N 74 08W
New Bedford Massachusetts U.S.A. 93 F2 41 38N 70 55W
New Bern North Carolina U.S.A. 91 K4 35 05N 77 04W
Newberry Michigan U.S.A. 92 C3 46 22N 85 30W
New Braunfels Texas U.S.A. 91 G2 29 43N 98 09W
New Britain Connecticut U.S.A. 93 F2 41 40N 72 47W
New Britain i. Papua New Guinea 45 O4 4 45S 150 30E
New Brunswick province Canada 89 V2 47 30N 66 00W
New Buffalo Michigan U.S.A. 92 C2 41 48N 86 44W
Newburgh New York U.S.A. 93 F2 41 30N 74 00W
NEW CALEDONIA 82
Newcastle Australia 78 I3 32 55S 151 46E
Newcastle Ontario Canada 93 E2 43 55N 78 35W
New Castle Pennsylvania U.S.A. 93 D2 41 00N 80 22W
Newcastle Wyoming U.S.A. 90 F5 43 52N 104 14W
Newcastle upon Tyne England United Kingdom 68 J7 54 59N 1 35W
New Delhi India 53 D5 28 37N 77 14E
New Dorp New York U.S.A. 94 B1 40 34N 74 06W
Newfoundland i. Newfoundland Canada 89 X2 48 15N 57 00W
Newfoundland province Canada 89 W4/Y2 52 30N 62 30W
Newfoundland Basin Atlantic Ocean 25 D11/E11 44 00N 40 00W
New Georgia i. Solomon Islands 82 C5 8 30S 157 30E
New Georgia Islands Solomon Islands 82 C5 8 00S 157 00E
New Georgia Sound (The Slot) Solomon Islands 82 D5 8 30S 158 30E
New Grant Trinidad and Tobago 96 T9 10 17N 61 19W
Newham bor. England United Kingdom 66 D3 51 30N 0 02E
New Hampshire state U.S.A. 93 F2 43 00N 72 00W
New Hanover i. Papua New Guinea 45 O5 2 30S 150 15E
New Haven Connecticut U.S.A. 93 F2 41 18N 72 55W
New Hebrides Trench Pacific Ocean 22 G6 15 00S 169 00E
New Hyde Park New York U.S.A. 94 D1 40 44N 73 42W
New Iberia Louisiana U.S.A. 91 H2 30 00N 91 51W
New Ireland i. Papua New Guinea 45 P5 3 15S 152 30E
New Jersey state U.S.A. 93 F1 40 00N 75 00W
New Liskeard Ontario Canada 93 E3 47 31N 79 41W
New London Connecticut U.S.A. 93 F2 41 21N 72 06W
Newman Australia 78 B5 23 20S 119 34E
New Mexico state U.S.A. 90 E3 35 00N 107 00W
New Milford Pennsylvania U.S.A. 93 E2 41 52N 75 44W
New Orleans Louisiana U.S.A. 91 H2 30 00N 90 03W
New Philadelphia Ohio U.S.A. 93 D2 40 31N 81 28W
Newport Australia 79 H3 33 39S 151 19E
Newport Wales United Kingdom 68 H3 51 35N 3 00W
Newport Maine U.S.A. 93 G2 44 50N 69 17W
Newport Rhode Island U.S.A. 93 F2 41 30N 71 19W
Newport Vermont U.S.A. 93 F2 44 56N 72 18W
Newport News Virginia U.S.A. 93 E1 36 59N 76 26W
New Providence i. The Bahamas 97 I5 25 00N 77 30W
New Rochelle New York U.S.A. 94 B2 40 55N 73 46W
Newry Northern Ireland United Kingdom 68 E6 54 11N 6 20W
New Siberian Islands Russia 57 Q10 75 00N 145 00E
New South Wales state Australia 78 G3/I3 32 00S 145 00E
New Springville New York U.S.A. 94 B1 40 35N 74 10W
New Territories admin. Hong Kong U.K. 51 B2 22 20N 114 00E
Newtownabbey Northern Ireland United Kingdom 68 F6 54 40N 5 54W
New Ulm Minnesota U.S.A. 92 B2 44 19N 94 28W
New Westminster British Columbia Canada 88 K2 49 10N 122 58W
New York New York U.S.A. 93 F2 40 40N 73 50W
New York state U.S.A. 93 E2/F2 43 00N 76 00W
Neyagawa Japan 46 G1 34 45N 135 36E
Neyrīz Iran 55 H4 29 14N 54 18E
Neyshābūr Iran 55 I6 36 13N 58 49E
Ngabang Indonesia 42 C4 0 15N 109 54E
Ngami, Lake Botswana 111 D3 21 00S 23 00E
Ngangla Ringco l. China 53 E6 31 40N 83 00E
Nganjuk Indonesia 42 P7 7 36S 111 56E
Nganze Co l. China 53 F6 31 00N 87 00E
Ngao Thailand 39 A3 18 45N 99 58E
Ngaoundéré Cameroon 112 H4 7 20N 13 35E
Ngathainggyaung Myanmar 38 B3 17 22N 95 04E
Ngau Chi Wan Hong Kong U.K. 51 C2 22 25N 114 10E
Ngau Kwu Long Hong Kong U.K. 51 A1 22 18N 113 58E
Ngauruhoe, Mount North Island New Zealand 79 C3 39 10S 175 38E
Ngau Tam Mei Hong Kong U.K. 51 B2 22 28N 114 04E
Ngau Tau Kok Hong Kong U.K. 51 C1 22 19N 114 13E
Ngawi Indonesia 42 P7 7 23S 111 22E
Negelē Ethiopia 110 G9 5 20N 39 35E
Nggatokae i. Solomon Islands 82 D5 8 50S 158 10E
Nggela Pile i. Solomon Islands 82 F4 9 10S 160 20E
Nggela Sule i. Solomon Islands 82 F4 9 00S 160 20E
Nghia Dan see Thai Hoa
Nghia Lo Vietnam 37 B4 21 36N 104 35E
Ngiap r. Laos 37 B3 18 45N 103 40E
Ngoc Linh mt. Vietnam 37 C3 15 02N 107 58E
Ngong Ping Hong Kong U.K. 51 A1 22 15N 113 54E
Nguigmi Niger 112 H5 14 19N 13 06E
Nguna i. Vanuatu 83 H4 17 29S 168 23E
Nguru Nigeria 112 H5 12 53N 10 30E
Nguyen Binh Vietnam 37 C4 22 41N 105 55E
Nha Trang Vietnam 37 C2 12 15N 109 10E
Nho Quan Vietnam 37 C4 20 20N 105 30E
Nhulunbuy Australia 78 F7 12 30S 136 56E
Niagara Falls tn. New York U.S.A. 93 E2 43 06N 79 04W
Niagara Falls tn. Ontario Canada 93 E2 43 05N 79 06W
Niamey Niger 112 F5 13 32N 2 05E
Niangara Zaïre 110 E8 3 45N 27 54E
Nias i. Indonesia 42 A4 1 00B 97 30E
Nibok Nauru 83 L2 0 30S 166 55E
Nibra India 52 K2 22 35N 88 15E
NICARAGUA 97 G2
Nice France 73 C1 43 42N 7 16E
Nicobar Islands India 53 G1 8 30N 94 00E
Nicosia Cyprus 54 D6 35 11N 33 23E
Nidd r. England United Kingdom 68 J6 54 02N 1 30W
Nied r. France 70 F1 49 15N 6 30E
Niedere Tauern mts. Austria 75 B2 47 00N 14 00E
Niedersachsen admin. Germany 71 A2 52 00N 9 00E
Nienburg Germany 71 A2 52 38N 9 13E
Niers r. Germany 70 F3 51 00N 6 00E
Nieuwegein Netherlands 70 E4 52 00N 5 05E
Nieuw Nickerie Surinam 102 F14 5 52N 57 00W
Nieuwpoort Belgium 70 B3 51 08N 2 45E
NIGER 112 G6/H6
Niger r. Nigeria 112 G4 5 30N 6 15E
Niger Delta Nigeria 104 5 00N 7 00E
NIGERIA 112 F4/H5
Niguria Islands Papua New Guinea 45 Q5 3 25S 154 30E
Niigata Japan 46 C2 37 58N 139 02E
Niihama Japan 46 B1 33 57N 133 15E
Niihau i. Hawaiian Islands 23 W18 21 50N 160 11W
Nii-jima i. Japan 46 C1 34 20N 139 15E
Nijkerk Netherlands 70 E4 52 12N 5 30E
Nijmegen Netherlands 70 E3 51 50N 5 52E
Nikko Japan 46 C2 36 45N 139 37E
Nikolayev Ukraine 58 C4 46 57N 32 00E
Nikolayevsk-na-Amure Russia 57 Q6 53 10N 140 44E
Nikol'skiy see Satlayev
Nikopol Ukraine 58 C4 45 34N 34 25E
Nikšić Montenegro Yugoslavia 74 C3 42 48N 18 56E
Nikumaroro (Gardner Island) i. Pacific Ocean 80 D3 3 00S 174 00W
Nila Solomon Islands 82 A6 7 10S 155 50E
Nile r. Egypt 110 F13 28 30N 30 40E
Nile Delta Egypt 104 31 00N 31 00E
Niles Michigan U.S.A. 92 C2 41 51N 86 15W
Nilgiri Hills India 53 D2 11 00N 76 30E
Nîmes France 73 B1 43 50N 4 21E
Nimule Sudan 110 F8 3 35N 32 03E
Nim Wan Hong Kong U.K. 51 A2 22 25N 113 56E
Ninepin Group Hong Kong U.K. 51 C1 22 15N 114 20E
Ninety East Ridge Indian Ocean 24 H4/H6
Ninety Mile Beach North Island New Zealand 79 B4 34 45S 172 58E
Nineveh hist. site Iraq 54 F6 36 24N 43 08E
Ningbo China 49 O4 29 54N 121 33E
Ninglang China 38 C5 27 15N 100 57E
Ningming China 37 C4 22 08N 107 06E
Ningnan China 38 C5 27 04N 102 50E
Ninh Binh Vietnam 37 C4 20 14N 106 00E
Ninh Giang Vietnam 37 C4 20 50N 106 00E
Ninh Hoa Vietnam 37 C2 12 28N 109 07E
Ninigo Group is. Papua New Guinea 45 L6 1 15S 142 15E
Ninove Belgium 70 D2 50 50N 4 02E
Niobrara r. U.S.A. 90 F5 42 00N 102 00W
Nioro du Sahel Mali 112 D6 15 12N 9 35W
Niort France 73 A2 46 19N 0 27W
Nipigon Ontario Canada 92 C3 49 02N 88 26W
Nipigon, r. Ontario Canada 92 C3 49 02N 88 26W
Nipigon, Lake Ontario Canada 92 C3/4 49 50N 88 30W
Niš Serbia Yugoslavia 74 D3 43 20N 21 54E
Nishi Japan 47 B2 35 26N 139 37E
Nishinomiya Japan 46 G1 34 44N 135 22E
Nishio Japan 46 J1 34 52N 137 02E
Nishiwaki Japan 46 F2 35 00N 134 58E
Niteroi Brazil 103 Q2 22 54S 43 06W
Nitra Slovakia 75 C2 48 19N 18 04E
Niuafo'ou Point Tonga 83 D1 21 03S 175 19W
Niue i. Pacific Ocean 80 D3 19 02S 169 55W
Nivelles Belgium 70 D2 50 36N 4 20E
Nizamabad India 53 D3 18 40N 78 05E
Nizhevertovsk Russia 57 J8 60 57N 76 40E
Nizhneangarsk Russia 57 M7 55 48N 109 35E
Nizhnekamsk Russia 56 H7 55 38N 51 49E
Nizhnekamskoye Vodokhranilische res. Russia 59 G6 56 00N 53 30E
Nizhnenkolymsk Russia 57 S9 68 34N 160 58E
Nizhniy Novgorod (Gork'iy) Russia 56 G7 56 20N 44 00E
Nizhniy Novgorod (Gor'kovskoya) Vodokhranilishche res. Russia 58 E6 57 00N 43 30E
Nizhniy Tagil Russia 56 I7 58 00N 59 58E
Nizhnyaya (Lower) Tunguska r. Russia 57 L8/M8 64 00N 94 00E
Nizké Tatry mts. Slovakia 75 C2/D2 49 00N 19 00E
Njoroveto Solomon Islands 82 B6 7 50S 156 40E
Nkongsamba Cameroon 112 G3 4 59N 9 53E
Nmai Hka r. Myanmar 38 B5 26 00N 98 05E
Noakhali Bangladesh 38 A4 22 52N 91 03E
Noatak Alaska U.S.A. 88 C6 67 33N 163 10W
Noatak r. Alaska U.S.A. 88 C6 67 33N 163 10W
Nobeoka Japan 46 B1 32 36N 131 40E
Nobi Japan 47 B1 35 11N 139 41E
Noda Japan 46 L2 35 57N 139 52E
Nogales Mexico 96 B6 31 20N 111 00W
Nogales Arizona U.S.A. 90 D3 31 20N 110 56W
Nogent France 67 C2 48 50N 2 30E
Noguera Ribagorzana r. Spain 72 C3 42 25N 0 45E
Noisy-le-Sec France 67 B2 48 53N 2 27E
Nojima-zaki c. Japan 46 L1 34 54N 139 54E
Nola Central African Republic 110 C8 3 28N 16 08E
Nomad Papua New Guinea 45 K3 6 18S 142 13E
Nome Alaska U.S.A. 88 B5 64 30N 165 30W
Nomoi i. Micronesia 80 B4 5 00N 146 00E
Nomuka i. Tonga 83 B2 20 15S 174 46W
Nomuka Group Tonga 83 B2 20 30S 174 30W
Nomukaiki i. Tonga 83 B2 20 16S 174 46W
Nong Bua Thailand 39 B3 15 53N 100 37E
Nong Bua Lamphu Thailand 39 B3 17 11N 102 29E
Nong Han Reservoir Thailand 39 B3 17 10N 104 10E
Nong Khai Thailand 39 B3 17 52N 102 44E
Nonouti Atoll Pacific Ocean 80 C3 1 00S 176 00E
Non Sung Thailand 39 B3 15 11N 102 19E
Nonthaburi Thailand 39 B2 13 48N 100 11E
Noord Beveland i. Netherlands 70 C3 51 35N 3 45E
Noord-Brabant admin. Netherlands 70 D3/E3 51 29N 5 00E
Noord-Holland admin. Netherlands 70 D4 52 30N 4 45E
Noordoost Polder Netherlands 70 E4 52 40N 5 45E
Noordwijk Netherlands 70 D4 52 15N 4 25E
Noorvik Alaska U.S.A. 88 C6 66 50N 161 14W
Noranda Québec Canada 93 E3 48 15N 79 00W
Nord admin. France 70 C2/D2 50 13N 4 03E
Norden Germany 71 A2 53 36N 7 13E
Nordenham Germany 71 A2 53 30N 8 29E
Norderney i. Germany 71 A2 53 00N 7 00E
Norderstedt Germany 71 A2 53 41N 9 58E
Nordfjord fj. Norway 69 B3 62 00N 5 15E
Nordfold Norway 69 D4 67 48N 15 20E
Nordfriesische Inseln (North Frisian Islands) is. Germany 71 A2 54 00N 8 00E
Nordhausen Germany 71 B2 51 31N 10 48E
Nordhorn Germany 71 A2 52 27N 7 05E
Nordkapp (North Cape) c. Norway 69 E5 71 11N 25 40E
Nordrhein-Westfalen admin. Germany 71 A2 52 00N 7 00E
Nordstrand i. Germany 71 A2 54 00N 8 00E
Nordvik Russia 57 N10 74 01N 111 30E
Nore r. Irish Republic 68 D4 52 25N 7 02W
Norfolk Nebraska U.S.A. 91 G5 42 01N 97 25W
Norfolk Virginia U.S.A. 93 E1 36 54N 76 18W
Norfolk Island Pacific Ocean 80 C2 29 05S 167 59E
Norfolk Island National Park Norfolk Island 81 K5 29 00S 167 56E
Norfolk Island Trough Pacific Ocean 22 G5 27 30S 166 00E
Norfolk Lake Arkansas U.S.A. 91 H4 36 00N 92 00W
Noril'sk Russia 57 K9 69 21N 88 02E
Normanby Island Papua New Guinea 45 O1 10 00S 151 00E
Normanton Australia 78 G6 17 40S 141 05E
Norman Wells tn. Northwest Territories Canada 88 J6 65 19N 126 46W
Norris Lake Tennessee U.S.A. 91 J4 36 00N 84 00W
Norristown Pennsylvania U.S.A. 93 E2 40 07N 75 20W
Norrköping Sweden 69 D2 58 35N 16 10E
Norseman Australia 78 C3 32 15S 121 47E
Norsup Vanuatu 83 G5 16 04S 167 24E
Northam Australia 78 B3 31 40S 116 40E
North American Basin Atlantic Ocean 25 C10 34 00N 55 00W
Northampton Australia 78 A4 28 27S 114 37E
Northampton England United Kingdom 68 K4 52 14N 0 54W
Northampton Massachusetts U.S.A. 93 F2 42 19N 72 38W
North Andaman i. Andaman Islands 38 A2 13 25N 92 55E
North Anna r. Virginia U.S.A. 93 E1 38 00N 77 00W
North Astrolabe Reef Fiji 83 C8 18 40S 178 30E
North Atlantic Ocean 25 D7/D11
North Australian Basin Indian Ocean 24 K5 14 00S 115 00E
North Barrackpore India 52 K3 22 46N 88 21E
North Battleford Saskatchewan Canada 88 N3 52 47N 108 17W
North Bay tn. Ontario Canada 93 E3 46 20N 79 28W
North Bergen New Jersey U.S.A. 94 B2 40 46N 74 02W
North Canadian r. U.S.A. 90 F4 36 00N 100 00W
North Cape North Island New Zealand 79 B4 34 25S 173 03E
North Cape see Nordkapp
North Carolina state U.S.A. 91 K4 36 00N 80 00W
North Channel British Isles 68 F7 55 20N 5 50W
North Channel Ontario Canada 93 D3 46 00N 83 00W
North Dakota state U.S.A. 90 F6 47 00N 102 00W
North Downs hills England United Kingdom 68 L3 51 13N 0 30W
North East Point Christmas Island 81 R3 10 24S 105 44E
Northeim Germany 71 A2 51 43N 9 59E
Northern Ireland United Kingdom 68 D6
Northern Lau Group Fiji 83 F9 17 20S 179 00W
NORTHERN MARIANAS 80 B4
Northern Range mts. Trinidad and Tobago 96 T10 10 47N 61 27W
Northern Territory territory Australia 78 E6/F5 19 00S 132 00E
North Esk r. Scotland United Kingdom 68 I8 56 50N 2 50W

North European Plain Europe **60** 54 00N 20 00E
North Fiji Basin Pacific Ocean **22** H6 18 00S 173 00E
North Frisian Islands *see* Nordfriesische Inseln
North Gauhati India **38** A5 26 15N 91 38E
North Head Australia **79** H2 33 49S 151 18E
North Hollywood California U.S.A. **95** A3 34 10N 118 22W
North Island New Zealand **79** B3/C3
NORTH KOREA 50 B4/D5
North Lakhimpur India **36** A7 27 12N 94 07E
North Little Rock Arkansas U.S.A. **91** H3 34 46N 92 16W
North Loup *r.* Nebraska U.S.A. **90** F5 42 00N 0 0 00W
North Platte Nebraska U.S.A. **90** F5 41 09N 100 45W
North Platte *r.* U.S.A. **90** F5 42 00N 103 00W
North Point Barbados **96** V13 13 20N 59 37W
North Point Hong Kong U.K. **51** C1 22 18N 114 12E
North Pole Arctic Ocean **20** 90 00N
North River *tn.* Manitoba Canada **89** Q4 58 55N 94 30W
North Sea Europe **64** C6
North Tuas Basin Singapore **41** A3 1 19N 103 39E
North Uist *i.* Scotland United Kingdom **68** D9 57 04N 7 15W
North West Cape Australia **78** A5 21 48S 114 10E
North West Christmas Island Ridge Pacific Ocean **23** J8 9 30N 170 00W
Northwestern Atlantic Basin Atlantic Ocean **25** B10 33 00N 70 00W
Northwest Highlands Scotland United Kingdom **68** F8/G10
Northwest Pacific Basin Pacific Ocean **22** F11 35 00N 150 00E
North West Point Christmas Island **81** P2 10 26S 105 33E
Northwest Territories *territory* Canada **88/89** M6 65 15N 115 00W
Northwood England United Kingdom **66** B3 51 36N 0 25W
North York Moors England United Kingdom **68** K6 55 22N 0 45W
Norton Kansas U.S.A. **90** G4 39 51N 99 53W
Norton Sound Alaska U.S.A. **88** C5 64 00N 162 30W
Norvegia, Cape Antarctica **21** 71 26S 122 25W
Norwalk California U.S.A. **95** B2 33 56N 118 04W
Norwalk Connecticut U.S.A. **93** F2 41 07N 73 25W
NORWAY 69 B3/F5
Norway House *tn.* Manitoba Canada **89** P3 53 59N 97 50W
Norwegian Basin Arctic Ocean **25** H13 67 00N 0 00
Norwegian Sea Arctic Ocean **20** 70 00N 5 00E
Norwich England United Kingdom **68** M4 52 38N 1 18E
Norwich Connecticut U.S.A. **93** F2 41 32N 72 05W
Noshiro Japan **46** D3 40 13N 140 00E
Nosop *r.* Southern Africa **111** D2 25 00S 20 30E
Nosy Bé *i.* Madagascar **111** I5 13 00S 47 00E
Notéc *r.* Poland **75** C3 53 00N 17 00E
Notre Dame Bay Newfoundland Canada **89** X2 49 40N 55 00W
Notre-Dame du Lac *tn.* Québec Canada **93** G3 47 38N 68 49W
Nottaway River Québec Canada **93** E4 51 00N 78 00W
Nottingham England United Kingdom **68** J4 52 58N 1 10W
Nottingham Island Northwest Territories Canada **89** T5 62 15N 77 30W
Nouadhibou Mauritania **112** B7 20 54N 17 01W
Nouakchott Mauritania **112** B6 18 09N 15 58W
Nouméa *i.* New Caledonia **82** V1 22 16S 166 26E
Nouvelle Caledonia *(New Caledonia) i.* Pacific Ocean **82** R6/X2 22 00S 165 00E
Nouzonville France **70** D1 49 49N 4 45E
Nova Friburgo Brazil **103** I8 22 16S 42 34W
Nova Iguaçu Brazil **103** I8 22 46S 43 23W
Novolazarevskaya *r.s.* Antarctica **21** 70 46S 11 50E
Novara Italy **74** A4 45 27N 8 37E
Nova Scotia *province* Canada **89** W1 44 30N 65 00W
Nova Scotia Basin Atlantic Ocean **25** C10 39 00N 55 00W
Novaya Zemlya *is.* Russia **57** H10 74 00N 55 00E
Novgorod Russia **56** F7 58 30N 31 20E
Novi Pazar Serbia Yugoslavia **74** D3 43 09N 20 29E
Novi Sad Serbia Yugoslavia **74** D4 45 15N 19 51E
Novocheboksarsk Russia **58** F6 56 05N 47 27E
Novocherkassk Russia **58** E4 47 25N 40 05E
Novo Hamburgo Brazil **103** G7 29 37S 51 07W
Novokazalinsk Kazakhstan **59** J4 45 48N 62 06E
Novokuybyshevsk Russia **58** G5 53 05N 49 59E
Novokuznetsk Russia **57** K6 53 45N 87 12E
Novomoskovsk Russia **58** D5 54 06N 38 15E
Novorossiysk Russia **56** F4 44 44N 37 46E
Novoshakhtinsk Russia **58** D4 47 46N 39 55E
Novosibirsk Russia **57** K7 55 04N 83 05E
Novosibirskiye Ostrova *(New Siberian Islands) is.* Russia **20** 75 00N 145 00E
Novotroitsk Russia **59** H5 51 11N 58 16E
Novvy Port Russia **57** J9 67 38N 72 33E
Novvy Urengoy Russia **57** J9 66 00N 77 20E
Nowai *r.* India **52** K2 22 39N 88 28E
Nowa Sól Poland **75** C3 51 49N 15 41E
Nowgong India **53** G5 26 20N 92 41E
Nowy Dwor Poland **75** D3 52 27N 20 41E
Nowy Sącz Poland **75** D2 49 39N 20 40E
Nuapapu *i.* Tonga **83** B4 18 42S 174 05W
Nubian Desert Sudan **110** F12 21 00N 33 00E
Nueces *r.* Texas U.S.A. **90** G2 28 00N 99 00W
Nueltin Lake Northwest Territories Canada **89** P5 60 30N 99 00W
Nueva Rosita Mexico **96** D5 27 58N 101 11W
Nueva San Salvador El Salvador **96** G2 13 40N 89 18W
Nuevitas Cuba **97** I4 21 34N 77 18W
Nuevo Casas Grandes Mexico **96** C6 30 22N 107 53W
Nuevo Laredo Mexico **96** E5 27 39N 99 30W
Nuku'alofa Tonga **83** D1 21 09S 175 14W
Nukubasaga *i.* Fiji **83** E10 16 20S 179 15W
Nukufetau *i.* Pacific Ocean **80** C3 7 00S 178 00E
Nuku Hiva *i.* Pacific Ocean **81** E3 8 56S 140 00W
Nukuilau Fiji **83** B9 17 53S 177 51E
Nukunono Atoll Pacific Ocean **80** D3 9 10S 171 55W
Nukunuku Tonga **83** D1 21 80S 175 10W
Nukuoro *i.* Micronesia **80** B4 4 00S 155 00E
Nukus Uzbekistan **59** H3 42 28N 59 07E
Nullarbor Plain Australia **78** D3 32 00S 128 00E
Num *i.* Irian Jaya Indonesia **44** F6 1 30S 135 15E
Numazu Japan **46** K2 35 08N 138 50E
Numedal *geog. reg.* Norway **69** C3 60 40N 9 00E
Nunivak Island Alaska U.S.A. **88** B5 60 00N 166 00W
Nunspeet Netherlands **70** E4 52 22N 5 47E
Nupani *i.* Solomon Islands **82** L3 10 11S 165 32E
Nura *r.* Kazakhstan **59** L5 51 00N 71 00E
Nurakita *i.* Pacific Ocean **80** C3 9 00S 179 00E
Nuremberg *see* Nürnberg
Nürnberg *(Nuremberg)* Germany **71** B2 49 27N 11 05E
Nürtingen Germany **71** A1 48 37N 9 20E
Nusa Tenggara Barat *admin.* Indonesia **42** E2 8 00S 117 00E
Nusa Tenggara Timur *admin.* Indonesia **43** F2 10 00S 122 00E
Nuseybin Turkey **54** F6 37 05N 41 11E
Nu Shan *mts.* China **38** B5 26 30N 99 00E
Nushki Pakistan **52** B5 29 33N 66 01E
Nutak Newfoundland Canada **89** W4 57 30N 61 59W
Nuthe *r.* Germany **67** E1 52 21N 13 07E
Nuuk *see* Godthåb
Nuussuaq *p.* Greenland **89** Y7 70 50N 53 00W
Nu'utele *i.* Western Samoa **82** B10 14 03S 171 22W
Nuuuli American Samoa **82** E12 14 19S 170 42W
Nyainqêntênglha Shan *mts.* China **48** G4/H5 30 00N 90 00E
Nyala Sudan **110** D10 12 01N 24 50E
Nyasa, Lake *(Lake Malawi)* Southern Africa **111** F5 12 00S 35 00E
Nyaungbitho Myanmar **38** B4 22 02N 96 11E
Nyaunglebin Myanmar **38** B3 17 59N 96 44E
Nyaung U Myanmar **38** A4 21 12N 94 55E
Nyíregyháza Hungary **75** D2 47 57N 21 43E
Nykøbing Denmark **69** C1 54 47N 11 53E
Nyköping Sweden **69** D2 58 45N 17 03E
Nyngan Australia **78** H3 31 34S 147 14E
Nyons France **73** C1 44 22N 5 08E
Nysa Poland **75** C3 50 30N 17 20E
Nysa *(Niesse) r.* Poland **75** B3 52 00N 14 00E
Nyūdō-zaki *c.* Japan **46** C2 40 00N 139 42E

O

Oahe, Lake U.S.A. **90** F6 45 00N 100 00W
Oahu *i.* Hawaiian Islands **23** X18-Y18 21 30N 158 10W
Oakes North Dakota U.S.A. **92** A3 46 08N 98 07W
Oak Hill *tn.* West Virginia U.S.A. **93** D1 37 58N 81 11W
Oakland California U.S.A. **90** B4 37 50N 122 15W
Oakland City Indiana U.S.A. **92** C1 38 21N 87 19W
Oak Ridge *tn.* Tennessee U.S.A. **91** J4 36 02N 84 12W
Oakville Ontario Canada **93** E2 43 27N 79 41W
Oamaru South Island New Zealand **79** B1 45 06S 170 58E
Oano Islands Pitcairn Islands **23** N5 23 32S 125 00W
Ōarai Japan **46** M3 36 18N 140 35E
Oates Land *geog. reg.* Antarctica **21** 70 00S 150 00E
Oaxaca Mexico **96** E3 17 05N 96 41W
Ob' *r.* Russia **57** I9 65 30N 66 00E
Oba Ontario Canada **89** S2 48 38N 84 17W
Obama Japan **46** G2 35 25N 135 45E
Oban Scotland United Kingdom **68** F8 56 25N 5 29W
Oberhausen Germany **71** A2 51 27N 6 50E
Oberösterreich *admin.* Austria **71** B1 48 00N 14 00E
Oberpfälzer Wald *see* Bohmer Wald
Oberursel Germany **71** A2 50 12N 8 35E
Ob', Gulf of Russia **57** J9 68 00N 74 00E
Obidos Brazil **102** F12 1 52S 55 30W
Obihiro Japan **46** D3 42 56N 143 10E
Obitsu *r.* Japan **47** C2 35 25N 139 53E
Ocala Florida U.S.A. **91** J2 29 11N 82 09W
Ocaña Colombia **102** C14 8 16N 73 21W
Ocatlán Mexico **96** D4 20 21N 102 42W
Ocean City Maryland U.S.A. **93** E1 38 21N 75 06W
Ochokovo Russia **56** L1 55 39N 37 30E
Ocho Rios Jamaica **97** Q8 18 24N 77 06W
Oconto Wisconsin U.S.A. **92** C2 44 55N 87 52W
Ōda Japan **46** B2 35 10N 132 29E
Odaejin North Korea **50** D5 41 23N 129 51E
Odate Japan **46** D3 40 18N 140 32E
Odawara Japan **46** L2 35 15N 139 08E
Odda Norway **69** B3 60 03N 6 34E
Ödemiş Turkey **74** E2 38 11N 27 58E
Odense Denmark **69** C2 55 24N 10 25E
Odenwald *mts.* Germany **71** A1 49 00N 9 00E
Oder *(Odra) r.* Europe **71** B2 52 00N 15 30E
Oder-Spree Kanal *can.* Germany **67** G1 52 21N 13 43E
Odessa Ukraine **58** C4 46 30N 30 46E
Odessa Delaware U.S.A. **93** E1 39 27N 75 40W
Odessa Texas U.S.A. **90** F3 31 50N 102 23W
Odiel *r.* Spain **72** A2 37 32N 7 00W
Odioñgan The Philippines **40** B3 12 24N 121 59E
Oekusi *see* Dili
Oema *i.* Solomon Islands **82** B7 6 40S 156 10E
Ofanto *r.* Italy **74** C3 41 00N 15 00E
Offenbach am Main Germany **71** A2 50 06N 8 46E
Offenburg Germany **71** A1 48 29N 7 57E
Ofolanga *i.* Tonga **83** B3 19 43S 174 29W
Ofu *i.* American Samoa **82** F12 14 11S 169 40W
Ofuna Japan **47** B2 53 21N 139 32E
Ofunato Japan **46** D2 39 04N 141 43E
Ogaden *geog. reg.* Africa **110** I9 7 00N 51 00E
Ōgaki Japan **46** H2 35 22N 136 36E
Ogano Japan **46** L2 35 55N 139 11E
Ogasawara Guntō *i.* Pacific Ocean **22** E10 27 30N 43 00E
Ogawa Japan **47** A3 35 43N 135 29E
Ogbomosho Nigeria **112** F4 8 05N 4 11E
Ogden Utah U.S.A. **90** D5 41 14N 111 59W
Ogdensburg New York U.S.A. **93** E2 44 42N 75 31W
Ogea Driki *i.* Fiji **83** F7 19 12S 178 25W
Ogea Levu *i.* Fiji **83** F7 19 09S 178 25W
Ogho Solomon Islands **82** B7 6 50S 156 50E
Ogilvie Mountains Yukon Territory Canada **88** H6 65 05N 139 00W
Ogoki *r.* Ontario Canada **89** R3 51 00N 87 00W
Ogooue *r.* Gabon **110** A7 0 30S 10 00E
Ogooué *r.* Gabon **112** G2 0 50S 9 50E
Ōhara Japan **46** M2 35 16N 140 22E
Ōhata Japan **46** D3 41 22N 141 11E
Ohio *r.* U.S.A. **92** C1 38 00N 88 00W
Ohio *state* U.S.A. **93** D2 40 00N 83 00W
'Ohonua Tonga **83** E1 21 22S 174 58W
Ohře *r.* Czech Republic **71** B2 50 00N 14 00E
Ohre *r.* Germany **71** B2 52 00N 11 00E
Ohridsko ozero *l.* Europe **74** D3 41 00N 21 00E
Oil City Pennsylvania U.S.A. **93** E2 41 26N 79 44W
Oise *r.* France **73** B2 49 10N 2 10E
Oistins Barbados **96** V12 13 04N 59 35W
Oistins Bay Barbados **96** V12 13 03N 59 34W
Ōita Japan **50** E1 33 15N 131 36E
Ojinaga Mexico **96** D5 29 35N 104 26W
Oka *r.* Russia **58** D5 55 00N 42 00E
Okaba Irian Jaya Indonesia **44** H2 8 06S 139 46E
Okanagan *r.* North America **90** C6 49 00N 119 00W
Okara Pakistan **53** C6 30 49N 73 31E
Okavango *r.* Southern Africa **111** C4 17 50S 20 00E
Okavango Basin Botswana **111** D4 19 00S 23 00E
Okaya Japan **46** C2 36 03N 138 00E
Okayama Japan **46** B1 34 40N 133 54E
Okazaki Japan **46** J1 34 58N 137 10E
Okeechobee, Lake Florida U.S.A. **91** J2 27 00N 81 00W
Okehampton England United Kingdom **73** A3 50 44N 4 00W
Okene Nigeria **112** G4 7 31N 6 14E
Okha Russia **57** Q6 53 35N 143 01E
Okhla India **52** M4 28 33N 77 16E
Okhotsk Russia **57** Q7 59 20N 143 15E
Okhotsk, Sea of Russia **57** Q7 55 00N 148 00E
Oki *is.* Japan **46** B2 36 05N 133 00E
Okinawa *i.* Japan **49** P4 26 30N 128 00E
Oklahoma *state* U.S.A. **91** G4 36 00N 98 00W
Oklahoma City Oklahoma U.S.A. **91** G4 35 28N 97 33W
Okpo Myanmar **38** B3 18 03N 95 43E
Oksapmin Papua New Guinea **45** K4 5 20S 142 12E
Oktyabr'skiy Russia **57** R6 52 43N 156 14E
Okushiri-tō *i.* Japan **46** C3 42 15N 139 30E
Olal Vanuatu **83** H5 16 05S 168 10E
Öland *i.* Sweden **69** D2 56 45N 51 50E
Olbia Italy **74** A3 40 56N 9 30E
Old Crow Yukon Territory Canada **88** H6 67 34N 139 43W
Oldenburg Germany **71** A2 53 08N 8 13E
Oldenzaal Netherlands **70** F4 52 19N 6 55E
Oldham England United Kingdom **68** I5 53 33N 2 07W
Old Harbour *tn.* Jamaica **97** Q7 17 56N 77 07W
Old Harbour Bay *tn.* Jamaica **97** Q7 17 54N 77 06W
Old Head of Kinsale *c.* Irish Republic **68** C3 51 40N 8 30W
Olds Alberta Canada **88** M3 51 50N 114 06W
Old Town Maine U.S.A. **93** G2 44 55N 68 41W
Olean New York U.S.A. **93** E2 42 05N 78 26W
Olekma *r.* Russia **57** O7 59 00N 121 00E
Olekminsk Russia **57** O8 60 25N 120 25E
Olenëk Russia **57** N9 68 28N 112 18E
Olenëk *r.* Russia **57** O10 72 00N 122 00E
Olhão Portugal **72** A2 37 01N 7 50W
Ólimbos *(Olympus) mt.* Greece **74** D3 40 05N 22 21E
Olinda Brazil **102** J11 8 00S 34 51W
Olivia Minnesota U.S.A. **92** B2 44 47N 94 58W
Olomouc Czech Republic **75** C2 49 38N 17 15E
Olongapo The Philippines **40** B3 14 49N 120 17E
Oloruа *i.* Fiji **83** F8 18 24S 178 45W
Olosega American Samoa **82** F12 14 12S 169 38W
Olpoy Vanuatu **83** F7 14 50S 166 35E
Olsztyn Poland **75** D3 53 48N 20 29E
Olt *r.* Romania **75** D1 44 00N 24 00E
Olten Switzerland **73** C2 47 22N 7 55E
O'luan-pi *c.* Taiwan **51** G4 21 54N 120 53E
Olutanga *i.* The Philippines **40** B2 7 23N 122 50E
Olympia Washington U.S.A. **90** B6 47 03N 122 53W
Olympus *mt.* Cyprus **54** D5 34 55N 32 52E
Olympus *see* Ólimbos
Olympus, Mount Washington U.S.A. **90** B6 47 49N 123 42W
Om' *r.* Russia **57** J7 55 00N 79 00E
Omagh Northern Ireland United Kingdom **68** D6 54 36N 7 18W
Omaha Nebraska U.S.A. **92** A2 41 15N 96 00W
OMAN 55 I2
Oman, Gulf of Iran/Oman **55** I3 24 30N 58 30E
Omba *see* Aoba
Omboué Gabon **112** G2 1 38S 9 20E
Omdurman Sudan **110** F11 15 37N 32 29E
Ome Japan **46** L2 35 48N 139 17E
Omihachiman Japan **46** H2 35 08N 136 04E
Ōmiya Japan **46** L2 35 54N 139 39E
Omo *r.* Ethiopia **110** G9 7 00N 37 00E
Omolon *r.* Russia **57** R9 65 00N 160 00E
Omoloy *r.* Russia **57** P9 69 00N 132 00E
Omona *i.* Solomon Islands **82** D6 7 30S 158 40E
Omsk Russia **57** J7 55 00N 73 22E
Ōmuta Japan **46** B1 33 02N 130 26E
Omutinskiy Russia **59** K6 56 30N 67 40E
Ondo Nigeria **112** F4 7 05N 4 55E
Oneata *i.* Fiji **83** F8 18 27S 178 30W
Onega, Lake *see* Ozero Onezhskoy
Oneonta New York U.S.A. **93** E2 42 28N 75 04W
Onetar Vanuatu **83** G7 14 16S 167 26E
Ongjin North Korea **50** B3 37 56N 125 21E
Onitsha Nigeria **112** G4 6 10N 6 47E
Ono Japan **46** F1 34 52N 134 55E
Ono *i.* Fiji **83** C8 18 53S 178 30E
Onoda Japan **50** E1 34 00N 131 11E
Ono-i-lau *i.* Fiji **83** F6 20 48S 178 45W
Onomichi Japan **46** B1 34 25N 33 11E
Onon *r.* Russia/Mongolia **49** M9 51 00N 114 00E
Onslow Australia **78** B5 21 41S 115 12E
Onsong North Korea **50** D6 42 55N 129 59E
Ontario California U.S.A. **90** C3 34 04N 117 38W
Ontario *province* Canada **89** Q3 51 00N 91 00W
Ontario, Lake Canada/U.S.A. **93** E2 43 45N 78 00W
Ontonagon Michigan U.S.A. **92** C3 46 52N 89 18W
Ontong Java Atoll Solomon Islands **82** E8 5 20S 159 30E
Oologah Lake Oklahoma U.S.A. **92** A1 36 00N 95 00W
Oostelijk Flevoland *geog. reg.* Netherlands **70** E4 52 30N 5 40E
Oostende Belgium **70** B3 51 13N 2 55E
Oosterhout Netherlands **70** D3 51 39N 4 52E
Oosterschelde *sd.* Netherlands **70** C3 51 30N 3 58E
Oost-Vlaanderen *admin.* Belgium **70** C3 51 10N 3 45E
Opala Zaïre **110** D7 0 40S 24 20E
Opava Czech Republic **75** C2 49 58N 17 55E
Open Bay Papua New Guinea **45** O4 4 45S 151 30E
Opochka Russia **69** F2 56 41N 28 42E
Opole Poland **75** C3 50 40N 17 56E
Oporto *see* Porto
Opotiki North Island New Zealand **79** C3 38 01S 177 17E
Optic Lake *tn.* Manitoba Canada **89** O3 54 47N 101 15W
Oradea Romania **75** D2 47 03N 21 55E
Oradell Reservoir New Jersey U.S.A. **94** B2 40 58N 74 00W
Orai India **53** D5 26 00N 79 26E
Oran Algeria **112** E10 35 45N 0 38W
Orán Argentina **103** E8 23 07S 64 16W
Orange Australia **78** H3 33 19S 149 10E
Orange France **73** B1 44 08N 4 48E
Orange California U.S.A. **95** C2 33 43N 117 54W
Orange New Jersey U.S.A. **94** B2 40 45N 74 14W
Orange Texas U.S.A. **91** H3 30 05N 93 43W
Orange *r.* Southern Africa **111** C2 28 30S 17 30E
Orangeburg South Carolina U.S.A. **91** J3 33 28N 80 53W
Orange Free State *admin.* Republic of South Africa **111** E2 27 30S 27 30E
Oranienburg Germany **71** B2 52 46N 13 15E
Oransbari Irian Jaya Indonesia **44** F6 1 16S 134 18E
Oras The Philippines **40** C3 12 10N 125 28E
Oravița Romania **75** D2 45 02N 21 43E
Orbigo *r.* Spain **72** A3 42 15N 5 45W
Orcadas *r.s.* Antarctica **21** 60 44S 44 44W
Orchies France **70** C2 50 28N 3 15E
Orcia *r.* Italy **74** B3 42 00N 11 00E
Ordu Turkey **58** D3 41 00N 37 52E
Ordzhonikidze *see* Vladikavkaz
Örebro Sweden **69** D2 59 17N 15 13E
Oregon *state* U.S.A. **90** B5 44 00N 120 00W
Oregon City Oregon U.S.A. **90** B6 45 21N 122 36W
Orekhovo-Zuyevo Russia **58** D6 55 47N 39 00E
Orël Russia **56** F6 52 58N 36 04E
Orem Utah U.S.A. **90** D5 40 20N 111 45W
Orenburg Russia **56** H6 51 50N 55 00E
Orense Spain **72** A3 42 20N 7 52W
Orient Bay *tn.* Ontario Canada **92** C3 49 23N 88 08W
Orihuela Spain **72** B2 38 05N 0 56W
Orillia Ontario Canada **93** E2 44 36N 79 26W
Orissa *admin.* India **53** E4 20 20N 83 00E
Oristano Italy **74** A2 39 54N 8 36E
Orizaba Mexico **96** E3 18 51N 97 08W
Orkney Islands Scotland United Kingdom **68** H11 59 00N 3 00W
Orlando Florida U.S.A. **91** J2 28 33N 81 21W
Orléans France **73** B2 47 54N 1 54E
Orly France **67** B1 48 44N 2 24E
Ormoc The Philippines **40** B3 11 01N 124 36E
Orne *r.* France **73** A2 48 50N 0 16W
Örnsköldsvik Sweden **69** D3 63 19N 18 45E
Orohena, Mount Tahiti **82** T9 17 37S 149 27W
Orona *(Hull Island) i.* Pacific Ocean **80** D3 4 35S 172 20W
Oropucha *r.* Trinidad and Tobago **96** T10 10 36N 61 05W
Oroquieta The Philippines **40** B2 8 31N 123 46E
Orpington England United Kingdom **66** D2 51 23N 0 05E
Orsay France **67** A1 48 42N 2 11E
Orsk Russia **56** H6 51 13N 58 35E
Orthez France **73** A1 43 29N 0 46W
Ortigueira Spain **72** A3 43 43N 8 13W
Ortoire *r.* Trinidad and Tobago **96** T9 10 16N 61 15W
Ortonville Minnesota U.S.A. **92** A3 45 18N 96 28W
Ortze *r.* Germany **71** B2 53 00N 10 00E
Orūmīyeh Iran **54** F6 37 40N 45 00E
Oruro Bolivia **102** D9 17 59S 67 08W
Osage *r.* U.S.A. **92** B1 38 00N 93 00W
Ōsaka Japan **46** G1 34 40N 135 30E
Ōsaka *pref.* Japan **46** G1 34 30N 135 10E
Ōsaka-wan *b.* Japan **46** G1 34 30N 135 10E
Osceola Iowa U.S.A. **92** B2 41 02N 93 46W
Osh Kirgyzstan **59** L3 40 37N 72 49E
Oshawa Ontario Canada **93** E2 43 53N 78 51W
Ō-shima *i.* Japan **46** C1 34 45N 139 25E
Oshkosh Wisconsin U.S.A. **92** C2 44 01N 88 32W
Oshogbo Nigeria **112** F4 7 50N 4 35E
Osijek Croatia **74** C4 45 33N 18 41E
Oskaloosa Iowa U.S.A. **92** B2 41 16N 92 40W
Oslo Norway **69** C2 59 56N 10 45E
Oslofjorden *fj.* Norway **69** C2 59 20N 10 37E
Osmaniye Turkey **54** E6 37 04N 36 15E
Osnabrück Germany **71** A2 52 17N 8 03E
Osorno Chile **103** C4 40 35S 73 14W
Oss Netherlands **70** E3 51 46N 5 31E
Ossa, Mount Australia **78** H1 41 52S 146 04E
Ostankino Russia **56** M2 55 50N 37 37E
Österdalälven *r.* Sweden **69** C3 61 40N 13 30E
Østerdalen *geog. reg.* Norway **69** C3 62 00N 10 30E
Osterode Germany **71** B2 51 44N 10 15E
Östersund Sweden **69** C3 63 10N 14 40E
Östervall Sweden **69** D3 62 20N 15 20E
Ostfriesische Inseln *(East Frisian Islands) is.* Germany **71** A2 53 00N 7 00E
Ostrava Czech Republic **75** C2 49 50N 18 15E
Ostróda Poland **75** C3 53 42N 19 59E
Ostrołęka Poland **75** D3 53 05N 21 32E
Ostrov Russia **69** F2 57 52N 28 20E
Ostrowiec Swietokrzyski Poland **75** D3 50 58N 21 22E
Ostrów Mazowiecki Poland **75** D3 52 50N 21 51E
Ostrów Wielkopolski Poland **75** C3 51 39N 17 50E
Oswego New York U.S.A. **93** E2 43 27N 76 31W
Ōta Japan **47** B3 33 15N 131 36E
Otaheite Bay Trinidad and Tobago **96** S9 10 15N 61 30W
Otaki North Island New Zealand **79** C2 40 46S 175 09E
Otakwa Irian Jaya Indonesia **44** G4 4 45S 137 10E
Otaru Japan **46** D3 43 14N 140 59E
Otava *r.* Czech Republic **71** B1 49 00N 13 00E
Otavalo Ecuador **102** B13 0 13N 78 15W
O' The Cherokees, Lake Oklahoma U.S.A. **92** B1 37 00N 95 00W
Otra *r.* Norway **69** B2 56 17N 7 30E
Otranto Italy **74** C3 40 08N 18 30E
Otranto, Strait of Adriatic Sea **74** C2/3 40 00N 19 00E
Otsego Michigan U.S.A. **92** C2 42 46N 85 42W
Ōtsu Japan **46** G2 35 00N 135 50E
Otsuki Japan **46** K2 35 38N 138 53E
Ottawa Illinois U.S.A. **92** C2 41 21N 88 51W
Ottawa Kansas U.S.A. **92** A1 38 35N 95 16W
Ottawa Ontario Canada **93** E3 45 24N 75 38W
Ottawa *r.* Ontario/Québec Canada **93** E3 46 00N 77 00W
Ottawa Islands Northwest Territories Canada **89** S4 59 10N 80 25W
Otter Rapids *tn.* Ontario Canada **93** D4 50 12N 81 40W
Ottumwa Iowa U.S.A. **92** B2 41 02N 92 26W
Otu Tolu Group Tonga **83** B2 20 20S 174 25W
Oua *i.* Tonga **83** B2 20 01S 174 44W
Ouaco New Caledonia **82** T3 20 50S 164 30E
Ouadda Central African Republic **110** D9 8 09N 22 20E
Ouagadougou Burkina **112** E5 12 20N 1 40W
Ouahigouya Burkina **112** E5 13 31N 2 20W
Ouargla Algeria **112** G9 32 00N 5 16E
Ouassel *r.* Algeria **72** C2 35 30N 2 00E
Oubangui *r.* Africa **112** I3 0 00 17 30E
Oudenaarde Belgium **70** C2 50 50N 3 37E
Oude Rijn *r.* Netherlands **70** D4 52 06N 4 46E

Rudolstadt Germany 71 B2 50 44N 11 20E
Rudow Germany 67 F1 52 24N 13 29E
Rueil-Malmaison France 67 A2 48 52N 2 12E
Rufiji *r.* Tanzania 111 G6 7 30S 38 40E
Rugao China 49 O5 32 27N 120 35E
Rugby England United Kingdom 68 J4 52 23N 1 15W
Rügen Germany 71 B2 54 00N 14 00E
Ruhr *r.* Germany 71 A2 51 00N 7 00E
Ruili China 38 B4 24 01N 97 52E
Ruislip England United Kingdom 66 B3 51 35N 0 25W
Rukuruku Bay Fiji 83 C10 16 41S 178 31E
Rukwa, Lake Tanzania 111 F6 8 00S 33 00E
Rumford Maine U.S.A. 93 F2 44 33N 70 34W
Rumoi Japan 46 D3 43 57N 141 40E
Runanga South Island New Zealand 79 B2 42 24S 171 15E
Rungis France 67 B2 48 45N 2 22E
Rupel *r.* Belgium 70 D3 51 05N 4 20E
Rur *r.* Germany 70 F2 51 00N 6 00E
Rurutu *i.* Pacific Ocean 81 E2 22 25S 151 20W
Ruse Bulgaria 74 E3 43 50N 25 59E
Rusk Texas U.S.A. 91 G3 31 49N 95 11W
Russas Brazil 102 J12 4 56N 38 02W
Russell Manitoba Canada 89 O3 50 47N 101 17W
Russell Kansas U.S.A. 90 G4 38 54N 98 51W
Russell Islands Solomon Islands 82 E4 9 00S 159 05E
RUSSIA 57 J8/M8
Russian Federation *see* RUSSIA
Rustavi Georgia 58 F3 41 34N 45 03E
Ruston Louisiana U.S.A. 91 H3 32 32N 92 39W
Ruteng Indonesia 43 F2 8 35S 120 28E
Ruth Nevada U.S.A. 90 D4 39 16N 114 59W
Rutland Vermont U.S.A. 93 F2 43 37N 72 59W
Rutland Island Andaman Islands 38 A2 11 25N 92 35E
Rutog China 48 E5 33 27N 79 43E
Ruvuma *(Rovuma)* *r.* Tanzania 111 G5 11 30S 38 00E
Ruwenzori, Mount Uganda/Zaire 104 0 23N 29 54E
Ruwenzori National Park Rwanda 110 E7 0 30S 29 30E
Ružomberok Slovakia 75 C2 49 04N 19 15E
RWANDA 110 F7
Ryazan' Russia 56 F6 54 37N 39 43E
Rybach'ye *see* Issyk-Kul'
Rybinsk *(Andropov)* Russia 56 F7 58 03N 38 50E
Rybinskoye Vodokhranilishche *res.* Russia 56 F7 59 00N 38 00E
Rybnik Poland 75 C3 50 07N 18 30E
Ryde Australia 79 G2 33 49S 151 06E
Rye New York U.S.A. 94 D2 40 58N 73 41W
Ryukyu Islands *(Nansei-shoto)* Japan 49 P4 27 30N 127 30E
Ryukyu Ridge Pacific Ocean 22 C10 25 50N 128 00E
Rzeszów Poland 75 D3 50 04N 22 00E
Rzhev Russia 58 C6 56 15N 34 18E

S
Sa Thailand 39 B3 18 33N 100 48E
Saale *r.* Germany 71 B2 50 00N 10 00E
Saalfeld Germany 71 B2 50 39N 11 22E
Saarbrücken Germany 71 A1 49 15N 6 58E
Saaremaa *i.* Estonia 69 E2 58 20N 22 00E
Saarland *admin.* Germany 71 A1 49 00N 6 00E
Saarlouis Germany 71 A1 49 19N 6 45E
Šabac Serbia Yugoslavia 74 C3 44 45N 19 41E
Sabadell Spain 72 C3 41 33N 2 07E
Sabah *admin.* Malaysia 42 E5 5 00N 115 00E
Sabaloka Cataract *(River Nile)* Sudan 110 F11 16 19N 32 40E
Sabanalarga Colombia 97 J2 10 38N 74 55W
Sabatai-baru Indonesia 43 G4 2 30N 128 10E
Sabhā Libya 110 B13 27 02N 14 26E
Sabi *r.* Zimbabwe/Mozambique 111 F3 20 30S 33 00E
Sabinas Mexico 96 D5 27 50N 101 09W
Sabinas Hidalgo Mexico 96 D5 26 33N 100 10W
Sabine *r.* U.S.A. 91 H3 30 00N 94 00W
Sabine, Mount Antarctica 21 72 00S 169 00W
Sabkhet el Bardawîl *l.* Egypt 54 N10 31 10N 33 35E
Sable, Cape Florida U.S.A. 91 J2 25 08N 80 07W
Sable Island Nova Scotia Canada 89 X1 43 57N 60 00W
Sabor *r.* Portugal 72 A3 41 22N 6 50W
Sabtang *i.* The Philippines 40 B5 20 20N 121 52E
Sabyā Saudi Arabia 54 F2 17 07N 42 39E
Sabzevār Iran 55 I6 36 15N 57 38E
Sachsen *admin.* Germany 71 B2 52 30N 11 30E
Sachsen-Anhalt *admin.* Germany 71 B2 51 00N 13 00E
Saclay France 67 A1 48 43N 2 09E
Sacramento California U.S.A. 90 B4 38 32N 121 30W
Sacramento Mountains U.S.A. 90 E3 33 00N 105 00W
Sadao Thailand 39 B1 6 39N 100 30E
Sadar Bazar India 52 L4 28 39N 77 12E
Sa Dec Vietnam 37 C2 10 19N 105 45E
Sadiya India 53 H5 27 49N 95 38E
Sado *r.* Portugal 72 A2 38 15N 8 30W
Sado-shima *i.* Japan 46 C2 38 20N 138 30E
Safi Morocco 112 D9 32 20N 9 17W
Safotu Western Samoa 82 A11 13 26S 172 24W
Safune Western Samoa 82 A11 13 26S 172 25W
Saga Japan 46 B1 33 16N 130 18E
Sagaing Myanmar 38 B4 21 55N 95 56E
Sagaing *admin.* Myanmar 38 A4/B4 23 40N 95 00E
Sagamihara Japan 46 L2 35 34N 139 22E
Sagami-nada *sea* Japan 46 L1 35 00N 139 30E
Sagami-wan *b.* Japan 46 L2 35 12N 139 20E
Saganthit Kyun *i.* Myanmar 38 B2 12 00N 98 30E
Sagar India 53 D4 23 50N 78 44E
Sagay The Philippines 40 B3 10 57N 123 25E
Saginaw Michigan U.S.A. 93 D2 43 25N 83 54W
Saginaw Bay Michigan U.S.A. 93 D2 44 00N 84 00W
Sag Sag Papua New Guinea 45 N4 5 34S 148 22E
Sagua la Grande Cuba 97 H4 22 48N 80 06W
Saguenay River Québec Canada 93 F3 48 00N 71 00W
Sagunto Spain 72 B2 39 40N 0 17W
Sahara Desert North Africa 108 D12/J12
Saharanpur India 53 D5 29 58N 77 33E
Sahiwal Pakistan 53 C6 30 41N 73 11E
Sahuaripa Mexico 96 C5 29 00N 109 13W
Sahuayo Mexico 96 D4 20 05N 102 42W
Saibai Island Australia 45 K2 9 23S 142 40E
Sai Buri Thailand 39 B1 6 45N 101 30E
Saïda *(Sidon)* Lebanon 54 O11 33 32N 35 22E
Saidor Papua New Guinea 45 M4 5 38S 146 28E
Saidpur Bangladesh 53 F5 25 48N 89 00E
Saigon *see* Ho Chih Minh
Saikhoa Ghat India 53 H5 27 46N 95 38E
Sai Kung Hong Kong U.K. 51 C2 22 23N 114 16E
Saimaa *l.* Finland 69 F3 61 15N 27 45E
St. Abb's Head *c.* Scotland United Kingdom 68 I7 55 55N 2 09W
Ste. Agathe des Monts Québec Canada 93 F3 46 03N 74 19W
St. Albans England United Kingdom 68 K3 51 46N 0 21W
St. Albans Vermont U.S.A. 93 F2 44 49N 73 07W
St-Amand-les-Eaux France 70 C2 50 27N 3 26E
St. Andrews Scotland United Kingdom 68 I8 56 20N 2 48W
Ste. Anne Manitoba Canada 92 A3 49 40N 96 40W
Ste. Anne de Beaupré Québec Canada 93 F3 47 02N 70 58W
St. Ann's Bay *tn.* Jamaica 97 Q8 18 26N 77 12W
St. Anthony Newfoundland Canada 89 X3 51 24N 55 37W
St. Augustine Florida U.S.A. 91 J2 29 54N 81 19W
St. Bees Head England United Kingdom 68 H6 54 31N 3 39W
St-Brieuc France 73 A2 48 31N 2 45W
St. Catherines Ontario Canada 93 E2 43 10N 79 15W
St-Chamond France 73 B2 45 29N 4 32E
St. Charles Missouri U.S.A. 92 B1 38 48N 91 29W
St. Claire, Lake North America 93 D2 43 00N 82 00W
St. Claire River North America 93 D2 43 00N 82 00W
St-Cloud France 67 A2 48 51N 2 11E
St. Cloud Minnesota U.S.A. 92 B3 45 34N 94 10W
St. Croix *i.* West Indies 97 L3 22 45N 65 00W
St. Croix *r.* U.S.A. 92 B3 46 00N 93 00W
St-Cyr-l'École France 67 A2 48 47N 2 03E
St. David's Head Wales United Kingdom 68 F3 51 55N 5 19W
St-Denis France 67 B2 48 57N 2 22E
St.-Dié France 73 C2 48 17N 6 57E
St.-Dizier France 73 B2 48 38N 4 58E
Sainte-Anne-des-Monts Québec Canada 89 V2 49 07N 66 29W
St. Elias, Mount Canada/U.S.A. 88 G5 60 12N 140 57W
Saintes France 73 A2 45 44N 0 38W
St.-Étienne France 73 B2 45 26N 4 23E
St. Fabien Québec Canada 93 G3 48 19N 68 51W
St.-Félicien Québec Canada 93 F3 48 38N 72 29W
Ste. Foy Québec Canada 93 F3 46 47N 71 18W
St. Francis *r.* U.S.A. 91 H4 35 00N 90 00W
St. Gallen Switzerland 73 C2 47 25N 9 23E
St.-Gaudens France 73 B1 43 07N 0 44E
St. George New York U.S.A. 94 B1 40 48N 74 06W
Saint George *i.* Alaska U.S.A. 88 B4 56 34N 169 31W
St. George, Cape Papua New Guinea 45 P4 4 52S 152 51E
St. Georges Québec Canada 93 F3 46 08N 70 40W
St. George's Grenada 97 L2 12 04N 61 44W
St. George's Channel British Isles 68 E3 52 00N 6 00W
St.-German en-Laye France 67 A2 48 54N 2 04E
St-Ghislain Belgium 70 C2 50 27N 3 49E
St-Girons France 73 B1 42 59N 1 08E
St. Helena *i.* Atlantic Ocean 25 H5 15 58S 5 43W
St. Helena Bay Republic of South Africa 111 C1 32 00S 17 30E
St. Helens England United Kingdom 68 I5 53 28N 2 44W
St. Helier Jersey Channel Islands 68 I1 49 12N 2 07W
St-Hubert Belgium 70 E2 50 02N 5 22E
St. Hyacinthe Québec Canada 93 F3 45 38N 72 57W
St. Ignace Michigan U.S.A. 93 D2 45 53N 84 44W
St. Ives Australia 79 G3 33 44S 151 10E
St. Jean Québec Canada 93 F3 45 18N 73 16W
St. Jean de Dieu Québec Canada 93 G3 48 00N 69 05W
St. Jean-de-Luz France 73 A1 43 23N 1 39W
St. Jean Port Joli Québec Canada 93 F3 47 13N 70 16W
St. Jerôme Québec Canada 93 F3 45 47N 74 01W
Saint John New Brunswick Canada 89 V2 45 16N 66 03W
St. John *r.* Liberia 112 D4 6 30N 9 40W
St. John's Antigua and Barbuda 97 L3 17 08N 61 50W
St. John's Newfoundland Canada 89 Y2 47 34N 52 41W
St-Joseph New Caledonia 82 V3 20 25S 166 36E
St Joseph Trinidad and Tobago 96 T10 10 39N 61 25W
St. Joseph Trinidad and Tobago 96 U9 10 39N 60 59W
St. Joseph Missouri U.S.A. 92 B1 39 45N 94 51W
St. Joseph Island Ontario Canada 93 D3 46 00N 84 00W
St. Kilda *i.* Scotland United Kingdom 68 C9 57 49N 8 34W
ST. KITTS-NEVIS 97 L3
St. Laurent French Guiana 102 G14 5 29N 54 03W
St. Lawrence, Gulf of Canada 89 W2 49 00N 62 30W
St. Lawrence Island Alaska U.S.A. 88 A5/B5 63 15N 169 50W
St. Lawrence River Canada/U.S.A. 89 V2 46 55N 55 24W
St. Lawrence Seaway North America 93 E2 44 00N 76 00W
St. Leonard New Brunswick Canada 93 G3 47 10N 67 55W
St-Lô France 73 A2 49 07N 1 05W
St-Louis New Caledonia 82 V1 22 13S 166 33E
St. Louis Senegal 112 B6 16 01N 16 30W
St. Louis Missouri U.S.A. 92 B1 38 40N 90 15W
ST. LUCIA 97 L2
St. Malo France 73 A2 48 39N 2 00W
St-Mandé France 67 B2 48 50N 2 26E
Ste. Marie Québec Canada 93 F3 46 26N 71 00W
St. Marys Ohio U.S.A. 93 D2 40 32N 84 22W
St. Matthew Island Alaska U.S.A. 88 A5 60 30N 172 30W
Saint Matthias Group *is.* Papua New Guinea 45 N6 1 40S 150 00E
St. Maur France 67 B2 48 48N 2 30E
St. Moritz Switzerland 73 C2 46 30N 9 51E
St.-Nazaire France 73 A2 47 17N 2 12W
St-Niklaas Belgium 70 D3 51 10N 4 09E
St.-Omer France 73 B3 50 45N 2 15E
St. Pacôme Québec Canada 93 G3 47 24N 69 58W
St. Pascal Québec Canada 93 G3 47 32N 69 48W
St. Paul Minnesota U.S.A. 92 B2 45 00N 93 10W
Saint Paul *i.* Alaska U.S.A. 88 A4 57 09N 170 18W
St. Paul *r.* Liberia 112 C4 7 10N 10 05W
St. Paul Rocks Atlantic Ocean 25 F7 0 23N 29 23W
St. Peter Minnesota U.S.A. 92 B2 44 21N 93 58W
St. Peter Port Guernsey Channel Islands 68 I1 49 27N 3 32W
St. Petersburg *(Leningrad, Sankt-Peterburg)* Russia 56 F7 59 55N 30 25E
St. Pierre Manitoba Canada 92 A3 49 28N 96 58W
Saint-Pierre & Miquelon *is.* Atlantic Ocean 89 X2 47 00N 56 20W
St. Pölten Austria 75 C2 48 13N 15 37E
St.-Quentin France 73 B2 49 51N 3 17E
St. Remy France 67 A1 48 42N 2 04E
St. Siméon Québec Canada 93 G3 47 50N 69 55W
St. Stephen New Brunswick Canada 89 V2 45 12N 67 18W
St. Thomas Ontario Canada 93 D2 42 46N 81 12W
St. Thomas *i.* West Indies 97 K3 18 00N 65 30W
St.-Tropez France 73 C1 43 16N 6 39E
St.-Truiden Belgium 70 E2 50 49N 5 11E
St. Vincent *i.* St. Vincent and The Grenadines 97 L2 13 15N 61 12W
ST. VINCENT AND THE GRENADINES 97 L2
St-Vith Belgium 70 F2 50 15N 6 07E
St Wendel Germany 70 F1 49 28N 7 10E
St.-Yvieix-la-Perche France 73 B2 45 31N 1 12E
Saipan *i.* Northern Marianas 80 B4 15 12N 145 43E
Saitama *pref.* Japan 46 L3 36 00N 139 30E
Sai Ying Pun Hong Kong U.K. 51 B1 22 17N 114 08E
Sai Yok Thailand 39 A2 14 26N 98 53E
Sa Kaeo Thailand 39 B2 13 48N 102 08E
Sakai Japan 46 G1 34 35N 135 28E
Sākākah Saudi Arabia 54 F4 29 59N 40 12E
Sakakawea, Lake North Dakota U.S.A. 90 F6 48 00N 103 00W
Sakarya *r.* Turkey 54 D7 40 05N 30 15E
Sakata Japan 46 C2 38 55N 139 51E
Sakchu North Korea 50 B5 40 24N 125 01E
Sakhalin *i.* Russia 57 Q6 50 00N 143 00E
Sakhalin Bay Russia 57 Q6 54 00N 141 00E
Sakhon Nakhon Thailand 39 B3 17 12N 104 09E
Sakura Japan 46 M2 35 43N 140 13E
Sakurai Japan 46 G1 34 54N 135 12E
Sala'ilua Western Samoa 82 A11 13 39S 172 33W
Salālah Oman 55 H2 17 00N 54 04E
Salelologa Western Samoa 82 A11 13 42S 172 10W
Salamanca Mexico 96 D4 20 34N 101 12W
Salamanca Spain 72 A3 40 58N 5 40W
Salani Western Samoa 82 B10 14 00S 171 35W
Salatiga Indonesia 42 P7 7 15S 110 34E
Salavat Russia 59 H5 53 22N 55 50E
Salay Gomez *i.* Pacific Ocean 23 P5 26 28S 105 28W
Saldus Latvia 69 E2 56 38N 22 30E
Salekhard Russia 57 I9 66 33N 66 35E
Salem India 53 D2 11 38N 78 08E
Salem Massachusetts U.S.A. 93 F2 42 32N 70 53W
Salem Oregon U.S.A. 90 B5 44 57N 123 01W
Salembu Besar *i.* Indonesia 42 D2 5 35S 114 26E
Salerno Italy 74 B3 40 40N 14 46E
Salgótarján Hungary 75 C2 49 05N 19 47E
Salgueiro Brazil 102 J11 8 04S 39 05W
Salihli Turkey 74 E2 38 29N 28 08E
Salima Malawi 111 F5 13 45S 34 29E
Salina Kansas U.S.A. 91 G4 38 53N 97 36W
Salinas Ecuador 102 A12 2 15S 80 58W
Salinas California U.S.A. 90 B4 36 39N 121 40W
Salinas Grandes *l.* Argentina 103 D6/E7 30 00S 65 00W
Salingyi Myanmar 38 B4 21 58N 95 07E
Salisbury England United Kingdom 68 J3 51 05N 1 48W
Salisbury Maryland U.S.A. 93 E1 38 22N 75 37W
Salisbury Island Northwest Territories Canada 89 T5 63 10N 77 20W
Salisbury Plain England United Kingdom 68 J3 51 10N 1 55W
Salmon Idaho U.S.A. 90 D6 45 11N 113 55W
Salmon *r.* Idaho U.S.A. 90 C6 45 00N 116 00W
Salmon River Mountains Idaho U.S.A. 90 C5/D6 45 00N 115 00W
Salo Finland 69 E3 60 23N 23 10E
Salon-de-Provence France 73 C1 43 38N 5 06E
Salonta Romania 75 D2 46 49N 21 40E
Salpausselka *geog. reg.* Finland 69 F3 61 40N 26 00E
Salt Jordan 54 O11 32 03N 35 44E
Salt *r.* Arizona U.S.A. 90 D3 34 00N 110 00W
Salt *r.* Missouri U.S.A. 92 B1 39 00N 91 00W
Salta Argentina 103 D8 24 46S 65 28W
Saltdal Norway 69 D4 67 06N 15 25E
Salten *geog. reg.* Norway 69 D4 67 05N 15 00E
Salt Fork *r.* Texas/Oklahoma U.S.A. 90 F3 35 00N 100 00W
Saltillo Mexico 96 D5 25 30N 101 00W
Salt Lake *tn.* India 52 K2 22 35N 88 23E
Salt Lake City Utah U.S.A. 90 D5 40 45N 111 55W
Salt Lakes India 52 K2 22 30N 88 20E
Salto Uruguay 103 F6 31 27S 57 50W
Salton Sea *l.* California U.S.A. 90 C3 33 00N 116 00W
Salvador Brazil 102 J10 12 58S 38 29W
Salween *(Nu Jiang)* *r.* China/Myanmar 38 B3 18 20N 97 30E
Salybia Trinidad and Tobago 96 T10 10 42N 61 02W
Salzach *r.* Europe 71 B1 48 00N 13 00E
Salzburg Austria 75 B2 47 48N 13 03E
Salzburg *admin.* Austria 71 B1 47 00N 13 00E
Salzgitter Germany 71 B2 52 13N 10 20E
Salzwedel Germany 71 B2 52 51N 11 10E
Samal *i.* The Philippines 40 C2 7 03N 125 44E
Samalaeulu Western Samoa 82 A11 13 26S 172 16W
Samales Group *is.* The Philippines 40 B2 6 00N 122 00E
Samani Japan 46 D3 42 07N 142 57E
Samar *i.* The Philippines 40 B3/C3 12 00N 125 00E
Samara *r.* Russia 59 G5 52 30N 53 00E
Samara *(Kuybyshev)* Russia 56 H6 53 10N 50 10E
Samarai Papua New Guinea 45 O1 10 36S 150 39E
Samara *(Kuybyshevskoye)* **Vodokhranilishche** *res.* Russia 58 F5/6 55 00N 45 00E
Samarinda Indonesia 42 E3 0 30S 117 09E
Samarkand Uzbekistan 59 K2 39 40N 66 57E
Sāmarrā' Iraq 54 F5 34 13N 43 52E
Samar Sea The Philippines 40 B3 12 00N 124 00E
Sambalpur India 53 E4 21 28N 84 04E
Sambas Indonesia 42 C4 1 22N 109 15E
Samboja Indonesia 42 E3 1 03S 117 04E
Sambor Cambodia 37 C2 12 46N 106 01E
Sambre *r.* France 70 C2 50 15N 4 00E
Samch'ŏk South Korea 50 D3 37 30N 129 10E
Samch'ŏnp'o South Korea 50 D2 35 00N 128 05E
Sam Ngao Thailand 39 A3 17 12N 99 02E
Sámos *i.* Greece 74 E2 37 00N 26 00E
Samothráki *i.* Greece 74 E3 40 00N 25 00E
Sampang Indonesia 42 Q7 7 13S 113 15E
Sampit Indonesia 42 D3 2 34S 112 59E
Samran *r.* Thailand 39 B2 14 40N 104 10E
Samrong Cambodia 37 B2 14 12N 103 31E
Sam Son Vietnam 37 C3 19 44N 105 53E
Samsun Turkey 54 E7 41 17N 36 22E
Samusu Western Samoa 82 B11 13 59S 171 22W
Samut Prakan Thailand 39 B2 13 38N 100 35E
Samut Sakhon Thailand 39 B2 13 31N 100 16E
Samut Songkhram Thailand 39 B2 13 25N 99 59E
San Mali 112 D5 13 21N 4 57W
San'ā Yemen Republic 54 F2 15 23N 44 14E
SANAE *(South African National Expedition)* *r.s.* Antarctica 21 70 18S 2 25W
Sanaga *r.* Cameroon 112 H3 4 30N 12 20E
Sanak Islands Alaska U.S.A. 88 C3 54 26N 162 40W
Sanana Indonesia 43 G3 2 03S 125 59E
Sanandaj Iran 55 G6 35 18N 47 01E
San Andrés Tuxtla Mexico 96 E3 18 28N 95 15W
San Angelo Texas U.S.A. 90 F3 31 28N 100 28W
San Antonio Chile 103 C6 33 35S 71 39W
San Antonio Texas U.S.A. 90 G2 29 25N 98 30W
San Antonio *r.* Texas U.S.A. 91 G2 29 00N 97 00W
San Antonio Abad Balearic Islands 72 D4 38 59N 1 19E
San Antonio Oeste Argentina 103 E4 40 45S 64 58W
San Augustin, Cape The Philippines 40 C2 6 17N 126 12E
San Bernado Chile 103 C6 33 37S 70 45W
San Bernardino California U.S.A. 90 C3 34 07N 117 18W
San Carlos Falkland Islands 25 M16 51 00S 58 50W
San Carlos Luzon The Philippines 40 B4 15 59N 120 22E
San Carlos Negros The Philippines 40 B3 10 30N 123 29E
San Carlos Venezuela 102 D14 9 39N 68 35W
San Carlos de Bariloche Argentina 103 C4 41 11S 71 23W
San Carlos del Zulia Venezuela 102 C14 9 01N 71 58W
San-chung Taiwan 51 H8 25 04N 121 29E
San Clemente Island California U.S.A. 90 C3 33 26N 117 36W
San Cristóbal Argentina 103 E6 30 20S 61 14W
San Cristóbal Mexico 96 F3 16 45N 92 40W
San Cristobal *(Makira)* Solomon Islands 82 G3 10 30S 161 40E
San Cristobal Venezuela 102 C14 7 46N 72 15W
Sanda Japan 46 G1 34 54N 135 12E
Sandai Indonesia 42 D3 1 15S 110 31E
Sandakan Malaysia 42 E5 5 52N 118 04E
Sandan Cambodia 37 C2 12 42N 106 03E
Sanday *i.* Scotland United Kingdom 68 I11 59 15N 2 30W
San Diego California U.S.A. 90 C3 32 45N 117 10W
Sandoway Myanmar 38 A3 18 28N 94 20E
Sandpoint *tn.* Idaho U.S.A. 90 C6 48 17N 116 34W
Sandspit British Columbia Canada 88 I3 53 14N 131 50W
Sandusky Ohio U.S.A. 93 D2 41 27N 82 42W
Sandwip *i.* Bangladesh 38 A4 22 30N 91 30E
Sandy Lake Ontario Canada 89 Q3 52 45N 93 00W
San Felipe Mexico 96 B6 31 03N 114 52W
San Felipe Venezuela 102 D15 10 25N 68 40W
San Feliú de Guixols Spain 72 C3 41 47N 3 02E
San Fernando Mexico 96 A5 29 59N 115 10W
San Fernando Spain 72 A2 36 28N 6 12W
San Fernando Luzon The Philippines 40 B4 15 02N 120 41E
San Fernando Luzon The Philippines 40 B4 16 39N 120 19E
San Fernando Trinidad and Tobago 96 T9 10 16N 61 28W
San Fernando California U.S.A. 95 A4 34 17N 118 27W
San Fernando de Apure Venezuela 102 D14 7 53N 67 15W
Sanford Florida U.S.A. 91 J2 28 49N 81 17W
San Francique Trinidad and Tobago 96 S9 10 05N 61 39W
San Francisco Argentina 103 E6 31 29S 62 06W
San Francisco Dominican Republic 97 J3 19 19N 70 15W
San Francisco California U.S.A. 90 B4 37 45N 122 27W
San Francisco del Oro Mexico 96 C5 26 52N 105 50W
San Francisco Javier Balearic Islands 72 D4 38 43N 1 26E
San Gabriel California U.S.A. 95 B3 34 06N 118 06W
San Gabriel Moutains California U.S.A. 95 B4/C3 34 18N 118 05W
San Gabriel Reservoir California U.S.A. 95 C3 34 12N 117 52W
San Gabriel River California U.S.A. 95 B2 33 58N 118 06W
Sangar Russia 57 O8 64 02N 127 30E
Sangerhausen Germany 71 B2 51 29N 11 18E
Sanggau Indonesia 42 D4 0 00 110 35E
Sangha *r.* Africa 112 I3 2 00N 17 00E
Sangju South Korea 50 D3 36 25N 128 08E
Sangker *r.* Cambodia 37 B2 12 40N 102 45E
Sangkhla Buri Thailand 39 A3 15 09N 98 32E
Sangkulirang Indonesia 42 E4 0 55N 118 01E
Sangli India 53 C3 16 55N 74 37E
Sangmélima Cameroon 112 H3 2 57N 11 56E
Sangpawng Bum *mts.* Myanmar 38 B5 26 30N 95 30E
Sangre de Cristo Mountains New Mexico U.S.A. 90 E4 37 00N 105 00W
Sangre Grande Trinidad and Tobago 96 T10 10 35N 61 08W
Sangu *r.* Bangladesh 38 A4 21 50N 92 25E
San Ildenfenso Peninsula The Philippines 40 B4 16 00N 122 00E
San Javier Bolivia 102 E9 16 22S 62 38W
San Joaquin *r.* California U.S.A. 90 B4 37 00N 120 00W
San Jorge *i.* Solomon Islands 82 E5 8 25S 159 35E
San José Balearic Islands 72 D4 38 55N 1 18E
San José Costa Rica 97 H1 9 59N 84 04W
San Jose Luzon The Philippines 40 B4 15 47N 120 59E
San Jose Mindoro The Philippines 40 B3 12 25N 121 03E
San José Uruguay 103 F6 34 27S 56 40W
San José California U.S.A. 90 B4 37 20N 121 55W
San Jose de Buenavista The Philippines 40 B3 10 45N 121 58E
San José del Cabo Mexico 96 C4 23 01N 109 40W
San Juan Argentina 103 D6 31 33S 68 31W
San Juán Peru 102 B9 15 22S 75 07W
San Juan Puerto Rico 97 K3 18 29N 66 08W
San Juan Trinidad and Tobago 96 T10 10 39N 61 27W
San Juan *r.* U.S.A. 90 D4 37 00N 110 00W
San Juan Bautista Balearic Islands 72 D4 39 05N 1 31E
San Juan de los Morros Venezuela 97 K1 9 53N 67 23W
San Juan Mountains Colorado U.S.A. 90 E4 37 50N 107 50W
San Julián Argentina 103 D3 49 17S 67 45W
Sānkrāil India 52 J2 22 33N 88 14E
Sankuru *r.* Zaire 111 D7 4 00S 23 30E
Sanlúcar de Barrameda Spain 72 A2 36 46N 6 21W

San Lucas Mexico **96** C4 22 50N 109 52W
San Luis Argentina **103** D6 33 20S 66 23W
San Luis Obispo California U.S.A. **90** B4 35 16N 120 40W
San Luis Potosí Mexico **96** D4 22 10N 101 00W
San Marcos Texas U.S.A. **91** G2 29 54N 97 57W
Sanmenxia China **49** M5 34 46N 111 17E
San Miguel El Salvador **96** G2 13 28N 88 10W
San Miguel de Tucumán Argentina **103** D7 26 47S 65 15W
Sanming China **49** N4 26 16N 117 35E
Sannan Japan **46** G2 35 05N 135 03E
San Pablo The Philippines **40** B3 14 03N 121 19E
San Pedro Argentina **103** E8 24 12S 64 55W
San Pedro Côte d'Ivoire **112** D3 4 45N 6 37W
San Pedro Dominican Republic **97** K3 18 30N 69 18W
San Pedro California U.S.A. **95** A1 33 45N 118 19W
San Pedro Bay California U.S.A. **95** A1 33 43N 118 12W
San Pedro Channel California U.S.A. **95** A1 33 43N 118 22W
San Pedro de las Colonias Mexico **96** D5 25 50N 102 59W
San Pedro Sula Honduras **96** G3 15 26N 88 01W
San Rafael Argentina **103** D6 34 35S 68 24W
San Rafael California U.S.A. **90** B4 37 58N 122 30W
San Remo Italy **74** A3 43 48N 7 46E
San Salvador El Salvador **96** G2 13 40N 89 10W
San Salvador *i.* The Bahamas **97** J4 24 00N 74 32W
San Salvador de Jujuy Argentina **103** D8 24 10S 65 48W
San Sebastián Spain **72** B3 43 19N 1 59W
San Severo Italy **74** C3 41 41N 15 23E
Santa Ana Bolivia **102** D10 13 46S 65 37W
Santa Ana El Salvador **96** G2 14 00N 89 31W
Santa Ana Mexico **90** D3 30 31N 111 08W
Santa Ana California U.S.A. **95** C2 33 44N 117 54W
Santa Ana *i.* Solomon Islands **82** H3 10 53S 162 28E
Santa Ana River California U.S.A. **95** C2 33 46N 117 54W
Santa Barbara Mexico **96** C5 26 48N 105 50W
Santa Barbara California U.S.A. **90** C3 33 29N 119 01W
Santa Catalina *i.* Solomon Islands **82** H3 10 55S 16 30E
Santa Catalina Island California U.S.A. **90** C3 33 25N 118 25W
Santa Catarina *admin.* Brazil **103** G7 27 00S 51 00W
Santa Clara Cuba **97** I4 22 25N 79 58W
Santa Cruz Bolivia **102** E9 17 50S 63 10W
Santa Cruz Canary Islands **112** B8 28 28N 16 15W
Santa Cruz Jamaica **97** Q8 18 03N 77 43W
Santa Cruz Luzon The Philippines **40** B3 14 16N 121 24E
Santa Cruz Marinduque The Philippines **40** B3 13 28N 122 03E
Santa Cruz California U.S.A. **90** B4 36 58N 122 03W
Santa Cruz Island California U.S.A. **90** C3 34 00N 119 40W
Santa Cruz Islands Solomon Islands **83** M3/N3 11 00S 166 30E
Santa Cruz *r.* Argentina **103** D2 50 00S 70 00W
Santa Eulalia del Rio Balearic Islands **72** D4 38 59N 1 33E
Santa Fé Argentina **103** E6 31 35S 60 50W
Santa Fé New Mexico U.S.A. **90** E4 35 41N 105 57W
Santa Isabel Solomon Islands **82** D6/E5 8 00S 159 00E
Santa Maria Brazil **103** G7 29 45S 53 40W
Santa Maria California U.S.A. **90** B3 34 56N 120 25W
Santa Maria *see* Gaua
Santa Marta Colombia **102** C15 11 18N 74 10W
Santa Monica California U.S.A. **95** A3 34 00N 118 25W
Santa Monica Moutains California U.S.A. **95** A3 33 07N 118 27W
Santana do Livramento Brazil **103** F6 30 52S 55 30W
Santander Colombia **102** B13 3 00N 76 25W
Santander Spain **72** B3 43 28N 3 48W
Sant' Antioco Italy **74** A2 39 04N 8 27E
Santañy Balearic Islands **72** E4 39 22N 3 07E
Santarém Brazil **102** G12 2 26S 54 41W
Santarém Portugal **72** A2 39 14N 8 40W
Santa Rosa Argentina **103** E5 36 37S 64 17W
Santa Rosa Honduras **96** G2 14 48N 88 43W
Santa Rosa California U.S.A. **90** B4 38 26N 122 43W
Santa Rosa New Mexico U.S.A. **90** F3 34 56N 104 42W
Santa Rosa Island California U.S.A. **90** B3 34 00N 120 05W
Santa Rosalia Mexico **96** B5 27 20N 112 20W
Santa Teresa Brazil **103** Q2 22 57S 43 12W
Santa Teresa Gallura Italy **73** C1 41 14N 9 12E
Santiago Chile **103** C6 33 30S 70 40W
Santiago Panama **97** H2 8 08N 80 59W
Santiago The Philippines **40** B4 16 45N 121 34E
Santiago de Compostela Spain **72** A3 42 52N 8 33W
Santiago de Cuba Cuba **97** I4 20 00N 75 49W
Santiago del Estero Argentina **103** E7 27 47S 64 15W
Santiago Ixcuintla Mexico **96** C4 21 50N 105 11W
San Tin Hong Kong U.K. **51** B3 22 30N 114 04E
Santi Nagar India **52** L4 28 40N 77 10E
Santo *(Luganville)* Vanuatu **83** G6 15 32S 167 32E
Santo Andre Brazil **103** H8 23 39S 46 29W
Santo Domingo Dominican Republic **97** K3 18 30N 69 57W
Santong He *r.* China **50** C6 42 00N 125 45E
Santos Brazil **103** H8 23 56S 46 22W
San Uk Ha Hong Kong U.K. **51** C3 22 30N 114 14E
San Vicente El Salvador **96** G2 13 38N 88 42W
San Vicente The Philippines **40** B4 18 30N 122 09E
São Bernardo do Campo Brazil **103** H8 23 45S 46 34W
São Borja Brazil **103** F7 28 35S 56 01W
São Cristovão Brazil **103** Q2 22 52S 43 15S
São Gonçalo Brazil **103** Q2 22 48S 43 08W
São João de Meriti Brazil **103** P2 22 47S 43 22W
São José Brazil **103** H7 27 35S 48 40W
São José do Rio Prêto Brazil **102** H8 20 50S 49 20W
São José dos Campos Brazil **103** H8 23 07S 45 52W
São Luís Brazil **102** I12 2 34S 44 16W
Saône *r.* France **73** B2 46 28N 4 55E
São Paulo Brazil **103** H8 23 33S 46 39W
São Paulo de Olivença Brazil **102** D12 3 34S 68 55W
São Paulo *admin.* Brazil **102** G8/H8 21 30S 50 00W
São Tomé *i.* Gulf of Guinea **112** G3 0 25N 6 35E
SÃO TOMÉ AND PRINCIPE **112** G3
São Vicente Brazil **103** H8 23 57S 46 23W
Saparua Indonesia **44** C5 3 35S 128 37E
Sape Indonesia **42** E2 8 35S 118 59E
Sappemeer Netherlands **70** F5 53 10N 6 47E
Sapporo Japan **46** D3 43 05N 141 21E
Sapudi *r.* Indonesia **42** R7 7 00S 114 15E
Sapulot Malaysia **42** E4 4 50N 117 00E
Saqqez Iran **55** G6 36 14N 46 15E
Saraburi Thailand **39** B2 14 32N 100 53E
Sarajevo Bosnia-Herzegovina **74** C3 43 52N 18 26E
Sarakhs Iran **55** J6 36 32N 61 07E
Saramati *mt.* India/Myanmar **38** B5 25 45N 95 02E
Saranac Lake *tn.* New York U.S.A. **93** F2 44 19N 74 10W
Sarang Papua New Guinea **45** L4 4 48S 145 40E
Sarangani *i.* The Philippines **40** C2 5 28N 125 28E
Saransk Russia **56** G6 54 12N 45 10E
Sarapui *r.* Brazil **103** P3 22 44S 43 17W
Sarapul Russia **59** G6 56 30N 53 49E
Sarasota Florida U.S.A. **91** J2 27 20N 82 32W
Sarata Ukraine **75** E2 46 00N 29 40E
Saratov Russia **56** G6 51 30N 45 55E
Saravan Iran **55** J4 27 25N 62 17E
Saravan Laos **37** C3 15 43N 106 24E
Sarawak *admin.* Malaysia **42** D4 1 00N 111 00E
Sarcelles France **67** B2 48 59N 2 22E
Sardegna *(Sardinia) i.* Italy **74** A2/A3 40 00N 9 00E
Sardindida Plain Kenya **110** G8/H8 2 00N 40 00E
Sardinia *see* Sardegna
Sar-e Pol Afghanistan **55** K6 36 13N 65 55E
Sargasso Sea Atlantic Ocean **25** B9 27 00N 66 00W
Sargeant Barbados **96** V12 13 05N 59 35W
Sargodha Pakistan **53** C6 32 01N 72 40E
Sarh Chad **110** C9 9 08N 18 22E
Sarikei Malaysia **42** D4 2 09N 111 31E
Sarimbun Reservoir Singapore **41** B5 1 26N 103 41E
Sarīr Calanscio *d.* Libya **110** D13 26 00N 22 00E
Sariwon North Korea **50** B4 38 30N 125 45E
Sark *i.* Channel Islands British Isles **68** I1 49 26N 2 22W
Sarmet Vanuatu **83** G5 16 11S 167 32E
Sarmi Irian Jaya Indonesia **44** H6 1 51S 138 45E
Sarmiento Argentina **103** D3 45 38S 69 08W
Sarnia Ontario Canada **93** D2 42 58N 82 23W
Sarolangun Indonesia **42** B3 2 14S 102 44E
Saronikós Kólpos *g.* Greece **74** D2 38 00N 23 00E
Sarpsborg Norway **69** C2 59 17N 11 06E
Sarraméa New Caledonia **82** U2 21 38S 165 50E
Sarrebourg France **73** C2 48 43N 7 03E
Sarreguemines France **73** C2 49 06N 6 55E
Sartène Corsica **73** C1 41 37N 8 58E
Sarthe *r.* France **73** A2 47 45N 0 30W
Sartrou-ville France **67** A2 48 56N 2 11E
Sary Ishikotrau *d.* Kazakhstan **59** M3/4 45 00N 77 00E
Sarysu *r.* Kazakhstan **59** K4 47 00N 67 30E
Sasamungga Solomon Islands **82** B6 7 05S 156 45E
Sasayama Japan **46** G2 35 03N 135 12E
Sasebo Japan **46** A1 33 10N 129 42E
Saskatchewan *province* Canada **88** N3 53 50N 109 00W
Saskatoon Saskatchewan Canada **88** N3 52 10N 106 40W
Sassandra Côte d'Ivoire **112** D3 4 58N 6 08W
Sassandra *r.* Côte d'Ivoire **112** D4 5 50N 6 55W
Sassari Italy **74** A3 40 43N 8 34E
Sassnitz Germany **71** B2 54 32N 13 40E
Sataua Western Samoa **82** A11 13 26S 172 40W
Satlayev *(Nikol'skiy)* Kazakhstan **69** K4 47 64N 67 26E
Satna India **53** E4 24 33N 80 50E
Satpura Range *mts.* India **53** C4/D4 21 40N 75 00E
Sattahip Thailand **39** B2 12 36N 100 56E
Satuk Thailand **39** B3 15 17N 103 20E
Satu Mare Romania **75** D2 47 48N 22 52E
Satun Thailand **39** B1 6 40N 100 01E
SAUDI ARABIA **94/95**
Sauer *(Sûre) r.* Europe **70** F1 49 45N 6 30E
Sault Ste. Marie Ontario Canada **93** D3 46 31N 84 20W
Sault Ste. Marie Michigan U.S.A. **93** D3 46 29N 84 22W
Saumlaki Indonesia **43** H2 7 59S 131 22E
Saumur France **73** A2 47 16N 0 05W
Saurimo Angola **111** D6 9 39S 20 24E
Savai'i *i.* Western Samoa **82** A11 13 44S 172 18W
Savanna Illinois U.S.A. **92** B2 42 06N 90 07W
Savannah Georgia U.S.A. **91** J3 32 04N 81 07W
Savannah *r.* U.S.A. **91** J3 33 00N 82 00W
Savannakhet Laos **37** B3 16 34N 104 45E
Savanna la Mar Jamaica **97** P8 18 13N 78 08W
Saverne France **71** A1 48 45N 7 22E
Savo *i.* Solomon Islands **82** E4 9 10S 159 50E
Savona Italy **74** A3 44 18N 8 28E
Savusavu Vanua Levu Fiji **83** D10 16 48S 179 20E
Savusavu Viti Levu Fiji **83** C9 17 34S 178 16E
Savusavu Bay Fiji **83** D10 16 48S 179 15E
Saw Myanmar **38** A4 21 12N 94 08E
Sawahlunto Indonesia **42** B3 0 41S 100 52E
Sawaleke Fiji **83** D9 17 59S 179 15E
Sawankhalok Thailand **39** A3 17 19N 99 50E
Sawara Japan **46** M2 35 52N 140 31E
Sawi Thailand **39** A2 10 15N 99 06E
Shawinigan Québec Canada **89** U2 46 33N 72 45W
Sawpit Canyon Reservoir California U.S.A. **95** C3 34 10N 117 59W
Sawu Sea Indonesia **43** F2 9 00S 122 00E
Sayabec Québec Canada **93** G3 48 35N 67 41W
Sayabouri *see* Xaignabouri
Sayanogorsk Russia **57** L6 53 00N 91 26E
Sayano-Shushenskoya Vodokhranilishche *res.* Russia **59** P5 52 00N 92 00E
Saylac Somalia **110** H10 11 21N 43 30E
Saynshand Mongolia **49** M7 44 58N 111 10E
Sayram Hu *l.* China **59** N3 44 45N 80 30E
Say'ūn Yemen Republic **55** G2 15 59N 48 44E
Scafell Pike *mt.* England United Kingdom **68** H6 54 27N 3 14W
Scandinavia *geog. reg.* Europe **60**
Scarborough England United Kingdom **68** K6 54 17N 0 24W
Scarsdale New York U.S.A. **94** B2 40 59N 73 49W
Sceaux France **67** B2 48 46N 218E
Schaerbeek Belgium **70** D2 50 52N 4 22E
Schaffhausen Switzerland **73** C2 47 42N 8 38E
Schagen Netherlands **70** D4 52 47N 4 47E
Schefferville *(Kawawachikamach)* Québec Canada **89** V3 54 50N 67 00W
Schelde *(Scheldt) r.* Netherlands **70** D3 51 15N 4 16E
Scheldt Estuary Europe **60** 51 30N 3 30E
Schenectady New York U.S.A. **93** F2 42 48N 73 57W
Schiedam Netherlands **70** D3 51 55N 4 25E
Schiermonnikoog *i.* Netherlands **70** F5 53 28N 6 10E
Schildow Germany **67** F2 52 40N 13 21E
Schleswig Germany **71** A2 54 32N 9 34E
Schleswig-Holstein *admin.* Germany **71** A2/B2 54 00N 10 00E
Schönebeck Germany **71** B2 52 01N 11 45E
Schöneberg Germany **67** F1 52 24N 13 22E
Schöneiche Germany **67** G1 52 28N 13 43E
Schönwalde Frankfurt Germany **67** F2 52 43N 13 26E
Schönwalde Potsdam Germany **67** E2 52 41N 13 27E
Schorndorf Germany **71** A1 48 48N 9 33E
Schoten Belgium **70** D3 51 15N 4 30E
Schouten Islands Papua New Guinea **45** L5 3 15S 144 30E
Schouwen *i.* Netherlands **70** C3 51 40N 3 50E
Schreiber Ontario Canada **92** C3 48 48N 87 17W
Schulzendorf Germany **67** G1 52 20N 13 34E
Schwäbisch Alb *mts.* Germany **71** A1/B1 48 00N 9 00E
Schwäbisch Gmünd Germany **71** A1 48 49N 9 48E
Schwabisch Hall Germany **71** A1 49 07N 9 45E
Schwandorf Germany **71** B1 49 20N 12 07E
Schwanebeck Germany **67** F2 52 40N 13 27E
Schwarze Elster *r.* Germany **71** B2 52 00N 13 00E
Schwarzwald *(Black Forest) mts.* Germany **71** A1 47 00N 8 00E
Schwarzwälder Hochwald *mts.* Germany **70** F1 49 00N 7 00E
Schwedt Germany **71** B2 53 04N 14 17E
Schweinfurt Germany **71** B2 50 03N 10 16E
Schwerin Germany **71** B2 53 38N 11 25E
Schwielowsee *l.* Germany **67** D1 52 19N 13 57E
Schwyz Switzerland **73** C2 47 02N 8 34E
Scilly, Isles of England United Kingdom **68** E1 49 56N 6 20W
Scioto *r.* Ohio U.S.A. **93** D1 40 00N 83 00W
Scoresbysund *(Ittoqqortoormiit) sd.* Greenland **89** EE7 70 30N 22 45W
Scotia Ridge Atlantic Ocean **25** C1 53 00S 50 00W
Scotia Sea Atlantic Ocean **25** C1 56 30N 50 00W
Scotland United Kingdom **68** F8
Scott Base *r.s.* Antarctica **21** 77 51S 166 45E
Scott Island Southern Ocean **22** H1 66 35S 180 00
Scottsbluff Nebraska U.S.A. **90** F5 41 52N 103 40W
Scranton Pennsylvania U.S.A. **93** E2 41 25N 75 40W
Scunthorpe England United Kingdom **68** K5 53 35N 0 39W
Sealdah India **52** K2 22 32N 88 22E
Seal River Manitoba Canada **89** P4 59 10N 97 00W
Seattle Washington U.S.A. **90** B6 47 35N 122 20W
Sebakung Indonesia **42** E3 1 36S 116 30E
Sebisseb *r.* Algeria **72** C2 35 30N 4 00E
Sebkra Sidi El Hani *salt l.* Tunisia **74** B2 35 30N 10 00E
Sedalia Missouri U.S.A. **92** B1 38 42N 93 15W
Sedan France **73** B2 49 42N 4 57E
Seddinsee *l.* Germany **67** G1 52 23N 13 42E
Segama *r.* Malaysia **40** A2 5 10N 118 30E
Segamat Malaysia **42** B4 2 30N 102 49E
Seghe Solomon Islands **82** C5 8 25S 157 50E
Ségou Mali **112** D5 13 28N 6 18W
Segovia Spain **72** B3 40 57N 4 07W
Segre *r.* Spain **72** C3 42 00N 1 10E
Segura *r.* Spain **72** B2 38 00N 1 00W
Sehulea Papua New Guinea **45** O2 9 59S 151 15E
Seine *r.* France **73** B2 49 15N 1 15E
Seki Japan **46** H2 35 30N 136 54E
Sekondi Takoradi Ghana **112** E3 4 59N 1 43W
Se Kong *r.* Cambodia **37** C2 13 45N 106 10E
Selaphum Thailand **39** B3 16 03N 103 59E
Selat Bali *sd.* Indonesia **42** R6 8 30S 114 30E
Selat Dampier *sd.* Irian Jaya Indonesia **44** D6 0 30S 131 15E
Selat Gaspar *sd.* Indonesia **42** C3 3 00S 107 00E
Selat Johor *sd.* Singapore/Malaysia **41** C5 1 27N 103 45E
Selat Jurong *sd.* Singapore **41** B3 1 18N 103 42E
Selat Lombok *sd.* Indonesia **42** E2 8 20S 116 00E
Selat Madura *sd.* Indonesia **42** Q7 7 30S 113 30E
Selat Melaka *see* Strait of Malacca
Selatpanjang Indonesia **42** B4 0 58N 102 40E
Selat Serasan *sd.* Indonesia **42** C4 2 00N 109 00E
Selat Sumba *sd.* Indonesia **43** F2 9 00S 120 00E
Selat Sunda *sd.* Indonesia **42** C2 5 50S 105 30E
Selat Wetar *sd.* Indonesia **44** B2 8 00S 126 15E
Selat Yapen *sd.* Irian Jaya Indonesia **44** G6 1 30S 136 15E
Seldovia Alaska U.S.A. **88** E4 59 29N 151 45W
Sele Irian Jaya Indonesia **44** D6 1 22S 131 06E
Selemdzha *r.* Russia **57** P6 52 30N 132 00E
Selenge *r.* Mongolia **49** K8 49 00N 102 00E
Seletar Singapore **41** D4 1 23N 103 52E
Seletar Reservoir Singapore **41** C4 1 24N 103 48E
Selety *r.* Kazakhstan **59** L5 52 50N 73 00E
Selima Oasis Sudan **110** E12 21 22N 29 19E
Selkirk Manitoba Canada **92** A4 50 10N 96 52W
Selma Alabama U.S.A. **91** I3 32 24N 87 01W
Selpele Irian Jaya Indonesia **44** D6 0 15S 130 15E
Sélune *r.* France **73** A2 48 40N 1 15W
Selvas *geog. reg.* South America **98** 7 00S 65 00W
Selwyn Mountains British Columbia Canada **88** I5 63 00N 131 00W
Selwyn Recreational Reserve Norfolk Island **81** K5 29 00S 167 55E
Semarang Indonesia **42** P7 6 58S 110 29E
Sematan Malaysia **42** C4 1 50N 109 48E
Sembakung *r.* Indonesia **42** E4 4 00N 117 00E
Sembawang Singapore **41** C5 1 27N 103 49E
Semenovskoye Russia **56** M1 55 39N 37 32E
Seminoe Reservoir Wyoming U.S.A. **90** E5 42 00N 106 00W
Seminole Oklahoma U.S.A. **91** G4 35 15N 96 40W
Semiozernoye Kazakhstan **59** J5 52 22N 64 06E
Semipalatinsk Kazakhstan **59** N5 50 26N 80 16E
Semirara Islands The Philippines **40** B3 12 00N 121 00E
Semitau Indonesia **42** D4 0 30N 111 59E
Semnān Iran **55** H6 35 30N 53 25E
Semo Fiji **83** B8 18 05S 177 24E
Semois *r.* Belgium **70** E1 49 40N 5 30E
Semuda Indonesia **42** D3 2 51S 112 58E
Sendai Honshu Japan **46** D2 38 16N 140 52E
Sendai Kyūshū Japan **46** B1 31 50N 130 17E
Seneca Lake New York U.S.A. **93** E2 43 00N 77 00W
SENEGAL **112** B5/C6
Sénégal *r.* Senegal/Mauritania **112** C6 16 45N 14 45W
Senftenberg Germany **71** B2 51 31N 14 01E
Senhor do Bonfim Brazil **102** I10 10 28S 40 11W
Senja *i.* Norway **69** D4 69 15N 17 20E
Senlis France **73** B2 49 12N 2 35E
Senmonorom Cambodia **37** C2 12 31N 107 41E
Sennar Sudan **110** F10 13 31N 33 38E
Sennar Dam Sudan **54** D1 13 20N 33 45E
Sennett Singapore **41** D3 1 20N 103 53E
Senobe Japan **46** G2 35 09N 135 25E
Sens France **73** B2 48 12N 3 18E
Senyavin Islands Pacific Ocean **22** G8 7 00N 161 30E
Seo de Urgel Spain **73** B1 42 22N 1 27E
Seoul *see* Sŏul
Sepanda Papua New Guinea **45** M3 7 20S 146 31E
Sepasu Indonesia **42** E4 0 42N 117 40E
Sepik *r.* Papua New Guinea **45** L4 4 15S 144 00E
Sept-Îles *tn.* Québec Canada **89** V3 50 10N 66 00W
Seraing Belgium **70** E2 50 37N 5 31E
Seram *(Ceram) i.* Indonesia **43** G3 3 30S 129 30E
Seram Sea Indonesia **43** G3/H3 2 30S 130 00E
Serang Indonesia **42** N7 6 07S 106 09E
Serangoon Singapore **41** D4 1 22N 103 52E
Serangoon Harbour Singapore **41** E4 1 23N 103 57E
Serbia *admin.* Yugoslavia **74** D3
Serdan Mexico **96** C5 28 40N 105 57W
Seremban Malaysia **42** B4 2 43N 102 57E
Serengeti National Park Tanzania **110** F7 2 30S 35 00E
Serenje Zambia **111** F5 13 12S 30 15E
Sergiev Posad *(Zagorsk)* Russia **56** F7 56 20N 38 10E
Sergino Russia **57** I8 62 30N 65 40E
Sergipe *admin.* Brazil **102** J10 11 00S 38 00W
Seria Brunei Darussalam **32** E4 4 39N 114 23E
Serikkembelo Indonesia **44** B5 3 20S 127 55E
Serov Russia **56** I7 59 42N 60 32E
Serowe Botswana **111** E3 22 25S 26 44E
Serpukhov Russia **58** D5 54 53N 37 25E
Serra Brazil **102** I9 20 06S 40 16W
Serra do Mar *mts.* Brazil **103** H7 27 30S 49 00W
Serra do Navio Brazil **102** G13 1 00N 52 05W
Sérrai Greece **74** D3 41 03N 23 33E
Serrania de Cuenca *mts.* Spain **72** B3 40 30N 2 15W
Serra Tumucumaque *mts.* Brazil **102** F13/G13 2 00N 55 00W
Serre *r.* France **70** C1 49 40N 3 52E
Serua *i.* Indonesia **44** D3 6 20S 130 02E
Serui Irian Jaya Indonesia **44** G6 1 53S 136 15E
Seruwai Indonesia **42** A4 4 10N 98 00E
Seruyan *r.* Indonesia **42** D3 2 20S 112 30E
Se San *r.* Cambodia **37** C2 13 40N 106 30E
Sesayap Indonesia **42** E4 3 34N 117 01E
Setagaya Japan **47** B3 35 37N 139 38E
Sète France **73** B1 43 25N 3 43E
Sete Lagoas Brazil **102** I9 19 29S 44 15W
Sete Pontes Brazil **103** Q2 22 51S 43 04W
Setesdal *geog. reg.* Norway **69** B2 59 30N 7 10E
Setit *r.* Sudan **110** G10 14 20N 36 15E
Seto Japan **46** J2 35 14N 137 06E
Seto-Naikai *sd.* Japan **46** B1 34 00N 132 30E
Settat Morocco **112** D9 33 04N 7 37W
Settlement *tn.* Christmas Island **81** R2 10 25S 105 41E
Setúbal Portugal **72** A2 38 31N 8 54W
Sevastopol' Ukraine **58** C3 44 36N 33 31E
Sevenoaks England United Kingdom **66** D2 51 16N 0 12E
Severn *r.* Ontario Canada **89** R4 55 10N 89 00W
Severn *r.* England United Kingdom **68** I4 52 30N 2 30W
Severnaya Sos'va *r.* Russia **56** I8 62 30N 62 00E
Severnaya Zemlya *(North Land) is.* Russia **57** L12 80 00N 95 00E
Severočsky *admin.* Czech Republic **71** B2 50 00N 14 00E
Severodonetsk Ukraine **58** D4 48 58N 38 29E
Severodvinsk Russia **56** F8 64 35N 39 50E
Severoural'sk Russia **59** J7 60 10N 59 56E
Sevier *r.* Utah U.S.A. **90** D4 39 00N 113 00W
Sevilla *(Seville)* Spain **72** A2 37 24N 5 59W
Seville *see* Sevilla
Sèvre *r.* France **73** A2 47 00N 1 10W
Sèvres France **67** A2 48 49N 2 13E
Seward Alaska U.S.A. **88** F5 60 05N 149 34W
Seward Peninsula Alaska U.S.A. **88** B5/C5 65 20N 165 00W
SEYCHELLES **24** E6
Seychelles Ridge Indian Ocean **24** E6/F5
Seym *r.* Russia/Ukraine **58** C5 51 00N 34 00E
Seymchan Russia **57** R8 62 54N 152 26E
Seymour Indiana U.S.A. **92** C1 38 57N 85 55W
Sézannes France **73** B2 48 44N 3 44E
Sfax Tunisia **112** H9 34 45N 10 43E
Sfîntu Gheorghe Romania **75** E2 45 51N 25 48E
's-Gravenhage *(Den Haag, The Hague)* Netherlands **70** D4 52 05N 4 16E
Shabaqua Ontario Canada **92** C3 48 35N 89 54W
Sha Chau *i.* Hong Kong U.K. **51** A2 22 21N 113 53E
Shache China **48** E6 38 27N 77 16E
Shackleton Ice Shelf Antarctica **21** 66 00S 100 00E
Shackleton Range Antarctica **21** 81 00S 20 00W
Shah Alam Malaysia **32** C4 3 02N 101 31E
Shahdara India **52** M4 28 40N 77 17E
Shahdol India **53** E4 23 19N 81 26E
Shahjahanpur India **53** D5 27 53N 79 55E
Shakhty Russia **58** E4 47 43N 40 16E
Shaki Nigeria **112** F4 8 39N 3 25E
Sha Lo Wan Hong Kong U.K. **51** A1 22 17N 113 54E
Sham Chung Hong Kong U.K. **51** C2 22 26N 114 17E
Sham Chun River Hong Kong U.K. **51** B3 22 30N 114 00E
Shamokin Pennsylvania U.S.A. **93** E2 40 45N 76 34W
Sham Shek Tsuen Hong Kong U.K. **51** A1 22 17N 113 53E
Sham Shui Po Hong Kong U.K. **51** B1 22 20N 114 09E
Sham Tseng Hong Kong U.K. **51** B2 22 22N 114 03E
Shangani *r.* Zimbabwe **111** E4 19 00S 29 00E
Shanghai China **49** O5 31 06N 121 22E
Shangqui China **49** N5 34 27N 115 07E
Shangrao China **49** N4 28 28N 117 54E
Shangshui China **49** M5 33 36N 114 38E
Shan State *admin.* Myanmar **38** B4 22 00N 98 00E
Shanngaw Range Myanmar **38** B5 26 10N 98 05E
Shannon *r.* Irish Republic **68** C4 53 30N 9 00W
Shantou China **49** N3 23 23N 116 39E
Shanyao China **51** E8 25 07N 118 44E
Shaoguan China **49** M3 24 54N 113 33E
Shaoxing China **49** O5 30 02N 120 35E
Shaoyang China **49** M4 27 10N 111 25E
Shaqrā' Saudia Arabia **55** G4 25 18N 45 15E
Sharon Pennsylvania U.S.A. **93** D2 41 46N 80 30W
Sharp Island Hong Kong U.K. **51** C2 22 22N 114 17E
Sharp Peak Hong Kong U.K. **51** D2 22 26N 114 22E
Shashi China **49** M5 30 16N 112 20E
Shasta Lake California U.S.A. **90** B5 40 45N 122 20W
Shasta, Mount California U.S.A. **90** B5 41 25N 122 12W
Sha Tau Kok Hong Kong U.K. **51** C3 22 33N 114 13E
Sha Tin Hong Kong U.K. **51** C2 22 22N 114 10E
Shatsky Rise Pacific Ocean **22** G11 34 00N 160 00E
Shau Kei Wan Hong Kong U.K. **51** C1 22 16N 114 13E
Shebelē *r.* Ethiopia/Somalia **110** H9 6 00N 44 00E
Sheberghān Afghanistan **55** K6 36 41N 65 45E
Sheboygan Wisconsin U.S.A. **92** C2 43 46N 87 44W

South Downs *hills* England United Kingdom **68** K2 50 50N 0 30W
South East Cape Australia **78** H1 43 38S 146 48E
Southeast Indian Basin Indian Ocean **24** J3 32 00S 108 00E
Southeast Indian Ridge Indian Ocean **24** H2/J2
South East Pacific Basin Pacific Ocean **23** Q2/Q3 53 00S 95 00W
Southend-on-Sea England United Kingdom **68** L3 51 33N 0 43E
Southern Alps *mts.* South Island New Zealand **79** A2/B2 43 07S 171 13E
Southern Honshu Ridge Pacific Ocean **22** E10 25 50N 142 30E
Southern Indian Lake Manitoba Canada **89** P4 57 00N 99 00W
Southern Lau Group Fiji **83** F8 18 30S 178 40W
Southern Ocean 22/23
Southern Uplands Scotland United Kingdom **68** G7/I7
South Esk *r.* Scotland United Kingdom **68** I8 56 40N 2 55W
South Fiji Basin Pacific Ocean **22** H5 25 00S 176 50E
South Gate *tn.* California U.S.A. **95** B2 33 56N 118 11W
South Georgia *i.* South Atlantic Ocean **25** E1 54 00S 36 30W
South Hatia Island Bangladesh **38** A4 22 40N 91 00E
South Haven Michigan U.S.A. **92** C2 42 25N 86 16W
South Head Australia **79** H2 33 50S 151 17E
South Indian Basin Indian Ocean **24** L3 55 00S 130 00E
South Island New Zealand **79** A1/B2
South Junction Manitoba Canada **92** A3 49 03N 95 44W
SOUTH KOREA 50 C2/D4
South Loup *r.* Nebraska U.S.A. **90** G5 42 00N 99 00W
South Nahanni *r.* Northwest Territories Canada **88** J5 61 30N 123 22W
South Negril Point *c.* Jamaica **97** P8 18 16N 78 22W
South Ockendon England United Kingdom **66** E3 51 32N 0 18E
South Orkney Islands Southern Ocean **21** 60 00S 45 00W
South Platte *r.* U.S.A. **90** F5 41 00N 103 00W
South Point Barbados **96** V12 13 02N 59 32W
South Pole Antarctica **21** 90 00S
Southport England United Kingdom **68** H5 53 39N 3 01W
South Sandwich Trench Atlantic Ocean **25** E1/F1 55 00S 30 00W
South Shetland Islands Southern Ocean **103** E0 62 00S 60 00W
South Sioux City Nebraska U.S.A. **92** A2 42 28N 96 24W
South Suburbs *(Behala)* India **52** K1 22 28N 88 18E
South Tuas Basin Singapore **41** A3 1 18N 103 39E
South Uist *i.* Scotland United Kingdom **68** D9 57 20N 7 15W
Southwark England United Kingdom **66** C3 51 30N 0 06W
Southwest Cape South Island New Zealand **79** A1 48 00S 168 00E
Southwest Indian Ridge Indian Ocean **24** D2/E3 40 00S 50 00E
South West Pacific Basin Pacific Ocean **23** K4 35 00S 155 00W
Sovetsk Lithuania **58** A6 55 02N 21 50E
Sovetskaya Gavan' Russia **57** Q5 48 57N 140 16E
Sozh *r.* Belarus **58** C5 53 00N 30 00E
Spa Belgium **70** E2 50 29N 5 52E
SPAIN 72 A2/C3
Spandau Germany **67** E2 52 32N 13 13E
Spanish Town Jamaica **97** R7 17 59N 79 58W
Sparks Nevada U.S.A. **90** C4 39 34N 119 46W
Spartanburg South Carolina U.S.A. **91** J3 34 56N 81 57W
Spárti Greece **74** D2 37 05N 22 25E
Spassk-Dal'niy Russia **57** P4 44 37N 132 37E
Spasskoye Kazakhstan **59** K5 52 07N 68 32E
Speightstown Barbados **96** V12 13 15N 59 39W
Spence Bay *tn.* Northwest Territories Canada **89** Q6 69 30N 93 20W
Spencer Iowa U.S.A. **92** A2 43 08N 95 08W
Spencer Gulf Australia **78** F3 34 00S 137 00E
Spey *r.* Scotland United Kingdom **68** H9 57 00N 4 30W
Speyer Germany **71** A1 49 18N 8 26E
Spiekeroog *i.* Germany **71** A2 53 47N 7 43E
Spijkenisse Netherlands **70** D3 51 52N 4 19E
Spin Bay Phillip Island **81** K1 29 07S 167 57E
Spirit River *tn.* Alberta Canada **88** L4 55 46N 118 51W
Spittal an der Drau Austria **75** B2 46 48N 13 30E
Split Croatia **74** C3 43 31N 16 28E
Spokane Washington U.S.A. **90** C6 47 40N 117 25W
Spoleto Italy **74** B3 42 44N 12 44E
Spong Cambodia **37** C2 13 27N 105 33E
Spratly Islands South China Sea **32** E5/F5 8 45N 111 54E
Spree *r.* Germany **71** B2 52 00N 14 00E
Springbok Republic of South Africa **111** C2 29 44S 17 56E
Springdale Newfoundland Canada **89** X2 49 30N 56 06W
Springfield Illinois U.S.A. **92** C1 39 49N 89 39W
Springfield Massachusetts U.S.A. **93** F2 42 07N 72 35W
Springfield Missouri U.S.A. **92** B1 37 11N 93 19W
Springfield Ohio U.S.A. **93** D1 39 55N 83 48W
Springfield Oregon U.S.A. **90** B5 44 03N 123 01W
Springsure Australia **78** H5 24 09S 148 04E
Springville New York U.S.A. **93** E2 42 31N 78 41E
Spurn Head *c.* England United Kingdom **68** L5 53 36N 0 07E
Squamish British Columbia Canada **88** K2 49 41N 123 11W
Sragen Indonesia **42** P7 7 24S 111 00E
Sredinnyy Range *mts.* Russia **57** R7 57 00N 158 00E
Srednekolymsk Russia **57** R9 67 27N 153 35E
Sre Khtum Cambodia **37** C2 12 11N 106 56E
Srepok *r.* Cambodia **37** C2 13 20N 106 40E
Sretensk Russia **57** N6 52 15N 117 52E
Sre Umbell Cambodia **37** B2 11 08N 103 46E
Sri Aman Malaysia **42** D4 1 13N 111 30E
Srikakulum India **53** E3 18 19N 84 00E
SRI LANKA 53 E1
Srimongal Bangladesh **38** A4 24 20N 91 40E
Srinagar Kashmir **53** C6 34 08N 74 50E
Srinagarind Reservoir Thailand **39** A2 14 35N 99 05E
Srinagarind National Park Thailand **39** A2/A3 15 00N 99 00E
Staaken Germany **67** E2 52 32N 13 06E
Stadskanaal *tn.* Netherlands **70** F4 53 00N 6 55E
Stafford England United Kingdom **68** I4 52 48N 2 07W
Stahnsdorf Germany **67** E1/F1 52 23N 13 13E
Staines England United Kingdom **66** B2 51 26N 0 30W
Stakhanov Ukraine **58** D4 48 34N 38 40E
Standish Michigan U.S.A. **93** D2 43 59N 83 58W
Stanley Falkland Islands **25** M16 51 45S 57 56W
Stanley *see* Chek Chue
Stanovoy Range *mts.* Russia **57** O7 56 00N 122 30E
Stara Planina *mts.* Europe **74** D3/E3 43 00N 23 00E
Stara Zagora Bulgaria **74** E3 42 25N 25 37E
Starbuck Island Pacific Ocean **81** E3 5 37S 155 55W
Stargard Szczeciński Poland **75** C3 53 21N 15 01E
Starnberger See *l.* Germany **71** B1 47 00N 11 00E
Starogard Gdański Poland **75** C3 53 58N 18 30E
Start Point *c.* England United Kingdom **68** H2 50 13N 3 38W
Staryy Oskol Russia **56** F6 51 20N 37 50E
State College Pennsylvania U.S.A. **93** E2 40 48N 77 52W
Staten Island New York U.S.A. **94** B1 40 35N 74 10W
Staunton Virginia U.S.A. **93** E1 38 10N 79 05W
Stavanger Norway **69** B2 58 58N 5 45E
Stavelot Belgium **70** E2 50 25N 5 56E
Staveren Netherlands **70** E4 52 53N 5 21E
Stavropol' Russia **56** G5 45 03N 41 59E
Stebbins Alaska U.S.A. **88** C5 63 32N 162 20W
Steels Point Norfolk Island **81** M5 29 01S 167 59E
Steen River *tn.* Alberta Canada **88** L4 59 40N 117 15W
Steenstrup Glacier Greenland **89** X8 75 00N 56 00W
Steenwijk Netherlands **70** F4 52 47N 6 07E
Steep Island Hong Kong U.K. **51** C1 22 16N 114 18E
Steep Point Christmas Island **81** R2 10 27S 105 44E
Steglitz Germany **67** F1 52 27N 13 19E
Steiermark *admin.* Austria **71** B1 47 00N 14 00E
Steigerwald Germany **71** B1 49 00N 10 00E
Stein Netherlands **70** E2 50 58N 5 45E
Steinbach Manitoba Canada **92** A3 49 32N 96 40W
Steinfurt Germany **71** A2 52 09N 7 21E
Stenay France **70** E1 49 29N 5 12E
Stendal Germany **71** B2 52 36N 11 52E
Stephenville Newfoundland Canada **89** X2 48 33N 58 34W
Stepney England United Kingdom **66** C3 51 31N 0 04W
Step' Shaidara *geog. reg.* Kazakhstan **59** K3 40 00N 65 00E
Sterling Colorado U.S.A. **90** F5 40 37N 103 13W
Sterling Illinois U.S.A. **92** C2 41 48N 89 43W
Sterlitamak Russia **56** H6 53 40N 55 59E
Steubenville Ohio U.S.A. **93** D2 40 22N 80 39W
Stevens Point *tn.* Wisconsin U.S.A. **92** C2 44 32N 89 33W
Stewart British Columbia Canada **88** I4 55 56N 130 01W
Stewart Yukon Territory Canada **88** H5 63 15N 139 15W
Stewart Crossing Yukon Territory Canada **88** H5 60 37N 128 37W
Stewart Hill Christmas Island **81** Q2 10 29S 105 36E
Stewart Island South Island New Zealand **79** A1 46 55S 167 55E
Steyr Austria **75** B2 48 04N 14 25E
Štip Macedonia (Former Yugoslav Republic) **74** D3 41 44N 22 12E
Stirling Scotland United Kingdom **68** H8 56 07N 3 57W
Stirling Alberta Canada **88** M2 49 34N 112 30W
St. Joseph, Lake Ontario Canada **89** Q3 51 30N 91 40W
Stockholm Sweden **69** D2 59 20N 18 05E
Stockport England United Kingdom **68** I5 53 25N 2 10W
Stockton California U.S.A. **90** B4 37 59N 121 20W
Stockton Lake *res.* Missouri U.S.A. **92** B1 38 00N 94 00W
Stockton-on-Tees England United Kingdom **68** J6 54 34N 1 19W
Stockyard Creek Norfolk Island **81** L5 29 02S 167 58E
Stoke-on-Trent England United Kingdom **68** I5 53 00N 2 10W
Stolberg Germany **71** A2 50 45N 6 15E
Stone Canyon Reservoir California U.S.A. **95** A3 34 07N 118 27W
Stonecutters Island Hong Kong U.K. **51** B1 22 18N 114 08E
Stonewall Manitoba Canada **92** A4 50 08N 97 20W
Stony Rapids *tn.* Saskatchewan Canada **88** N4 59 14N 103 48W
Stora Lulevatten *l.* Sweden **69** D4 67 20N 19 00E
Størdal Norway **69** C3 63 18N 11 48E
Støren Norway **69** C3 63 03N 10 16E
Storm Lake *tn.* Iowa U.S.A. **92** A2 42 39N 95 11W
Stornoway Scotland United Kingdom **68** E10 58 12N 6 23W
Storsjön *l.* Sweden **69** C3 63 10N 14 10E
Storuman Sweden **69** D4 65 05N 17 10E
Stour *r.* England United Kingdom **68** L4 51 10N 1 10E
Straits of Florida *sd.* Florida U.S.A. **91** J1 25 00N 80 00W
Strakonice Czech Republic **71** B1 49 16N 13 54E
Stralsund Germany **71** B2 54 18N 13 06E
Stranraer Scotland United Kingdom **68** F6 54 55N 5 02W
Strasbourg France **73** C2 48 35N 7 45E
Stratford Ontario Canada **93** D2 43 22N 81 00W
Strathfield Australia **79** G2 33 52S 151 06E
Straubing Germany **71** B1 48 53N 12 35E
Strausberg Germany **71** B2 52 34N 13 53E
Streatham England United Kingdom **66** C2 51 26N 0 07W
Streator Illinois U.S.A. **92** C2 41 07N 88 53W
Stredočesky *admin.* Czech Republic **71** B2 50 00N 14 00E
Stretto di Messina *sd.* Italy **74** C2 38 00N 15 00E
Strickland *r.* Papua New Guinea **45** J3 7 30S 141 45E
Strimón *r.* Greece **74** D3 41 00N 23 00E
Strogino Russia **56** L2 55 49N 37 46E
Stromboli *mt.* Italy **74** C2 38 48N 15 15E
Stronsay *i.* Scotland United Kingdom **68** I11 59 07N 2 37W
Stroudsburg Pennsylvania U.S.A. **93** E2 41 00N 75 12W
Stuart Highway *rd.* Australia **78** E6 20 00S 135 00E
Stubaler Alpen *mts.* Austria **71** B1 47 00N 11 00E
Stubbings Point Christmas Island **81** Q1 10 34S 105 38E
Stung Chikreng *r.* Cambodia **37** B2 13 30N 104 30E
Stung Chinit *r.* Cambodia **37** C2 12 25N 105 15E
Stung Pursat *r.* Cambodia **37** B2 12 20N 103 15E
Stung Sen *r.* Cambodia **37** C2 13 30N 105 10E
Stung Sreng *r.* Cambodia **37** B2 14 00N 103 50E
Stung Stong *r.* Cambodia **37** B2 13 20N 104 50E
Stung Treng Cambodia **37** C2 13 31N 105 59E
Stura di Demonte *r.* Italy **73** C1 44 00N 7 00E
Sturgeon Falls *tn.* Ontario Canada **93** E3 46 22N 79 57W
Sturgeon Lake Ontario Canada **92** B3/4 50 00N 91 00W
Sturgeon Landing Saskatchewan Canada **89** O3 54 18N 101 49W
Sturt Creek *r.* Australia **78** D6 18 00S 127 30E
Stuttgart Germany **71** A1 48 47N 9 12E
Stykkishólmur Iceland **69** H7 65 05N 22 44W
Suakin Sudan **110** G11 19 08N 37 17E
Su-ao Taiwan **51** H7 24 33N 121 48E
Subang Indonesia **42** N7 6 32S 107 45E
Subansiri *r.* China/India **38** A5 28 00N 94 15E
Subotica Serbia Yugoslavia **74** C4 46 04N 19 41E
Suceava Romania **75** E2 47 37N 26 18E
Suck *r.* Irish Republic **68** C5 53 40N 8 30W
Sucre Bolivia **102** D9 19 05S 65 15W
Sucy-en-Brie France **67** C2 48 49N 231E
SUDAN 110 E8/F11
Sudbury Ontario Canada **93** D3 46 30N 81 01W
Sudd *swamp* Africa **104** 7 00N 30 00E
Sudety Reseniky *mts.* Europe **75** C3 50 40N 16 00E
Sudr Egypt **54** D4 29 40N 32 42E
Sue *r.* Sudan **110** E9 7 00N 28 00E
Suez *see* El Suweis
Suez Canal *(Qanâ el Suweis)* Egypt **109** S4 31 30N 32 20E
Suez, Gulf of Egypt **54** D4 29 56N 32 32E
Sugar Loaf *see* Pão de Açúcar
Suginami Japan **47** B3 35 41N 139 40E
Sugut *r.* Malaysia **40** A2 6 00N 117 00E
Sühbaatar Mongolia **49** L9 50 10N 106 14E
Suhl Germany **71** B2 50 37N 10 43E
Suir *r.* Irish Republic **68** D4 52 15N 7 05W
Suita Japan **46** G1 34 46N 135 30E
Sukabumi Indonesia **42** N7 6 55S 106 50E
Sukadana Indonesia **42** C3 1 15S 109 57E
Sukaraja Indonesia **42** D3 2 10S 110 35E
Sukaraja Indonesia **42** O7 7 30S 109 15E
Sukhona *r.* Russia **56** G8 60 00N 45 00E
Sukhothai Thailand **39** A3 17 00N 99 51E
Sukhumi Georgia **58** E3 43 01N 41 01E
Sukkertoppen Greenland **89** Y6 65 25N 53 00W
Sukkur Pakistan **52** B5 27 42N 68 54E
Sulaiman Range *mts.* Pakistan **52** B5/C6 30 00N 70 00E
Sulawesi *i.* Indonesia **43** F3 2 00S 120 00E
Sulawesi Selatan *admin.* Indonesia **43** E3 2 30S 119 00E
Sulawesi Tengah *admin.* Indonesia **43** F3 1 20S 122 00E
Sulawesi Tenggara *admin.* Indonesia **43** F3 4 00S 123 00E
Sulawesi Utara *admin.* Indonesia **43** F4 0 30N 123 00E
Sulaymānīyah Iraq **55** G6 35 32N 45 27E
Sullana Peru **102** A12 4 52S 80 39W
Sultanpur India **53** E5 26 15N 82 04E
Sulu Archipelago The Philippines **40** B2 6 00N 121 00E
Sulu Sea The Philippines/Malaysia **40** A2/B2 8 00N 120 00E
Sumatera *i.* Indonesia **42** A4 0 00 100 00E
Sumatera Barat *admin.* Indonesia **42** B3 1 30S 100 30E
Sumatera Selatan *admin.* Indonesia **42** B3 3 00S 104 00E
Sumatera Utara *admin.* Indonesia **42** A4 1 30N 99 00E
Sumbawa Besar Indonesia **42** E2 8 30S 117 25E
Sumburgh Head *c.* Scotland United Kingdom **68** J12 59 51N 1 16W
Sumedang Indonesia **42** N7 6 54S 107 55E
Sumenep Indonesia **42** Q7 7 01S 113 51E
Sumgait Azerbaijan **58** F3 40 35N 49 38E
Sumida Japan **47** C3 35 42N 139 49E
Summit Lake *tn.* British Columbia Canada **88** K4 58 45N 124 45W
Sumoto Japan **46** F1 34 20N 134 53E
Sumprabum Myanmar **38** B5 26 38N 97 36E
Sumy Ukraine **58** C5 50 55N 34 49E
Sunan North Korea **50** B4 39 12N 125 40E
Sunbury England United Kingdom **66** B2 51 24N 0 25W
Sunbury Pennsylvania U.S.A. **93** E2 40 52N 76 47W
Sunch'ŏn North Korea **50** B4 39 23N 125 59E
Sunch'ŏn South Korea **50** C2 34 56N 127 28E
Sunderland England United Kingdom **68** J6 54 55N 1 23W
Sundsvall Sweden **69** D3 62 22N 17 20E
Sungai Api Api *r.* Singapore **41** E4 1 22N 103 56E
Sungai Bedok *r.* Singapore **41** E3 1 20N 103 57E
Sungai Buloh Besar *r.* Singapore **41** B5 1 26N 103 43E
Sungai Changi *r.* Singapore **41** E4 1 23N 103 59E
Sungai Jurong *r.* Singapore **41** B3 1 19N 103 44E
Sungai Kangkar *r.* Singapore **41** B4 1 25N 103 43E
Sungai Mandai *r.* Singapore **41** C5 1 26N 103 46E
Sungai Pandan *r.* Singapore **41** C3 1 18N 103 45E
Sungai Pang Sua *r.* Singapore **41** C4 1 24N 103 45E
Sungai Peng Siang *r.* Singapore **41** B4 1 23N 103 44E
Sungaipenuh Indonesia **42** B3 2 00S 101 28E
Sungai Petani Malaysia **42** B5 5 38N 100 28E
Sungai Punggol *r.* Singapore **41** D4 1 24N 103 53E
Sungai Rochor *r.* Singapore **41** D3 1 18N 103 52E
Sungai Seletar Reservoir Singapore **41** D4 1 24N 103 51E
Sungai Sembawang *r.* Singapore **41** C5 1 26N 103 48E
Sungai Serangoon *r.* Singapore **41** D4 1 23N 103 55E
Sungai Simpang *r.* Singapore **41** D5 1 27N 103 51E
Sungai Tampines *r.* Singapore **41** E4 1 22N 103 57E
Sungai Tengah *r.* Singapore **41** B4 1 23N 103 43E
Sungai Whampoa *r.* Singapore **41** D3 1 20N 103 51E
Sung Kong *i.* Hong Kong U.K. **51** C1 22 11N 114 17E
Sung Men Thailand **39** B3 18 03N 100 10E
Sunland California U.S.A. **95** A4 34 15N 118 17W
Sunset Beach *tn.* California U.S.A. **95** B1 33 43N 118 04W
Sunset Peak Hong Kong U.K. **51** A1 22 15N 113 57E
Sunshine Island Hong Kong U.K. **51** B1 22 16N 114 03E
Suntar Russia **57** N8 62 10N 117 35E
Sunyani Ghana **112** E4 7 22N 2 18W
Suoi Rut Vietnam **37** C4 20 48N 105 08E
Suō-nada *b.* Japan **46** B1 33 50N 131 30E
Suong Cambodia **37** C2 11 55N 105 43E
Superior Wisconsin U.S.A. **92** B3 46 42N 92 05W
Superior, Lake Canada/U.S.A. **92** C3 48 00N 88 00W
Suphan Buri Thailand **39** B2 14 28N 100 07E
Sūr Oman **55** I3 22 34N 59 32E
Sura *r.* Russia **58** F6 55 00N 46 30E
Surabaya Indonesia **42** Q7 7 14S 112 45E
Surakarta Indonesia **42** P7 7 32S 110 50E
Suramana Indonesia **43** E3 0 51S 119 37E
Surat India **53** C4 21 10N 72 54E
Surat Thani Thailand **39** A1 9 09N 99 20E
Sûre *(Sauer) r.* Europe **70** E1 49 45N 6 30E
Surendranagar India **53** C4 22 44N 71 43E
Surgut Russia **57** J8 61 13N 73 20E
Surigao The Philippines **40** C2 9 47N 125 29E
Surin Thailand **39** B2 14 53N 103 29E
SURINAM 102 F13
Surma *r.* Bangladesh/India **38** A4 24 50N 91 45E
Surrey *county* England United Kingdom **66** C2 51 25N 0 14W
Surte *(Sirte)* Libya **110** C14 31 13N 16 35E
Surui *r.* Brazil **103** Q3 22 40S 43 08W
Surulangun Indonesia **42** B3 2 35S 102 47E
Surulere Nigeria **109** V3 6 30N 3 25E
Susitna *r.* Alaska U.S.A. **88** E5 62 10N 150 15W
Suska Solomon Islands **82** B7 6 50S 156 53E
Susono Japan **46** K2 35 11N 138 50E
Susquehanna River U.S.A. **93** E2 40 00N 77 00W
Susubona Solomon Islands **82** E5 8 17S 159 29E
Susuman Russia **57** Q8 62 46N 148 08E
Sutherland Australia **79** G1 34 02S 151 03E
Sutlej *r.* Pakistan **53** C6 30 00N 73 00E
Sutton Québec Canada **93** F3 45 05N 72 36W
Sutton England United Kingdom **66** C2 51 22N 0 12W
Suva Fiji **83** C8 18 08S 178 25E
Suvasvesi *l.* Finland **69** F3 62 40N 28 10E
Suwannaphum Thailand **39** B3 15 36N 103 46E
Suwarrow *i.* Pacific Ocean **81** D3 15 00S 161 00W
Suwŏn South Korea **50** C3 37 16N 126 59E
Suzhou Anhui China **49** N5 33 38N 117 02E
Suzhou Jiangsu China **49** O5 31 21N 120 40E
Suzuka Japan **46** H1 34 52N 136 37E
Suzuka-sanmyaku *mts.* Japan **46** H1/2 35 00N 136 20E
Suzu-misaki *c.* Japan **46** C2 37 30N 137 21E
Svalbard *(Spitsbergen) i.* Arctic Ocean **20** 79 00N 15 00E
Svay Chek Cambodia **37** B2 13 50N 102 59E
Svay Rieng Cambodia **37** C2 11 05N 105 48E
Svendborg Denmark **71** B3 55 04N 10 38E
Sverdlovsk Ukraine **58** D4 48 05N 39 37E
Sverdlovsk *see* Yekaterinburg
Svobodnyy Russia **57** O6 51 24N 128 05E
Swains Island Pacific Ocean **80** D3 11 03S 171 06W
Swale *r.* England United Kingdom **68** J6 54 15N 1 30W
Swanley England United Kingdom **66** D2 51 24N 0 12E
Swansea Wales United Kingdom **68** H3 51 38N 3 57W
SWAZILAND 111 F2
SWEDEN 69 C2/E4
Sweetwater *tn.* Texas U.S.A. **90** F3 32 27N 100 25W
Swellendam Republic of South Africa **111** D1 34 01S 20 26E
Swiebodzin Poland **75** C3 52 15N 15 31E
Swift Current *tn.* Saskatchewan Canada **88** N3 50 17N 107 49W
Swindon England United Kingdom **68** J3 51 34N 1 47W
Świnoujście Poland **75** B3 53 55N 14 18E
SWITZERLAND 73 C2
Sydney Australia **78** I3 33 55S 151 10E
Sydney Nova Scotia Canada **89** W2 46 10N 60 10W
Sydney Bay Norfolk Island **81** K4 29 03S 167 56E
Sydney Island *see* Manra
Syktyvkar Russia **56** H8 61 42N 50 45E
Sylhet Bangladesh **53** G4 24 53N 91 51E
Sylt Germany **71** A2 54 00N 8 00E
Syowa *r.s.* Antarctica **21** 69 00S 39 35E
Syracuse New York U.S.A. **93** E2 43 03N 76 10W
Syr-Dary'ya *r.* Asia **59** L3 43 30N 66 30E
SYRIA 54 E6
Syrian Desert Middle East **54** E5 32 30N 39 20E
Syzran' Russia **56** G6 53 10N 48 29E
Szczecin Poland **75** B3 53 25N 14 32E
Szczecinek Poland **75** C3 53 42N 16 41E
Szeged Hungary **75** D2 46 15N 20 09E
Székesfehérvár Hungary **75** C2 47 11N 18 22E
Szolnok Hungary **75** D2 47 10N 20 10E
Szombathely Hungary **75** C2 47 14N 16 38E

T

Taal, Lake The Philippines **40** B3 14 00N 121 00E
Tabaquite Trinidad and Tobago **96** T9 10 23N 61 18W
Tabar Islands Papua New Guinea **45** O5 2 45S 151 45E
Tabas Iran **55** I5 33 37N 56 54E
Taber Alberta Canada **88** M2 49 48N 112 09W
Tabiteuea *i.* Pacific Ocean **80** C3 1 25S 174 50E
Tablas *i.* The Philippines **40** B3 12 00N 121 00E
Tablas Plateau The Philippines **40** B2 9 00N 122 00E
Tablas Strait The Philippines **40** B3 12 00N 122 00E
Table Rock Lake Missouri U.S.A. **91** H4 36 38N 93 17W
Tábor Czech Republic **75** B2 49 25N 14 39E
Tabora Tanzania **111** F7 5 01S 32 48E
Tabrīz Iran **55** G6 38 05N 46 18E
Tabūk Saudi Arabia **54** E4 28 33N 36 36E
Tabuk The Philippines **40** B4 17 25N 121 28E
Tabwemasana *mt.* Vanuatu **83** F6 15 20S 166 40E
Tabwewa Fiji **83** E10 16 28S 179 58W
Ta-chia Taiwan **51** G7 24 20N 120 34E
Tachikawa Japan **46** L2 35 42N 139 28E
Tacloban The Philippines **40** C3 11 15N 125 01E
Tacna Peru **102** C9 18 00S 70 15W
Tacoma Washington U.S.A. **90** B6 47 16N 122 30W
Tadine New Caledonia **82** W2 21 31S 167 53E
Tadmur Syria **54** E5 34 40N 38 10E
T'aean South Korea **50** C3 36 48N 126 17E
T'aebaek-Sanmaek *mts.* North Korea/South Korea **50** D3/4 38 00N 128 20E
Taedong *r.* North Korea **50** B4 39 00N 1225 30E
Taegu South Korea **50** D2 35 52N 128 36E
Taeha-dong South Korea **50** E3 37 40N 130 50E
Taejŏn South Korea **50** C3 36 20N 127 26E
Tafalla Spain **73** A1 42 32N 1 41W
Tafila Jordan **54** O10 30 52N 35 36E
Tafna *r.* Algeria **72** B2 35 00N 2 00W
Taga Western Samoa **82** A11 13 44S 172 27W
Taganrog Russia **56** F5 47 14N 38 55E
Tagaytay The Philippines **40** B3 14 05N 12 055E
Tagbilaran The Philippines **40** B2 9 38N 123 53E
Tagig The Philippines **40** B3 14 31N 121 03E
Tagula Papua New Guinea **45** P1 11 21S 153 11E
Tagula Island Papua New Guinea **45** P1 11 30S 153 30E
Tagum The Philippines **40** C2 7 25N 125 54E
Tahara Japan **46** J1 34 40N 137 18E
Tahat, Mount Algeria **112** G7 23 18N 5 33E
Tahiti *i.* French Polynesia **81** E3 17 30S 148 30W
Tahoe, Lake U.S.A. **90** C4 39 00N 120 00W
Tahoua Niger **112** G5 14 57N 5 19E
Tahta Egypt **54** D4 26 47N 31 31E
Tahuna Indonesia **43** G4 3 33N 125 33E
Tai'an China **49** N6 36 15N 117 10E
T'ai-chung Taiwan **51** G7 24 09N 124 40E
Tai Lam Chung Hong Kong U.K. **51** B2 22 22N 114 01E

The Hague see 's-Gravenhage
Thelon r. Northwest Territories Canada 89 O5 64 40N 102 30W
Thepa r. Thailand 39 B1 6 30N 100 55E
The Pas Manitoba Canada 89 O3 53 49N 101 14W
Thermaïkós Kólpos g. Greece 74 D2/3 40 00N 22 50E
Thermopolis Wyoming U.S.A. 90 E5 43 39N 108 12W
Thessalon Ontario Canada 93 D3 46 15N 83 34W
Thessaloniki Greece 74 D3 40 38N 22 58E
Thetford Mines Québec Canada 93 F3 46 06N 71 18W
Thiais France 67 B2 48 45N 2 24E
Thief River Falls tn. Minnesota U.S.A. 92 A3 48 12N 96 48W
Thiers France 73 B2 45 51N 3 33E
Thiès Senegal 112 B5 14 49N 16 52W
Thika Kenya 110 G7 1 03S 37 05E
Thimphu Bhutan 53 F5 27 32N 89 43E
Thingangyun Myanmar 38 B3 16 47N 96 12E
Thio New Caledonia 82 V2 21 36S 166 12E
Thionville France 73 C2 49 22N 6 11E
Thira i. Greece 74 E2 36 00N 25 00E
Thívai Greece 74 D2 38 19N 23 19E
Thnot r. Cambodia 37 B2 11 30N 104 45E
Thoeng Thailand 39 B3 19 43N 100 10E
Tholen i. Netherlands 70 D3 51 33N 4 05E
Thomasville Georgia U.S.A. 91 J3 30 50N 83 59W
Thompson Manitoba Canada 89 P4 55 45N 97 54W
Thomson Singapore 41 D4 1 21N 103 50E
Thomson r. Australia 78 G5 24 00S 143 30E
Thong Hoe Singapore 41 B5 1 25N 103 43E
Thongwa Myanmar 38 B3 16 45N 96 34E
Thonze Myanmar 38 B3 17 36N 95 48E
Thouars France 73 A2 46 59N 0 13W
Three Kings Islands North Island New Zealand 79 B4 34 10S 172 07E
Three Mile Bay tn. New York U.S.A. 93 E2 44 04N 76 12W
Three Pagodas Pass Myanmar/Thailand 39 A3 15 20N 98 21E
Three Points, Cape Ghana 112 E3 4 43N 2 06W
Three Sisters Islands Solomon Islands 82 G3 10 10S 162 00E
Thu Dau Mot Vietnam 37 C2 10 59N 106 39E
Thuln Belgium 70 D2 50 21N 4 18E
Thule (Qaanaaq) Greenland 89 V8 77 30N 69 00W
Thun Switzerland 73 C2 46 46N 7 38E
Thunder Bay tn. Ontario Canada 92 C3 48 27N 89 12W
Thung Salaeng Luang National Park Thailand 39 B3 16 40N 100 50E
Thung Song Thailand 39 A1 8 10N 99 41E
Thüringen admin. Germany 71 B2 50 30N 11 00E
Thüringer Wald hills Germany 71 B2 50 00N 10 00E
Thurso Scotland United Kingdom 68 H10 58 35N 3 32W
Thurso r. Scotland United Kingdom 68 H10 58 15N 3 35W
Thurston Island Antarctica 21 70 00S 100 00W
Tian'anmen China 47 G1 40 50N 116 26E
Tiandong China 36 D6 23 50N 106 35E
Tianjin China 49 N6 39 08N 117 12E
Tianshifu China 50 B5 41 20N 124 22E
Tianshui China 49 L5 34 25N 105 58E
Tiarel Tahiti 82 T9 17 32S 149 20W
Tiaret Algeria 72 C2 35 20N 1 20E
Tiber r. Italy 74 B3 42 00N 12 00E
Tiberias Israel 54 O11 32 48N 35 32E
Tiberias, Lake (Sea of Galilee) Israel 54 O11 32 45N 35 30E
Tibesti mts. Chad 110 C12 21 00N 17 00E
Tibet Autonomous Region see Xizang Zizhiqu
Tiburón i. Mexico 96 B5 28 30N 112 30W
Ticao i. The Philippines 40 B3 12 00N 123 00E
Ticino r. Italy/Switzerland 73 C2 45 00N 9 00E
Ticul Mexico 96 G4 20 22N 89 31W
Tidore Indonesia 43 G4 J0 40N 127 25E
Tiel Netherlands 70 E3 51 53N 5 26E
Tieling China 50 A6 42 19N 123 52E
Tielt Belgium 70 C3 51 00N 3 20E
Tienen Belgium 70 D2 50 48N 4 56E
Tyan Shan (Tian-Shan') mts. China 59 M3/N3 41 00N 76 00E
Tien Yen Vietnam 37 C4 21 19N 107 25E
Tierra Blanca Mexico 96 E3 18 28N 96 21W
Tietar r. Spain 72 A3 40 07N 5 15W
Tiffin Ohio U.S.A. 93 D2 41 07N 83 11W
Tifu Indonesia 43 G3 3 41S 126 24E
Tiga New Caledonia 82 W2 21 10S 167 52E
Tigris r. Iraq 55 G5 32 00N 46 00E
Tikrit Iraq 54 F5 34 36N 43 42E
Tijuana Mexico 96 A6 32 29N 117 10W
Tijuca Brazil 103 P2 22 56S 43 16W
Tijuca National Park Brazil 103 P2 22 58S 43 17W
Tikhoretsk Russia 58 E4 45 52N 40 07E
Tikopia i. Solomon Islands 83 O1 12 10S 168 50E
Tiksi Russia 57 O10 71 40N 128 45E
Tilak Nagar India 52 L4 28 38N 77 07E
Tilburg Netherlands 70 E3 51 34N 5 05E
Tillsonburg Ontario Canada 93 D2 42 53N 80 44W
Tilomar Indonesia 43 G2 9 22S 125 09E
Timaru South Island New Zealand 79 B2 44 24S 171 15E
Timbira r. Brazil 103 Q3 22 40S 43 12W
Timbuktu see Tombouctou
Timbunke Papua New Guinea 45 K4 4 10S 143 30E
Timimóun Algeria 112 F8 29 15N 0 14E
Timişoara Romania 75 D2 45 45N 21 15E
Timişul r. Romania/Yugoslavia 75 D2 45 00N 21 00E
Timmins Ontario Canada 93 D3 48 30N 81 20W
Timor i. Indonesia 43 F2-G2 9 00S 125 00E
Timor Sea Indonesia 78 D7 10 45S 126 00E
Timor Timur admin. Indonesia 43 G2 8 00S 126 00E
Timsâh, Lake see Bahra el Timsâh
Tinakula i. Solomon Islands 82 L3 10 28S 165 40E
Tindouf Algeria 112 D8 27 42N 8 10W
Tineg r. The Philippines 40 B4 17 00N 120 00E
Tinh Gia Vietnam 37 C3 19 27N 105 38E
Tinos i. Greece 74 E2 37 00N 25 00E
Tinputz Papua New Guinea 45 Q4 5 36S 155 02E
Tinsukia India 38 B5 27 28N 95 20E
Tiranë Albania 74 C3 41 20N 19 49E
Tir'at el Ismâ'ilîya can. Egypt 109 R3 30 32N 31 48E
Tir'at el Mansûrîya r. Egypt 109 R4 31 12N 31 38E
Tiraz Mountains Namibia 111 C2 25 30S 16 30E
Tiree i. Scotland United Kingdom 68 E8 56 30N 6 55W
Tîrgoviste Romania 75 E1 44 56N 25 27E
Tîrgu Jiu Romania 75 D2 45 03N 23 18E
Tîrgu Mureş Romania 75 D2 46 33N 24 34E
Tirol admin. Austria 71 B1 47 00N 11 00E
Tirso r. Italy 74 A2 40 00N 9 00E
Tiruchchirāppalli India 53 D2 10 50N 78 41E
Tirunelveli India 53 D1 8 45N 77 43E
Tirupati India 53 D2 13 39N 79 25E
Tiruppur India 53 D2 11 05N 77 20E
Tisdale Saskatchewan Canada 88 O3 52 51N 104 01W
Tisza r. Hungary/Yugoslavia 75 D2 46 00N 20 00E
Titāgarh India 52 K2 22 44N 88 22E
Titograd Montenegro Yugoslavia 74 C3 42 28N 19 17E
Titova Mitrovica Serbia Yugoslavia 74 D3 42 54N 20 52E
Titovo Užiče Serbia Yugoslavia 74 C3 43 52N 19 50E
Titov Veles Macedonia (Former Yugoslav Republic) 74 D3 41 43N 21 49E
Tiu Chung Chau i. Hong Kong U.K. 51 C1/2 22 20N 114 19E
Tiu Keng Leng Hong Kong U.K. 51 C1 22 18N 114 15E
Tiverton Rhode Island U.S.A. 93 F2 41 38N 71 13W
Tivoli Italy 74 B3 41 58N 12 48E
Tiwaka r. New Caledonia 82 U2 20 52S 165 10E
Tizimím Mexico 96 G4 21 10N 88 09W
Tizi Ouzou Algeria 112 F10 36 44N 4 05E
Tiznit Morocco 112 D8 29 43N 9 44W
Tlemcen Algeria 112 E9 34 53N 1 21W
Toad River tn. British Columbia Canada 88 J4 59 00N 125 10W
Toak Vanuatu 83 H5 16 20S 168 28E
Toamasina Madagascar 111 I4 18 10S 49 23E
Toa Payoh Singapore 41 D4 1 20N 103 51E
Toba Japan 46 H1 34 29N 136 51E
Tobago i. Trinidad and Tobago 97 L2 11 15N 60 40W
Tobermory Ontario Canada 93 D3 45 15N 81 39W
Tobi i. Caroline Islands 43 H4 3 01N 131 10E
Tobi-shima i. Japan 46 C2 39 12N 139 32E
Toboali Indonesia 42 C3 3 00S 106 30E
Tobol r. Russia 57 I7 56 00N 66 00E
Tobol'sk Russia 57 I7 58 15N 68 12E
Tochigi pref. Japan 46 L3 36 20N 139 40E
Toco Trinidad and Tobago 96 U10 10 49N 60 57W
Tocopilla Chile 103 C8 22 05S 70 10W
Tofonga i. Tonga 83 B3 19 58S 174 29W
Tofua i. Tonga 83 A3 19 45S 175 05W
Toga i. Vanuatu 83 F8 13 26S 166 41E
Tōgane Japan 46 M2 35 34N 140 22E
TOGO 112 F4
Tohiea, Mount Tahiti 82 R9 17 33S 149 48W
Tŏkchŏk-Kundo is. South Korea 50 C3 37 15N 126 00E
Tokelau Islands Pacific Ocean 80 D3 9 00S 168 00W
Toki Japan 46 J2 35 25N 137 12E
Tokoname Japan 46 H1 34 50N 136 50E
Tokorozawa Japan 47 C2 35 47N 139 28E
Tokrau r. Kazakhstan 59 M4 48 00N 75 00E
Toku i. Tonga 83 B4 18 20S 174 10W
Tokushima Japan 46 B1 34 03N 134 34E
Tokuyama Japan 46 B1 34 03N 131 48E
Tōkyō Japan 47 C3 35 35N 139 40E
Tōkyō pref. Japan 46 L2 35 35N 139 40E
Tokyo Bay see Tōkyō-wan
Tōkyō-wan (Tokyo Bay) Japan 46 L2 35 30N 139 50E
Tolbukhin see Dobrich
Toledo Spain 72 B2 39 52N 4 02W
Toledo The Philippines 40 B3 10 24N 123 39E
Toledo Ohio U.S.A. 93 D2 41 40N 83 35W
Toliara Madagascar 111 H3 23 20S 43 41E
Tolitoli Indonesia 43 F4 1 05N 120 50E
Tollygunge India 52 K2 22 30N 88 19E
Tolo Channel Hong Kong U.K. 51 C2 22 28N 114 17E
Tolo Harbour Hong Kong U.K. 51 C2 22 26N 114 14E
Tolosa Spain 72 B3 43 09N 2 04W
Tolsan South Korea 50 C2 34 36N 127 43E
Toluca Mexico 96 E3 19 20N 99 40W
Tol'yatti Russia 56 G6 53 32N 49 24E
Tom' r. Russia 59 O5 55 00N 86 30E
Tomakomai Japan 46 D3 42 39N 141 33E
Tomanivi (Mount Victoria) mt. Fiji 83 C9 17 37S 178 01E
Tomar Portugal 72 A2 39 36N 8 25W
Tomaszów Mazowiecka Poland 75 D3 51 33N 20 00E
Tomatlán Mexico 96 C3 19 54N 105 18W
Tombigbee r. U.S.A. 91 I3 32 00N 88 00W
Tombouctou (Timbuktu) Mali 112 E6 16 49N 2 59W
Tombua Angola 111 B4 15 49S 11 53E
Tomini Indonesia 43 F4 0 50N 120 30E
Tomioka Japan 46 K3 36 14N 138 45E
Tomo New Caledonia 82 V2 21 57S 166 10E
Tomogashima-suidō sd. Japan 46 F1/G1 34 15N 134 00E
Tomotu Noi i. Solomon Islands 83 M3 10 50S 166 00E
Tom Price, Mount Australia 78 B5 22 49S 117 51E
Tomsk Russia 57 K7 56 30N 85 05E
Tonala Mexico 96 F3 16 08N 93 41W
Tondano Indonesia 43 F4 1 19N 124 50E
Tønder Denmark 71 A2 54 57N 8 53E
Tone-gawa r. Japan 46 M2 35 51N 140 09E
TONGA 83
Tonga i. 80 D2
Tong'an China 51 F8 24 43N 118 07E
Tongatapu i. Tonga 83 D1 21 09S 175 16W
Tongatapu Group Tonga 83 A1
Tonga Trench Pacific Ocean 22 I5 20 00S 173 00W
Tongchuan China 49 L6 35 05N 109 02E
Tongeren Belgium 70 E2 50 47N 5 28E
Tong Fuk Hong Kong U.K. 51 A1 22 14N 113 56E
Tonghae South Korea 50 D3 37 33N 129 07E
Tonghai China 49 K3 24 07N 104 45E
Tonghua China 49 P7 41 42N 125 45E
Tongking, Gulf of China/Vietnam 37 C3/4 19 00N 107 00E
Tongling China 49 N5 30 58N 117 48E
Tongnae South Korea 50 D2 35 11N 129 05E
Tongoa (Kuwaé) i. Vanuatu 83 H5 16 54S 168 34E
Tongren China 36 D7 27 44N 109 10E
Tongzi China 36 D7 28 08N 106 49E
Tonle Basak r. Cambodia 37 C2 11 00N 105 05E
Tonle Sap l. Cambodia 37 B2 13 00N 104 00E
Tonle Sap r. Cambodia 37 B2 12 00N 104 50E
Tonopah Nevada U.S.A. 90 C4 38 05N 117 15W
Tønsberg Norway 69 C2 59 16N 10 25E
Tonumea i. Tonga 83 B2 20 25S 174 54W
Tooele Utah U.S.A. 90 D5 40 32N 112 18W
Toowoomba Australia 78 I4 27 35S 151 54E
Topeka Kansas U.S.A. 92 A1 39 02N 95 41W
Torbali Turkey 74 E2 38 07N 27 08E
Torbay England United Kingdom 68 H2 50 27N 3 30W
Tordesillas Spain 72 A3 41 30N 5 00W
Torhout Belgium 70 C3 51 04N 3 06E
Toride Japan 46 M2 35 54N 140 07E
Torino (Turin) Italy 74 A4 45 04N 7 40E
Tormes r. Spain 72 A3 41 03N 5 58W
Torne älv r. Sweden 69 E4 67 03N 23 02E
Torne-träsk l. Sweden 69 D4 68 14N 19 40E
Torngat Mountains Newfoundland/Québec Canada 89 W4 59 00N 64 15W
Tornio Finland 69 E4 65 50N 24 10E
Toronto Ontario Canada 93 E2 43 42N 79 46W
Tororo Uganda 110 F8 0 42N 34 12E
Toros Dağlari mts. Turkey 54 D6 37 10N 33 10E
Torquay England United Kingdom 73 A3 50 28N 3 30W
Torrance California U.S.A. 95 A2 33 50N 118 20W
Torre del Greco Italy 74 B3 40 46N 14 22E
Torrelavega Spain 72 B3 43 21N 4 03W
Torrens, Lake Australia 78 F3 31 00S 137 50E
Torreón Mexico 96 D5 25 34N 103 25W
Torres Islands Vanuatu 83 F8 13 20S 166 35E
Torres Strait Australia 78 G7/8 10 00S 142 30E
Torrington Connecticut U.S.A. 93 F2 41 48N 73 08W
Tortosa Spain 72 C3 40 49N 0 31E
Toruń Poland 75 C3 53 01N 18 35E
Tosa-wan b. Japan 46 B1 33 20N 133 40E
Toshima Japan 47 B3 35 43N 139 41E
Totoya i. Fiji 83 E8 18 56S 179 50W
Totsuka Japan 47 B2 35 23N 139 32E
Tottori Japan 46 B2 35 32N 134 12E
Toudao Jiang r. China 50 C6 42 20N 127 00E
Touggourt Algeria 112 G9 33 08N 6 04E
Touho New Caledonia 82 U3 20 45S 165 15E
Toul France 73 C2 48 41N 5 54E
Tou-liu Taiwan 51 G6 23 42N 120 32E
Toulon France 73 C1 43 07N 5 55E
Toulouse France 73 B1 43 33N 1 24E
Toungoo Myanmar 38 B3 18 57N 96 26E
Tourakom Laos 37 B3 18 25N 102 31E
Tourcoing France 73 B3 50 44N 310E
Tournai Belgium 70 C2 50 36N 3 24E
Tours France 73 B2 47 23N 0 42E
Tovu Fiji 83 E8 18 59S 179 48W
Tower Hamlets England United Kingdom 66 C3 51 30N 0 02W
Town Creek Norfolk Island 81 L4 29 03S 167 57E
Townsville Australia 78 H6 19 13S 146 48E
Toyama Japan 46 C2 36 42N 137 14E
Toyoake Japan 46 H2 35 02N 136 55E
Toyohashi Japan 46 J1 34 46N 137 22E
Toyokawa Japan 46 J1 34 47N 137 24E
Toyonaka Japan 46 G1 34 48N 135 35E
Toyooka Japan 46 F2 35 35N 134 48E
Toyota Japan 46 J2 35 05N 137 09E
Tozeur Tunisia 112 G9 33 55N 8 07E
Trâblous (Tripoli) Lebanon 54 O12 34 27N 35 50E
Trabzona Turkey 54 E7 41 00N 39 43E
Tracy Québec Canada 93 F3 45 59N 73 04W
Trail British Columbia Canada 88 L2 49 04N 111 39W
Tralee Irish Republic 68 B4 52 16N 9 42W
Trang Thailand 39 A1 7 30N 98 33E
Trang r. Thailand 39 A1 8 00N 99 30E
Tranninh see Xiangkhoang Plateau
Transantarctic Mountains Antarctica 21
Transvaal province Republic of South Africa 111 E3/F3 24 30S 28 00E
Trápani Italy 74 B2 38 02N 12 32E
Trapeang Veng Cambodia 37 B2 13 50N 105 58E
Trat Thailand 39 B2 12 16N 102 30E
Traunstein Germany 71 B1 47 52N 12 39E
Traverse City Michigan U.S.A. 92 C2 44 46N 85 38W
Travers, Mount South Island New Zealand 79 B2 42 01S 172 44E
Tra Vinh Vietnam 37 C1 9 57N 106 20E
Treasury Islands Solomon Islands 82 A6 7 20S 155 30E
Treinta-y-Tres Uruguay 103 G6 33 16S 54 17W
Trelew Chile 103 D4 43 13S 65 15W
Templinersee l. Germany 67 E1 52 21N 13 02E
Trencín Slovakia 75 C2 48 53N 18 00E
Treng Cambodia 37 B2 12 50N 102 57E
Trenque Lauquen Argentina 103 E5 35 56S 62 43W
Trent r. England United Kingdom 68 K5 53 10N 0 50W
Trento Italy 74 B4 46 04N 11 08E
Trenton Ontario Canada 93 E2 44 07N 77 34W
Trenton New Jersey U.S.A. 93 F2 40 15N 74 43W
Trepassey Newfoundland Canada 89 Y2 46 45N 53 20W
Treptow Germany 67 F1 52 29N 13 27E
Tres Arroyos Argentina 103 E5 38 26S 60 17W
Três Lagoas Brazil 102 G8 20 46S 51 43W
Trevanion i. Solomon Islands 82 L3 10 40S 165 40E
Treviso Italy 74 B4 45 40N 12 15E
Trichur India 53 D2 10 32N 76 14E
Trier Germany 71 A1 49 45N 6 39E
Trieste Italy 74 B4 45 39N 13 47E
Tríkkala Greece 74 D2 39 33N 21 46E
Trindade i. Atlantic Ocean 25 F4 20 30S 29 20W
Trinidad Bolivia 102 E10 14 46S 64 50W
Trinidad Cuba 97 H4 21 48N 80 00W
Trinidad Colorado U.S.A. 90 F4 37 11N 104 31W
Trinidad i. Trinidad and Tobago 97 L2 11 00N 61 30W
TRINIDAD AND TOBAGO 97 L2
Trinity r. U.S.A. 91 G3 32 00N 96 00W
Trinity Hills Trinidad and Tobago 96 T9 10 07N 61 07W
Trinity Islands Alaska U.S.A. 88 E4 56 45N 154 15W
Tripoli see Trâblous
Trípolis Greece 74 D2 37 31N 22 22E
Tripura Mizoram admin. India 53 G4 23 40N 92 30E
Tristan da Cunha i. Atlantic Ocean 25 G2 37 15S 12 30W
Trivandrum India 53 D1 8 30N 76 57E
Trnava Slovakia 75 C2 48 23N 17 35E
Trobriand Islands Papua New Guinea 45 O2 8 30S 151 00E
Troisdorf Germany 71 A2 50 49N 7 09E
Trois-Pistoles Québec Canada 93 G3 48 08N 69 10W
Trois-Rivières tn. Québec Canada 93 F3 46 21N 72 34W
Troitsk Russia 59 J5 54 08N 61 33E
Troitsko Pechorsk Russia 59 H7 62 40N 56 08E
Trollhätten Sweden 69 C2 58 17N 12 20E
Trollheimen mts. Norway 69 B3 63 00N 9 00E
Tromsø Norway 69 D4 69 42N 19 00E
Trondheim Norway 69 C3 63 36N 10 23E
Trondheimsfjorden fj. Norway 69 C3 63 40N 10 30E
Trout Lake Northwest Territories Canada 88 K5 61 00N 121 30W
Trouville France 73 B2 49 22N 0 05E
Troy Alabama U.S.A. 91 I3 31 49N 86 00W
Troy New York U.S.A. 93 F2 42 43N 73 43W
Troy hist. site Turkey 54 C6 39 55N 26 17E
Troyes France 73 B2 48 18N 4 05E
Truc Giang see Ban Tre
Trujillo Peru 102 B11 8 06S 79 00W
Trujillo Spain 72 A2 39 28N 5 53W
Trujillo Venezuela 102 C14 9 20N 70 38W
Truk Islands Caroline Islands 80 B4 7 30N 152 30E
Truro Nova Scotia Canada 89 W2 45 24N 63 18W
Truro England United Kingdom 68 F2 50 16N 5 03W
Truyère r. France 73 B1 44 55N 2 47E
Tsangpo see Yarlung Zangbo Jiang
Tsavo National Park Kenya 110 G7 3 30S 38 00E
Tselinograd see Akmola
Tseung Kwan O Hong Kong U.K. 51 C1 22 19N 114 14E
Tshane Botswana 111 D3 24 05S 21 54E
Tshuapa r. Zaïre 110 D7 1 00S 23 00E
Tsimlyanskoye Vodokhranilishche res. Russia 58 E4 47 30N 43 00E
Tsing Chau Tsai Hong Kong U.K. 51 B2 22 20N 114 02E
Tsing Yi Hong Kong U.K. 51 B2 22 21N 114 06E
Tsing Yi i. Hong Kong U.K. 51 B2 22 20N 114 00E
Tsin Shui Wan Hong Kong U.K. 51 C1 22 14N 114 12E
Tsu Japan 46 H1 34 41N 136 30E
Tsuchiura Japan 46 M3 36 05N 140 11E
Tsuen Wan Hong Kong U.K. 51 B2 22 22N 114 06E
Tsugaru-kaikyō sd. Japan 46 D4 41 30N 140 30E
Tsumeb Namibia 111 C4 19 13S 17 42E
Tsuna Japan 46 F1 34 26N 134 53E
Tsunashima Japan 47 B3 35 13N 139 38E
Tsuru Japan 46 K2 35 36N 138 54E
Tsuruga Japan 46 C2 35 40N 136 05E
Tsurugi-zaki Japan 46 L2 35 08N 139 37E
Tsuruoka Japan 46 C2 38 42N 139 50E
Tsushima Japan 46 H2 35 11N 136 45E
Tsushima i. Japan 46 A1 34 30N 129 20E
Tsuyama Japan 46 B2 35 04N 134 01E
Tsz Wan Shan Hong Kong U.K. 51 C2 22 21N 114 12E
Tua r. Papua New Guinea 45 L3 6 30S 144 30E
Tua r. Portugal 72 A3 41 20N 7 30W
Tual Indonesia 43 H2 5 38S 132 40E
Tuamotu Archipelago is. Pacific Ocean 81 E3 15 00S 145 00W
Tuamotu Ridge Pacific Ocean 23 L6 19 00S 144 00W
Tuan Giao Vietnam 37 B4 21 35N 103 25E
Tuas Singapore 41 A3 1 19N 103 40E
Tuasivi Western Samoa 82 A11 13 38S 172 08W
Tuba r. Russia 59 P5 54 00N 94 00E
Tuban Indonesia 42 Q7 6 55S 112 01E
Tubbataha Reefs The Philippines 40 A2 9 00N 120 00E
Tübingen Germany 71 A1 48 32N 9 04E
Tubize Belgium 70 D2 50 42N 4 12E
Tubou Fiji 83 F8 18 13S 178 49W
Tubruq Libya 110 D14 32 05N 23 59E
Tubuai i. Pacific Ocean 81 E2 23 23S 149 27W
Tubuai Islands Pacific Ocean 81 E2 23 23S 149 27W
Tucheng Taiwan 51 H7 24 52N 121 49E
Tuchitua Yukon Territory Canada 88 J5 61 20N 129 00W
Tucson Arizona U.S.A. 90 D3 32 15N 110 57W
Tucumcari New Mexico U.S.A. 90 F4 35 11N 103 44W
Tucupita Venezuela 102 E14 9 02N 62 04W
Tucuruí Brazil 102 H12 3 42S 49 44W
Tudela Spain 72 B3 42 04N 1 37W
Tuen Mun Hong Kong U.K. 51 A2 22 23N 113 57E
Tufi Papua New Guinea 45 N2 9 08S 149 20E
Tugaske Sasketchewan Canada 88 N3 50 54N 106 15W
Tuguegarao The Philippines 40 B4 17 36N 121 44E
Tujunga California U.S.A. 95 B3 34 14N 118 16W
Tuktoyaktuk Northwest Territories Canada 88 I6 69 24N 133 01W
Tukums Latvia 69 E2 56 58N 23 10E
Tula American Samoa 82 E12 14 15S 170 35W
Tula Hidalgo Mexico 96 E4 20 01N 99 21W
Tula Tamaulipas Mexico 96 E4 23 00N 99 41W
Tula Russia 56 F6 54 11N 37 38E
Tulaghi Solomon Islands 82 F4 9 03S 160 10E
Tulcán Ecuador 102 B13 0 50N 77 48W
Tulcea Romania 75 E2 45 10N 28 50E
Tuleki i. Solomon Islands 83 N4 9 50S 167 05E
Tulkarm Jordan 54 O11 32 19N 35 02E
Tullamore Irish Republic 68 D5 53 16N 7 30W
Tulle France 73 B2 45 16N 1 46E
Tuloma r. Russia 69 G4 69 00N 32 00E
Tulsa Oklahoma U.S.A. 91 G4 36 07N 95 58W
Tuluá Colombia 102 B13 4 05N 76 12W
Tulun Russia 57 M6 54 32N 100 35E
Tulungagung Indonesia 42 P6 8 10S 111 48E
Tulun Islands (Carteret Islands) Papua New Guinea 45 Q4 4 40S 155 30E
Tumaco Colombia 102 B13 1 51N 78 46W
Tumen (Tuman) r. China 50 D6 42 00N 129 00E
Tumbes Peru 102 A12 3 37S 80 27W
Tumen China 50 D6 421 56N 129 47E
Tumkur India 53 D2 13 20N 77 06E
Tumpat Malaysia 39 B1 6 02N 102 10E
Tunapuna Trinidad and Tobago 96 T10 10 38N 61 23W
Tunduru Tanzania 111 G5 11 08S 27 21E
Tundzha r. Bulgaria 74 E3 42 00N 25 00E
Tungabhadra r. India 53 D3 16 00N 77 00E
Tung-chiang Taiwan 51 G5 22 26N 120 30E
Tung Lung Chau l. Hong Kong U.K. 51 C1 22 15N 114 17E
Tungsten Northwest Territories Canada 88 J5 62 25N 128 40W
Tungua i. Tonga 83 B2 20 00S 174 45W
Tunis Tunisia 112 H10 36 50N 10 13E
TUNISIA 112 G9/H9
Tunja Colombia 102 C14 5 33N 73 23W
Tunnsjøen l. Norway 69 C3 64 45N 13 25E
Tuong Duong Vietnam 37 B3 19 14N 104 34E
Tupelo Mississippi U.S.A. 91 I3 34 15N 88 43W
Tupiza Bolivia 102 D8 21 27S 65 45W
Tupper Lake tn. New York U.S.A. 93 F2 44 14N 74 29W
Túquerres Colombia 102 B13 1 06N 77 37W
Tura Russia 57 M8 64 20N 100 17E
Tura r. Russia 59 J6 58 00N 63 00E
Turda Romania 75 D2 46 35N 23 50E
Turfan see Turpan
Turfan Depression China 48 G7 42 40N 89 30E
Turgay r. Kazakhstan 59 J4 50 00N 64 00E
Turgutlu Turkey 74 E2 38 30N 27 43E
Turia r. Spain 72 B2 39 45N 0 55W
Turin see Torino
Turkana, Lake Ethiopia/Kenya 110 G8 4 00N 36 00E
Turkestan Kazakhstan 59 K3 43 17N 68 16E
TURKEY 54 D6
TURKMENISTAN 59 H3/J2

Vijosë *r.* Albania **74** D3 40 30N 20 00E
Vikna *I.* Norway **69** C3 64 55N 10 55E
Vilaine *r.* France **73** A2 47 50N 1 50W
Vila Nova de Gaia Portugal **72** A3 41 08N 8 37W
Vila Pedro Brazil **103** P2 22 49S 43 20W
Vila Real Portugal **72** A3 41 17N 7 45W
Vila Velha Brazil **102** I8 20 23S 40 18W
Vilhelmina Sweden **69** D3 64 38N 16 40E
Vilhena Brazil **102** E10 12 40S 60 08W
Villa Constitución Mexico **96** B5 25 05N 111 45W
Villahermosa Mexico **96** F3 18 00N 92 53W
Villalba Spain **72** A3 43 17N 7 41W
Villa María Argentina **103** E6 32 25S 63 15W
Villa Montes Bolivia **102** E8 21 15S 63 30W
Villanueva Mexico **96** D4 22 24N 102 53W
Villaricca Chile **103** C5 39 15S 72 15W
Villarrobledo Spain **72** B2 39 16N 2 36W
Villa Unión Argentina **103** D7 29 27S 62 46W
Villa Unión Mexico **96** C4 23 10N 106 12W
Villavicencio Colombia **102** C13 4 09N 73 38W
Villefranche-sur-Saône France **73** B2 46 00N 4 43E
Villejuif France **67** B2 48 47N 2 23E
Villeneuve d'Ascq France **70** C2 50 37N 3 10E
Villeneuve St. Georges France **67** B1 48 43N 2 27E
Villeneuve-sur-Lot France **73** B1 44 25N 0 43E
Villeparisis France **67** C2 48 56N 2 37E
Villeurbanne France **73** B2 45 46N 4 54E
Villingen-Schwenningen Germany **71** A1 48 03N 8 28E
Vilnius Lithuania **69** F1 54 40N 25 19E
Vilnya *r.* Lithuania **69** F1 54 00N 25 00E
Vils *r.* Germany **71** B1 48 00N 12 00E
Vilvoorde Belgium **70** D2 50 56N 4 25E
Vilyuy *r.* Russia **57** O8 64 00N 123 00E
Vilyuysk Russia **57** O8 63 46N 121 35E
Viña del Mar Chile **103** C6 33 02S 71 35W
Vinaroz Spain **72** C3 40 29N 0 28E
Vincennes France **67** B2 48 51N 2 27E
Vincennes Indiana U.S.A. **92** C1 38 42N 87 30W
Vincent, Point Norfolk Island **81** J6 28 59S 167 55E
Vindelälven *r.* Sweden **69** D4 65 15N 18 15E
Vindhya Range *mts.* India **53** C4 23 00N 75 00E
Vineland New Jersey U.S.A. **93** E1 39 29N 75 02W
Vinh Vietnam **37** C3 18 42N 105 41E
Vinh Giat Vietnam **37** C2 12 41N 109 20E
Vinh Linh Vietnam **37** C3 17 04N 107 00E
Vinh Loi *see* Bac Lieu
Vinh Long Vietnam **37** C2 10 15N 105 59E
Vinh Yen Vietnam **37** C4 21 18N 105 36E
Vinkovci Croatia **74** C4 45 16N 18 49E
Vinnitsa Ukraine **58** B4 49 11N 28 30E
Vinson Massif *mts.* Antarctica **21** 78 02S 22 00W
Vipiteno Italy **74** B4 46 54N 11 27E
Viqueque Indonesia **44** B2 9 00S 125 30E
Virac The Philippines **40** B3 13 35N 124 14E
Virache *(Vœune Sai)* Cambodia **37** C2 13 59N 106 48E
Virgin *r.* U.S.A. **90** D4 37 00N 114 00W
Virginia Minnesota U.S.A. **92** B3 47 30N 92 28W
Virginia *state* U.S.A. **91** K4 38 00N 77 00W
Virginia Beach *tn.* Virginia U.S.A. **91** K4 36 51N 75 59W
Virgin Islands West Indies **97** L3 18 00N 64 30W
Viroqua Wisconsin U.S.A. **92** B2 43 33N 90 54W
Virovitica Croatia **74** C4 45 50N 17 25E
Virton Belgium **70** E1 49 34N 5 32E
Vis *i.* Croatia **74** C3 43 00N 16 00E
Visalia California U.S.A. **90** C4 36 20N 119 18W
Visayan Sea The Philippines **40** B3 11 00N 123 00E
Visby Sweden **69** D2 57 32N 18 15E
Viscount Melville Sound Northwest Territories Canada **89** P7 74 10N 105 00W
Viseu Portugal **72** A3 40 40N 7 55W
Vishakhapatnam India **53** E3 17 42N 83 24E
Visoqo Fiji **83** D10 16 12S 179 41E
Vitebsk Belarus **75** F4 55 10N 30 14E
Viterbo Italy **74** B3 42 24N 12 06E
Vi Thanh Vietnam **37** C1 9 47N 105 26E
Vitichi Bolivia **102** D8 20 14S 65 22W
Viti Levu *i.* Fiji **83** B9/C9 17 30S 178 00E
Viti Levu Bay Fiji **83** C9 17 25S 178 15E
Vitim Russia **57** N7 59 28N 112 35E
Vitim *r.* Russia **57** N7 58 00N 113 00E
Vitória Brazil **102** I8 20 20S 40 18W
Vitoria Spain **72** B3 42 51N 2 40W
Vitória da Conquista Brazil **102** I10 14 53S 40 52W
Vitry-le-François France **73** B2 48 44N 4 36E
Vitry-sur-Seine France **67** B2 48 47N 2 24E
Vityaz Trench Pacific Ocean **22** G7 9 30S 170 00E
Vivi *r.* Russia **57** L9 61 00N 96 00E
Viwa *i.* Fiji **83** A9 17 10S 176 45E
Vize *i.* Russia **57** J11 79 30N 77 00E
Vizianagaram India **53** E3 18 07N 83 30E
Vladikavkaz *(Ordzhonikidze)* Russia **56** G4 43 02N 44 43E
Vladimir Russia **56** G7 56 08N 40 25E
Vladivostok Russia **57** P4 43 09N 131 53E
Vlieland *i.* Netherlands **70** D5 53 16N 5 00E
Vlissingen Netherlands **70** C3 51 27N 3 35E
Vlorë Albania **74** C3 40 29N 19 29E
Vltava *r.* Czech Republic **75** B2 49 00N 14 00E
Vo Dat Vietnam **37** C2 11 08N 107 33E
Vœune Sai *see* Virache
Vogelkop *see* Doberai Peninsula
Vogelsberg *mts.* Germany **71** A2 50 00N 9 00E
Voh New Caledonia **82** T3 20 57S 164 44E
Voi Kenya **110** G7 3 23S 38 35E
Vokhma *r.* Russia **58** F6 58 00N 45 30E
Volendam Netherlands **70** E4 52 30N 5 04E
Volga *r.* Russia **56** G5/6 50 00N 45 00E
Volgodonsk Russia **56** G5 47 35N 42 08E
Volgograd Russia **56** G5 48 45N 44 30E
Volgogradskoye Vodokhranilishche *res.* Russia **58** E4 50 00N 45 30E
Volkhov *r.* Russia **58** C6 59 00N 31 30E
Volksrust Republic of South Africa **111** E2 27 22S 29 54E
Vologda Russia **56** F7 59 10N 39 55E
Vólos Greece **74** D2 39 22N 22 57E
Vol'sk Russia **58** F5 52 04N 47 22E
Volta, Lake Ghana **112** E4 7 30N 0 30W
Volta Redonda Brazil **103** I8 22 31S 44 05W
Volturno *r.* Italy **74** B3 41 00N 14 00E
Volzhskiy Russia **56** G5 48 48N 44 45E
Vomo *i.* Fiji **83** B9 17 30S 177 15E
Vona Vona *i.* Solomon Islands **82** C5 8 15S 157 05E
Voorburg Netherlands **70** D4 52 04N 4 22E
Voorst Netherlands **70** F4 52 10N 6 10E
Vopnafjördur Iceland **69** J7 65 46N 14 50W
Vorarlberg *admin.* Austria **71** A1 47 00N 10 00E
Vorderrhein *r.* Switzerland **73** C2 46 45N 9 15E
Vordingborg Denmark **71** B3 55 01N 11 55E
Voríai Sporadhes *is.* Greece **74** D2 39 00N 24 00E
Vorkuta Russia **57** I9 67 27N 64 00E
Vorna *r.* Russia **58** E5 52 00N 42 30E
Voronezh Russia **56** F6 51 40N 39 13E
Voroshilovgrad *see* Lugansk
Vørterkaka Nunatak *mt.* Antarctica **21** 71 45S 32 00E
Võrtsjärv *l.* Estonia **69** F2 58 15N 26 10E
Võru Estonia **69** F2 57 46N 26 52E
Vosges *mts.* France **73** C2 48 10N 6 50E
Voss Norway **69** B3 60 38N 6 25E
Vostochnyy Russia **57** P4 42 52N 132 56E
Vostok *r.s.* Antarctica **21** 78 27S 106 49E
Vostok Island Pacific Ocean **81** E3 10 05S 152 23W
Votkinsk Russia **59** G6 57 00N 54 00E
Votkinskoye Vodokhranilishche Russia **59** H6 57 00N 55 30E
Votua Fiji **83** C10 16 40S 178 42E
Vouga *r.* Portugal **72** A3 40 45N 8 15W
Vouziers France **70** D1 49 25N 4 41E
Voxnan Sweden **69** D3 61 22N 15 39E
Vrangelya *(Wrangel) i.* Russia **57** T10 61 30N 180 00
Vranje Serbia Yugoslavia **74** D3 42 33N 21 54E
Vratsa Bulgaria **74** D3 43 12N 23 32E
Vrbas *r.* Bosnia-Herzegovina **74** C3 44 00N 17 00E
Vršac Serbia Yugoslavia **74** D4 45 07N 21 19E
Vryburg Republic of South Africa **111** D2 26 57S 24 44E
Vuaqava *i.* Fiji **83** F8 18 52S 178 54W
Vught Netherlands **70** E3 51 40N 5 18E
Vukovar Croatia **74** C4 45 19N 19 01E
Vulavu Solomon Islands **82** E5 8 30S 159 50E
Vunadadir Papua New Guinea **45** P4 4 22S 152 15E
Vung Cam Ranh *b.* Vietnam **37** C2 11 45N 109 20E
Vung Da Nang *b.* Vietnam **37** C3 16 10N 108 30E
Vung Rach Gia *b.* Vietnam **37** B2 10 00N 105 55E
Vung Tau Vietnam **37** C2 10 21N 107 04E
Vunidawa Fiji **83** C9 17 50S 178 20E
Vunisea Fiji **83** C7 19 04S 178 10E
Vyatka *r.* Russia **56** G7 58 00N 50 00E
Vyaz'ma Russia **58** C6 55 12N 34 17E
Vyborg Russia **56** E8 60 45N 28 41E
Vychegda *r.* Russia **56** H8 62 00N 52 00E
Vyshniy-Volochek Russia **58** C6 57 34N 34 23E

W

Wa Ghana **112** E5 10 07N 2 28W
Waal *r.* Netherlands **70** E3 51 50N 5 07E
Waala New Caledonia **82** S4 19 45S 163 38E
Waalwijk Netherlands **70** E3 51 42N 5 04E
Wabag Papua New Guinea **45** K4 5 28S 143 40E
Wabana Newfoundland Canada **89** Y2 47 40N 52 58W
Wabao New Caledonia **82** W2 21 35S 167 58E
Wabash Indiana U.S.A. **92** C2 40 47N 85 48W
Wabash *r.* North America **91** I4 38 00N 87 30W
Wabowden Manitoba Canada **89** P3 54 57N 98 38W
Wabush Lake *tn.* Newfoundland Canada **89** V3 52 45N 66 50W
Waco Texas U.S.A. **91** G3 31 33N 97 10W
Wadayama Japan **46** F2 35 22N 134 49E
Waddeneilanden *(West Frisian Islands)* Netherlands **70** D5/E5 53 25N 5 15E
Waddenzee *sea* Netherlands **70** D5/E5 53 15N 5 15E
Waddington, Mount British Columbia Canada **88** J3 51 22N 125 14W
Wadi al Masīlah *r.* Yemen Republic **55** H2 16 00N 50 00E
Wadi Araba *r.* Israel **54** O10 30 30N 35 10E
Wadi el 'Arish *r.* Egypt **54** N9/10 30 05N 33 50E
Wâdi el Gafra Egypt **109** R2 30 16N 31 46E
Wadi Halfa Sudan **110** F12 21 55N 31 20E
Wad Medani Sudan **110** F10 14 24N 33 30E
Waesch, Mount Antarctica **21** 77 00S 127 30W
Waflia Indonesia **44** B5 3 11S 126 03E
Wagaru Myanmar **38** B3 15 59N 97 45E
Wageningen Netherlands **70** E3 51 58N 5 40E
Wager Bay Northwest Territories Canada **89** R6 66 00N 89 00W
Wagga Wagga Australia **78** H2 35 07S 147 24E
Wagin Australia **78** B3 33 20S 117 15E
Waglan Island Hong Kong U.K. **51** C1 22 10N 114 18E
Wah Pakistan **53** C6 33 50N 72 44E
Waha Libya **110** C13 28 10N 19 57E
Wahai Indonesia **43** G3 2 48S 129 29E
Wahiawa Hawaiian Islands **23** X18 21 35N 158 05W
Wahpeton North Dakota U.S.A. **92** A3 46 16N 96 36W
Waialua Hawaiian Islands **23** X18 21 35N 158 08W
Waibeem Irian Jaya Indonesia **44** E6 0 29S 132 59E
Waihi North Island New Zealand **79** C3 37 57S 175 44E
Waikaremoana, Lake North Island New Zealand **79** C3 38 46S 177 06E
Waikato *r.* North Island New Zealand **79** C3 37 25S 174 45E
Waikelo Indonesia **42** E2 9 30S 119 50E
Wailagi Lala *i.* Fiji **83** E10 16 45S 179 11W
Wailuku Hawaiian Islands **23** Y18 20 54N 156 30W
Waimate South Island New Zealand **79** B2 44 44S 171 03E
Waingapu Indonesia **43** F2 9 40S 120 16E
Wainunu Bay Fiji **83** C10 16 56S 178 53E
Wainwright Alberta Canada **88** M3 52 49N 110 52W
Wainwright Alaska U.S.A. **88** D7 70 39N 160 10W
Waipawa North Island New Zealand **79** C3 39 57S 176 35E
Wairiki Fiji **83** D10 16 50S 180 00
Wairoa North Island New Zealand **79** C3 39 03S 177 25E
Waitaki *r.* South Island New Zealand **79** B2 44 45S 170 30E
Waitara North Island New Zealand **79** B3 39 00S 174 14E
Wajima Japan **46** C2 37 23N 136 53E
Wajir Kenya **110** H8 1 46N 40 05E
Wakasa-wan *b.* Japan **46** C2 35 40N 135 30E
Wakatipu, Lake South Island New Zealand **79** A1 45 06S 168 31E
Wakaya Fiji **83** D9 17 39S 179 01E
Wakayama Japan **46** G1 34 12N 135 10E
Wakefield Rhode Island U.S.A. **93** F2 41 26N 71 30W
Wake Island Pacific Ocean **80** C4 19 18N 166 36E
Wakkanai Japan **46** D4 45 26N 141 43E
Wako Japan **47** B4 35 46N 139 37E
Waku Papua New Guinea **45** N3 6 09S 149 05E
Wakunai Papua New Guinea **45** Q4 5 52S 155 10E
Walaha Vanuatu **83** G6 15 24S 167 42E
Wałbrzych Poland **75** C3 50 48N 16 19E
Walcheren *i.* Netherlands **70** C3 51 30N 3 30E
Waldorf Maryland U.S.A. **93** E1 38 38N 76 56W
Wales United Kingdom **68** G4
Wales Alaska U.S.A. **88** B6 65 38N 168 09W
Walingai Papua New Guinea **45** M3 6 17S 147 43E
Walker Lake Nevada U.S.A. **90** C4 38 40N 118 43W
Walkerton Ontario Canada **93** D2 44 08N 81 10W
Wallaceburg Ontario Canada **93** D2 42 34N 82 22W
Wallaroo Australia **78** F3 33 57S 137 36E
Walla Walla Washington U.S.A. **90** C6 46 05N 118 18W
WALLIS AND FUTUNA *is.* Pacific Ocean **80** D3 13 00S 177 00E
Walsall England United Kingdom **68** J4 52 35N 1 58W
Walsenburg Colorado U.S.A. **90** F4 37 36N 104 48W
Waltham Forest *bor.* England United Kingdom **66** C3 51 36N 0 00
Walthamstow England United Kingdom **66** C3 51 34N 0 01W
Walton-on-Thames England United Kingdom **66** B2 51 24N 0 25W
Walvis Bay *tn.* Namibia **111** B3 22 59S 14 31E
Walvis Ridge Atlantic Ocean **25** I3/4 30 00S 3 00E
Wamba *r.* Zaire **111** C6 6 30S 17 30E
Wamena Irian Jaya Indonesia **44** H5 3 50S 138 38E
Wamlana Indonesia **43** G3 3 05S 126 31E
Wamma *r.* Irian Jaya Indonesia **44** F5 3 15S 134 45E
Wamulan Indonesia **44** B5 3 37S 126 13E
Wanaka, Lake South Island New Zealand **79** A2 44 28S 169 09E
Wanapiri Irian Jaya Indonesia **44** F4 4 29S 135 42E
Wando South Korea **50** C2 34 22N 126 40E
Wandsworth *bor.* England United Kingdom **66** C2 51 27N 0 11W
Wanganui North Island New Zealand **79** C3 39 56S 175 03E
Wanganui *r.* North Island New Zealand **79** C3 39 30S 175 00E
Wang Chau *i.* Hong Kong U.K. **51** C1 22 20N 114 22E
Wangerooge *i.* Germany **71** A2 53 47N 7 54E
Wang Saphung Thailand **39** B3 17 22N 101 41E
Wang Toi Shan Hong Kong U.K. **51** B2 22 26N 114 05E
Wan Hsa-la Myanmar **38** B4 20 26N 98 40E
Wanon Niwat Thailand **39** B3 17 38N 103 50E
Wansee Germany **67** E1 52 24N 13 09E
Wanstead England United Kingdom **66** D3 51 34N 0 02E
Wanxian China **49** L5 30 54N 108 20E
Waparen Indonesia **44** B5 3 10S 126 59E
Wapotin Indonesia **44** B5 3 05S 126 41E
Warangal India **53** D3 18 00N 79 35E
Warburg Germany **71** A2 51 28N 9 10E
Wardha *r.* India **53** D4 20 30N 79 00E
Ward Hunt, Cape Papua New Guinea **45** N2 8 04S 148 08E
Waregem Belgium **70** C2 50 53N 3 26E
Waremme Belgium **70** E2 50 42N 5 15E
Waren Germany **71** B2 53 32N 12 42E
Waren Irian Jaya Indonesia **44** G5 2 13S 136 24E
Warendorf Germany **71** A2 51 57N 8 00E
Warin Chamrap Thailand **39** B3 15 11N 104 51E
Warmare Irian Jaya Indonesia **44** E6 0 53S 133 57E
Warnow *r.* Germany **71** B2 53 00N 12 00E
Warrego *r.* Australia **78** H4 27 30S 146 00E
Warren Michigan U.S.A. **93** D2 42 30N 83 02W
Warren Ohio U.S.A. **93** D2 41 15N 80 49W
Warren Pennsylvania U.S.A. **93** E2 41 52N 79 09W
Warrensburg Missouri U.S.A. **92** B1 38 46N 93 44W
Warrior Reefs Australia **45** K2 9 50S 143 10E
Warrnambool Australia **78** G2 38 23S 142 03E
Warroad Minnesota U.S.A. **92** A3 48 54N 95 20W
Warsaw *see* Warszawa
Warszawa *(Warsaw)* Poland **75** D3 52 15N 21 00E
Warta *r.* Poland **75** C3 52 00N 17 00E
Waru Indonesia **44** D5 3 26S 130 37E
Warwick Australia **78** I4 28 12S 152 00E
Warwick Rhode Island U.S.A. **93** F2 41 42N 71 23W
Wasaga Beach *tn.* Ontario Canada **93** D2 44 31N 80 02W
Washburn Wisconsin U.S.A. **92** B3 46 41N 90 53W
Washington Pennsylvania U.S.A. **93** D2 40 11N 80 16W
Washington *state* U.S.A. **90** B6 47 00N 120 00W
Washington D.C. District of Columbia U.S.A. **93** E1 38 55N 77 00W
Wash, The *b.* England United Kingdom **68** L4 52 55N 0 10E
Wasian Irian Jaya Indonesia **44** E6 1 51S 133 21E
Wasior Irian Jaya Indonesia **44** F5 2 38S 134 27E
Wasiri Indonesia **44** B3 7 36S 126 38E
Wasmes Belgium **70** C2 50 25N 3 51E
Wassenaar Netherlands **70** D4 52 07N 4 23E
Wasua Papua New Guinea **45** K2 8 18S 142 57E
Wasum Papua New Guinea **45** N3 6 03S 149 20E
Watam Papua New Guinea **45** L5 3 55S 144 30E
Watampone Indonesia **43** F3 4 33S 120 20E
Waterbury Connecticut U.S.A. **93** F2 41 33N 73 03W
Waterbury Vermont U.S.A. **93** F2 44 21N 72 46W
Waterfall *tn.* Australia **79** G1 34 08S 151 00E
Waterfall *tn.* Christmas Island **81** R2 10 28S 105 43E
Waterford Irish Republic **68** D4 52 15N 7 06W
Waterloo Belgium **70** D2 50 43N 4 24E
Waterloo Trinidad and Tobago **96** T9 10 28N 61 28W
Waterloo Iowa U.S.A. **92** B2 42 30N 92 20W
Waterton Lakes National Park Alberta Canada **90** D6 49 00N 114 00W
Watertown New York U.S.A. **93** E2 43 57N 75 56W
Watertown South Dakota U.S.A. **92** A2 44 54N 97 08W
Waterville Maine U.S.A. **93** G2 44 34N 69 41W
Watford England United Kingdom **66** B3 51 39N 0 24W
Watkins Glen New York U.S.A. **93** E2 42 23N 76 53W
Watseka Illinois U.S.A. **92** C2 40 46N 87 45W
Wat Sing Thailand **39** B3 15 18N 100 02E
Watson Lake *tn.* Yukon Territory Canada **88** J5 60 07N 128 49W
Watten France **70** B2 50 50N 2 13E
Wattrelos Belgium **70** C2 50 40N 3 14E
Wau Papua New Guinea **45** M3 7 22S 146 40E
Wau Sudan **110** E9 7 40N 28 04E
Waukegan Illinois U.S.A. **92** C2 42 21N 87 52W
Waukesha Wisconsin U.S.A. **92** C2 43 01N 88 14W
Wausau Wisconsin U.S.A. **92** C2 44 58N 89 40W
Wauwatosa Wisconsin U.S.A. **92** C2 43 04N 88 02W
Waveney *r.* England United Kingdom **68** M4 52 30N 1 30E
Wavre Belgium **70** D2 50 43N 4 37E
Wawa Ontario Canada **93** D3 48 04N 84 49W
Wawoi *r.* Papua New Guinea **45** K3 7 00S 142 30E
Waya *i.* Fiji **83** B9 17 19S 177 09E
Wayakuba Indonesia **44** B6 0 50S 127 48E
Wayao China **38** B5 25 29N 99 19E
Wayasewa *i.* Fiji **83** B9 17 20S 177 09E
Waycross Georgia U.S.A. **91** J3 31 12N 82 22W
Wayne New Jersey U.S.A. **94** A2 40 55N 74 15W
Waynesboro Virginia U.S.A. **93** E1 38 04N 78 54W
Wé New Caledonia **82** W3 20 55S 167 56E
Weald, The *geog. reg.* England United Kingdom **68** L3 51 05N 0 25E
Wear *r.* Durham England United Kingdom **68** J6 54 40N 1 50W
Webster City Iowa U.S.A. **92** B2 42 30N 93 50W
Weddell Island Falkland Islands **25** L16 51 55S 61 30W
Weddell Sea Southern Ocean **21** 71 00S 40 00W
Wedding Germany **67** F2 52 33N 13 21E
Weert Netherlands **70** E3 51 15N 5 42E
Weiden Germany **71** B1 49 40N 12 10E
Weifang China **49** N6 36 44N 119 10E
Wei He *r.* China **49** L5 34 00N 106 00E
Weimar Germany **71** B2 50 59N 11 20E
Weining China **38** C5 26 50N 104 22E
Weipa Australia **78** G7 12 35S 141 56E
Weissensee Germany **67** F2 51 12N 11 05E
Weishan China **38** C5 25 15N 100 20E
Weisse Elster *r.* Germany **71** B2 51 00N 12 00E
Weissenfels Germany **71** B2 51 12N 11 58E
Weisswasser *tn.* Germany **71** B2 51 31N 14 38E
Weixi China **38** B5 27 19N 99 20E
Weiyuang Jiang *r.* China **38** C4 23 45N 100 50E
Weizhou Dao *i.* China **37** C4 21 00N 109 01E
Wejherowo Poland **75** C3 54 36N 18 12E
Welland Ontario Canada **93** E2 45 59N 79 14W
Welland *r.* England United Kingdom **68** K4 52 50N 0 00
Wellesley Islands Australia **78** F6 16 30S 139 00E
Wellington Kansas U.S.A. **91** G4 37 17N 97 25W
Wellington North Island New Zealand **79** B2 41 17S 174 46E
Wellsboro Pennsylvania U.S.A. **93** E2 41 45N 77 18W
Wellsford North Island New Zealand **79** B3 36 18S 174 31E
Wels Austria **75** B2 48 10N 14 02E
Wembley England United Kingdom **66** B3 51 33N 0 18W
Wendesi Irian Jaya Indonesia **44** F5 2 33S 134 17E
Wenshan China **37** B4 23 22N 104 20E
Wensum *r.* England United Kingdom **68** M4 52 45N 1 10E
Wenyu He *r.* China **47** H2 40 02N 116 32E
Wenzhou China **49** O4 28 02N 120 40E
Werder Germany **67** D1 52 23N 12 56E
Weri Irian Jaya Indonesia **44** E5 3 15S 132 30E
Wernigerode Germany **71** B2 51 51N 10 48E
Werra *r.* Germany **71** B2 51 00N 10 00E
Wertach *r.* Germany **71** B1 48 00N 10 00E
Wesel Germany **71** A2 51 39N 6 37E
Weser *est.* Germany **71** A2 53 00N 8 00E
Weser *r.* Germany **71** A2 53 00N 8 00E
Wessel, Cape Australia **44** G1 11 01S 136 46E
Wessel Islands Australia **44** G1 11 28S 136 29E
West Allis Wisconsin U.S.A. **92** C2 43 01N 88 00W
West Antarctica *geog. reg.* Antarctica **21** 80 00S 120 00W
West Australian Basin Indian Ocean **24** I4/J5 20 00S 100 00E
West Bank *territory* Israel **54** O11 32 00N 35 00E
West Bengal *admin.* India **53** F4 22 00N 88 00E
Westbourne Manitoba Canada **92** A4 50 08N 98 33W
Westbrook *tn.* Maine U.S.A. **93** F2 43 41N 70 22W
West Caroline Basin Pacific Ocean **22** D8 3 00N 136 00E
West Chester Pennsylvania U.S.A. **93** E1 39 58N 75 37W
West Covina California U.S.A. **95** C3 34 04N 117 56W
West End Point Phillip Island **81** K1 29 07S 167 56E
Westerland Germany **71** A2 54 54N 8 19E
Western Australia *state* Australia **78** A5/D3 25 00S 117 00E
Western Ghats *mts.* India **53** C2/3 15 30N 74 00E
WESTERN SAHARA **112** C7/8
WESTERN SAMOA **80** D3
Western Sayan *mts.* Russia **57** L6 52 30N 92 30E
Western Yamuna Canal India **52** L4 28 40N 77 08E
Westerschelde *sd.* Netherlands **70** C3 51 20N 3 45E
Westerwald *geog. reg.* Germany **71** A2 50 00N 8 00E
West European Basin Atlantic Ocean **25** G11 47 00N 18 00W
West Falkland *i.* Falkland Islands **25** L16 51 00S 60 40W
Westfield Massachusetts U.S.A. **93** F2 42 07N 72 45W
West Fork White River Indiana U.S.A. **92** C1 39 00N 87 00W
West Frisian Islands *see* Waddeneilanden
West Ham England United Kingdom **66** D3 51 32N 0 01E
West Ice Shelf Antarctica **21** 66 00S 85 00E
West Indies *is.* Caribbean Sea **97** J4/K4 22 00N 69 00W
West Kingsdown England United Kingdom **66** D2 51 20N 0 16E
West Lamma Channel Hong Kong U.K. **51** B1 22 10N 114 00E
West Los Angeles California U.S.A. **95** A3 34 02N 118 25W
West Marianas Basin Pacific Ocean **22** D9 16 00N 137 30E
West Memphis Arkansas U.S.A. **91** H4 35 09N 90 11W
Westminster California U.S.A. **95** C2 33 45N 117 59W
Westminster *bor.* England United Kingdom **66** C2 51 30N 0 09W
Weston West Virginia U.S.A. **93** D1 39 03N 80 28W
West Palm Beach *tn.* Florida U.S.A. **91** J2 26 42N 80 05W
West Plains *tn.* Missouri U.S.A. **92** B1 36 44N 91 51W
Westport Irish Republic **68** B5 53 48N 9 32W
Westport Connecticut U.S.A. **93** F2 41 09N 73 22W
Westray *i.* Scotland United Kingdom **68** I11 59 18N 3 00W
West Rift Valley Africa **104** 0 00 30 00E
West Siberian Lowland Russia **57** J7/J8 60 00N 75 00E
West Terschelling Netherlands **70** E5 53 22N 5 13E
West Virginia *state* U.S.A. **93** D1 39 00N 81 00W
West-Vlaanderen *admin.* Belgium **70** B3 51 10N 3 00E
Wetaskiwin Alberta Canada **88** M3 52 57N 113 20W
Wetzlar Germany **71** A2 50 33N 8 30E
Wevelgem Belgium **70** C2 50 48N 3 12E
Wewak Papua New Guinea **45** K5 3 35S 143 35E
Wexford Irish Republic **68** E4 52 20N 6 27W
Wey *r.* England United Kingdom **66** B2 51 18N 0 30W
Weybridge England United Kingdom **66** B2 51 22N 0 28W
Weyburn Saskatchewan Canada **88** O2 49 39N 103 51W

150

Weymouth England United Kingdom 68 I2 50 37N 2 25W
Weymouth Massachusetts U.S.A. 93 F2 42 14N 70 58W
Whakatane North Island New Zealand 79 C3 37 58S 176 59E
Whangarei North Island New Zealand 79 B3 35 43S 174 19E
Wharfe r. England United Kingdom 68 J5 53 50N 1 50W
Wharton Basin Indian Ocean 24 I5/J5 15 00S 100 00E
Wharton Hill Christmas Island 81 Q1 10 31S 105 39E
Wheaton Minnesota U.S.A. 92 A3 45 49N 96 30W
Wheeler Lake Alabama U.S.A. 91 I3 34 00N 87 00W
Wheeling West Virginia U.S.A. 93 D2 40 05N 80 43W
Whitby Ontario Canada 93 E2 43 52N 78 56W
White r. U.S.A. 91 H4 35 00N 92 00W
White Bay Newfoundland Canada 89 X3 50 30N 55 15W
Whitecourt Alberta Canada 88 L3 54 10N 115 38W
Whitehaven England United Kingdom 68 H6 54 33N 3 35W
Whitehorse Yukon Territory Canada 88 H5 60 41N 135 08W
Whiteland Indiana U.S.A. 92 C1 39 32N 86 05W
Whiteman Range Papua New Guinea 45 N4 5 45S 149 45E
White Mountains New Hampshire U.S.A. 93 F2 44 00N 72 00W
White Nile see Bahr el Abiad
White Nile Dam Sudan 110 F11 14 18N 32 20E
White River tn. Ontario Canada 92 C3 48 35N 85 16W
White Sea Russia 56 F9 66 00N 37 30E
White Volta r. Ghana 112 E4/5 9 30N 1 30W
Whitney Ontario Canada 93 E3 45 29N 78 15W
Whitney, Mount California U.S.A. 90 C4 36 35N 118 17W
Whittier California U.S.A. 95 B2 33 58N 118 02W
Whyalla Australia 78 F3 33 04S 137 34E
Wiang Chai Thailand 39 A3 19 56N 99 58E
Wiarton Ontario Canada 93 D2 44 44N 81 10W
Wichita Kansas U.S.A. 91 G4 37 43N 97 20W
Wichita r. Texas U.S.A. 90 F3 33 00N 100 00W
Wichita Falls tn. Texas U.S.A. 90 G3 33 55N 98 30W
Wick Scotland United Kingdom 68 H10 58 26N 3 06W
Wicklow Mountains Irish Republic 68 E5 53 00N 6 20W
Wide Bay Papua New Guinea 45 P4 5 15S 152 00E
Wien (Vienna) Austria 75 C2 48 13N 16 22E
Wiener Neustadt Austria 75 C2 47 49N 16 15E
Wieprz r. Poland 75 D3 51 00N 23 00E
Wierden Netherlands 70 F4 52 21N 6 35E
Wiesbaden Germany 71 A2 50 05N 8 15E
Wigan England United Kingdom 68 I5 53 33N 2 38W
Wijchen Netherlands 70 E3 51 48N 5 44E
Wil Switzerland 73 C2 47 28N 9 03E
Wildau Germany 67 G1 52 18N 13 38E
Wilhelm II Land geog. reg. Antarctica 21 70 00S 90 00E
Wilhelm, Mount Papua New Guinea 45 L4 5 46S 144 59E
Wilhelm-Pieck-Stadt-Guben Germany 71 B2 51 59N 14 42E
Wilhelmshaven Germany 71 A2 53 32N 8 07E
Wilkes-Barre Pennsylvania U.S.A. 93 E2 41 15N 75 50W
Wilkes Land geog. reg. Antarctica 21 68 00S 105 00E
Willemstad Curaçao 97 K2 12 12N 68 56W
Willerbroek Belgium 70 D3 51 04N 4 22E
Willesden England United Kingdom 66 C3 51 33N 0 14W
Williamsburg Virginia U.S.A. 93 E1 37 17N 79 43W
Williams Lake tn. British Columbia Canada 88 K3 52 08N 122 09W
Williamson West Virginia U.S.A. 93 D1 37 42N 82 16W
Williamsport Pennsylvania U.S.A. 93 E2 41 16N 77 03W
Williamstown Kentucky U.S.A. 93 D1 38 39N 84 32W
Williston North Dakota U.S.A. 90 F6 48 09N 103 39W
Williston Lake British Columbia Canada 88 K4 56 00N 124 00W
Willmar Minnesota U.S.A. 92 A3 45 06N 95 03W
Willow Springs tn. Missouri U.S.A. 92 B1 36 59N 91 59W
Wilmersdörf Germany 67 F1 52 28N 13 16E
Wilmington Delaware U.S.A. 93 E1 39 46N 75 31W
Wilmington North Carolina U.S.A. 91 K3 34 14N 77 55W
Wilson North Carolina U.S.A. 91 K4 35 43N 77 56W
Wilson Strait Solomon Islands 82 B6 7 50S 156 30E
Wiluna Australia 78 C4 26 37S 120 12E
Wimbledon England United Kingdom 66 C2 51 25N 0 13W
Wimereux France 70 A2 50 46N 1 37E
Winchester England United Kingdom 68 J3 51 04N 1 19W
Winchester Virginia U.S.A. 91 K4 39 11N 78 12W
Windhoek Namibia 111 C3 22 34S 17 06E
Wind River Range mts. Wyoming U.S.A. 90 E5 43 00N 109 00W
Windsor England United Kingdom 66 A2 51 29N 0 38W
Windsor Ontario Canada 93 D2 42 18N 83 00W
Windward Islands Lesser Antilles 97 L2 12 30N 62 00W
Windward Passage Cuba/Haiti 97 J3/J4 20 00N 73 00W
Wingham Ontario Canada 93 D2 43 45N 81 19W
Winisk Lake Ontario Canada 89 R3 52 30N 87 30W
Winisk River Ontario Canada 89 R4 54 50N 87 00W
Winkler Manitoba Canada 92 A3 49 12N 97 55W
Winnebago, Lake Wisconsin U.S.A. 92 C2 44 00N 88 00W
Winnemucca Nevada U.S.A. 90 C5 40 58N 117 45W
Winnipeg Manitoba Canada 92 A3 49 53N 97 10W
Winnipeg, Lake Manitoba Canada 89 P3 52 30N 97 30W
Winnipegosis, Lake Manitoba Canada 89 O3 52 10N 100 00W
Winnipesaukee, Lake New Hampshire U.S.A. 93 F2 43 00N 72 00W
Winona Minnesota U.S.A. 92 B2 44 02N 91 37W
Winschoten Netherlands 70 G5 53 07N 7 02E
Winslow Arizona U.S.A. 90 D4 35 01N 110 43W
Winston-Salem North Carolina U.S.A. 91 J4 36 05N 80 18W
Winterswijk Netherlands 70 F3 51 58N 6 44E
Winterthur Switzerland 73 C2 47 30N 8 45E
Winton Australia 78 G5 22 22S 143 00E
Wirmaf Indonesia 44 D4 4 45S 131 45E
Wiscasset Maine U.S.A. 93 G2 44 01N 69 41W
Wisconsin r. Wisconsin U.S.A. 91 H5 45 00N 90 00W
Wisconsin state U.S.A. 92 B2/C3 45 00N 90 00W
Wisconsin Rapids tn. Wisconsin U.S.A. 92 C2 44 24N 89 50W
Wisła r. Poland 75 D3 53 00N 19 00E
Wisłok r. Poland 75 D3 50 00N 22 00E

Wismar Germany 71 B2 53 54N 11 28E
Wissembourg France 73 C2 49 02N 7 57E
Witham r. England United Kingdom 68 K5 53 05N 0 10W
Wittenberg Germany 71 B2 51 53N 12 39E
Wittenberge Germany 71 B2 52 59N 11 45E
Wittlich Germany 71 A1 49 59N 6 54E
Wittstock Germany 71 B2 53 10N 12 30E
Witu Islands Papua New Guinea 45 N4 4 45S 148 30E
Wlingi Indonesia 42 Q6 8 07S 112 12E
Włocławek Poland 75 C3 52 39N 19 01E
Woerden Netherlands 70 D4 52 05N 4 53E
Woitape Papua New Guinea 45 M2 8 30S 147 15E
Woking England United Kingdom 66 A2 51 20N 0 34W
Wolf-Bay tn. Québec Canada 89 W3 50 14N 60 40W
Wolfen Germany 71 B2 51 41N 12 17E
Wolfenbüttel Germany 71 B2 52 10N 10 33E
Wolfsberg Austria 75 B2 46 50N 14 50E
Wolfsburg Germany 71 B2 52 27N 10 49E
Wolin Poland 71 B2 53 51N 14 38E
Wollaston Lake Saskatchewan Canada 89 O4 58 20N 103 00W
Wollaston Lake tn. Saskatchewan Canada 89 O4 58 05N 103 38W
Wollongong Australia 78 I3 34 25S 150 52E
Wolverhampton England United Kingdom 68 I4 52 36N 2 08W
Wompah Australia 78 G4 29 04S 142 05E
Wong Chuk Hang Hong Kong U.K. 51 C1 22 15N 114 10E
Wong Chuk Yuen Hong Kong U.K. 51 B2 22 26N 114 06E
Wŏnju South Korea 50 C3 37 24N 127 52E
Wonogiri Indonesia 42 P7 7 38S 110 52E
Wonosobo Indonesia 42 O7 7 21S 109 56E
Wŏnsan North Korea 50 C4 39 07N 127 26E
Woodbridge New Jersey U.S.A. 94 A1 40 33N 74 16W
Wood Buffalo National Park Alberta Canada 88 M4 60 00N 113 00W
Woodford England United Kingdom 66 D3 51 37N 0 02E
Woodlands tn. Manitoba Canada 92 A3 50 12N 97 40W
Woodlands tn. Singapore 41 C5 1 26N 103 47E
Woodlark Island Papua New Guinea 45 P2 9 10S 152 50E
Woods, Lake of the Ontario Canada 92 B3 49 15N 94 45W
Woodstock New Brunswick Canada 89 V2 46 10N 67 36W
Woodstock Ontario Canada 93 D2 43 07N 80 46W
Woodstock Vermont U.S.A. 93 F2 43 37N 72 33W
Woodsville New Hampshire U.S.A. 93 F2 44 08N 72 02W
Woodville North Island New Zealand 79 C2 40 21S 175 52E
Woodward Oklahoma U.S.A. 90 G4 36 26N 99 25W
Wooi Indonesia 44 B6 1 40S 127 57E
Woollahra Australia 79 H2 33 53S 151 15E
Woolwich England United Kingdom 66 D2 51 29N 0 04E
Woonsocket Rhode Island U.S.A. 93 F2 42 00N 71 30W
Wooster Ohio U.S.A. 93 D2 40 46N 81 57W
Worcester Republic of South Africa 111 C1 33 39S 19 26E
Worcester England United Kingdom 68 I4 52 11N 2 13W
Worcester Massachusetts U.S.A. 93 F2 42 17N 71 48W
Workington England United Kingdom 68 H6 54 39N 3 33W
Worland Wyoming U.S.A. 90 E5 44 01N 107 58W
Wormhoudt France 70 B2 50 53N 2 28E
Worms Germany 71 A1 49 38N 8 23E
Woronora Reservoir Australia 79 F1 34 07S 150 56E
Woronora River Australia 79 G1 34 07S 151 00E
Worthing Barbados 96 V12 13 05N 59 35W
Worthing England United Kingdom 68 K2 50 48N 0 23W
Worthington Minnesota U.S.A. 92 A2 43 37N 95 36W
Wotu Indonesia 43 F3 2 34S 120 46E
Wounpouko Vanuatu 83 F7 14 50S 166 34E
Wousi Vanuatu 83 F6 15 20S 166 39E
Wrangell Alaska U.S.A. 88 I4 56 28N 132 23W
Wrangell Mountains Alaska U.S.A. 88 G5 62 00N 143 00W
Wrath, Cape Scotland United Kingdom 68 G10 58 37N 5 01W
Wrexham England United Kingdom 68 H5 53 03N 3 00W
Wright Peak Antarctica 21 73 15S 94 00W
Wright Point Christmas Island 81 R2 10 29S 105 42E
Wrigley Northwest Territories Canada 88 K5 63 16N 123 39W
Wrocław Poland 75 C3 51 05N 17 00E
Wuhai China 49 L6 39 40N 106 40E
Wuhan China 49 M5 30 35N 114 19E
Wuhu China 49 N5 31 23N 118 25E
Wukari Nigeria 112 G4 7 49N 9 49E
Wulian Geng mts. China 38 C5 28 00N 104 00E
Wuliang Shan mts. China 38 C4 24 00N 101 00E
Wuliaru i. Indonesia 44 D3 7 30S 131 00E
Wuluhan Indonesia 42 Q6 8 20S 113 30E
Wulur Indonesia 44 C3 7 09S 128 39E
Wumeng Shan mts. China 38 C5 26 20N 104 00E
Wuning Myanmar 38 B5 27 02N 98 25E
Wuntho Myanmar 38 A4 23 54N 95 41E
Wupper r. Germany 70 G3 51 00N 7 00E
Wuppertal Germany 71 A2 51 15N 7 10E
Wurno Nigeria 112 G5 13 18N 5 29E
Würtzburg Germany 71 A1 49 48N 9 57E
Wusul Jiang (Ussuri) r. China 49 Q8 47 00N 134 00E
Wutongqiao China 49 K4 29 21N 103 48E
Wuvulu Island Papua New Guinea 45 K6 1 44S 142 50E
Wuxi China 49 O5 31 35N 120 19E
Wuyi Shan mts. China 49 N4 26 00N 116 30E
Wuzhi Shan mts. China 37 C3 18 50N 109 45E
Wuzhou China 49 M3 23 30N 111 21E
Wye r. England United Kingdom 68 H4 51 58N 2 35W
Wyndham Australia 78 D6 15 30S 128 09E
Wyoming state U.S.A. 90 E5 43 00N 108 00W

X

Xaanfuun Somalia 110 J10 10 27N 51 15E
Xaidulla China 53 D7 36 27N 77 46E
Xaignabouri (Sayabouri) Laos 37 B3 19 18N 101 46E
Xam Nua Laos 37 B4 20 28N 104 05E
Xánthi Greece 74 D3 41 07N 24 56E
Xa Song Luy Vietnam 37 C2 11 12N 108 22E

Xe Bangfai r. Laos 37 C3 17 00N 105 10E
Xé Banghiang r. Laos 37 C3 16 15N 105 30E
Xé Don r. Laos 37 C3 15 50N 106 10E
Xé Kaman r. Laos 37 C3 15 00N 107 00E
Xé Kong r. Laos 37 C3 16 00N 107 00E
Xepenehe New Caledonia 82 W3 20 45S 167 10E
Xépôn Laos 37 C3 16 43N 106 20E
Xiaguan China 49 K4 25 33N 100 09E
Xiamen China 49 N3 24 28N 118 05E
Xi'an China 49 L5 34 16N 108 54E
Xiangfan China 49 M5 32 05N 112 03E
Xiangkhoang Laos 37 B3 19 23N 103 29E
Xiangkhoang Plateau (Tranninh) Laos 37 B3 19 10N 103 30E
Xiang Ngeun Laos 37 B3 19 46N 102 16E
Xiangtan China 49 M4 27 48N 112 55E
Xiangyun China 38 C5 25 29N 100 37E
Xianyang China 49 L5 34 22N 108 42E
Xianyou China 51 E8 25 23N 118 40E
Xichang China 38 C5 27 55N 102 23E
Xide China 36 C7 28 19N 102 32E
Xigaze China 48 G5 29 18N 88 50E
Xi Jiang r. China 49 M3 23 30N 111 00E
Xinbin China 50 B5 41 41N 124 55E
Xingtai China 49 M6 37 08N 114 29E
Xingyi China 38 C5 25 29N 104 48E
Xinhuang China 38 D7 27 20N 109 10E
Xining China 49 K6 36 35N 101 55E
Xinjiang Uygur Zizhiqu (Sinkiang Uighur Autonomous Region) admin. China 48 F6/G7 41 00N 85 00E
Xinjin China 49 O6 39 25N 121 58E
Xinying China 37 C3 19 05N 110 00E
Xiqing Shan mts. China 49 K5 34 00N 102 30E
Xizang Zizhiqu (Tibet Autonomous Region) admin. China 48 F5/H5 33 30N 85 00E
Xizhuang China 47 G1 39 51N 116 20E
Xochimilco Mexico 96 E3 19 08N 99 09W
Xuan Vietnam 37 C4 20 22N 105 10E
Xuanhua China 49 N7 40 36N 115 01E
Xuan Loc Vietnam 37 C2 10 49N 107 16E
Xuanwei China 38 C5 26 12N 104 11E
Xuchang China 49 M5 34 03N 113 48E
Xuwen China 49 M3 20 25N 110 08E
Xuzhou China 49 N5 34 17N 117 18E

Y

Yaba Indonesia 44 B6 0 25S 127 27E
Yaba Nigeria 109 V3 6 30N 3 24E
Yablonovy Range mts. Russia 57 M6/N6 51 30N 110 00E
Yabrūd Syria 54 P11 33 58N 36 39E
Yacata i. Fiji 83 E9 17 15S 179 33W
Yacheng China 37 C3 18 30N 109 12E
Yadua i. Fiji 83 C10 16 50S 178 18E
Yagasa i. Fiji 83 F8 18 56S 178 28W
Yahagi-gawa r. Japan 46 J2 35 20N 137 10E
Yaizu Japan 46 C1 34 54N 138 20E
Yakima Washington U.S.A. 90 B6 46 37N 120 30W
Yakima r. Washington U.S.A. 90 B6 47 00N 120 00W
Yakutat Alaska U.S.A. 88 H4 59 29N 139 49W
Yakutsk Russia 57 O8 62 10N 129 50E
Yala Thailand 39 B1 6 40N 101 10E
Yalewa Kalou i. Fiji 83 B10 16 43S 177 50E
Yalong Jiang r. China 38 C5 28 30N 101 25E
Yalu r. China/North Korea 49 P7 42 00N 127 00E
Yamagata Japan 46 D3 38 16N 140 16E
Yamaguchi Japan 46 B1 34 10N 131 28E
Yamal Peninsula Russia 57 I10/J10 72 00N 70 00E
Yamanashi pref. Japan 46 K2 35 40N 138 48E
Yaman-Tau mt. Russia 59 H5 54 58N 59 00E
Yamato Japan 47 A2 35 29N 139 27E
Yamato-takada Japan 46 G1 34 31N 135 43E
Yambio Sudan 110 E8 4 34N 28 21E
Yambol Bulgaria 74 E3 42 28N 26 30E
Yamburg Russia 57 J9 68 19N 77 09E
Yamethin Myanmar 38 B4 20 24N 96 08E
Yamoussoukro Côte d'Ivoire 112 D4 6 50N 5 20W
Yamuna r. India 53 D5 26 00N 79 00E
Yamunanagar India 53 D6 30 07N 77 17E
Yana r. Russia 57 P9 69 00N 135 00E
Yanbian China 38 C5 26 55N 101 36E
Yanbu'al Bahr Saudi Arabia 54 E3 24 07N 38 04E
Yandina Solomon Islands 82 E4 9 05S 159 15E
Yandoon Myanmar 38 B3 17 01N 95 38E
Yanfeng China 38 C5 25 50N 101 11E
Yangcheng China 49 O5 33 23N 120 10E
Yangdon admin. Myanmar 38 B3 17 10N 96 00E
Yangdon (Rangoon) Myanmar 38 B3 16 47N 96 10E
Yanglin China 38 C5 25 11N 103 10E
Yangquan China 49 M6 37 52N 113 29E
Yangtze see Jinsha Jiang or Chang Jiang
Yangwu China 38 C4 23 53N 102 12E
Yanji China 49 P7 42 52N 129 32E
Yanjin China 38 C5 28 04N 104 20E
Yanjing China 49 J4 29 01N 98 38E
Yan Kit Singapore 41 E4 1 21N 103 58E
Yankton South Dakota U.S.A. 92 A2 42 53N 97 24W
Yanshan China 38 C5 23 36N 104 24E
Yantai China 49 O6 37 30N 121 22E
Yanuca i. Fiji 83 C8 18 24S 178 00E
Yanuca i. Fiji 83 E10 16 30S 179 43W
Yanuya i. Fiji 83 B9 17 05S 177 05E
Yanyuan China 38 C5 27 25N 101 34E
Yao Japan 46 G1 34 36N 135 37E
Yao'an China 38 C5 25 27N 101 15E
Yaotsu Japan 46 J2 35 29N 137 10E
Yaoundé Cameroon 112 H3 3 51N 11 31E
Yapero Irian Jaya Indonesia 44 G4 4 58S 137 14E
Yap Islands Pacific Ocean 80 A4 9 30N 138 09E
Yap Trench Pacific Ocean 22 D8 10 00N 139 00E
Yaqaga i. Fiji 83 C10 16 35S 178 36E
Yaqeta i. Fiji 83 B9 17 03S 177 17E
Yaqui r. Mexico 96 C5 28 00N 109 50W
Yaren Nauru 83 L1 0 32S 166 55E
Yaritagua Venezuela 97 K2 10 05N 69 07W
Yarlung Zangbo Jiang (Tsangpo) r. China 48 H4 29 00N 92 30E
Yarmouth Nova Scotia Canada 89 V1 43 50N 66 08W
Yaroslavl' Russia 56 F7 57 34N 39 52E
Yaroua i. Fiji 83 F9 17 44S 178 39W
Yarumal Colombia 102 B14 6 59N 75 25W
Yasawa i. Fiji 83 B10 16 50S 177 30E
Yasawa Group Fiji 83 B9/10 16 50S 177 25E
Yasothon Thailand 39 B3 15 48N 104 13E
Yaté New Caledonia 82 V1 22 09S 167 00E
Yathkyed Lake Northwest Territories Canada 89 P5 62 30N 97 30W

Yatsushiro Japan 46 B1 32 32N 130 35E
Yau Ma Tei Hong Kong U.K. 51 C1 22 18N 114 10E
Yau Tong Hong Kong U.K. 51 C1 22 18N 114 14E
Yauza r. Russia 56 M5 55 45N 37 43E
Yavu i. Fiji 83 E10 16 30S 179 43W
Yaw r. Myanmar 38 A4 21 10N 94 45E
Yawatahama Japan 46 B1 33 27N 132 24E
Ya Xian China 49 L2 18 25N 109 27E
Yayuan China 50 C5 41 48N 126 31E
Yazd Iran 55 H5 31 54N 54 22E
Yazoo r. Mississippi U.S.A. 91 H3 33 00N 90 00W
Ye Myanmar 38 B3 15 15N 97 50E
Yekaterinburg (Sverdlovsk) Russia 56 I7 56 52N 60 35E
Yelets Russia 58 D5 52 35N 38 30E
Yell i. Shetland Islands United Kingdom 68 J12 60 35N 1 10W
Yellowknife Northwest Territories Canada 88 M5 62 30N 114 29W
Yellow Sea (Huang Hai) China 49 O6 35 30N 122 30E
Yellowstone r. U.S.A. 90 E6 46 00N 108 00W
Yellowstone Lake Wyoming U.S.A. 90 D5 44 30N 110 20W
Yellowstone National Park Wyoming U.S.A. 90 D5 44 00N 11 30W
YEMEN REPUBLIC 54 F2
Yenakiyevo Ukraine 58 D4 48 14N 38 15E
Yenangyaung Myanmar 38 A4 20 28N 94 54E
Yen Bai Vietnam 37 B4 21 43N 104 54E
Yenisey r. Russia 57 K8 64 00N 87 30E
Yenisey, Gulf of Russia 57 J10/K10 72 30N 80 00E
Yeniseysk Russia 57 L7 58 27N 92 13E
Yeppoon Australia 78 I5 23 05S 150 42E
Yerevan Armenia 58 E3 40 10N 44 31E
Yermolayevo Russia 59 H5 52 46N 55 54E
Yesil r. Turkey 54 E7 41 00N 36 25E
Yeu Myanmar 38 A4 22 49N 95 26E
Yevpatoriya Ukraine 58 C4 45 12N 33 20E
Yew Tree Singapore 41 C4 1 23N 103 45E
Ye Xian China 49 N6 37 10N 119 55E
Yiannitsá Greece 74 D3 40 46N 22 24E
Yibin China 49 K4 28 42N 104 36E
Yichang China 49 M5 30 46N 111 20E
Yichun China 36 E7 27 45N 114 22E
Yin r. Myanmar 38 B3 19 50N 95 20E
Yinchuan China 49 L6 38 30N 106 19E
Yingde China 36 E6 24 12N 113 20E
Yingjiang China 38 B4 24 43N 98 00E
Yingkou China 49 O7 40 40N 122 17E
Ying Pun Hong Kong U.K. 51 B2 22 28N 114 06E
Yining China 48 F7 43 50N 81 28E
Yio Chu Kang Singapore 41 D4 1 23N 103 51E
Yipinglang China 38 C5 25 11N 101 59E
Yirga 'Alem Ethiopia 100 G8 6 48N 38 22E
Yishan China 36 D6 24 35N 108 35E
Yishun Singapore 41 C5/D5 1 25N 103 50E
Yiyang China 49 M4 28 39N 112 10E
Yoakum Texas U.S.A. 91 G2 29 18N 97 20W
Yobi Irian Jaya Indonesia 44 H6 1 48S 138 04E
Yobi Yapen Island Irian Jaya Indonesia 44 G6 1 45S 136 23E
Yogyakarta Indonesia 42 P7 7 48S 110 24E
Yoichi Japan 46 D3 43 14N 140 47E
Yōka Japan 46 F2 35 25N 134 40E
Yokadouma Cameroon 112 I3 3 26N 15 06E
Yokaichi Japan 46 H2 35 05N 136 11E
Yōkaichiba Japan 46 M2 35 40N 140 30E
Yokkaichi Japan 46 H1 34 58N 136 38E
Yokohama Japan 47 B2 35 27N 139 38E
Yokosuka Japan 47 B2 35 18N 139 38E
Yokote Japan 46 D2 39 20N 140 31E
Yola Nigeria 112 H4 9 14N 12 32E
Yonago Japan 46 B2 35 27N 133 20E
Yonaguni i. Japan 51 I7/J7 24 29N 123 00E
Yonan North Korea 50 C3 37 55N 126 11E
Yŏng-an North Korea 50 D5 41 10N 129 25E
Yongchun China 51 E8 25 18N 118 13E
Yongde China 38 B4 24 00N 99 16E
Yŏngdŏk South Korea 50 D3 36 23N 129 23E
Yŏnghŭng North Korea 50 C4 39 31N 127 18E
Yŏnghŭng-man b. North Korea 50 C4 39 15N 127 30E
Yŏngju South Korea 50 D3 36 50N 128 40E
Yongping China 38 B5 25 29N 99 34E
Yongsheng China 38 C5 26 41N 100 48E
Yonkers New York U.S.A. 94 B2 40 56N 73 52W
Yonki Dam Papua New Guinea 45 M3 6 05S 146 05E
Yonne r. France 73 B2 48 00N 3 15E
Yorii Japan 46 L3 36 07N 139 12E
York England United Kingdom 68 J5 53 58N 1 05W
York Pennsylvania U.S.A. 93 E1 39 57N 76 44W
York, Cape Australia 78 G7 10 42S 142 32E
York Factory tn. Manitoba Canada 89 Q4 57 08N 92 25W
Yorkshire Wolds hills England United Kingdom 68 K6 54 00N 0 45W
Yorkton Saskatchewan Canada 89 O3 51 12N 102 29W
Yosemite National Park California U.S.A. 90 C4 37 30N 119 00W
Yoshino-Kumano National Park Japan 46 G1/H1 34 15N 136 00E
Yoshkar-Ola Russia 58 F6 56 38N 47 52E
Yŏsu South Korea 50 C2 34 50N 127 30E
Youghal Irish Republic 68 D3 51 51N 7 50W
You Jiang r. China 49 L3 23 30N 107 00E
Youngstown Ohio U.S.A. 93 D2 41 05N 80 40W
Ypres see Ipres
Ysef see Ijzer
Ytterhogdal Sweden 69 C3 62 10N 14 55E
Yuanjiang China 38 C4 23 35N 102 04E
Yuan Jiang (Hong, Merah, Song-koi) r. China/Vietnam 38 C4 23 00N 103 20E
Yüan-li Taiwan 51 G6 24 26N 120 40E
Yüan-lin Taiwan 51 G6 23 57N 120 33E
Yuanling China 36 E7 28 30N 110 12E
Yuba City California U.S.A. 90 B4 39 09N 121 36W
Yūbari Japan 46 D3 43 04N 141 59E
Yucatan p. Mexico 96 G3 19 00N 89 00W
Yucatan Basin Caribbean Sea 23 R9 20 00N 85 00W
Yuci China 49 M6 37 40N 112 44E
Yuen Long Hong Kong U.K. 51 B2 22 26N 114 02E
Yuexi China 36 C7 29 00N 103 00E
Yugakir Plateau Russia 57 R9 66 30N 156 00E
Yugawara Japan 46 L2 35 09N 139 06E
YUGOSLAVIA 74 D3
Yu Jiang r. China 49 L3 23 00N 109 00E
Yü-kitka l. Finland 69 F4 66 15N 28 30E
Yukon Delta Alaska U.S.A. 88 C5 62 45N 164 00W